HISTORY

OF THE

UNITED STATES,

FROM THE

DISCOVERY OF THE AMERICAN CONTINENT.

BY

GEORGE BANCROFT.

VOL. V.

BOSTON:
LITTLE, BROWN AND COMPANY,
1857.

RIVERSIDE, CAMBRIDGE:
PRINTED BY H. O. HOUGHTON AND COMPANY.

CONTENTS.

CHAPTER I.

THE CONTINENT OF EUROPE, 1763.

CHAPTER II.

THE CONTINENT OF EUROPE—FRANCE, 1763.

CHAPTER III.

ENGLAND AND ITS DEPENDENCIES. 1763.

CHAPTER IV.

ENGLAND AND ITS DEPENDENCIES CONTINUED. 1763.

CHAPTER V.

CHARLES TOWNSHEND PLEDGES THE MINISTRY OF BUTE TO TAX AMERICA BY THE BRITISH PARLIAMENT, AND RESIGNS. February—April, 1763.

CHAPTER VI.

THE TRIUMVIRATE MINISTRY PURSUE THE PLAN OF TAXING AMERICA BY PARLIAMENT. April—May, 1763.

CHAPTER VII.

PONTIAC'S WAR.—THE TRIUMVIRATE MINISTRY CONTINUED. May—September, 1763.

CHAPTER VIII.

THE TREASURY ENTER A MINUTE FOR AN AMERICAN STAMP TAX.—MINISTRY OF GRENVILLE AND BEDFORD. May—September, 1763.

CHAPTER IX.

ENFORCEMENT OF THE ACTS OF NAVIGATION.—GRENVILLE'S ADMINISTRATION CONTINUED. October, 1763—April, 1764.

CHAPTER X.

HOW AMERICA RECEIVED THE PLAN OF A STAMP ACT.—GRENVILLE'S ADMINISTRATION CONTINUED. April—December, 1764.

CHAPTER XI.

THE TWELFTH PARLIAMENT OF GREAT BRITAIN PASSES THE STAMP ACT.—GRENVILLE'S ADMINISTRATION CONTINUED. January—April, 1765.

CHAPTER XII.

THE MINISTRY OFFEND THE KING AS WELL AS THE COLONIES.—GRENVILLE'S ADMINISTRATION CONTINUED. April—May 1765.

CHAPTER XIII.

THE DAY-STAR OF THE AMERICAN UNION. April—May, 1765.

CHAPTER XIV.

SOUTH CAROLINA FOUNDS THE AMERICAN UNION. June—July, 1765.

CHAPTER XV.

THE DUKE OF CUMBERLAND FORMS A MINISTRY.—THE ROCKINGHAM WHIGS. June—July, 1765.

CHAPTER XVI.

HOW THE STAMP-OFFICERS WERE HANDLED IN AMERICA.—ROCKINGHAM'S ADMINISTRATION. August—September, 1765.

CHAPTER XVII.

AMERICA REASONS AGAINST THE STAMP ACT.—ROCKINGHAM'S ADMINISTRATION CONTINUED. September, 1765.

CHAPTER XVIII.

THE COLONIES MEET IN CONGRESS.—ROCKINGHAM'S ADMINISTRATION. Oct. 1765.

CHAPTER XIX.

AMERICA ANNULS THE STAMP ACT.—ROCKINGHAM'S ADMINISTRATION CONTINUED. October—December, 1765.

CHAPTER XX.

PARLIAMENT LEARNS THAT AMERICA HAS RESISTED.—ROCKINGHAM'S ADMINISTRATION CONTINUED. December, 1765—January, 1766.

CHAPTER XXI.

HAS PARLIAMENT THE RIGHT TO TAX AMERICA?—ROCKINGHAM'S ADMINISTRATION CONTINUED. January, 1766.

CHAPTER XXII.

PARLIAMENT AFFIRMS ITS RIGHT TO TAX AMERICA.—ROCKINGHAM'S ADMINISTRATION CONTINUED. February, 1766.

CHAPTER XXIII.

THE REPEAL OF THE STAMP ACT.—ROCKINGHAM'S ADMINISTRATION CONTINUED
February, 1766.

CHAPTER XXIV.

THE HOUSE OF LORDS GIVE WAY WITH PROTESTS.—ROCKINGHAM'S ADMINISTRATION CONTINUED. February—May, 1766.

THE

AMERICAN REVOLUTION.

EPOCH SECOND

HOW GREAT BRITAIN ESTRANGED AMERICA.

1763—1774.

HOW GREAT BRITAIN ESTRANGED AMERICA.

CHAPTER I.

THE CONTINENT OF EUROPE.

1763.

THE successes of the Seven Years' War were the 1763
triumphs of Protestantism. For the first time since the breach made in the church by Luther, the great Catholic powers, attracted by a secret consciousness of the decay of old institutions, banded themselves together to arrest the progress of change. In vain did the descendants of the feudal aristocracies lead to the field superior numbers; in vain did the Pope bless their banners as though uplifted against unbelievers; no God of battles breathed life into their hosts, and the resistless heroism of the earlier chivalry was no more. A wide-spread suspicion of insincerity weakened the influence of priestcraft, which relapsed from confident menace into a decorous compromise with skepticism. The Catholic monarchies, in their struggle against innovations, had encountered overwhelming

CHAP. I. 1763. defeat; and the cultivated world stood ready to welcome a new era. The forms of religion, government, military service, and industry, which lent to the social organization of the Middle Age a compacted unity, were undermined; and the venerable fabric, clinging to the past, hung over the future as

> A mighty rock,
> Which has, from unimaginable years,
> Sustained itself with terror and with toil
> Over a gulf; and with the agony
> With which it clings, seems slowly coming down.

The dynasties which received their consecration from the Roman church, would cease to array themselves in arms against the offspring of the reformers; in the long tumultuous strife, Protestantism had fulfilled its political ends, and was never again to convulse the world.

But from Protestantism there came forth a principle of all-pervading energy, the common possession of civilized man, and the harbinger of new changes in the state. The life-giving truth of the Reformation was the right of private judgment. This personal liberty in affairs of conscience had, by the illustrious teachings of Descartes, been diffused through the nations which adhered to the old faith, under the more comprehensive form of philosophical freedom. Every where throughout intelligent Europe and America, the separate man was growing aware of the inhering right to the unfettered culture and enjoyment of his whole moral and intellectual being. Individuality was the groundwork of new theories in politics, ethics, and industry.

In Europe, where the human mind groped its way through heavy clouds of tradition, inquisitive activity assumed universally the form of doubt. From discussions on religion, it turned to the analysis of institutions and opinions. Having, in the days of Luther and Calvin, pleaded the Bible against popes and prelates and the one indivisible church, it now invoked the authority of reason, and applied it to every object of human thought; to science, speculative philosophy, and art; to the place of our planet in the order of the heavens and the nature and destiny of the race that dwells on it; to every belief and every polity inherited from the past; to the priestly altar which the veneration of centuries had glorified; to the royal throne which the Catholic church had hallowed, and which the social hierarchy of feudalism had required as its head. Skepticism was the method of the new reform; its tendency, revolution. Sad era for European humanity! which was to advance towards light and liberty only through universal distrust; and, before faith could be inspired by genial love to construct new governments, was doomed to gaze helplessly as its received institutions crumbled away. The Catholic system embraced all society in its religious unity; Protestantism broke that religious unity into sects and fragments; philosophy carried analysis through the entire range of human thought and action, and appointed each individual the arbiter of his own belief and the director of his own powers. Society would be organized again; but not till after the recognition of the rights of the individual. Unity would once more be restored, but not through the canon and feudal law; for the new Catholic element was the people.

CHAP. I. 1763.

CHAP. I. 1763. Yet Protestantism, albeit the reform in religion was the seed-plot of democratic revolutions, had at first been attended by the triumph of absolute monarchy throughout continental Europe; where even the Catholic powers themselves grew impatient of the authority of the Pope over their temporal affairs. The Protestant king, who had just been the ally of our fathers in the Seven Years' War, presented the first great example of the passage of feudal sovereignty into unlimited monarchy, resting on a standing military force. Still surrounded by danger, his inflexible and uncontrolled will stamped the impress of harshness even on his necessary policy, of tyranny on his errors of judgment, and of rapine and violence on his measures for aggrandizement. Yet Prussia, which was the favorite disciple of Luther and the child of the Reformation, while it held the sword upright, bore with every creed and set reason free. It offered a shelter to Rousseau, and called in D'Alembert and Voltaire as its guests; it set Semler to hold the Bible itself under the light of criticism; it breathed into the boldly thoughtful Lessing widest hopes for the education of the race to a universal brotherhood on earth; it gave its youth to the teachings of Immanuel Kant, who, for power of analysis and universality, was inferior to none since Aristotle. "An army and a treasure do not constitute a power," said Vergennes; but Prussia had also philosophic liberty. All freedom of mind in Germany hailed the peace of Hubertsburg as its own victory.[1] In every question of public law, Frederic, though full of respect for the rights of possession, continuing to noble birth its prescriptive posts and almost

[1] I. F. Fries: Geschichte der Philosophie, ii. 495.

leaving his people divided into castes, made the welfare of the kingdom paramount to privilege. He challenged justice under the law for the humblest against the highest. He among Protestants set the bright pattern of the equality of Catholics in worship and in civil condition. To heal the conflict of franchises in the several provinces of his realm, he planned a general code, of which the faults are chiefly due to the narrowness of the lawyers of his day. His ear was open to the sorrows of the poor and the complaint of the crushed; and as in time of war he shared peril and want with the common soldier, in peace the peasant that knocked at his palace gate was welcome to a hearing. "I love the lineage of heroes," he would say, "but I love merit more." "Patents of nobility are but phantoms; true worth is within." As he studied the history of the human race, the distinctions of rank vanished before his eyes; so that he would say, "Kings are nothing but men, and all men are equal." Thus he arraigned the haughtiness of hereditary station, yet without forming purposes or clear conceptions of useful change. Not forfeiting the affection of his people, and not exciting their restless impatience, he yet made no effort to soften the glaring contrast between his philosophy and the political constitution of his kingdom. In the age of doubt he was its hero. Full of hope for the people, yet distrusting them for their blind superstitions; scoffing at the arrogance of the nobility and the bigoted pride of legitimate kings, yet never devising their overthrow; rejecting atheism as an absurdity[1], yet never achieving the serene repose of an unwavering faith;

[1] Supplement aux Oeuvres posthumes de Frederic II. À Cologne, iii. 380.

CHAP. I. 1763. passionate against those who held that human thought and the human soul are but forms of matter, yet never inspired with the sense of immortality; confiding neither in the capacity of the great multitude, nor the wisdom of philosophers, nor the power of religion, nor the disposition of kings, nor the promise of the coming age, he moved through the world as the colossal genius of skepticism, questioning the past which he knew not how to reform. Holding no colonies, he could calmly watch their growth to independence; indulging an antipathy against the king of England, he might welcome the experiment of the widely-extending American commonwealth, but not with confidence in its happy course.

If the number of active minds in cultivated Prussia was not yet large enough to give to forming opinion a popular aspect, in Russia, the immense empire which was extending itself along the Baltic and the Euxine, and had even crossed the Pacific to set up its banners in Northwestern America, free inquiry had something of solitary dignity as the almost exclusive guest of the empress. First of the great powers of Europe in population, and exceeding all of them together in extent of European lands, the great Slavonic State was not proportionably strong and opulent. More than two-thirds of its inhabitants were bondsmen and slaves, thinly scattered over vast domains. The slave held the plough; the slave bent over the anvil, or threw the shuttle; the slave wrought the mines. The nobles, who directed the labor on their estates, in manufactures, or the search for ores, read no books from abroad, and as yet had no native literature. The little science that faintly gleamed on the interior was diffused through the priests of the Greek church, themselves bred up in superstition; so that the Slavonic race, which was neither Protestant nor Catholic—which had neither been ravaged by the wars of religion, nor educated by the discussions of creeds—a new and rising power in the world, standing on the confines of Europe and Asia, not wholly Oriental and still less of the West, displayed the hardy but torpid vigor of a people not yet vivified by intelligence, still benumbed by blind belief, ignorance, and servitude. Its political unity existed in the strength of its monarchy, which organized its armies and commanded them without control; made laws, and provided for their execution; appointed all officers, and displaced them at will; directed the internal administration and the relations with foreign powers. The sovereign who held these absolute prerogatives was Catherine, a princess of a German Protestant house. Her ambition had secured the throne by adopting her husband's religion, conniving at his deposition, and not avenging his murder. Her love of pleasure solicited a licentiousness of moral opinion; her passion for praise sought to conciliate the good will of men of letters; so that she blended the adoption of the new philosophy with the grandeur, the crimes, and the voluptuousness of Asiatic despotism. If she invaded Poland, it would be under the pretext of protecting religious freedom; if she moved towards the Bosphorus, she would surround herself with the delusive halo of some imaginary restoration of the liberties of ancient Greece. At home respecting the property of the nobles, yet seeking to diminish the number of slaves;[1] an apparent devotee to the faith of the Greek church, yet giving religious

[1] Storch: Economie Politique, iv. 252.

CHAP. I. 1763. freedom to the Catholic and the Protestant, and even printing the Koran for the Mussulmans of her dominions: abroad, she bent neither to France nor to England. Her policy was thoroughly true to the empire that adopted her, and yet imbued with the philosophy of western Europe. With deserts near at hand to colonize, with the Mediterranean inviting her flag, she formed no wish of conquering Spanish colonies on the Pacific; and we shall find her conduct towards England, in its relations with America, held in balance between the impulse from the liberal systems of thought which she made it her glory to cherish, and the principle of monarchy which flattered her love of praise and was the basis of her power.

Soon after the peace of Hubertsburg, the youthful heir to the Austrian dominions, which, with Prussia and Russia, shaped the politics of eastern and northern Europe, was elected the successor to the Imperial crown of Germany. As an Austrian prince, it was the passion of Joseph the Second to rival Frederic of Prussia. His mother, Maria Theresa, was a devotee in her attachment to the church. The son, hating the bigotry in which he was nurtured, inclined to skepticism and unbelief. The mother venerated with an absurd intensity of deference the prerogatives of an unmixed aristocratic descent; the son affected to deride all distinctions of birth, and asserted the right to freedom of mind with such integrity, that he refused to impair it when afterwards it came to be exercised against himself. But, in the conflict which he provoked with the past, he mixed philanthropy with selfishness, and his hasty zeal to abolish ancient abuses was subordinate to a passion for sequestering political immunities, and concentrating all power in his own hands. As a reformer, he therefore failed in every part of his dominions; and as he brought no enduring good to Hungary, but rather an example of violating its constitution, so we shall find the Austrian court the only great European power which, both as an ally of England and an enemy to republics, remained inflexibly opposed to America. Yet the efforts of Joseph the Second, ill-judged and vain as they were, illustrate the universality of the new influence.[1]

The German empire, of which he was so soon to be the head, was the creature and the symbol of the Middle Ages. Its life was gone. The forms of liberty were there, but the substance had perished under the baleful excess of aristocracy. The emperor was an elective officer, but his constituents were only princes. Of the nine electors, three were Roman Catholic Archbishops, owing their rank to the choice of others; but their constituents were of the unmixed nobility, to whom entrance into the electoral chapters was exclusively reserved. The sovereignty of the empire resided, not in the emperor, but in the great representative body of the whole country, or Diet, as it was called, which was composed of the emperor himself, of about one hundred independent prelates and princes, and of delegates from nine and forty independent towns. These last, besides the free cities of Bremen and Hamburg, had internally not only municipal liberties, but self-government, and were so many little republics, dotted throughout the land, from the Rhine to the Danube. But in the Diet, their votes counted as

[1] Klopstock: An den Kaiser, Werke, ii. 51.

CHAP. I.

1763.

nothing. As the people on the one side were not heard, so the dignity of the Imperial crown on the other brought no substantial power; and as the hundred princes were never disposed to diminish their separate independence, it followed that the German empire was but a vain shadow. The princes and nobles parcelled out the land, and ruled it in severalty with an authority which there was none to dispute, to guide, or to restrain.

Nobility throughout Germany was strictly a caste. The younger son of a subordinate and impoverished noble family would not have wedded with the wealthiest plebeian heiress. Various chapters and ecclesiastical preferments were accessible to those only who were of unmixed aristocratic ancestry. It followed, that, in the breast of the educated commoner, no political passion was so strong as the hatred of nobility; for nowhere in the world was the pride of birth so great as in the petty German principalities. The numerous little princes—absolute within their own narrow limits over a hopeless people, whose fortunes they taxed at will, whose lives and services they not only claimed for the service of the state and of themselves, but as merchantable property which might be transferred to others—made up for the small extent of their dominions by an excess of self-adulation; though, after all, as was said of them by one of the greatest German poets, who was ready to praise merit wherever found, they were but "demi-men, who, in perfectly serious stupidity, thought themselves beings of a higher nature than we."[1] But their pride was a

[1] Klopstock: Fürstenlob.
Halbmenschen, die sich, in vollem, dummen Ernst für höhere Wesen halten als uns.

pride which licked the dust, for "almost all of them were venal and pensionary."[1] CHAP. I. 1763.

The United Provinces of the Netherlands, the forerunner of nations in religious tolerance, were, from the origin of their confederacy, the natural friends of intellectual freedom. Here thought ranged through the wide domain of speculative reason. Here the literary fugitive found an asylum, and the boldest writings, which in other countries circulated by stealth, were openly published to the world. But in their European relations, the Netherlands were no more a great maritime power. They had opulent free ports in the West Indies, colonies in South America, Southern Africa, and the East Indies, with the best harbor in the Indian Ocean: their paths, as of old, were on the deep, and their footsteps in many waters. They knew they could be opulent only through commerce, and their system of mercantile policy was liberal beyond that of every nation in Europe. Even their colonial ports were less closely shut against the traffic with other countries. This freedom bore its fruits: they became wealthy beyond compare, reduced their debt, and were able so to improve their finances, that their funds, bearing only two per cent. interest, rose considerably above par. Ever the champions of the freedom of the seas, at the time of their greatest naval power, they had in their treaty of 1674 with England, embodied the safety of neutrals in time of war, limiting contraband articles of trade, and making goods on shipboard as safe as the ships that bore

[1] The authority is an English Lord Chancellor, speaking his mind to an English Duke. Hardwicke to Newcastle, 10th Sept., 1751; in Coxe's Pelham Administration, ii. 410. "Almost all the princes of Europe are become venal and pensionary."

CHAP. I. 1763. them. But the accession of the Stadtholder,[1] William of Orange to the throne of England was fatal to the political weight of the Netherlands. From the rival of England they became her ally, and almost her subordinate; and guided by her policy, they exhausted their means in land forces and barriers against France, leaving their navy to decline, and their fleets to disappear from the ocean. Hence arose the factions by which their counsels were distracted and their strength paralysed. The friends of the Stadtholder, who in 1763 was a boy of fifteen, sided with England, desired the increase of the army, were averse to expenditures for the navy, and forfeiting the popular favor which they once enjoyed, inclined more and more towards monarchical interests. The Patriots saw in their weakness at sea a state of dependence on Great Britain; they cherished a deep sense of the wrongs unatoned for and unavenged, which England, in the pride of strength, and unmindful of treaties, had in the last war inflicted on their carrying-trade and their flag; they grew less jealous of France; they opposed the increase of the army—longed to restore the maritime greatness of their country; and including much of the old aristocratic party among the merchants, they were fervid lovers of their country and almost republicans.

The kingdom from which the United Provinces had separated, which Philip the Second had made the citadel of Catholicism—in which Loyola had organized his "Society of Jesus" as a spiritual army against

[1] Offenbar war's aber der Republik nicht vortheilhaft, dass ihr General-Capitain zugleich auch König in England war. Spittler's Europäische Staaten—Geschichte, i. 564, 565.

Protestantism and modern philosophy, might seem to have been inaccessible to the ameliorating influence of a more enlightened public reason. The territory was compact and almost insulated; and since the Cortes had ceased to be assembled, the government was that of absolute monarchy, controlled by no national representation, or independent judiciary, or political institution. "The royal power," says its apologist and admirer,[1] "moved majestically in the orbit of its unlimited faculties." The individual to whom these prerogatives were confided, was the bigoted, ignorant, kindly Charles III. A fond husband, a gentle master, really wishing well to his subjects, he had never read a book, not even in his boyhood with his teachers. He indulged systematically his passion for the chase, crossing half his kingdom to hunt a wolf; and chronicling his achievements as a sportsman. He kept near his person the prayer-book and playthings of his childhood as amulets; and yielding his mind to his confessors, he never strayed beyond the established paths in politics and religion. Yet the light that shone in his time penetrated even his palace: externally, he followed the direction of France; at home, the mildness of his nature, and some good sense, and even his timidity, made him listen to the counsels of the most liberal of his ministers; so that in Spain also criminal law was softened, the use of torture discountenanced, and the papal power and patronage more and more restrained. The fires of the Inquisition were extinguished, though its ferocity was not subdued;

[1] Sans representation nationale donc, sans aucun corps ou institution politique quelconque qui pût le contrôler, le pouvoir royal tournoit majestueusement dans l'orbite de ses facultés illimitées. A l'aspect d'un tel bonheur, qui auroit pu croire, &c., &c. Muriel: Gouvernement de Charles III. Roi d'Espagne. Introduction, 9.

CHAP. I. 1763. and even the Jesuits, as reputed apologists of resistance and regicide when kings are unjust, were on the point of being driven from the most Catholic country of Europe.

Spain ranked as the fourth European power in extent of territory, the fifth in revenue, while its colonies exceeded all others of the world beside; embracing nearly all South America, except Brazil and the Guianas; all Mexico and Central America; California, which had no bounds on the north; Louisiana, which came to the Mississippi, and near its mouth beyond it; Cuba, Porto Rico, and part of Hayti; and mid-way between the Pacific and the Indian Ocean, the Marianna and Philippine groups of isles; in a word, the countries richest in soil, natural products, and mines, and having a submissive population of nearly twenty millions of souls.

In the midst of this unexampled grandeur of possession, Spain, which with Charles V. and Philip II. had introduced the mercantile system of restrictions, was weak, and poor, and wretched. It had no canals, no good roads, no manufactures. There was so little industry, or opportunity of employing capital, that though money was very scarce, the rate of interest was as low at Madrid as in Holland. Almost all the lands were entailed in perpetuity, and were included in the immense domains of the grandees. These estates, never seen by their owners, were poorly cultivated and ill managed; so that almost nothing fell to the share of the masses. Except in Barcelona and Cadiz, the nation every where presented the most touching picture of misery and poverty.

And Spain, which by its laws of navigation reserved to itself all traffic with its colonies, and desired to make the Gulf of Mexico and the Caribbean its own close seas, allowed but four and thirty vessels, some of them small ones, to engage in voyages between itself and the Continent of America on the Atlantic side, and all along the Pacific; while but four others plied to and fro between Spain and the West India Isles. Having admirable harbors on every side, and a people on the coasts, especially in Biscay and Catalonia, suited to life at sea, all its fisheries, its coasting trade, its imports and exports, and all its colonies, scarcely employed sixteen thousand sailors. Such were the fruits of commercial monopoly, as illustrated by its greatest example.[1]

The political relations of Spain were analogous. From a consciousness of weakness it leaned on the alliance with France; and the deep veneration of the Catholic king for the blood of the Bourbons confirmed his attachment to the Family Compact. Besides, like France—and more than France—he had griefs against England. The English, in holding the Rock of Gibraltar, hurled at him a perpetual insult; England encroached on Central America; England encouraged Portugal to extend the bounds of Brazil; England demanded a ransom for the Manillas; England was always in the way, defying, subduing, overawing; sending its ships into forbidden waters; protecting its smugglers; ever ready to seize the Spanish colonies themselves. The court of Spain was so wrapt up in veneration of the kingly power, that by its creed such a monarch of such an empire ought to be invincible; it dreamed of a new and more successful Armada, and

[1] From information obtained for the French Government, in the Archives des Affaires Étrangères.

CHAP. I. 1763. hid its unceasing fears under gigantic propositions of daring; but the king, chastened by experience, had all the while an unconfessed misgiving; and slyly timid, delighted in intrigue and menace, affected to be angry at the peace, and was perpetually stimulating France to undertake a new war, of which he yet carefully avoided the outbreak.

CHAPTER II.

THE CONTINENT OF EUROPE—FRANCE.

1763.

FRANCE, the "beautiful kingdom" of central Europe, was occupied by a most ingenious people, formed of blended elements, and still bearing traces not only of the Celtic but of the German race, of the culture of Rome, and the hardihood of the Northmen. In the habit of analysis it excelled all nations; its delight in logical exactness and in precision of outline and expression of thought, gave the style alike to its highest efforts and to its ordinary manufactures; to its poetry and its prose; to the tragedies of Racine and the pictures of Poussin, as well as to its products of taste for daily use, and the adornment of its public squares with a careful regard to fitness and proportion. Its severe method in the pursuit of mathematical science corresponded to its nicety of workmanship in the structure of its ships of war, its canals, its bridges, its fortifications, and its public buildings. Light-hearted, frivolous and vain, no people were more ready to seize a new idea, and to pursue it with rigid dialectics to all its con- CHAP. II. 1763.

CHAP. II. 1763. sequences; none were so eager to fill, and as it were to burden the fleeting moment with pleasure; and none so ready to renounce pleasure, and risk life for a caprice, or sacrifice it for glory. Self-indulgent, they abounded in offices of charity. Often exhibiting the most heartless egoism, they were also easily inflamed with a most generous enthusiasm. Seemingly lost in profligate sensuality, they were yet capable of contemplative asceticism. To the superficial observer, they were a nation of atheists; and yet they preserved the traditions of their own Bossuet and Calvin, of Descartes and Fenelon.

In this most polished and cultivated land,—whose government had just been driven out from North America, whose remaining colonies collectively had but about seventy thousand white persons, whose commerce with the New World could only be a consequence of American Independence,—two opposite powers competed for supremacy; on the one side monarchy, claiming to be absolute; on the other, free thought, which was becoming the mistress of the world.

Absolute power met barriers on every side. The arbitrary Central will was circumscribed by the customs and privileges of the provinces, and the independence of its own agents. Many places near the king were held by patent; the officers of his army were poorly paid, and often possessed of large private fortunes; the clergy, though named by him, held office irrevocably, and their vast revenues, of a hundred and thirty millions of livres annually, were their own property. His treasury was always in need of money, not by taxes only, but by loans, which require the credit that rests on an assured respect for law. Former kings had in their poverty made a permanent sale of the power of civil and criminal justice; so that the magistrates were triply independent, being themselves wealthy, holding their office of judges as a property, and being irremovable. The high courts of justice, or parliaments as they were called, were also connected with the power of legislation; for as they enforced only those laws which they themselves had registered, so they assumed the right of refusing to register laws; and if the king came in person to command their registry, they would still remonstrate, even while they obeyed.

But the great impairment of royal power was the decay of the faith on which it had rested. France was no more the France of the Middle Age. The caste of the nobility, numbering, of both sexes and all ages, not much more than one hundred thousand souls, was overtopt in importance by the many millions of an industrious people; and its young men, trained by the study of antiquity, sometimes imbibed republican principles from the patriot writings of Greece and Rome. Authority, in its feeble conflict with free opinion, did but provoke licentiousness, and was braved with the invincible weapons of ridicule. Freedom was the vogue, and it had more credit than the king. Skepticism found its refuge in the social circles of the capital; and infusing itself into every department of literature and science, blended with the living intelligence of the nation. Almost every considerable house in Paris had pretensions as a school of philosophy. Derision of the established church was the fashion of the world; many waged warfare against every form of religion, and against religion itself,

CHAP. II. 1763. while some were aiming also at the extermination of the throne. The new ideas got abroad in remonstrances and sermons, comedies and songs, books and epigrams.

On the side of modern life, pushing free inquiry to the utmost contempt of restraint, though not to total unbelief, Voltaire employed his peerless wit and activity. The Puritans of New England changed their hemisphere to escape from bishops, and hated prelacy with the rancor of faction; Voltaire waged the same warfare with widely different weapons, and, writing history as a partisan, made the annals of his race a continuous sarcasm against the hierarchy of the Roman Catholic church. His power reached through Europe; he spoke to the free thinkers throughout the cultivated world. In the age of skepticism he was the prince of scoffers; when philosophy hovered round saloons, he excelled in reflecting the brilliantly licentious mind of the intelligent aristocracy. His great works were written in retirement, but he was himself the spoiled child of society. He sunned himself in its light, and dazzled it by concentrating its rays. He was its idol, and he courted its idolatry. Far from breaking with authority, he loved the people as little as he loved the Sorbonne. The complaisant courtier of sovereigns and ministers, he could even stand and wait for smiles at the toilet of the French king's mistress, or prostrate himself in flattery before the Semiramis of the north; willing to shut his eyes on the sorrows of the masses, if the great would but favor men of letters. He it was, and not an English poet, that praised George the First of England as a sage and a hero who ruled the

CHAP. II. 1763.

universe by his virtues;[1] he could address Louis the Fifteenth as a Trajan; and when the French king took a prostitute for his associate, it was the aged Voltaire who extolled the monarch's mistress as an adorable Egeria.[2] "The populace which has its hands to live by," such are the words, and such the sentiments of Voltaire, and as he believed of every landholder, "the people has neither time nor capacity for self-instruction; they would die of hunger before becoming philosophers. It seems to me essential that there should be ignorant poor.[3] Preach virtue to the lower classes; when the populace meddles with reasoning, all is lost."[4]

The school of Voltaire did not so much seek the total overthrow of despotism as desire to make his philosophy its counsellor; and shielded the vices of a libidinous oligarchy by proposing love of self as the cornerstone of morality. The great view which pervades his writings is the humanizing influence of letters, and not the regenerating power of truth. He welcomed, therefore, every thing which softened barbarism, refined society, and stayed the cruelties of superstition; but he could not see the hopeful coming of popular power, nor hear the footsteps of Providence along the line of centuries, so that he classed the changes in the government of France among accidents and anecdotes. Least of all did he understand the tendency of his own untiring labors. He would have hated the thought of hastening a democratic revolution; and, in mocking the follies and vices of French institutions, he harbored

Au Roi d'Angleterre, George 1er, en lui envoyant la tragédie d'Œdipe.

[2] Voltaire à Madame la Comtesse du Barri, 20 Juin, 1773.

[3] "Il me paraît essentiel qu'il y ait des gueux ignorans."

[4] "Quand la populace se mêle de raisonner, tout est perdu." Voltaire a M. Damilaville, 1er Avril, 1766.

CHAP. II. 1763. no purpose of destroying them. "Spare them," he would say, "though they are not all of gold and diamonds. Take the world as it goes; if all is not good, all is passable."[1]

Thus skepticism proceeded unconsciously in the work of destruction, invalidating the past, yet unable to construct the future. For good government is not the creation of skepticism. Her garments are red with blood, and ruins are her delight; her despair may stimulate to voluptuousness and revenge; she never kindled with the disinterested love of man.

The age could have learnt, from the school of Voltaire, to scoff at its past; but the studious and observing Montesquieu discovered "the title deeds of humanity," as they lay buried under the rubbish of privileges, conventional charters, and statutes. His was a generous nature that disdained the impotence of epicureanism, and found no resting-place in doubt. He saw that society, notwithstanding all its revolutions, must repose on principles that do not change; that Christianity, which seems to aim only at the happiness of another life, also constitutes man's blessedness in this.[2] He questioned the laws of every nation to unfold to him the truth that had inspired them; and behind the confused masses of positive rules, he recognised the anterior existence and reality of justice. Full of the inquiring spirit of his time, he demanded tolerance for every opinion; and to him belongs the

[1] Le monde comme il va; Vision de Babouc.

[2] Chose admirable! La Religion Chrétienne, qui ne semble avoir d'objet que la félicité de l'autre vie, fait encore notre bonheur dans celle-ci. Esprit des Lois, Livre xxiv. chapitre iii.

peaceful and brilliant glory of leading the way to a milder and more effective penal code. Shunning speculative conjecture, he limited his reasonings to the facts in European political life, and though he failed to discover, theoretically, the true foundation of government, he revived and quickened faith in the principles of political liberty, and showed to the people of France how monarchy may be tempered by a division of its power, and how republics, more happy than those of Italy, may save themselves from the passionate tyranny of a single senate.

CHAP. II. 1763.

That free commerce would benefit every nation, is a truth which Montesquieu[1] is thought to have but imperfectly perceived. The moment was come when the languishing agriculture of his country would invoke science to rescue it from oppression by entreating the liberty of industry and trade. The great employment of France was the tillage of land, than which no method of gain is more grateful in itself, or more worthy of freemen,[2] or more happy in rendering service to the whole human race.[3] No occupation is nearer heaven. But authority had invaded this chosen domain of labor; as if protection of manufactures needed restrictions on the exchanges of the products of the earth, the withering prohibition of the export of grain had doomed large tracts of land[4] to lie desolately fallow. Indirect taxes, to the number of at least ten thousand,[5] bringing with them custom-houses between provinces, and custom-houses on the frontier, and a hundred thou-

[1] Montesquieu: Esprit des Lois. Livre xx. chap. xxiii.

[2] Cicero de Officiis.

[3] Cicero de Senectute.

[4] Boisguillebert: Traité de la Nature, Culture, Commerce, et Intérêt des Grains, &c. &c. chap. vii.

[5] Boisguillebert: Factum de la France, chap. vi. Economistes, 290.

CHAP. II. 1763. sand tax-gatherers, left little "to the peasant[1] but eyes to weep with." The treasury was poor, for the realm was poor; and the realm was poor because the husbandman was poor.[2] While every one, from the palace to the hovel, looked about for a remedy to this system of merciless and improvident spoliation, there arose a school of upright and disinterested men,[3] who sought a remedy for the servitude of labor by looking beyond the precedents of the statute book, or forms of government, to universal principles and the laws of social life; beyond the power of the people or the power of princes, to the power of nature.[4] They found that man in society renounces no natural right, but remains the master of his person and his faculties, with the right to labor and to enjoy or exchange the fruits of his labor. Exportation has no danger,[5] for demand summons supplies; dearness need not appal, for high prices, quickening production, as manure does the soil, are their own certain, as well as only cure. So there should be no restriction on commerce[6] and industry, internal or external; competition should supersede monopoly, and private freedom displace the regulating supervision of the state.

Such was "the liberal and generous"[7] system of the political economists who grouped themselves round the calm and unpretending Quesnai, startling the world by their axioms and tables of rustic economy,[8] as

[1] Blanqui: Histoire de l'Economie Politique, ii. 54.

[2] Quesnai: Maximes Générales du Gouvernement. Edition of the "Physiocrates" of Eugene Daire, 83.

[3] Blanqui: Hist. de l' Econ. Pol. ii. 94.

[4] Hence their name; not democrats, but "physiocrates."

[5] Quesnai: Maximes Générales du Gouvernement, xvi.

[6] F. Quesnai: Maximes Générales du Gouvernement, xxv.

[7] Adam Smith's Wealth of Nations, Book iv. ch. 9.

[8] Marmontel: Livre cinquième, Œuvres i. 149, 150.

though a discovery had been made like that of the alphabet or of metallic coin.[1]

1763. The new ideas fell, in France, on the fruitful genius of Turgot, who came forward in the virgin purity of philosophy to take part in active life. He was well-informed and virtuous,[2] most amiable,[3] and of a taste the most delicate and sure; a disinterested man, austere, yet holding it to be every man's business to solace those who suffer; wishing the effective accomplishment of good, not his own glory in performing it. For him the human race was one great whole,[4] composed, as the Christian religion first taught, of members of one family under a common Father; always, through calm and through "agitations," through good and through ill, through sorrow and through joy, on the march, though at "a slow step,"[5] towards a greater perfection.

To further this improvement of the race, opinion, he insisted, must be free, and liberty conceded to industry in all its branches and in all its connections. "Do not govern the world too much," he repeated, in the words of an earlier statesman. Corporations had usurped the several branches of domestic trade and manufactures; Turgot vindicated the poor man's right to the free employment of his powers. Statesmen, from the days of Philip the Second of Spain, had fondly hoped to promote national industry and wealth by a system of prohibitions and restrictions, and had only succeeded in deceiving nations into mutual antipathies, which did but represent the hatreds and envy of avarice: Turgot would solve questions of trade abstractly from countries as well as from provinces, and make it

[1] Marquis de Mirabeau, the elder.
[2] D'Alembert to Voltaire.
[3] Voltaire to D'Alembert.
[4] Notice sur la vie et les œuvrages de Turgot, xxviii. &c. &c.
[5] À pas lents.

CHAP. II. 1763.

free between man and man, and between nation and nation; for commerce is neither a captive to be ransomed, nor an infant to be held in leading-strings. Thus he followed the teachings of nature, living as one born not for himself, but for the service of truth and the welfare of mankind.[1]

In those days the people toiled and suffered, with scarce a hope of a better futurity even for their posterity. In life Turgot employed his powers and his fortune as a trust, to relieve the sorrows of the poor; but, under the system of uncontrolled individual freedom, the laborer, from the pressure of competition, might underbid his fellow laborer till his wages should be reduced to a bare support.[2] Thus the skeptical philosopher, the erudite magistrate, the philanthropic founder of the science of political economy, proposed what they could for human progress. From the discipleship of Calvin, from the republic of Geneva, from the abodes of poverty, there sprung up a writer, through whom the "ignorant poor" breathed out their wrongs, and a new class gained a voice in the world of published thought. With Jean Jacques Rousseau truth was no more to employ the discreet insinuations of academicians; nor seek a hearing by the felicities of wit; nor compromise itself by exchanging flattery for the favor of the great; nor appeal to the interests of the industrial classes. Full of weaknesses and jealousies, shallow and inconsiderate, betrayed by poverty into shameful deeds, yet driven by remorse to make atonement for

[1] Secta fuit servare modum, finemque tenere,
Naturamque sequi, patriæque impendere vitam;
Non sibi, sed toti genitum se credere mundo.
Motto of Condorcet: Vie de Turgot.

[2] Turgot sur la Formation et la Distribution des Richesses. § vi. Œuvres i. 10.

his vices, and possessing a deep and real feeling for humanity, in an age of skepticism and in the agony of want, tossed from faith to faith, as from country to country, he read the signs of death on the features of the past civilization; and in tones of sadness, but not of despair—clinging always to faith in man's spiritual nature, and solacing the ills of life by trust in God[1]—he breathed the spirit of revolution into words of flame. Fearlessly questioning all the grandeurs of the world—despots and prelates, and philosophers and aristocrats, and men of letters; the manners, the systems of education, the creeds, the political institutions, the superstitions of his time;—he aroused Europe to the inquiry, if there did not exist a people. What though the church cursed his writings with its ban, and parliaments burned them at the gibbet by the hangman's hand? What though France drove him from her soil, and the republic of his birth disowned her son? What though the men of letters hooted at his wildness, and the humane Voltaire himself led the cry against this "savage charlatan,"[2] "this beggar," who sought "fraternal union among men" by setting "the poor to plunder all the rich?" Without learning or deep philosophy, from the woes of the world in which he had suffered, from the wrongs of the down-trodden which he had shared,[3] he derived an eloquence which went to the heart of Europe. He lit up the darkness

[1] See Rousseau to Voltaire.

[2] "Un je ne sais quel charlatan sauvage." Voltaire: Siècle de Louis XV. chap. xliii.

[3] Rousseau: Confessions; Partie I., Livre iv. "Il me fit entendre qu'il cachoit son vin à cause des aides; quil cachoit son pain à cause de la taille; et qu'il seroit un homme perdu, si l'on pouvoit se douter quil ne mourût pas de faim. Tout ce qu'il me dit à ce sujet, me fit une impression, qui ne s'effacera jamais. Ce fut là le germe de cette haine inextinguible qui se dévelopa depuis dans mon coeur contre les vexations qu' éprouve le malheureux peuple et contre ses oppresseurs.

CHAP. II. 1763. of his times with flashes of sagacity; and spoke out the hidden truth, that the old social world was smitten with inevitable decay; that if there is life still on earth, "it is the masses alone that live."[1]

At the very time when Bedford and Choiseul were concluding the peace that was ratified in 1763, Rousseau, in a little essay on the social compact, published to the millions, that while true legislation has its source in divinity, the right to exercise sovereignty belongs inalienably to the people; but rushing eagerly to the doctrine which was to renew the world, he lost out of sight the personal and individual freedom of mind. The race as it goes forward, does not let fall one truth, but husbands the fruits of past wisdom for the greater welfare of the ages to come. Before government could grow out of the consenting mind of all, there was need of all the teachers who had asserted freedom for the reason of each separate man. Rousseau claimed power for the public mind over the mind of each member of the state, which would make of democracy a homicidal tyranny. He did not teach that the freedom, and therefore the power, of the general mind, rests on the freedom of each individual mind; that the right of private judgment must be confirmed before the power of the collective public judgment can be justified; that the sovereignty of the people presupposes the entire personal freedom of each citizen. He demanded for his commonwealth the right of making its power a religion, its opinions a creed, and of punishing every dissenter with exile or death;[2] so that his precepts

[1] The phrase is from Cousin.

[2] Rousseau: Du Contrat Social, livre iv. chap. viii. "Il y a donc une profession de foi purement civile dont il appartient au souverain de fixer les articles. . . Sans

were at once enfranchising and despotic, involving revolution, and constituting revolution an exterminating despotism. This logical result of his lessons was at first less observed. His fiery eloquence, and the concerted efforts of men of letters who fashioned anew the whole circle of human knowledge, overwhelmed the priesthood and the throne. The ancient forms of the state and the church were still standing; but monarchy and the hierarchy were as insulated columns, from which the building they once belonged to had crumbled away; where statues, formerly worshipped, lay mutilated and overthrown, among ruins that now sheltered the viper and the destroyer.

CHAP. II.

1763.

pouvoir obliger personne à les croire, il peut bannir de l'état quiconque ne les croit pas. . . Que, si quelqu'un, après avoir reconnu publiquement ces mêmes dogmes, se conduit comme ne les croyant pas, qu'il soit puni de mort."

CHAPTER III.

ENGLAND AND ITS DEPENDENCIES.

1763.

CHAP. III. 1763. North of the channel that bounded France, liberty was enjoyed by a wise and happy people, whose domestic character was marked by moderation, and, like its climate, knew but little of extremes. The opinions on religion and on government which speculative men on the continent of Europe were rashly developing without qualification or reserve, were derived from England. She rose before the philosophers as the asylum of independent thought, and upon the nations as the home of revolution, where liberty emanated from discord and sedition. There free opinion had carried analysis boldly to every question of faith as well as of science. English free-thinkers had led the way in the reaction of Protestant Europe against the blind adoration of the letter of the Bible. English Deists, tracing Christianity to reason and teaching that it was as old as creation, were the forerunners of the German Rationalists. English treatises on the human understanding were the sources of the materialism of France. In the atmosphere of England

Voltaire ripened the speculative views which he published as English Letters; there Montesquieu sketched a government which should make liberty its end; and from English writings and example Rousseau derived the idea of a social compact. Every Englishman discussed public affairs; busy politicians thronged the coffee-houses; petitions were sent to parliament from popular assemblies; cities, boroughs, and counties framed addresses to the king: and yet, such was the stability of the institutions of England amidst the factious conflicts of parties, such her loyalty to law even in her change of dynasties, such her self-control while resisting power, such the fixedness of purpose lying beneath the restless enterprise of her intelligence, that the ideas which were preparing radical changes in the social system of other monarchies, held their course harmlessly within her borders, as winds playing capriciously round some ancient structure whose massive buttresses tranquilly bear up its roof, and towers, and pinnacles, and spires.

The Catholic kingdoms sanctified the kingly power by connecting it with the church and deriving its title-deed directly from heaven; Prussia was as yet the only great modern instance of a warlike state resting on an army; England limited her monarchy by law. Her constitution was venerable from its antiquity. Some traced it to Magna Charta, some to the Norman conquest, and some to the forests of Germany, where acts of legislation were debated and assented to by the people and by the nobles; but it was at the revolution of 1688, that the legislature definitively assumed the sovereignty by dismissing a monarch from the kingdom, as a landlord might dis-

CHAP. III. 1763. miss a farmer from his holding. In England, monarchy, in the Catholic sense, had gone off; the dynasty on its throne had abdicated the dignity of hereditary right and the sanctity of divine right, and wore the crown in conformity to a statute, so that its title was safe only with the constitution. The framework of government had for its direct end, not the power of its chief, but personal liberty and the security of property. The restrictions, which had been followed by such happy results, had been established under the lead of the aristocracy, to whom the people, in its gratitude for security against arbitrary power and its sense of inability itself to reform the administration, had likewise capitulated; so that England was become an aristocratic republic[1] with the king as the emblem of a permanent executive.

In the Catholic world, the church, as the independent interpreter of the divine will, placed itself above the state, and might interpose to protect itself and the people against feudal tyranny by appeals to that absolute truth which it claimed and was acknowledged to represent. In England, the church had no independent power; and its connection with the state was purchased by its subordination. None but conformists could hold office; but in return, the church, in so far as it is a civil establishment, was the creature of parliament; a statute enacted the articles of its creed, as well as its book of prayer; it was not even intrusted with a co-ordinate power to reform its own abuses; any attempt to have done so would have been

[1] Une nation où la rèpublique se cache sous la forme de la monarchie. Montesquieu: i. 105.

treated as a usurpation; amendment could proceed only from parliament. The convocations of the church were infrequent, and if laymen were not called to them, it was because the assembly was merely formal. Through parliament the laity ruled the church. It seemed, indeed, as if the bishops were still elected; but it was only in appearance; the crown, which gave leave to elect, named also the person to be chosen, and obedience to its nomination was enforced by the penalties of a premunire.

The laity, too, had destroyed the convents and monasteries which, under other social forms, had been the schools, the poor-houses, and the hostelries of the land; and all the way from Netley Abbey to the rocky shores of Northumberland, and even to the remote loneliness of Iona, had filled the country with the ruins of buildings, which once rose in such numbers and such beauty of architecture that they seemed like a concert of voices engaged in a hymn of praise. And the property of the church, which had been enjoyed by the monasteries that undertook the performance of the parochial offices, had now fallen into the hands of impropriators; so that the fund set apart for charity, instruction, and worship, often became the plunder of laymen, who took the great tithes and left a remaining pittance to their vicars.

The lustre of spiritual influence was tarnished by this strict subordination to the temporal power. The clergy had never slept so soundly over the traditions of the church; and the dean and chapter, at their cathedral stalls, seemed like strangers encamped among the shrines, or lost in the groined aisles which the fervid genius of men of a different age and a heartier faith had fashioned; filling the choir with

CHAP. III. 1763. religious light from the blended colors of storied windows, imitating the graceful curving of the lambent flame in the adornment of the tracery, and carving in stone every flower and leaf of the garden to embellish the light column, whose shafts soared upwards, as if to reach the sky.

The clergy were Protestant and married. Their great dignitaries dwelt in palaces, and used their vast revenues not to renew cathedrals, or beautify chapels, or build new churches, or endow schools; the record of their wealth was written in the rolls of the landed gentry, into which the fortunes they accumulated introduced their children; so that the church, though it was represented among the barons, never came in conflict with the landed aristocracy with which its interests were identified.

The hereditary right of the other members of the House of Lords was such a privilege as must, in itself, always be hateful to a free people;[1] and yet, in England, it was not so. In France, the burgesses were preparing to overthrow the peerage; but in England there was no incessant struggle to be rid of it. The reverence for its antiquity was enhanced by pleasing historical associations. But for the aid of the barons, Magna Charta would not have been attained; and but for the nobility and gentry, the revolution of 1688 would not have succeeded. A sentiment of gratitude was, therefore, blended in the popular mind with submission to rank.

Besides, nobility was not a caste, but rather an

[1] Les prérogatives odieuses par elles-mêmes, et qui dans un état libre, doivent toujours être en danger. Montesquieu.

CHAP. III. 1763.

office, personal and transmissible to but one. The right of primogeniture made its chief victims in the bosom of the families which it kept up, and which themselves set the leading example of resignation to its injustice. Not younger sons only, who might find employment in public office, or at the bar, or in the church, the army, or navy, or in mercantile adventures and pursuits; the daughters of the great landed proprietors, from a delicate sense of self-sacrifice, characteristic of the sex, applauded the rule by which they were disinherited, and placed their pride in upholding a system which left them dependent or destitute. In the splendid houses of their parents they were bred to a sense of their own poverty, and were bred to endure that poverty cheerfully. They would not murmur against the system, for their sighs might have been taunted as the repinings of selfishness. They all revered the head of the family, and by their own submission taught the people to do so. Even the mother who might survive her husband, after following him to his tomb in the old manorial church, returned no more to the ancestral mansion, but vacated it for the heir; and the dowager must be content with her jointure, which might often be paid grudgingly as to one

Long wintering on a young man's revenue.

As the daughters of the nobility were left poor, and most of them necessarily remained unmarried, or wedded persons of inferior birth, so the younger sons became commoners; and though they were in some measure objects of jealousy, because they so much engrossed the public patronage, yet, as they really were commoners, and entered the body of the people, they

CHAP. III. 1763. kept up between classes a sympathy unknown in any other country. Besides, the road to the honors of the peerage, as all knew, lay open to all. It was a body, constantly invigorated by recruits from some among the greatest men of England. Had it been left to itself, it would have perished long before. Once, having the gentle Addison for a supporter of the measure, it voted itself to be a close order, but was saved by the House of Commons from consummating its selfish purpose, where success would have prepared its ruin; and it remained that the poorest man who ever struggled upwards in the rude competition of the law, might come to preside in the House of Lords. So the peerage was doubly connected with the people; the larger part of its sons and daughters descended to the station of commoners, and commoners were at all times making their way to the peerage. In no country was rank so privileged, or classes so blended.

The peers, too, were, like all others, amenable to the law; and though the system of finance bore evidence of their controlling influence in legislation, yet the houses, lands, and property of the peers were not exempt from taxation. The law, most unequal as it certainly was, yet such as it was, applied equally to all.

One branch of the legislature was reserved to the hereditary aristocracy of landholders; the House of Commons partook of the same character: it represented every blade of grass in the kingdom, but not every laborer; the land of England, but not her men. No one but a landholder was qualified to be elected into that body; and most of those who were chosen were scions of the great families. Sons of peers, even the oldest son, while his father lived, could sit in the House of Commons; and there might be, and usually were, many members of one name.

Nor was the condition of the elective franchise uniform. It was a privilege; and the various rights of election depended on capricious charters or immemorial custom rather than on reason.

Of the five hundred and fifty-eight members, of whom the House of Commons then consisted, the counties of England, Wales, and Scotland elected one hundred and thirty-one as knights of the shires. These owed their election to the good will of the owners of great estates in the respective counties; for it was a usage that the tenant should vote as his landlord directed, and his compliance was certain, for the ballot was unknown, and the vote was given by word of mouth or a show of hands. The representatives of the counties were, therefore, as a class, country gentlemen, independent of the court. They were, comparatively free from corruption, and some of them fervidly devoted to English liberty.

The remaining four hundred and twenty-seven members, "citizens and burgesses," were arbitrarily distributed among cities, towns, and boroughs, with little regard to the wealth or to the actual numbers of the inhabitants. The bare name of Old Sarum, where there was not so much as the ruins of a town, and scarce so much housing as a sheep-cot, or more inhabitants than a shepherd, sent as many representatives to the grand assembly of law-makers as the whole county of Yorkshire, so numerous in people and powerful in riches.[1] The lord of the borough

[1] The illustration is in substance, and almost in words, from Locke.

CHAP. III.

1763.

of Newport, in the Isle of Wight, in like manner named two members, while Bristol elected no more; the populous capital of Scotland but one; and Manchester none. Two hundred and fifty-four members had such small constituencies, that about five thousand seven hundred and twenty-three votes sufficed to choose them. Fifty-six were elected by so few that, had the districts been equally divided, six and a half votes would have sufficed for each member. In an island counting more than seven and a half millions of people, and at least a million and a half of mature men, no one could pretend that it required more than ten thousand voters to elect the majority of the House of Commons. But, in fact, it required the consent of a far less number.

London, and Bristol, and perhaps a few more of the larger places, made independent selections; but they were so few, independence seemed to belong to London alone. The boroughs were nearly all dependent on some great proprietor, or on the crown. The burgage tenures belonged to men of fortune; and as the elective power attached to borough houses, the owner of those houses could compel their inhabitants to elect whom he pleased. The majority of the members were able to command their own election, sat in parliament for life as undisturbed as the peers, and bequeathed to their children the property and influence which secured their seats. The same names occur in the rolls of parliament, at the same places, from one generation to another.

The exclusive character of the representative body was completed by the prohibition of the publication of the debates, and by the rule of conducting all important negotiations with closed doors. Power was with the few. The people was swallowed up in the lords and commons. CHAP. III. 1763.

Such was the parliament whose favor conferred a secure tenure of office, whose judgment was the oracle of British statesmen. In those days they never indulged in abstract reasoning, and cared little for general ideas. Theories and philosophy from their lips would have been ridiculed or neglected; for them the applause at St. Stephen's weighed more than the approval of posterity, more than the voice of God in the soul. That hall was their arena of glory, their battle-field for power. They pleaded before that tribunal, and not in the forum of humanity. They studied its majorities, to know on which side was "the best of the lay" in the contest of factions for office. How to meet parliament was the minister's chief solicitude; and sometimes, like the spendthrift at a gaming-table, he would hazard all his political fortunes on its one decision. He valued its approval more than the affections of mankind, and could boast that this servitude, like obedience to the Divine Law, was perfect freedom.[1]

The representation in parliament was manifestly inadequate, and might seem to introduce that unmixed aristocracy which is the worst government under the sun. But the English system was so tempered with popular franchises that faithful history must place it among the very best which the world had seen. If no considerable class desired to introduce open and avowed republicanism, no British statesman of that century had as yet been suspected of deliberately

[1] "Perfect freedom." Burke: Thoughts on the Cause of the Present Discontents.

CHAP. III. 1763. planning how to narrow practical liberty, by substituting the letter of the constitution for its vital principle. It was the custom of parliament to listen with deference to the representations of the opulent industrial classes, and the House of Commons was sympathetic with the people.

Hence the inconsistency involved in the English electoral system, which was altogether a domestic question and not likely to be reformed by any influence from within, was less considered than the fact, that the country, alone among monarchies, really possessed a legislative constitution. In the pride of comparison with France and Spain, it was a part of the Englishman's nationality to maintain the perfection of British institutions, and to look down with scorn on all the kingdoms of the Continent, as lands of slaves. Every Englishman, in the comparison, esteemed himself as his own master and lord, having no fear of oppression, obeying no laws but such as he seemed to have assisted in making, and reasoning on politics with that free inquiry which, in a despotism, leads to revolution. The idea of the perfection of representative government veiled the inconsistencies of practice. It was received as yet without much question, that every independent man had, or might have, a vote; that every man was governed by himself; and that the people of England, as a corporate body, exercised legislative power.

Men considered, too, the functions of parliament, and especially of the House of Commons. It protected the property of every man by taking from the executive the power of taxation, and establishing the ideal principle, that taxes could be levied only with the consent of the people. It maintained the supremacy of the civil power by making the grants for the army and navy annual, limiting the number of troops that might be kept up, and keeping the control over their discipline by leaving even the mutiny bill to expire once a year. Thus it guarded against danger from a standing army, of which it always stood in dread. All appropriations, except the civil list for maintaining the dignity of the crown, it made specific and only for the year. As the great inquest of the nation, it examined how the laws were executed, and was armed with the power of impeachment. By its control of the revenue, it was so interwoven with the administration, that it could force the king to accept, as advisers, even men who had most offended him; so that it might seem doubtful if he named, or if parliament designated the ministers.

The same character of aristocracy was imprinted on the administration. The king reigned, but, by the theory of the constitution, was not to govern.[1] He appeared in the Privy Council on occasions of state; but Queen Anne was the last of the English monarchs to attend the debates in the House of Lords, or to preside at a meeting of the ministry. In the cabinet, according to the rule of aristocracy, every question was put to vote, and after the vote the dissentients must hush their individual opinions, and present the appearance of unanimity. The king himself must be able to change his council, or must yield. Add to this, that the public offices were engrossed by a small group of families, that favor dictated appointments of

[1] The phrase, "The king reigns but does not govern," may be found in Bolingbroke, who wished that the patriot king should "govern as well as reign."

CHAP. III. 1763. bishops in the church, of officers in the navy, and still more in the army, in which even boys at school held commissions, and we shall find that the aristocracy of England absorbed all the functions of administration.

Yet, even here, the spirit of aristocracy was reined in. Every man claimed a right to sit in judgment on the administration; and the mighty power of public opinion,[1] embodied in a free press, pervaded, checked, and, in the last resort, nearly governed the whole.

Nor must he who will understand the English institutions leave out of view the character of the enduring works which had sprung from the salient energy of the English mind. Literature had been left to develope itself. William of Orange was foreign to it; Anne cared not for it; the first George knew no English; the second, not much. Devotedness to the monarch is not impressed on English literature; but it willingly bore the mark of its own aristocracy.

> Envy must own I live among the great,

was the boast of the most finished English poet of the eighteenth century.

Neither the earlier nor the later literature put itself at war with the country or its classes. The philosophy of Bacon, brilliant with the richest lustre of a creative imagination and extensive learning, is marked by moderation as well as grandeur; and, like that principle of English institutions which consults

[1] "He who, speculating on the British constitution, should omit from his enumeration the mighty power of public opinion, embodied in a free press, which pervades, and checks, and perhaps, in the last resort, nearly governs the whole, would give but an imperfect view of the government of England."—Speech, at Liverpool, of Canning, who died before the reform of parliament.

precedents and facts rather than theories, it prepared the advancement of science by the method of observation. Newton was a contented member of a university, and never thought to rebel against the limits that nature has set to the human powers in the pursuit of science.

The inmost character of the English mind, in the various epochs of its history, was imprinted on its poetry. Chaucer recalled the joyous heroism, and serious thought, and mirth, and sadness, that beguiled the pious pilgrimages, or lent a charm to the hospitality of Catholic England. Spencer threw the dim halo of allegory round the monotonous caprices of departing chivalry. Shakespeare, "great heir of fame," rising at the proud moment of the victory of English nationality and Protestant liberty over all their enemies, seeming to be master of every chord that vibrates in the human soul, and knowing all that can become the cottage or the palace, the town or the fields and forests, the camp or the banqueting hall, unfolded the panorama of English history, and embodied in "easy numbers" all that is wise, and lovely, and observable in English manners and social life, proud of his countrymen and his country, to him

> This land of such dear souls, this dear, dear land,
> Dear for her reputation through the world.

Milton, with his heroic greatness of mind, was the stately representative of English republicanism, eager to quell the oppressor, but sternly detesting libertinism and disorder, and exhorting to "patience," even in the days of the later Stuarts. Dryden, living through the whole era of revolutions, yielded to the social influences of his time, and reproduced in his verse the

CHAP. III. 1763. wayward wavering of the English court between Protestantism and the Roman Catholic religion, between voluptuousness and faith; least read, because least proudly national. And Pope was the cherished poet of English aristocratic life, as it existed in the time of Bolingbroke and Walpole; flattering the great with sarcasms against kings; an optimist, proclaiming order as the first law of Heaven. None of all these, not even Milton, provoked to the overthrow of the institutions of England.

Nor had the skepticism of modern philosophy penetrated the mass of the nation, or raised vague desires of revolution. It kept, rather, what was held to be the best company. It entered the palace during the licentiousness of the two former reigns; and though the court was now become decorous and devout, still the nobility, and those who, in that day, were called "the great," affected free-thinking as a mark of high breeding, and laughed at the evidence of piety in any one of their order. But the spirit of the people rebelled against materialism; if worship, as conducted in the parish church, had no attractive warmth, they gathered round the preacher in the fields, eager to be assured that they had within themselves a spiritual nature and a warrant for their belief in immortality; yet, under the moderating influence of Wesley, giving the world the unknown spectacle of a fervid reform in religion, combined with unquestioning deference to authority in the state.

English metaphysical philosophy itself bore a character of moderation analogous to English institutions. In open disregard to the traditions of the Catholic church, Locke had denied that thought implies an immaterial substance; and Hartley and the chillingly repulsive Priestley asserted that the soul was but of flesh and blood; but the more genial Berkeley, armed with "every virtue," insisted rather on the certain existence of the intellectual world alone; while from the bench of English bishops the inimitable Butler pressed the analogies of the material creation itself into the service of spiritual life, and, with the authority of reason, taught the supremacy of conscience. If Hume embodied the logical consequences of the sensuous philosophy in the most skilfully constructed system of idealism which the world had ever known, his own countryman, Reid, in works worthy to teach the youth of a republic, illustrated the active powers of man and the reality of right; Adam Smith found a criterion of duty in the universal sentiment of mankind; and the English Dissenter, Price, enforced the eternal, necessary, and unchanging distinctions of morality. So philosophic freedom in England rebuked its own excesses, and, self-balanced and self-restrained, never sought to throw down the august fabric which had for so many centuries stood before Europe as the citadel of liberty.

CHAP. III. 1763.

The blended respect for aristocracy and for popular rights was impressed upon the courts of law. They were charged with the protection of every individual without distinction, securing to the accused a trial by sworn men, who were taken from among his peers, and held their office for but one short term of service. And especially the judges watched over the personal liberty of every Englishman, with power on the instant to set free any one illegally imprisoned, even though in custody by the king's express command.

At the same time the judiciary, with a reputation

CHAP. III. 1763. for impartiality, in the main well deserved, was by its nature conservative, and by its constitution the associate and the support of the House of Lords. Westminster Hall, which had stood through many revolutions and many dynasties, and was become venerable from an unchanged existence of five hundred years, sent the first officer in one of its courts, from however humble an origin he might have sprung, to take precedence of the nobility of the realm, and act as president of the chamber of peers. That branch of the legislature derived an increase of its dignity from the great lawyers whom the crown, from time to time, was accustomed to ennoble; and moreover, it formed, of itself, a part of the judicial system. The House of Commons, whose members, from their frequent elections, best knew the temper of the people, possessed exclusively the right to originate votes of supply; but the final judgment on all questions of law respecting property rested with the House of Lords.

The same cast of aristocracy, intermingled with popularity, pervaded the systems of education. From climate, compact population, and sober national character, England was capable beyond any other country in the world of a system of popular education. Nevertheless it had none. The mass of its people was left ignorant how to write or read.

But the benevolence of Catholic ages, emulated also in later times, had benefited science by endowments, which in their conception were charity schools; founded by piety for the education of poor men's sons; where a place might sometimes be awarded to favor, but advancement could be obtained only by merit; and the sons of the aristocracy, having no seminaries of their own, grouped themselves as at Eton, or Westminster, or Harrow, or Winchester, round the body of the scholars on the foundation; submitting like them to the accustomed discipline, even to the use of the rod, at which none rebelled, since it fell alike on all.

The same constitution marked the universities. The best scholars on the foundation were elected from the public schools to the scholarships in the several colleges; and formed the continuing line of succession to their appointments as well as the central influence of industry, order, and ambition, round which the sons of the opulent clustered. Thus the genius of the past claimed the right to linger in the streets of Mediaeval Oxford; and the sentiment of loyalty, as in earlier days, still hovered over the meadows of Christ Church and the walks of Maudlin; but if the two universities were both loyal to the throne and devoted to the church, it was from their own free choice; and not from deference to authority or command. They had proved their independence and had resisted kings. If they were swayed on the surface by ministerial influences, they were at heart intractable and self-determined. The king could neither appoint their officers, nor prescribe their studies, nor control their government, nor administer their funds. The endowments of the colleges, which, in their origin, were the gifts of piety and charity, were held as property, independent of the state; and were as sacred as the estates of any one of the landed gentry. The sons of the aristocracy might sometimes be prize-men at Oxford or wranglers at Cambridge; but if they won collegiate honors, it was done fairly by merit alone. In the pursuit, the eldest sons of peers stood on no vantage ground over

CHAP. III. 1763. the humblest commoner; so that the universities in their whole organization, at once upheld the institutions of England, and found in them the security of their own privileges.

It might be supposed that the gates of the cities would have been barred against the influence of the aristocracy. But it was not so. That influence was interwoven with the prosperity of the towns. Entails were not perpetual; but land was always in the market; estates were often encumbered; and the national debt, which was intimately connected with all private credit and commercial transactions, was also in fact a mortgage upon all the soil of the kingdom. The swelling expenses of the government increased its dependence on the moneyed class; and the leading minister needed the confidence of the city as well as of the country and the court. Besides, it was not uncommon to see a wealthy citizen, toiling to amass yet greater wealth that he might purchase land and found a family, or giving his richly dowered daughter in marriage to a peer.

Every body formed a part of the aristocratic organization: a few desired to enter the higher class; the rest sought fortune in serving it.

Moreover; the interests of the trade of the nation had precedence of the political interests of the princes. The members of the legislature watched popular excitements and listened readily to the petitions of the merchants; and these in their turn did not desire to see one of their own number charged with the conduct of the finances as chancellor of the exchequer; but wished rather for some member of the aristocracy, friendly to their interests. They preferred to speak through such an one, and rebelled against the necessity of doing so, as little as they did at the employment of a barrister to plead their cause in the halls of justice. CHAP III. 1763.

But if aristocracy was not excluded from towns, still more did it pervade the rural life of England. The climate not only enjoyed the softer atmosphere that belongs to the western side of masses of land, but was further modified by the proximity of every part of it to the sea. It knew neither long continuing heat nor cold; and was more friendly to daily employment throughout the whole year, within doors or without, than any in Europe. The island was "a little world" of its own; with a "happy breed of men" for its inhabitants, in whom the hardihood of the Norman was intermixed with the gentler qualities of the Celt and the Saxon, just as nails are rubbed into steel to temper and harden the Damascus blade. They loved country life, of which the mildness of the clime increased the attractions; since every grass and flower and tree that had its home between the remote north and the neighborhood of the tropics would live abroad, and such only excepted as needed a hot sun to unfold their bloom, or concentrate their aroma, or ripen their fruit, would thrive in perfection: so that no region could show such a varied wood. The moisture of the sky favored a soil not naturally very rich; and so fructified the earth, that it was clad in perpetual verdure. Nature had its attractions even in winter. The ancient trees were stripped indeed of their foliage; but showed more clearly their fine proportions, and the undisturbed nests of the noisy rooks among their boughs; the air was so mild, that the flocks and herds still grazed on the freshly springing herbage; and the

CHAP. III. 1763. deer found shelter enough by crouching amongst the fern; the smoothly shaven grassy walk was soft and yielding under the foot; nor was there a month in the year in which the plough was idle. The large landed proprietors dwelt often in houses which had descended to them from the times when England was gemmed all over with the most delicate and most solid structures of Gothic art. The very lanes were memorials of early days, and ran as they had been laid out before the conquest; and in mills for grinding corn, water-wheels revolved at their work just where they had been doing so for at least eight hundred years. Hospitality also had its traditions; and for untold centuries Christmas had been the most joyous of the seasons.

The system was so completely the ruling element in English history and English life, especially in the country, that it seemed the most natural organization of society, and was even endeared to the dependent people. Hence the manners of the aristocracy, without haughtiness or arrogance, implied rather than expressed the consciousness of undisputed rank; and female beauty added to its loveliness the blended graces of dignity and humility—most winning, where acquaintance with sorrow had softened the feeling of superiority, and increased the sentiment of compassion.

Yet the privileged class defended its rural pleasures and its agricultural interests with impassioned vigilance. The game laws parcelling out among the large proprietors the exclusive right of hunting, which had been wrested from the king as too grievous a prerogative, were maintained with relentless severity; and to steal or even to hamstring a sheep[1] was as much punished by death as murder or treason. During the reign of George the Second, sixty-three new capital offences had been added to the criminal laws, and five new ones, on the average, continued to be discovered annually;[2] so that the criminal code of England, formed under the influence of the rural gentry, seemed written in blood, and owed its mitigation only to executive clemency.

But this cruelty, while it encouraged and hardened offenders,[3] did not revolt the instinct of submission in the rural population. The tenantry, for the most part without permanent leases, holding lands at a moderate rent, transmitting the occupation of them from father to son through many generations,

> With calm desires that asked but little room,

clung to the lord of the manor as ivy to massive old walls. They loved to live in his light, to lean on his support, to gather round him with affectionate deference rather than base cowering; and, by their faithful attachment, to win his sympathy and care; happy when he was such an one as merited their love. They caught refinement of their superiors, so that their cottages were carefully neat, with roses and honeysuckles clambering to their roofs. They culti-

[1] "Recently a boy was hanged for hamstringing some sheep which a butcher intended to have stolen." Sir William Meredith: Debates, 9th May, 1770, in Cavendish, ii. 12.

[2] "Previous to the Revolution, the number of capital offences did not exceed 50. During the reign of George II. 63 new ones were added; and at the present moment they amount to no fewer than 154." Ibid. "Let a gentleman only come down to this House and say that a man has done so and so but cannot be hanged for it, the cry is, 'Oh, let us make a law, and hang him up immediately!'" Speech of Sir William Meredith, 27th Nov. 1770; in Cavendish, ii. 89.

[3] Charles Fox: in Cavendish, ii. 12.

CHAP. III. 1763. vated the soil in sight of the towers of the church, near which reposed the ashes of their ancestors for almost a thousand years. The whole island was mapped out into territorial parishes, as well as into counties, and the affairs of local interest, the assessment of rates, the care of the poor and of the roads, were settled by elected vestries or magistrates, with little interference from the central government. The resident magistrates were unpaid, being taken from among the landed gentry ; and the local affairs of the county, and all criminal affairs of no uncommon importance, were settled by them in a body at their quarterly sessions, where a kind-hearted landlord often presided, to appal the convicted offender by the solemn earnestness of his rebuke, and then to show him mercy by a lenient sentence.

Thus the local institutions of England shared the common character; they were at once the evidence of aristocracy and the badges of liberty.

The climate, so inviting to rural life, was benign also to industry of all sorts. Nowhere could labor apply itself so steadily, or in the same time achieve so much; and it might seem that the population engaged in manufactures would have constituted a separate element not included within the aristocratic system; but the great manufacture of the material not produced at home was still in its infancy. The weaver toiled in his own cottage, and the thread which he used was with difficulty supplied to him sufficiently by the spinners at the wheel of his own family and among his neighbors. Men had not as yet learned by machinery to produce, continuously and uniformly, from the down of cotton, the porous cords of parallel filaments; to attenuate them by gently drawing them out; to twist and extend the threads as they are formed; and to wind them regularly on pins of wood as fast as they are spun. At that time the inconsiderable cotton manufactures of Great Britain, transported from place to place on pack-horses, did not form one two-hundredth part of the present production, and were politically of no importance. Not yet had art done more than begin the construction of channels for still-water navigation. Not yet had Wedgwood fully succeeded in changing, annually, tens of thousands of tons of clay and flint into brilliantly glazed and durable ware, capable of sustaining heat, cheap in price, and beautiful and convenient in form. Not yet had the mechanics of England, after using up its forests, learned familiarly to smelt iron with pit coal, or perfected the steam-engines that were to do the heavy work in mining coal and to drive machinery in workshops.

Let the great artificers of England, who work in iron or clay, adopt science as their patron; let the cotton-spinners, deriving their raw material from abroad, perfect their manufacture by inventive plebeian genius, and so prosper as to gather around their mills a crowded population; and there will then exist a powerful, and opulent, and numerous class, emancipated from aristocratic influence, thriving independently outside of the old society of England.

But, in 1763, the great manufactures of the realm were those of wool and the various preparations from heepskins and hides, far exceeding in value all others of all kinds put together; and for these the land-owner furnished all the raw material; so that his prosperity was bound up in that of the manufacturer. The manu-

CHAP. III.

1763.

facture of wool was cherished as the most valuable of all. It had grown with the growth and wealth of England, and flourished in every part of the island; at Kidderminster, and Wilton, and Norwich, not less than in the West Riding of Yorkshire. It had been privileged by King Stephen, and regulated by the iron-hearted Richard. Its protection was as much a part of the statute-book as the game laws, and was older than Magna Charta itself. To foster it was an ancient custom of the country, coeval with the English constitution, and it was so interwoven with the condition of life in England that it seemed to form an intimate dependency of the aristocracy. The land-owner, whose rich lawns produced the fleece, sympathized with the industry that wrought it into beautiful fabrics. Mutual confidence was established between the classes of society; no chasm divided its orders.

Thus unity of character marked the constitution and the social life of England. The sum of the whole was an intense nationality in its people. They were happy in their form of government, and were justly proud of it; for they enjoyed more perfect freedom than the world up to that time had known. In spite of all the glaring defects of their system, Greece, in the days of Pericles or Phocion, had not been blessed with such liberty. Italy, in the fairest days of her ill-starred republics, had not possessed such security of property and person, so pure an administration of justice, such unlicensed expression of thought.

These benefits were held by a firm tenure; safe against revolutions and sudden changes in the state; the laws reigned, and not men; and the laws had been the growth of centuries, yielding to amendment only by the gradual method of nature, when opinions exercising less instant influence should slowly infuse themselves through the public mind into legislation; so that the English constitution, though like all things else perpetually changing, changed like the style of architecture along the aisles of its own cathedrals, where the ponderous severity of the Norman age melts in the next, almost imperceptibly, into the more genial pointed arch and the seemingly lighter sheaf of columns, yet without sacrificing the stately majesty of the proportions or the massive durability of the pile.

The English knew this, and were boastfully conscious of it. As a people, they cared not to hear of the defects in the form of their constitution. They looked out upon other states, and compared their own condition with that of the peoples on the continent, abjectly exposed to the sway of despots; they seemed to enjoy liberty in its perfection, and lost sight of the actual inadequacy of their system in their joy at its ideal purity. They felt that they were great, not by restraining laws, not by monopoly, but by liberty and labor. Liberty was the cry of the whole nation; and every opposition, from whatever selfish origin it might spring, took this type, always demanding more than even a liberal government would concede. Liberty and industry gave England its nationality and greatness. As a consequence, they thought themselves superior to every other nation. The Frenchman loved France, and when away from it, longed to return to it, as the only country where life could be thoroughly enjoyed. The German, in whom the sentiment of his native soil was enfeebled by its divisions into so many states and sovereignties, gained enlargement in his sphere of vision, and at home had

CHAP. III. 1763.

a curiosity for all learning; away from home, had eyes for every thing. The Englishman, wherever he went, was environed by an English atmosphere. He saw the world abroad as if to perceive how inferior it was to the land of his birth. The English statesmen, going from the classical schools to the universities—brought up in a narrow circle of classical and mathematical learning, with no philosophical training or acquaintance with general principles, travelled as Englishmen. They went young to the House of Commons; and were so blinded by admiration of their own country, they thought nothing blameworthy that promoted its glory, its power, or its welfare. They looked out upon the surrounding sea as their wall of defence

> Against the envy of less happier lands.

The great deep seemed to them their inheritance, inviting them every where to enter upon possession of it as their rightful domain. They looked beyond the Atlantic, and not content with their own colonies, they counted themselves defrauded of their due as the sole representatives of liberty, so long as Spain should hold exclusively such boundless empires. Especially to them the House of Bourbon was an adder, that might at any time be struck at, whenever it should rear its head. To promote British interests, and command the applause of the British Senate, they were ready to infringe on the rights of other countries,[1] and even on those of the outlying dominions of the crown.

[1] When Aristotle, in Polit. i. 1, wrote βαρβαρων δ'ἑλληνας αρχειν εικος, the Greek of that day reasoned just like an Englishman of the eighteenth century.

CHAPTER IV.

ENGLAND AND ITS DEPENDENCIES, CONTINUED.

1763.

CHAP. IV. 1763.

So England was one united nation. The landed aristocracy was the sovereign, was the legislature, was the people, was the state. The separate influence of each of the great component parts of English society may be observed in the British dominions outside of Great Britain.

From the wrecks of the empire of the Great Mogul, a monopolizing company of English merchants had gained dominion in the East; with factories, subject provinces, and territorial revenues on the coast of Malabar, in the Carnatic, and on the Ganges. They despised the rivalry of France, whose East India Company was hopelessly ruined, and whose feeble factories were in a state of confessed inferiority;—and with eager zeal they pushed forward their victories, openly avowing gain as the sole end of their alliances and their trade, of their warfare and their civil rule.

In America, the middling class, chiefly rural people, with a few from the towns of England, had

CHAP. IV. 1763. founded colonies in the forms of liberty; and themselves owned and cultivated the soil.

Ireland, whose government was proposed as a model for the British colonies, and whose history is from this time intimately connected with the course of events in America, had been seized by the English oligarchy.

The island was half as large as England, with a still milder climate, and a more fertile soil. From the midst of its wild mountain scenery in the west gushed numerous rivers, fed by the rains which the sea breeze made frequent. These, now forming bogs and morasses, now expanding into beautiful lakes, now rushing with copious volume and swift descent, offered along their courses waterpower without limit, and near the sea formed deep and safe harbors. The rich limestone plains under the cloudy sky were thickly covered with luxuriant grasses, whose unequalled verdure vied in color with the emerald.

Centuries before the Christian era, the beautiful region had been occupied by men of one of the Celtic tribes, who had also colonized the Highlands of Scotland. The Normans, who in the eighth century planted commercial towns on its sea coast, were too few to maintain separate municipalities. The old inhabitants had been converted to Christianity by apostles of the purest fame, and abounded in churches and cathedrals, in a learned, liberal, and numerous clergy. Their civil government was an aristocratic confederacy[1] of septs or families and their respective chiefs; and the remote land seemed set

[1] Hallam's Constitutional History of England, iii. 461. The whole of the eighteenth chapter is devoted to the Constitution of Ireland.

apart by nature as the safe abode of an opulent, united and happy people.

CHAP. IV. 1763.

In the reign of Henry the Second of England, and in his name, English barons and adventurers invaded Ireland; and before the end of the thirteenth century its soil was parcelled out among ten English families.

As the occupation became confirmed, the English system of laws was continued to the English colonists living within the pale which comprised the four counties of Dublin, Louth, Meath, and Kildare. In the Irish parliament, framed ostensibly after the model of the English constitution, no Irishman could hold a seat: it represented the intruders only, who had come to possess themselves of the land of the natives, now quarrelling among themselves about the spoils, now rebelling against England, but always united against the Irish.

When Magna Charta was granted at Runnymede, it became also the possession and birthright of the Norman inhabitants of Ireland; but to the "mere Irish" its benefits were not extended, except by special charters of enfranchisement or denization, of which the sale furnished a ready means of exaction.

The oligarchy of conquerors in the process of time began to amalgamate with the Irish; they had the same religion; they inclined to adopt their language, dress, and manners; and to speak for the rights of Ireland more warmly than the Irish themselves. To counteract this tendency of "the degenerate English," laws were enacted so that the Anglo-Irish could not intermarry with the Celts, nor permit them to graze their lands, nor present them to benefices, nor receive them into religious houses, nor entertain their bards. The mere Irish were considered as out of the king's allegiance; in

CHAP. IV. 1763. war they were accounted rebels; in peace, the statute book called them Irish enemies; and to kill one of them was adjudged no felony.

During the long civil wars in England, English power declined in Ireland. To recover its subordination, in the year 1495, the tenth after the union of the Roses, the famous statute of Drogheda,[1] known as Poyning's Law, from the name of the Lord Deputy who obtained its enactment, reserved the initiative in legislation to the crown of England. No parliament could from that time "be holden in Ireland till the king's lieutenant should certify to the king, under the great seal of the land, the causes and considerations, and all such acts as it seems to them ought to be passed thereon, and such be affirmed by the king and his council, and his license to summon a parliament be obtained." Such remained the rule of Irish parliaments,[2] and began to be regarded as a good precedent for America.

The change in the relations of England to the See of Rome, at the time of the reform, served to amalgamate the Celtic Irish and the Anglo-Norman Irish; for the Catholic lords within the pale, as well as Catholic Ireland, adhered to their ancient religion.

The Irish resisted the act of supremacy; and the accession of Queen Elizabeth brought the struggle to a crisis. She established the Protestant Episcopal Church by an act of what was called an Irish parliament, in which the Celtic Irish had no part, and English retainers, chosen from select counties and boroughs and new boroughs made for the occasion,

[1] 1495: 10 Henry VII. Compare too the explanatory Act of 3 and 4 Philip and Mary.

[2] Speech of Sir John Davis in Leland, ii. 581.

held the ascendant over the Anglo-Norman Irish. The laws of supremacy and uniformity were adopted, in the words of the English statutes; the common prayer was appointed instead of mass, and was to be read in the English language, or, where that was not known, in the Latin. CHAP. IV. 1763

The Anglican prelates and priests, divided from the Irish by the insuperable barrier of language, were quartered upon the land, shepherds without sheep, pastors without people; strangers to the inhabitants, wanting not them but theirs. The churches went to ruin; the benefices fell to men who were held as foreigners and heretics, and who had no care for the Irish, but to compel them to pay tithes.[1] The inferior clergy were men of no parts or erudition, and were as immoral as they were illiterate.[2] No pains were taken to make converts, except by penal laws; and the Norman-Irish and Celtic-Irish now became nearer to one another, drawn by common sorrows, as well as by a common faith; for "the people of that country's birth, of all degrees, were papists, body and soul."[3]

The Anglican church in Ireland represented the English interest. Wild and incoherent attempts at self-defence against relentless oppression were followed by the desolation of large tracts of country, new confiscations of land, and a new colonial garrison in the train of the English army. Even the use of parliaments was suspended for seven and twenty years.

The accession of James the First, with the counsels

[1] Des pasteurs sans ouailles. Histoire de l'Irlande. Par l'Abbé MacGheogan, iii. 422.

[2] Edmund Spencer: View of the State of Ireland, in Ancient Irish Histories, i. 139–143. "Generally bad, licentious, and most disordered. 143. Only they take the tithes and offerings, and gather what fruit they may." 140.

[3] Sidney papers in Hallam, iii. 498.

CHAP. IV. 1763. of Bacon, seemed to promise Ireland some alleviation of its woes; for the pale was broken down; and when the king, after a long interval, convened a parliament, it stood for the whole island. But in the first place, the law tolerated only the Protestant worship; and when colonies were planted on lands of six counties in Ulster escheated to the crown, the planters were chiefly Presbyterians from Scotland, than whom none more deeply hated the Catholic religion. And next the war of chicane succeeded to the war of arms and hostile statutes. Ecclesiastical courts wronged conscience; soldiers practised extortions; the civil courts took away lands. Instead of adventurers despoiling the old inhabitants by the sword, there came up discoverers, who made a scandalous traffic of pleading the king's title against the possessors of estates to force them to grievous compositions,[1] or to effect the total extinction of the interests of the natives in their own soil.[2]

This species of subtle ravage, continued with systematic iniquity in the next reign, and carried to the last excess of perfidy, oppression and insolence, inspired a dread of extirpation, and kindled the flames of the rising of 1641.

To suppress this rebellion, when it had assumed the form of organized resistance, large forfeitures of lands were promised to those who should aid in reducing the island. The Catholics had successively against them, the party of the king, the Puritan parliament of England, the Scotch Presbyterians among themselves, the fierce, relentless energy of Cromwell, a unanimity of

[1] Lelands's History of Ireland.
[2] Edmund Burke to Sir Hercules Langrishe. 3 Jan. 1792.

CHAP. IV. 1763.

hatred, quickened by religious bigotry; greediness after confiscated estates, and the pride of power in the Protestant interest. Modern History has no parallel[1] for the sufferings of the Irish nation from 1641 to 1660.

At the restoration of Charles II. a declaration of settlement confirmed even the escheats of land, decreed by the republican party for the loyalty of their owners to the crown. It is the opinion of an English historian,[2] that "upon the whole result the Irish Catholics, having previously held about two-thirds of the kingdom, lost more than one-half of their possessions by forfeitures on account of their rebellion. * * * They were diminished also by much more than one-third through the calamities of that period."

Even the favor of James II. wrought the Catholic Irish nothing but evil, for they shared his defeat; and after their vain attempt to make of Ireland his independent place of refuge, and a gallant resistance, extending through a war of three years, the Irish at Limerick capitulated to the new dynasty, obtaining the royal promise of security of worship to the Roman Catholics, and the continued possession of their estates, free from all outlawries or forfeitures. Of these articles, the first was totally disregarded; the second was evaded. New forfeitures followed to the extent of more than a million of acres; and at the close of the seventeenth century, the native Irish, with the Anglo-Irish Catholics, possessed not more than a seventh of their own island.

The maxims on which the government of Ireland

[1] Clarendon. Hallam: "The sufferings of that nation, from the outset of the rebellion to its close, have never been surpassed but by those of the Jews in their destruction by Titus."

[2] Hallam's Constitutional History, iii. 527, 528.

CHAP. IV. 1763. was administered by Protestant England after the revolution of 1688, brought about the relations by which that country and our own reciprocally affected each other's destiny: Ireland assisting to people America, and America to redeem Ireland.

The inhabitants of Ireland were four parts[1] in five, certainly more than two parts in three,[2] Roman Catholics. Religion established three separate nationalities; the Anglican Churchmen, constituting nearly a tenth of the population; the Presbyterians, chiefly Scotch-Irish; and the Catholic population, which was a mixture of the old Celtic race, the untraceable remains of the few Danish settlers, and the Normans and first colonies of the English.

In settling the government, England intrusted it exclusively to those of "the English colony," who were members of its own church; so that the little minority ruled the island. To facilitate this, new boroughs were created; and wretched tenants, where not disfranchised, were so coerced in their votes at elections, that two-thirds of the Irish House of Commons were the nominees of the large Protestant proprietors of the land.

In addition to this, an act of the English parliament rehearsed the dangers to be apprehended from the presence of popish recusants in the Irish parliament, and

[1] Boulter to the Archbishop of Canterbury, i. 210: "There are, probably, in this kingdom five Papists to at least one Protestant." Durand to Choiseul, 30 July, 1767. Angleterre T. 474, "la proportion est au moins de quatre centre un." So Arthur Young: "500,000 Protestants, two million Catholics." Tour in Ireland, ii. 33.

[2] Burke says, more than two to one.

[3] "The people, saving a few British planters here and there, which were not a tenth part of the remnant, obstinate recusants." Bedell to Laud, in Burnet's Bedell. The civil wars changed the proportion.

required of every member the new oaths of allegiance and supremacy and the declaration against transubstantiation.[1] But not only were Roman Catholics excluded from seats in both branches of the legislature; a series of enactments, the fruit of relentless perseverance, gradually excluded "papists" from having any votes in the election of members to serve in parliament.[2]

The Catholic Irish, being disfranchised, one enactment pursued them after another till they suffered under a universal, unmitigated, indispensable, exceptionless disqualification.[3] In the courts of law, they could not gain a place on the bench, nor act as a barrister, or attorney, or solicitor,[4] nor be employed even as a hired clerk, nor sit on a grand jury, nor serve as a sheriff or a justice of the peace, nor hold even the lowest civil office of trust and profit, nor have any privilege in a town corporate, nor be a freeman of such corporation, nor vote at a vestry. If papists would trade and work, they must do it even in their native towns as aliens. They were expressly forbidden to take more than two apprentices in whatever employment, except in the linen manufacture only. A Catholic might not marry a Protestant[5]—the priest who should celebrate such a marriage was to be hanged;[6] nor be a guardian to any child, nor educate his own child, if the mother declared herself a Protest-

[1] 3 William and Mary, c. ii. An act for the abrogating the oath of supremacy in Ireland, and appointing other oaths. Plowden's Historical Review, i. 197.

[2] 7 and 9 William III. "It was resolved, *nemine contradicente*, that the excluding of papists from having votes for the electing of members to serve in parliament, was necessary to be made into a law." This was accomplished by the statutes of 1703, 1715, 1727.

[3] Edmund Burke.

[4] 9 William III. c. xiii.

[5] 7 and 9 William III. and 2 Anne.

[6] 12 Geo. I.

CHAP. IV. 1763.

ant; or even if his own child, however young, should profess to be a Protestant.

None but those who conformed to the established church were admitted to study at the universities, nor could degrees be obtained but by those who had taken all the tests, oaths, and declarations. No Protestant in Ireland might instruct a papist.[1] Papists could not supply their want by academies and schools of their own;[2] for a Catholic to teach, even in a private family or as usher to a Protestant, was a felony, punishable by imprisonment, exile, or death. Thus "papists" were excluded from all opportunity of education at home, except by stealth and in violation of law. It might be thought that schools abroad were open to them; but, by a statute of King William,[3] to be educated in any foreign Catholic school was an "unalterable and perpetual outlawry."[4] The child sent abroad for education, no matter of how tender an age, or himself how innocent, could never after sue in law or equity, or be guardian, executor, or administrator, or receive any legacy or deed of gift; he forfeited all his goods and chattels, and forfeited for his life all his lands. Whoever sent him abroad, or maintained him there, or assisted him with money or otherwise, incurred the same liabilities and penalties. The crown divided the forfeiture with the informer; and when a person was proved to have sent abroad a bill of exchange or money, on him rested the burden of proving that the remittance was innocent, and he must do so before justices without the benefit of a jury.[5]

[1] 7 William III.

[2] 8 Anne.

[3] 4 William and Mary, c. iv. Act to restrain foreign education.

[4] Edmund Burke.

[5] Edmund Burke's Fragment of a Tract on the Popery Laws.

The Irish Catholics were not only deprived of their liberties, but even of the opportunity of worship, except by connivance. Their clergy, taken from the humbler classes of the people,[1] could not be taught at home, nor be sent for education beyond seas, nor be recruited by learned ecclesiastics from abroad. Such priests as were permitted to reside in Ireland were required to be registered, and were kept like prisoners at large within prescribed limits. All "papists" exercising ecclesiastical jurisdiction, all monks, friars, and regular priests, and all priests not then actually in parishes, and to be registered, were banished from Ireland[2] under pain of transportation, and, on a return, of being hanged, drawn, and quartered.[3] Avarice was stimulated to apprehend them by the promise of a reward;[4] he that should harbor or conceal them was to be stripped of all his property. When the registered priests were dead, the law, which was made perpetual, applied to every popish priest.[5] By the laws of William and of Anne, St. Patrick, in Ireland, in the eighteenth century, would have been a felon. Any two justices of the peace might call before them any Catholic, and make inquisition as to when he heard mass, who were present, and what Catholic schoolmaster or priest he knew of; and the penalty for refusal to answer was a fine or a year's imprisonment. The Catholic priest, abjuring his religion, received a pension[6] of thirty, and afterwards of forty, pounds.[7] And, in spite of these laws, there were, it

CHAP. IV.

1763.

[1] Edmund Burke's Letter to a Peer in Ireland on the Penal Laws against Irish Catholics, 21 February, 1782.

[2] 7 and 9 William III. c. xxvi.

[3] 2 Anne.

[4] 8 Anne.

[5] Edmund Burke's Fragments of a Tract on the Popery Laws, c. ii.

[6] 8 Anne.

[7] 11 and 12 Geo. III. c. xxvii.

CHAP. IV. 1763. is said, four thousand Catholic clergymen in Ireland, and the Catholic worship gained upon the Protestant, so attractive is sincerity when ennobled by persecution, even though "the laws did not presume a papist to exist there, and did not allow them to breathe but by the connivance of the government."[1]

The Catholic Irish had been plundered of six-sevenths of the land by iniquitous confiscations; every acre of the remaining seventh was grudged them by the Protestants. No nonconforming Catholic could buy land, or receive it by descent, devise, or settlement; or lend money on it, as the security; or hold an interest in it through a Protestant trustee; or take a lease of ground for more than thirty-one years. If, under such a lease, he brought his farm to produce more than one-third beyond the rent, the first Protestant discoverer might sue for the lease before known Protestants, making the defendant answer all interrogatories on oath; so that the Catholic farmer dared not drain his fields, nor inclose them, nor build solid houses on them. If in any way he improved their productiveness, his lease was forfeited. It was his interest rather to deteriorate the country, lest envy should prompt some one to turn him out of doors.[2] In all these cases the forfeitures were in favor of Protestants. Even if a Catholic owned a horse worth more than five pounds, any Protestant might take it away.[3] Nor was natural affection or parental authority respected. The son of a Catholic landholder, however dissolute or however young, if he

[1] Plowden's Historical Review, i 322. Saul to O'Connor in Appendix to Plowden, i. 265.

[2] Compare Durand, of the French Embassy in London, to Choiseul, 30 July, 1767. French Archives, Angleterre, cccxxiii.

[3] 7 William III.

would but join the English church, could revolt against his father, and turn his father's estate in fee-simple into a tenancy for life, becoming himself the owner, and annulling every agreement made by the father, even before his son's conversion.

The dominion of the child over the property of the Popish parent was universal. The Catholic father could not in any degree disinherit his apostatizing son; but the child, in declaring himself a Protestant, might compel his father to confess upon oath the value of his substance, real and personal, on which the Protestant court might out of it award the son immediate maintenance, and after the father's death, any establishment it pleased. A new bill might at any time be brought by one or all of the children, for a further discovery. If the parent, by his industry, improved his property, the son might compel a new account of the value of the estate, in order to a new disposition. The father had no security against the persecution of his children but by abandoning all acquisition or improvement.[1]

Ireland, of which by far the greater part had been confiscated since the reign of Henry VIII., and much of it more than once, passed away from the ancient Irish. The proprietors in fee were probably fewer than in an equal area in any part of Western Europe, Spain only excepted. The consequence was, an unexampled complication of titles. The landlord in chief was often known only as having dominion over the estate; leases of large tracts had been granted for very long terms of years; these were again subdivided to those who subdivided them once

[1] Burke on the Penal Laws.

CHAP. IV. 1763. more, and so on indefinitely. Mortgages brought a new and numerous class of claimants. Thus humane connection between the tenant and landlord was not provided for. Leases were in the last resort most frequently given at will; and then what defence had the Irish Catholic against his Protestant superior? Hence the thatched mud cabin, without window or chimney; the cheap fences; the morass undrained; idleness in winter; the tenant's concealment of good returns: for to spend his savings in improving his farm would have been giving them to his immediate landlord.

To the native Irish the English oligarchy appeared not in the attitude of kind proprietors, whom residence and a common faith, long possession and hereditary affection united with the tenantry, but as men of a different race and creed, who had acquired the island by force of arms, rapine, and chicane, and derived revenues from it by the employment of extortionate underlings or overseers.

This state of society, as a whole, was what ought not to be endured, and the English were conscious of it. The common law respects the right of self-defence; yet the Irish Catholics, or Popish recusants as they were called, were, by one universal prohibition,[1] forbidden using or keeping any kind of weapons whatsoever, under penalties which the Crown could not remit. Any two justices might enter a house and search for arms, or summon any person whomsoever, and tender him an oath, of which the repeated refusal was punishable as treason.

[1] Irish statutes, 1695: Act for the security of Government.

CHAP. IV.

1763

Such was the Ireland of the Irish;—a conquered people, whom the victors delighted to trample upon, and did not fear to provoke.[1] Their industry within the kingdom was prohibited or repressed by law, and then they were calumniated as naturally idle. Their savings could not be invested on equal terms in trade, manufactures, or real property; and they were called improvident. The gates of learning were shut on them, and they were derided as ignorant. In the midst of privations they were cheerful. Suffering for generations under acts which offered bribes to treachery, their integrity was not debauched; no son rose against his father, no friend betrayed his friend. Fidelity to their religion, to which afflictions made them cling more closely, chastity, and respect for the ties of family, remained characteristics of the down-trodden race. America as yet offered it no inviting asylum, though her influence was soon to mitigate its sorrows and relax its bonds.

Relief was to come through the conflicts of the North American colonies with Great Britain. Ireland and America, in so far as both were oppressed by the commercial monopoly of England, had a common cause; and while the penal laws against the Catholics did not affect the Anglo-Irish, they suffered equally with the native Irish from the mercantile system. The restrictions of the acts of trade[2] extended not to America only, but to the sister kingdom. It had harbors, but it could not send a sail across the Atlantic, nor ship directly to the colonies, even in English vessels, any thing but "servants, and horses, and

[1] Edmund Burke to Sir H. Langrishe.

[2] Acts "to which we never consented." Dean Swift.

CHAP. IV. 1763. victuals,"[1] and at last linens;[2] nor receive sugar, or coffee, or other colonial produce, but from England.

Its great staple was wool; its most important natural manufacture was the woollen. "I shall do all that lies in my power to discourage the woollen manufactures of Ireland," said William of Orange.[3] The exportation of Irish woollens to the colonies and to foreign countries was prohibited;[4] and restrictive laws so interfered with the manufacture that it seemed probable, Irishmen would not be able to wear a coat of their own fabric.[5]

In the course of years the "English colonists" themselves began to be domiciliated in Ireland;[6] and with the feeling that the country in which they dwelt was their home, there grew up discontent that it continued to be treated as a conquered country. Proceeding by insensible degrees, they at length maintained openly the legislative equality of the two kingdoms. In 1692, the Irish House of Commons claimed "the sole and undoubted right to prepare and resolve the means of raising money."[7] In 1698,[8] Molyneux, an Irish Protestant, and member for the University of Dublin, asserted, through the press,[9] the perfect and reciprocal independence of the Irish and English parliaments; that Ireland was not bound by the acts of a legislative body in which it was not represented. Two replies were written to the tract, which was also formally condemned by the English House of

[1] Navigation acts of Charles II.

[2] 1704, 3 and 4 Anne, c. x. 1714, 1 Geo. I. c. xxvi.

[3] Speech to the Commons, 2 July, 1698.

[4] 10 and 11, William III. c. x. and the statute of 1732.

[5] Edmund Burke to ******, ***** & Co. Bristol. Westminster, 2 May, 1778.

[6] Edmund Burke.

[7] Journals of Irish House of Commons for 21 Oct., 1692.

[8] Plowden's Hist Review, i. 203.

[9] Molyneux: Case of Ireland, &c. &c.

Commons. When[1] in 1719 the Irish House of Lords denied for Ireland the judicial power of the House of Lords of Great Britain, the British parliament, making a precedent for all its outlying dominions, enacted, that "the king, with the consent of the parliament of Great Britain, had, hath, and of right ought to have full power and authority to make laws and statutes of force to bind the people and the kingdom of Ireland!"[2] CHAP. IV. 1763.

But the opposite opinion was confirmed among the Anglo-Irish statesmen. The Irish people set the example of resisting English laws by voluntary agreements to abstain from using English manufactures,[3] and the patriot party had already acquired strength and skill, just at the time when the British parliament, by its purpose of taxing the American colonies, provoked their united population to raise the same questions, and in their turn to deny its power.

But besides the conforming Protestant population, there was in Ireland another class of Protestants who shared in some degree the disqualifications of the Catholics. To Queen Anne's bill for preventing the further growth of Popery,[4] a clause was added in England,[5] and ratified by the Irish parliament, that none should be capable of any public employment, or of being in the magistracy of any city, who did not receive the sacrament according to the English test act;[6] thus disfranchising the whole body of Pres-

[1] Journals of the House of Commons, 22 June, 1698.

[2] 5 Geo. I. c. i.

[3] Dean Swift's State of Ireland.

[4] 2 Anne.

[5] Burnet's History of His Own Times. Curry's Historical and Critical Review, ii. 235. Plowden's Historical Review, i. 213.

[6] Burnet's History of His Own Times.

CHAP. IV. 1763. byterians. At home, where the Scottish nation enjoyed its own religion, the people were loyal: in Ireland, the disfranchised Scotch Presbyterians, who still drew their ideas of Christian government from the Westminster Confession, began to believe that they were under no religious obligation to render obedience to the British government. They could not enter the Irish parliament to strengthen the hands of the patriot party; nor were they taught by their faith to submit in patience, like the Catholic Irish. Had all Ireland resembled them, it could not have been kept in subjection. But what could be done by unorganized men, constituting only about a tenth of the people, in the land in which they were but sojourners? They were willing to quit a soil which was endeared to them by no traditions; and the American colonies opened their arms to receive them. They began to change their abode as soon as they felt oppression;[1] and every successive period of discontent swelled the tide of emigrants. Just after the peace of Paris, "the Heart of Oak" Protestants of Ulster, weary of strife with their landlords, came over in great numbers;[2] and settlements on the Catawba, in South Carolina, dated from that epoch.[3] At different times in the eighteenth century, some had found homes in New-England, but they were most numerous south of New-York, from New-Jersey to

[1] Boulter to the Duke of Newcastle, 23 Nov. 1728: "The whole North is in a ferment at present, and people every day engaging one another to go the next year to the West Indies. The humor has spread like a contagious distemper; and the people will hardly hear anybody that tries to cure them of their madness. The worst is, that it affects only Protestants, and reigns chiefly in the North." Plowden's Historical Review, i. 276. Compare, too, Dean Swift's Letters.

[2] James Gordon's History of Ireland, ii. 241.

[3] The parents of Andrew Jackson, the late President of the United States, reached South Carolina in 1764.

CHAP. IV. 1763.

Georgia. In Pennsylvania they peopled many counties, till, in public life, they already balanced the influence of the Quakers. In Virginia, they went up the valley of the Shenandoah; and they extended themselves along the tributaries of the Catawba, in the beautiful upland region of North Carolina. Their training in Ireland had kept the spirit of liberty and the readiness to resist unjust government as fresh in their hearts, as though they had just been listening to the preachings of Knox, or musing over the political creed of the Westminster Assembly. They brought to America no submissive love for England; and their experience and their religion alike bade them meet oppression with prompt resistance. We shall find the first voice publicly raised in America to dissolve all connection with Great Britain came, not from the Puritans of New-England, or the Dutch of New-York, or the planters of Virginia, but from Scotch-Irish Presbyterians.

CHAPTER V.

CHARLES TOWNSHEND PLEDGES THE MINISTRY OF BUTE TO TAX AMERICA BY THE BRITISH PARLIAMENT, AND RESIGNS.

FEBRUARY—APRIL, 1763.

CHAP. V. 1763. Feb.

AT the peace of 1763 the fame of England was exalted throughout Europe above that of all other nations. She had triumphed over those whom she called her hereditary enemies, and retained half a continent as the monument of her victories. Her American dominions stretched without dispute from the Atlantic to the Mississippi, from the Gulf of Mexico to Hudson's Bay; and in her older possessions that dominion was rooted as firmly in the affections of the colonists as in their institutions and laws. The ambition of British statesmen might well be inflamed with the desire of connecting the mother country and her transatlantic empire by indissoluble bonds of mutual interest and common liberties.

But the Board of Trade had long been angry with provincial assemblies for claiming the right of free deliberation. For several years[1] it had looked forward to peace as the moment when the colonies were to feel the superiority of the parent land.[2] Now that

[1] C. Calvert to Lieut. Governor Sharpe, 19th January, 1760.

[2] C. Calvert to Lieut. Governor Sharpe, March, 1763.

the appointed time had come, the Earl of Bute, with the full concurrence of the king, making the change which had long been expected,[1] assigned to Charles Townshend the office of first lord of trade, with the administration of the colonies. Assuming larger powers than had ever been exercised by any of his predecessors except Halifax,[2] called also to a seat in the cabinet, and enjoying direct access to the king on the affairs of his department, he, on the twenty-third of February, became secretary of state for the colonies in all but the name.[3] 1763. Feb.

In the council, in which Townshend took a place, there was Bute, its chief, having the entire confidence of his sovereign; the proud restorer of peace, fully impressed with the necessity of bringing the colonies into order,[4] and ready to give his support to the highest system of authority of Great Britain over America. Being at the head of the Treasury, he was, in a special manner, responsible for every measure connected with the finances; and though he was himself a feeble man of business, yet his defects were in a measure supplied by Jenkinson, his able, indefatigable and confidential private secretary.—There was

[1] Jasper Mauduit, Massachusetts, agent to Mr. Secretary Oliver, 12 March, 1763: "I am now to mention a change which has long been expected, and has at length taken place. Lord Sandys is removed from the board of trade, and Mr. Charles Townshend is put at the head of it."

[2] "It appears, upon Mr. Townshend's entry upon his office, the board of trade did notify their appointment to all the American governments, as well of the old established as the new acquired colonies; and did transmit to them, at the same time, copies of the order in council, of the 11th March, 1752; and the explanatory letters of the secretary of state, as the rule of their future correspondence." Paper by the Earl of Hillsborough, in the Lansdowne House manuscripts.

[3] Rigby to Bedford, 23 February, 1763, in the Bedford Correspondence, iii. 210.

[4] Knox, agent of Georgia. In Extra-official State Papers, ii. 29.

CHAP. V. 1763. Feb.

Mansfield,[1] the illustrious jurist, who had boasted publicly of his early determination never to engage in public life, "but upon whig principles;"[2] and, in conformity to them, had asserted that an act of parliament in Great Britain could alone prescribe rules for the reduction of refractory colonial assemblies.[3]—There was George Grenville, then first Lord of the Admiralty, bred to the law; and ever anxious to demonstrate that all the measures which he advocated reposed on the British Constitution, and the precedents of 1688; eager to make every part of the British empire tributary to the prosperity of Great Britain, and making the plenary authority of the British Legislature the first article of his political creed.—There was the place as Keeper of the Privy Seal for Bedford, the head of the house of Russell, and the great representative of the landed aristocracy of Great Britain, absent from England at the moment, but, through his friends, ready to applaud the new colonial system, to which he had long ago become a convert.—There was the weak and not unamiable Halifax, so long the chief of the American administration, heretofore baffled by the colonies, and held in check by Pitt; willing himself to be the instrument to carry his long cherished opinions of British omnipotence into effect.—There was the self-willed, hot-tempered Egremont, using the patronage of his office to enrich his family and friends; the same who had menaced Maryland, Pennsylvania and North Carolina—obstinate and impatient of contradiction, igno-

[1] Lord Campbell's Lives of the Chief Justices, ii. 459–460.

[2] Murray's speech in his own defence before the Lords of the Privy Council in 1753.

[3] Opinion of Sir Dudley Rider and Hon. William Murray, Attorney and Solicitor General, in October, 1744.

rant of business, passionate, and capable of cruelty in defence of authority; at variance with Bute, and speaking of his colleague, the Duke of Bedford, as "a headstrong, silly wretch."[1]

CHAP. V. 1763. Feb,

To these was now added the fearless, eloquent and impetuous Charles Townshend, trained to public life, first in the Board of Trade, and then as secretary at war—a statesman who entered upon the gravest affairs with all the courage of eager levity, and with a daring purpose of carrying difficult measures with unscrupulous speed. No man in the House of Commons was thought to know America so well; no one was so resolved on making a thorough change in its constitutions and government. "What schemes he will form," said the proprietary of Pennsylvania,[2] "we shall soon see." But there was no disguise about his schemes. He was always for making thorough work of it with the colonies.

James the Second, in attempting the introduction of what was called order into the New World, had employed the prerogative. Halifax and Townshend, in 1753, had tried to accomplish the same ends by the royal power, and had signally failed. It was now settled that no tax could be imposed on the inhabitants of a British plantation but by their own assembly, or by an act of parliament;[3] and though the ministers readily employed the name and authority of the king, yet, in the main, the new system was to be enforced by the transcendental power of the British parliament.

[1] Egremont to George Grenville, in the Grenville Papers, i. 475: "That headstrong, silly wretch."

[2] Thomas Penn to James Hamilton, 11 Feb. 1763.

[3] Opinion of Sir Philip Yorke and Sir Clement Wearg.

CHAP. V. 1763. Feb.

On his advancement, Townshend became at once the most important man in the House of Commons; for Fox commanded no respect, and was preparing to retire to the House of Lords; and Grenville, offended at having been postponed, kept himself sullenly in reserve. Besides; America, which had been the occasion of the war, became the great subject of consideration at the peace; and the minister who was charged with its government took the lead in public business.

Townshend carried with him into the cabinet and the House of Commons the experience, the asperities and the prejudices of the Board of Trade; and his plan for the interference of the supreme legislature derived its character from the selfish influences under which it had been formed, and which aimed at obtaining an unlimited, lucrative and secure patronage.

The primary object was, therefore, a revenue, to be disposed of by the British ministry, under the sign manual of the king. The ministry would tolerate no further "the disobedience of long time to royal instructions," nor bear with the claim of "the lower houses of assemblies" in the colonies to the right of deliberating on their votes of supply, like the parliament of Great Britain. It was announced "by authority"[1] that there were to be "no more requisitions from the king," but instead of such requisitions an immediate taxation of the colonies by the British legislature.

The first charge upon that revenue was to be the civil list, that all the royal officers in America, the judges in every court not less than the executive, might be wholly superior to the assemblies, and de-

[1] Cecil Calvert, Secretary in England for Maryland, to H. Sharpe, Lieutenant Governor of Maryland, 1 March, 1763.

pendent on the king's pleasure alone for their appointment to office, their continuance in it, and the amount and payment of their emoluments; so that the corps of persons in the public employ might be a civil garrison, set to keep the colonies in dependence, and to sustain the authority of Great Britain.

The charters were obstacles, and, in the opinion of Charles Townshend, the charters should fall, and one uniform system of government[1] be substituted in their stead. The little republics of Connecticut and Rhode Island, which Clarendon had cherished, and every ministry of Charles II. had spared, were no longer safe. A new territorial arrangement of provinces was in contemplation; Massachusetts itself was to be restrained in its boundaries, as well as made more dependent on the king.

This arbitrary policy required an American standing army, and that army was to be maintained by

[1] This part of the scheme was not at once brought out. The evidence of its existence in idea is, therefore, not to be found in the journals of parliament; but see Almon's Biographical Anecdotes of most Eminent Persons, ii. 83: "To make a new division of the colonies;" "to make them all royal governments." See also Chas. Townshend's speech in the House of Commons, on the third of June, 1766; "It has long been my opinion," &c. &c. See also the communication from Governor Wentworth, of New Hampshire, to Dr. Langdon, as narrated in Gordon's American Revolution, i. 142–144. Compare also Richard Jackson to Lieutenant Governor Hutchinson, 18 Nov. 1766. Charles Townshend "has often turned that matter, the alteration of the constitutions in America, in his thoughts, and was once inclined that way." This can hardly refer to any other moment than Townshend's short career as first lord of trade. Compare, further, the letter of Governor Bernard to Halifax, of 9 November, 1764, where the idea of these constitutional alterations is most fully developed, and where it is said, "This business seems only to have waited for a proper time." See, too, the many letters from the colonies, just before the peace, strongly recommending the changes. Lieut. Gov. Colden's paper on the same subject. So, too, the queries of the Rev. Dr. Samuel Johnson, of Connecticut, sent, in 1760, to the Archbishop of Canterbury, and Secker to Johnson. R. Jackson to Hutchinson, 13 Aug. 1764, and Hutchinson to Jackson, 15 October, 1764, relate to the same subject. The purpose against Rhode Island and Connecticut was transmitted through successive ministries till the Declaration of Independence.

CHAP. V. 1763. Feb.

those whom it was to oppress. To complete the system, the navigation acts were to be strictly enforced. It would seem that the execution of so momentous a design must have engaged the attention of the whole people of England, and of the civilized world. But so entirely was the British government of that day in the hands of the few, and so much was their curiosity engrossed by what would give influence at court, or secure votes in the House of Commons, that the most eventful measures ever adopted in that country were entered upon without any observation on the part of the historians and writers of memoirs at the time. The ministry itself was not aware of what it was doing. And had some seer risen up to foretell that the charter of Rhode Island derived from its popular character a vitality that would outlast the unreformed House of Commons, the faithful prophet would have been scoffed at as a visionary madman.

The first memorable opposition came from the General Assembly of New-York. In the spirit of loyalty and the language of reverence they pleaded with the king[1] concerning the colonial court of judicature, which exercised the ample authorities of the two great courts of King's Bench and Common Pleas, and also of the Barons of the Exchequer. They represented that this plenitude of uncontrolled power in persons who could not be impeached in the colony, and who, holding their offices during pleasure, were

[1] The Representation of the General Assembly at New-York to the King, concerning the Administration of Justice in that Province, 11th Dec. 1762. In Lansdowne House MSS.

CHAP. V. 1763. Feb.

consequently subject to the influence of governors, was to them an object of terror; and, from tenderness to the security of their lives, rights, and liberties, as well as fortunes, they prayed anxiously for leave to establish by law the independence and support of so important a tribunal. They produced, as an irrefragable argument, the example given in England after the accession of King William the Third, and they quoted the declaration of the present king himself, that he "looked upon the independency and uprightness of the judges as essential to the impartial administration of justice, one of the best securities to the rights and liberties of the subject, and as most conducive to the honor of the crown."[1] And, citing these words, which were the king's own to parliament on his coming to the throne, they express confidence in his undiscriminating liberality to all his good subjects, whether at home or abroad. But the voice of the Assembly, "supplicating with the most respectful humility," was unheeded; and the treasury board, at which Lord North had a seat, decided not only that the commission of the chief justice of New-York should be at the king's pleasure, but the amount and payment of his salary also.[2] And this momentous precedent, so well suited to alarm the calmest statesmen of America, was decided as quietly as any ordinary piece of business. The judiciary of a continent was,

[1] The king's speech to both houses of parliament, 3 March, 1761, recommending making the commissions of the judges perpetual during their good behavior, notwithstanding any future demise of the crown, &c. Annual Register, iv. 243.

[2] Dyson, Secretary of the Treasury, to J. Pownall, Secretary of the Board of Trade, 29 Dec. 1762, in Treasury Letter Book, xxii. 353. Dyson to auditor of plantations, ib. Compare, as to the fact of the allowance, Lieut. Gov. Colden to board of trade, New-York, 8 July, 1763, and Chief Justice Smyth, of New Jersey, to Hillsborough, 20 Nov. 1768.

CHAP. V. 1763. Mar.

by ministerial acts, placed in dependence on the crown avowedly for political purposes. The king, in the royal provinces, was to institute courts, name the judges, make them irresponsible but to himself, remove them at pleasure, regulate the amount of their salaries, and pay them by warrants under the sign manual, out of funds which were beyond the control of the several colonies, and not even supervised by the British parliament. The system introduced into New-York was to be universally extended.

While the allowance of a salary to the chief justice of New-York was passing through the forms of office, Welbore Ellis, the successor of Charles Townshend as secretary at war, brought forward the army estimates[1] for the year, including the proposition of twenty regiments as a standing army for America.

The country members would have grudged the expense; but Charles Townshend, with a promptness which in a good cause would have been wise and courageous, explained the plan of the ministry,[2] that these regiments were, for the first year only, to be supported by England,[3] and ever after by the colonies

[1] Journals of the House of Commons, xxiv. 506.

[2] "I understand part of the plan of the army is, and which I very much approve, to make North America pay its own army." Rigby to the Duke of Bedford, 23 February, 1763, in Bedford Correspondence, iii. 210. Compare, too, Calvert, resident secretary of Maryland in London, to Horatio Sharpe, deputy governor of Maryland, 1 March, 1763. "I am by authority informed that a scheme is forming for establishing 10,000 men, to be British Americans standing force there, and paid by the colonies."

[3] Jasper Mauduit, agent of the province of Massachusetts, to the speaker of the House of Representatives, 12 March, 1763, to be found in Massachusetts' Council Letter Book of Entries, i. 384, relates, that, a few days before, the secretary at war had proposed an establishment of twenty regiments for America, to be supported the first year by England, afterwards by the colonies. Compare, too, same to same, 11 Feb., 1764. See also, the accounts received in Charleston, S. C., copied into Weyman's N. Y. Gazette, 4 July, 1763, 238, 2, 2, and 3:

themselves. With Edmund Burke[1] in the gallery for one of his hearers, he dazzled country gentlemen by playing before their eyes the image of a revenue to be raised in America. The House of Commons listened with complacency to a plan which, at the expense of the colonies, would give twenty new places of colonels, that might be filled by members of their own body.

On the Report to the House, Pitt wished only that more troops had been retained in service; and as if to provoke France to distrust, he called "the peace hollow and insecure, a mere armed truce for ten years."[2] The support of Pitt prevented any opposition to the plan.

Two days after, on the ninth day of March, 1763, Charles Townshend came forward with a part of the scheme for taxing America by act of parliament. The existing duty on the trade of the continental colonies with the French and Spanish islands was, from its excessive amount, wholly prohibitory, and had been regularly evaded by a treaty of connivance between the merchants on the one side, and the custom-house officers and their English patrons on the other; for the custom-house officers were "quartered upon" by those through whom they gained their places. The minister proposed to reduce the

"Charlestcn, S. C., June 14th.—It is pretty certain that twenty British regiments, amounting to 10,000 effective men, are allotted to this continent and the British islands; some of them are to come here, but from whence, and their number, is equally uncertain. There are letters in town which positively say, that these troops are to be paid the first year only by Great Britain, and that every article of expense afterwards is to be defrayed by the colonies."

[1] Burke's speech on American Taxation.

[2] Walpole's Memoirs of the Reign of George the Third, i. 247. Rigby to the Duke of Bedford, 10 March, 1763. In Correspodence of Duke of Bedford, iii. 218.

CHAP. V. 1763. Mar.

duty and enforce its collection; and he did it with such bold impetuosity that, "short as the term was, it seemed that he would carry it through before the rising of parliament."[1] The house was impatient for it; heavy complaints were made, that the system of making all the revenue offices in America sinecure places, had led to such abuses, that an American annual revenue of less than two thousand pounds cost the establishment of the customs in Great Britain between seven and eight thousand pounds a year.[2]

Lord North and Charles Yorke were members of the committee who introduced into the House of Commons this first bill, having for its object an American revenue by act of Parliament.[3] A stamp act and other taxes were to follow, till a sufficient revenue should be obtained from America to defray the expenses of its army.[4]

[1] Jasper Mauduit to Mr. Secretary Oliver. London, 23 March, 1763. "Some days ago the First Lord of Trade proposed lowering the duties on French molasses from 6d to 2d per gallon, in order the more effectually to secure the payment; and, short as the term is, he will probably carry it through before the rising of parliament." See Jasper Mauduit to the Speaker of the House of Representatives of the Province of Massachusetts Bay.

[2] Grenville to Horace Walpole, 8 Sept. 1763, in Grenville Papers, ii. 114.

[3] Journals of the House of Commons, xxix. 609.

[4] That the ministry of Bute had in view specially an American stamp tax is in itself probable, as the revenue without it would have been notoriously insufficient for their avowed object; and a stamp tax had long been very generally spoken of as the most eligible by those who wished to draw a parliamentary revenue from America. Besides, as we shall see, Townshend expressed himself violently in favor of the stamp tax when it came up; and though he voted for its repeal, he insisted he had been, and was still for it. Bute, and all the other members of his cabinet who remained alive, opposed the repeal. Add to this the belief of the time, as contained in a letter from London, dated March 27, 1763, and printed in Weyman's New-York Gazette for Monday, 30 May, 1763. Number 233, 3, 1.

"I cannot, however, omit mentioning a matter much the subject of conversation here, which, if carried into execution, will, in its consequences, greatly affect the colonies. It is the quartering sixteen regiments in America, to be supported at the expense of the Provinces. The inutility of these troops in time of peace, though evidently apparent, might not be complained of by the people of America, was

CHAP. V. 1763. Mar.

At the same time, as if to exhibit in the most glaring manner the absence of all just ground for parliamentary taxation, the usual "compensation for the expenses of the several provinces," according to their "active vigor and strenuous efforts," was voted without curtailment; and amounted to more than seven

the charge defrayed by England. But to lay that burden on the plantations, already exhausted in the prosecution of an expensive war, is what I believe you would not have thought of. The money, it is said, will be levied by act of parliament, and raised on a stamp duty, excise on rum distilled on the continent, and a duty on foreign sugar and molasses, &c.; by reducing the former duty on these last mentioned articles, which it is found impracticable to collect, to such a one as will be collected. This manner of raising money, except what may arise on the foreign sugars, &c., I apprehend will be thought greatly to diminish even the appearance of the subject's liberty, since nothing seems to be more repugnant to the general principles of freedom than the subjecting a people to taxation by laws in the enactment of which they are not represented."

This view is corroborated by many circumstances. "The stamp act was not originally Mr. Grenville's." Such is the testimony of Richard Jackson, in a letter to Lieutenant Governor Hutchinson of 26 December, 1765, quoted in Gordon's History of the American Revolution, i. 157. Gordon had an opportunity of examining the correspondence of Hutchinson. The letter which he cited should now be among the records of Massachusetts, but I searched for it there in vain. Yet I see no reason for doubting the accuracy of the quotation. Richard Jackson, from his upright character and his position as a friend of Grenville, and soon as a confidential officer of the Exchequer, was competent to give decisive evidence.

In a debate in the House of Commons in the thirteenth parliament, Sir William Meredith, speaking in the presence of Grenville, intimates that Grenville adopted the measure of the stamp act at the suggestion of another. See the Reports by Cavendish, i. 499.

Horace Walpole, a bitter enemy of Grenville's, yet says, in a note to his Memoirs of Geo. III. iii. 32, that the stamp act was a measure of Bute's ministry, at the suggestion of his secretary, Jenkinson, who afterwards brought it into the treasury for Grenville's adoption. Bute personally, as we know from Knox, wished to bring the colonies "into order;" but as every body about him wished the same, he probably thought not much about the matter, but left it to others, and especially to Charles Townshend.

Finally, Jenkinson himself, in the debate in the House of Commons of 15th May, 1777, condemned the tea act as impolitic, &c., &c. "Then, turning to the stamp act, he said that measure was not Mr. Grenville's; if the act was a good one, the merit of it was not due to Mr. Grenville; if it was a bad one, the errors of it, or the ill-policy of it, did not belong to him. The measure was not his." See Almon's Parliamentary Register, vii. 214.

It admits of no question, that Bute's ministry resolved on raising an American revenue by parliamentary taxes on America. When the decisive minute of the Treasury Board on the subject was ordered, will appear below.

CHAP. V. 1763. Mar. hundred thousand dollars. The appropriation was the most formal recognition that even in the last year of the war, when it was carried on beyond their bounds, the colonies had contributed to the common cause, more than their just proportion.

The peace, too, the favorite measure of the ministry and the king,[1] had been gratefully welcomed in the New World. "We in America," said Otis[2] to the people of Boston, on being chosen moderator at their first town meeting in 1763, "have abundant reason to rejoice. The heathen are driven out and the Canadians conquered. The British dominion now extends from sea to sea, and from the great rivers to the ends of the earth. Liberty and knowledge, civil and religious, will be co-extended, improved and preserved to the latest posterity. No constitution of government has appeared in the world so admirably adapted to these great purposes as that of Great Britain. Every British subject in America is, of common right, by act of Parliament, and by the laws of God and nature, entitled to all the essential privileges of Britons. By particular charters, particular privileges are justly granted, in consideration of undertaking to begin so glorious an empire as British America. Some weak and wicked minds have endeavored to infuse jealousies with regard to the colonies; the true interests of Great Britain and her plantations are mutual; and what God in his providence has united, let no man dare attempt to pull asunder." Such was the unanimous voice of the colonies. Fervent attachment to England was joined with love for the English constitution, as it had been imitated

[1] Bernard to Egremont, 16 Feb. 1763.

[2] Hutchinson's History of Massachusetts, iii. 101, 102.

in America, at the very time when the ministry of Bute was planning the thorough overthrow of colonial liberty.

CHAP. V. 1763 Mar.

But George Grenville would not be outdone by Charles Townshend in zeal for British interests. He sought to win the confidence of Englishmen by considering England as the head and heart of the whole empire, and by making all other parts of the king's dominion serve but as channels to convey wealth and vigor to that head. Ignorant of colonial affairs, his care of them had reference only to the increase of the trade and revenue of Great Britain.[1] He meant well for the British public, and was certainly indefatigable.[2] He looked to the restrictions in the statute book for the source of the maritime greatness of England; and did not know that if British commerce flourished beyond that of Spain, which had an equal population, still greater restrictions, and still more extensive colonies, it was only because England excelled in freedom. His mind bowed to the superstition of the age. He did not so much embrace as worship the navigation act with idolatry as the palladium of his country's greatness; and regarded connivance at the breaches of it by the overflowing commerce of the colonies with an exquisite jealousy.[3] Placed at the head of the admiralty, he was eager and importunate to unite his official influence, his knowledge of the law, and his place as a leader in the House of Commons, to restrain American inter-

[1] Knox Semi-official Papers, ii. 32.

[2] Duke of Grafton's Autobiography. Part I. MS.

[3] Burke's Speech on American Taxation.

CHAP. V. 1763. Mar.

course by new powers to vice-admiralty courts, and by a curiously devised system,[1] which should bribe the whole navy of England to make war on colonial trade. Accordingly, at a time when the merchants were already complaining of the interruption of their illicit dealings with the Spanish main, he recommended to Bute the more rigid enforcement of the laws of navigation; and on the very day on which the bill for a regular plantation revenue was reported to the house, he was put on a committee to carry his counsel into effect. March had not ended when a bill was brought in,[2] giving authority to employ the ships, seamen and officers of the navy as custom-house officers and informers. The measure was Grenville's own, and it was rapidly carried through; so that in three short weeks it became lawful, from the mouth of the St. Lawrence to Cape Florida, for each commander of an armed vessel to stop and examine, and, in case of suspicion, to seize every merchant ship approaching the colonies; while avarice was stimulated by hope of large emoluments, to make as many seizures, and gain in the vice-admiralty courts the condemnation of as many vessels as possible. It was Grenville who introduced a more than Spanish sea guard of British America; it was he who first took energetic measures to enforce the navigation acts.

[1] Smith's Wealth of Nations, Book I. chap. v.: "The mercantile system, in its nature and essence, is a system of restraint and regulation, and such as could scarce fail to be agreeable to a laborious and plodding man of business, who had been accustomed to regulate the different departments of public offices, and to establish the necessary checks and controls for confining each to its proper sphere, &c." This, and what follows, applies to Grenville as well as to Colbert.

[2] Journals of the House of Commons, xxix. 609. Statutes at large, vii. 443. 3 George III. chap. xxii. Lieut. Governor Hutchinson's private letter to R. Jackson, 17 Sept. 1763. Admiral Colville to Lieut. Gov. Colden, 14 Oct. 1763; also Egremont's Circular of 9 July, 1763.

The supplies voted for the first year of peace amounted to seventy millions of dollars; and the public charges pressed heavily on the lands and the industry of England. New sources of revenue were required; and, happily for America, an excise on cider and perry, by its nature affecting only the few counties where the apple was much cultivated, divided the country members, inflamed opposition, and burdened the estates of some in the House of Lords. Pitt opposed the tax as "intolerable." The defence of it fell upon Grenville, who treated the ideas of his brother-in-law on national expenses with severity. He admitted that the impost was odious. "But where," he demanded, "can you lay another tax? Tell me where; tell me where;" and Pitt made no answer, but by humming audibly—

Gentle shepherd, tell me where.

"The house burst out into a fit of laughter which continued some minutes."[1] Grenville, very warm, stood up to reply; when Pitt, "with the most contemptuous look and manner," rose from his seat, made the chairman a low bow, and walked slowly out of the house.[2] Yet the ministry persevered, though the cider counties were in a flame; the city of London, proceeding beyond all precedent, petitioned Commons, Lords, and King against the measure; and the cities of Exeter and Worcester instructed their members to oppose it. The House of Lords divided upon it; and two protests against it appeared on their journals.[3] Thus, an English tax, which came afterwards to be regarded as

[1] Anecdotes and Speeches of the Earl of Chatham, i. 369, 370. Walpole's Memoirs of Geo. III.

[2] Rigby to the Duke of Bedford, 10 March, 1763. Correspondence III. 218.

[3] Journals of House of Lords, of March 29 and March 30.

CHAP. V. 1763. Mar. proper, met with turbulent resistance. No one uttered a word for America. The bill for raising a revenue there was quietly read twice and committed.[1] But yet "this matter," observed Calvert, "may be obstructed under a Scotch premier minister, the Earl of Bute, against whom a strong party is forming." The ministry itself was crumbling. The king was Bute's friend; but his majority in "the king's parliament" was broken and unmanageable. The city of London, the old aristocracy, the House of Lords, the mass of the House of Commons, the people of England, the people of the colonies, the cabinet, all disliked him; the politicians, whose friendship he thought to have secured by favor, gave him no hearty support; nearly every member of the cabinet which he himself had formed was secretly or openly against him. "The ground I tread upon," said he, "is hollow;"[2] he might well be "afraid of falling;" and if he persisted, of injuring the king by his fall. Charles Townshend made haste to retire from the cabinet; and his bill for raising a revenue in the plantations was, on the twenty-ninth of March,[3] postponed.

Had Bute continued longer at the head of affairs, the government must soon have been at the mercy of a successful opposition:[4] had he made way unreservedly for a sole minister in his stead, the aristocratic party might have recovered and long retained the entire control of the administration.[5] By his instances to retire, made a half a year before, the king had been so troubled, that he frequently sat for hours together

[1] Journals of House of Commons, xxix. 606, 614, 617.

[2] Adolphus i.

[3] Journals of House of Commons, xxix. 623.

[4] Bute to one of his friends, in Adolphus i. 117.

[5] Fox to the Duke of Cumberland, in Albemarle's Memoirs of Rockingham, i. 131.

CHAP. V. 1763. Mar.

leaning his head upon his arm without speaking;[1] and at last when he consented to a change, it was on condition that in the new administration there should be no chief minister.

For a moment Grenville, to whom the treasury was offered, affected to be coy. "My dear George," said Bute, as if he had been the dictator, "I still continue to wish for you preferable to other arrangements; but if you cannot forget old grievances, and cordially take the assistance of all the king's friends, I must in a few hours put other things in agitation;"[2] and Grenville, "with a warm sense" of obligation, accepted the "high and important situation" destined for him by the king's goodness and his lordship's friendship,[3] promising not "to put any negative"[4] upon those whom the king might approve as his colleagues in the ministry.

Bute next turned to Bedford, announcing the king's "abiding determination never, upon any account, to suffer those ministers of the late reign, who had attempted to fetter and enslave him, to come into his service while he lived to hold the sceptre."[5] "Shall titles and estates," he continued, "and names like a Pitt, that impose on an ignorant populace, give this prince the law?"[6] And he solicited Bedford to accept the post of president of the council, promising, in that case, the privy seal to Bedford's brother-in-law, Lord Gower.

[1] Grenville's Narrative, in the Grenville Papers, i. 435.
[2] Bute to G. Grenville, in Grenville Papers, ii. 33–39.
[3] G. Grenville to Bute, in Grenville Papers, ii. 33–39.
[4] Ibid. 38.
[5] Bute to Bedford, 2d April, 1763, in Wiffen's Memoirs of the House of Russell, ii. 522. Lord John Russell's Correspondence of John, 4th Duke of Bedford, iii. 224.
[6] Wiffen, ii. 523. Bedford Cor. iii. 225.

CHAP. V. 1763. April.

While the answer was waited for, it was announced to the foreign ministers that the king had confided the executive powers of government to a triumvirate, consisting of Grenville, as the head of the treasury and chancellor of the exchequer, and of Egremont and Halifax, the two secretaries of state. After making this arrangement, Bute resigned, having established, by act of parliament, a standing army in America, and bequeathing to his successor his pledge to the House of Commons, to provide for the support of that army after the current year, by taxes on America.

CHAPTER VI.

THE TRIUMVIRATE MINISTRY PURSUE THE PLAN OF TAXING AMERICA BY PARLIAMENT.

April, May, 1763.

CHAP. VI. 1763. April.

George the Third was revered by his courtiers as realizing the idea of a patriot king.[1] He would "espouse no party, rule "by no faction," and employ none but those who would conduct affairs on his own principles. The watchword of his friends was "a coalition of parties," in the spirit of dutiful obedience, so that he might select ministers from among them all, and he came to the throne resolved "to begin to govern as soon as he should begin to reign."[2] Yet the established constitution was more immovable than his designs. Pitt did not retire from the ministry till the country was growing weary of "his German war," and a majority in the British cabinet opposed his counsels. Newcastle, so long the representative of a cabal of the oligarchy, which had once been more respected than the royal authority itself,[3] did not aban-

[1] The Annual Register: Gov. Bernard, in a speech to the Legislature of Massachusetts.

[2] Bolingbroke's Patriot King, 77.

[3] Bolingbroke on the Spirit of Patriotism, Works, iii. 18, 19.

CHAP. VI. 1763. April. don office till he had lost weight with parliament and the people; and the favorite, Bute, after making the peace with general approbation, had no option but to retire from a place which neither his own cabinet, nor the nation, nor either house of parliament, was willing he should hold. In the midst of changing factions the British constitution stood like adamant.

Grenville, who was never personally agreeable to the king,[1] was chosen to succeed Bute in the ministry, because, from his position, he seemed dependent on the court. He had no party, and was aware of it.[2]—No man had more changed his associates: entering life as a patriot, accepting office of Newcastle, leaving Newcastle with Pitt, and remaining in office when Pitt and Temple were driven out. The head of his own house now regarded him with lively hatred, and one of his younger brothers had repudiated his conduct as base;[3] so that he derived no strength from his family. Moreover, he loved office, and loved it for its emoluments,[4] and so inordinately, that, even against the utmost endeavors of his own brothers, he had for many years nourished a rankling grudge against Pitt, and secretly questioned his friendship, honor, and good faith, because Pitt had conferred upon him the very lucrative office of treasurer of the navy, at a time when he himself was lusting after the still more enormously lucrative one of paymaster to the forces.[5] And, in 1762, he had suffered himself to

[1] Autobiography of the Duke of Grafton: "There may be good reason for believing that his [George Grenville's] manners were never agreeable to His Majesty."

[2] Grenville's own remark to the king, in his Diary.

[3] James Grenville to Temple, 3 Nov. 1762. In Grenville Papers, i. 409.

[4] Knox: Extra Official Papers, ii. 34.

[5] G. Grenville's Narrative, in the Grenville Papers, i. 439.

CHAP. VI. 1763. April.

be summarily thrust out of the office of secretary of state, and had accepted another from avarice,[1] and in the hope of still higher preferment.[2]

Yet Grenville was no venal adventurer, and in his love of money retained the cold austerity that marked his character. He never grew giddy with the hazards of the stock-market, nor made himself a broker of office, nor jobbed in lottery-tickets and contracts. His desire was for solid and sure places; a tellership in the exchequer, or the profits of a light-house, the rich sinecures which English law and English usages tolerated; so that even in the indulgence of his strongest passion, he kept a good conscience, and men regarded him as a model of integrity,[3] and the resolute enemy of corruption. Nor was he aware that the craving for wealth led him to penurious parsimony. He was the second son; and his childless elder brother, whose title would fall to his family, could break the entail of some part of his great possessions;[4] so Grenville saved always all his emoluments from public office, pleading that it was a disinterested act, which only enriched his children;[5] as if a miser hoards money for any others than his heirs.

His personal deportment was always grave and formally solemn and forbidding; and in an age of dissoluteness, his apathy in respect of pleasure made him

[1] Horace Walpole's George the Third, i.

[2] Fragment in the Grenville Papers, i. 484.

[3] Walpole's George III. i. 338, 339. Walpole then "entertained a most favorable opinion of his integrity." Soon afterwards he had a bitter quarrel with Grenville, and from that hour spoke very ill of him. Ibid i. 343. This must be borne in mind; towards no man of his time does Walpole show himself so peevishly bitter as towards Grenville, often coloring and distorting facts, and always swayed by an invincible disgust.

[4] Grenville's Narrative, in the Grenville Papers.

[5] Knox: Extra-official Papers, ii. 35.

CHAP. VI. 1763. April. appear a paragon for sanctity of morals. Bishops praised him for his constant weekly attendance at the morning service. He was not cruel; but the coldness of his nature left him incapable of compassion. He had not energetic decision, although he was obstinately self-interested: as a consequence, he was not vengeful; but when evil thoughts towards others rose up within his breast, they rather served to trouble his own peace with the gall of bitterness. He would also become unhappy, and grievously repine at disappointment or the ill success of his plans, even while his self-love saved him from remorse. Nor was he one of the king's friends, nor did he seek advancement by unworthy flattery of the court.[2] A good lawyer, and trained in the best and most liberal political school of his day, it was ever his pride to be esteemed a sound Whig,[3] making the absolute supremacy of parliament the test of his consistency and the essential element of his creed; and he rose to eminence through the laborious gradations of public service, by a thorough knowledge of its constitution[4] and an indefatigable attention to all its business. Just before his death, after a service in the House of Commons of about thirty years,[5] he said with pride that to that house he owed all his distinction; and such was the flattering self-conceit of this austere and rigidly inflexible man, that he ascribed all his eminence to his own merits, which he never regarded as too highly rewarded. Gratitude, therefore, found no place in his nature;

[1] Bishop Newton's Autobiography, in Newton's Works, i.

[2] Burke, in his speech on American Taxation.

[3] "I know that Mr. Grenville, as a sound whig, bore me no good will." Hume, in Burton's life of Hume.

[4] Edmund Burke.

[5] Grenville, in Cavendish.

CHAP. VI. 1761. April.

but now that he was at that period of life when the gentler passions are quiet, and ambition rules without restraint, he was so much like the bird that croaks whilst enjoying the fullest meal, that towards those even who had benefited him most, there remained in his heart something like a harsh willingness to utter reproach for their not having succeeded in doing more. And when he looked back upon the line of his predecessors in office; upon Bute, Newcastle, Devonshire, Waldegrave, and even Pelham, under whom he had been trained, it was easy for him to esteem himself superior to them all. Yet Grenville wanted the elements of true statesmanship and greatness: he had neither a creative mind to devise a system of policy, nor active powers to guide an administration. His nature inclined him not to originate measures, but to amend, and alter, and regulate. He had neither salient traits nor general comprehensiveness of mind; neither the warm imagination, which can arrange and vivify various masses of business, nor sagacity to penetrate the springs of public action and the consequences of measures. In a word, he was a dull, plodding pedant in politics; a painstaking, exact man of business, capable of counting[1] the Manilla ransom if it had ever been paid. In his frequent, long, and tedious speeches, it has been said that a trope[2] never passed his lips; but he abounded in repetitions and explanatory self-justification. He would have made a laborious and an upright judge,

[1] Dr. Johnson's Thoughts on the Late Transactions Respecting Falkland's Islands. First edition: "Let him (George Grenville) not be depreciated in his grave. He had powers not universally possessed. Could he have enforced payment of the Manilla ransom, he could have counted it." Boswell's Life of Johnson, chap. xxv.

[2] Knox: Extra-official Papers.

CHAP. VI. 1763. April. or an impartial and most respectable speaker of the House of Commons; but at the head of an administration, he could be no more than the patient and methodical executor of plans "devolved"[1] upon him by the statute-book of England or by his predecessors in office. The stubbornness with which he was wont to adhere to them sprung from the weakness of pride and obstinacy, that were parts of his nature, not from the vigor of a commanding will,[2] which never belonged to him.

With the bequest of Bute's office, the new minister inherited also the services of his efficient private secretary, Charles Jenkinson, who now became the principal Secretary of the Treasury. He was a man of rare ability. An Oxford scholar without fortune, and at first destined for the Church, he entered life on the side of the whigs; but using an immediate opportunity of becoming known to George the Third while Prince of Wales, he devoted himself to his service. He remained always a friend and a uniform favorite of the king. Engaged in the most important scenes of political action, and rising to the highest stations, he moved with so soft a step, that he seemed to pass on as noiselessly as a shadow; and history was hardly aware of his presence. He had the singular talent of being employed in the most delicate and disagreeable personal negotiations, and fulfilling such trusts so calmly as to retain the friendship of those whom he seemed commissioned to wound. Except at first, when still very poor, he never showed a wish for office, till the time arrived when it seemed to seek him; and

[1] Edmund Burke on American Taxation.

[2] The elder Pitt had a very strong will, and was by no means obstinate: Grenville had a feeble will, and was very obstinate.

CHAP. VI. 1763. April.

he proved how an able man may quietly gain every object of his ambition, if he is but so far the master of his own mind as to make desire wait upon opportunity and fortune. His old age was one of dignity, cheered by the unabated regard of the king; and in the midst of physical sufferings, soothed and made happy by the political success of one son and the affectionate companionship of another. The blot on his life was his conduct respecting America; the thorough measures which Charles Townshend had counselled with dangerous rashness, and which George Grenville in part resisted, Jenkinson was always ready to carry forward with tranquil collectedness.

The king wished to see Townshend at the head of the admiralty.[1] "My nephew Charles," reasoned Newcastle,[2] "will hardly act under George Grenville;" and it proved so. A sharp rivalry existed between the two, and continued as long as both lived; each of them, in the absence of Pitt, aiming to stand first in the House of Commons, and in the Government. But Townshend, though, for the present, he declined office, took care to retain the favor of the king by zeal against popular commotions.[3] The Duke of Bedford, too, refused to join the ministry after the advancement of Egremont and Grenville, who, at the time of his negotiating the peace, had shown him so much ill-will. He advised the employment of the old whig aristocracy. "I know," said he, "the administration cannot last; should I take in it the place of

[1] Bute to Beford, 2 April, 1763, in Wiffen and Bedford Correspondence.

[2] Newcastle to Pitt, 9 April 1763, in Chatham Correspondence, ii. 221.

[3] Gilly Williams to George Selwin, in Jesse's George Selwin, i. 189.

CHAP. VI. 1763. April. President of the Council, I should deserve to be treated like a madman."[1] So unattractive was Grenville!

The triumvirate, of whom not one was beloved by the people, became "a general joke,"[2] and was laughed at as a three-headed monster,[3] quieted by being gorged with patronage and office. The business of the session was rapidly brought to a close. Grenville's bill for the effectual enforcement of the acts of navigation received the royal assent. The scheme of taxing the colonies did but lie over for the next session; but at the prorogation, the king's speech announced the purpose of improving the revenue, which, as the debates during the session explained, had a special reference to America. "It was not "the wish of this man or that man;"[4] each house of parliament, and nearly every body in Great Britain, was eager to throw a part of the public burdens on the increasing opulence of the New World.

The new ministry, at the outset, was weakened by its own indiscreet violence. In the speech at the close of the session, the king vauntingly arrogated merit for the peace which Frederic of Prussia had concluded, after being left alone by England. Wilkes, a man who shared the social licentiousness of his day, in the forty-fifth number of a periodical paper called the North Briton, exposed the fallacy. The king, thinking one

[1] Bedford to Bute, Paris, 7 April, 1763, in Wiffen, ii. 525, and in Bedford Correspondence, iii. 228.

[2] Walpole to Mann, 30 April, 1763.

[3] Wilkes to Lord Temple, in Grenville Papers.

[4] Speech of Cornwall, brother-in-law of Charles Jenkinson, in the House of Commons, in Cavendish Debates, i. 91.

CHAP. VI. 1763. April.

of his subjects had given him the lie, applied[1] to the ministry for the protection to which every Englishman had a right. How to proceed became a question. Grenville,[2] as a lawyer, knew, and "declared that general warrants were illegal;" but conforming to "long established precedents," Halifax, as one of the secretaries of state, issued a general warrant for the arrest of all concerned in a publication which calm judgment[3] pronounces unworthy of notice, but which all parties at that day branded as a libel.

Wilkes was arrested; but on the doubtful plea that his privilege as a member of parliament had been violated, he was set at liberty by the popular Chief Justice Pratt. The opponents of the ministry hastened to renew the war of privilege against prerogative, with the advantage of being defenders of the constitution on a question affecting a vital principle of personal freedom. The cry for "Wilkes and Liberty" was heard in all parts of the British dominion."[4]

In the midst of the confusion, Grenville set about confirming himself in power[5] by diligence in the public business. "His self-conceit," said Lord Holland afterwards,"[6] "as well as his pride and obstinacy, established him." For the joint secretary of the treasury he selected an able and sensible lawyer, Thomas Whately, in whom he obtained a firm defender and political friend. His own secretary as Chancellor of

[1] Grenville, in Knox's Considerations on the Present State of the Nation. 48.

[2] Grenville's Speeches in the House of Commons, 16 December, 1768, and 3 February, 1769, in Wright's Cavendish Debates, i. 110, 160.

[3] Mahon's History of England, iv.

[4] Hutchinson's History of the Province of Massachusetts Bay, iii. 163.

[5] Grenville's Account of himself to Knox.

[6] Lord Holland to George Selwyn.

CHAP. VI. 1763. April. the Exchequer was Richard Jackson; and the choice is very strong evidence that though he entered upon his task blindly, as it proved, and in ignorance[1] of the colonies, yet his intentions were fair;[2] for Jackson was a liberal member of the House of Commons, a good lawyer, not eager to increase his affluent fortune, frank, independent, and abhorring intrigue. He was, moreover, better acquainted with the state of America, and exercised a sounder judgment on questions of colonial administration, than, perhaps, any man in England. His excellent character led Connecticut and Pennsylvania to make him their agent; and he gave the latter province even better advice than Franklin himself. He was always able to combine affection for England with uprightness and fidelity to his American employers.

To a mind like Grenville's, the protective system had irresistible attractions. He saw in trade the foundation of the wealth and power of his country, and embraced all the prejudices of the mercantile system; he wished by regulations and control to advance the commerce and public credit, which really owed their superiority to the greater liberty of England. He prepared to recharter the bank of England, to connect it still more closely with the funding system; to sustain the credit of the merchants, which faltered under the revulsion consequent on the return to peace; to bind more firmly the restrictions of the commercial monopoly; to increase

[1] That Grenville was very ignorant as to the colonies we have a witness in Knox, who himself had held office in Georgia, and knew America from his own observation.

[2] "The best in the world." Burke and the Duke of Grafton both vouch for Grenville's good intentions.

the public revenue, and in its expenditure to found a system of frugality. CHAP. VI.

America, with its new acquisitions—Florida, and the valley of the Mississippi, and Canada—lay invitingly before him. The enforcing the navigation acts was peculiarly his own policy, and was the first leading feature of his administration. His predecessors had bound him by their pledges to provide for the American army by taxes on the colonies; and to find sources of an American revenue, was his second great object. This he combined with the purpose[1] of so dividing the public burdens between England and America as to diminish the motive to emigrate from Great Britain and Ireland;[2] for, in those days, emigration[3] was considered an evil. 1763. April.

In less than a month after Bute's retirement, Egremont, who still remained Secretary of State for the southern department, asked the advice of the Lords of Trade on the organization of governments in the newly acquired territories, the military force to be kept up in America, and in what mode least burthensome and most palatable to the colonies, they can contribute towards the support of the additional expense which must attend their civil and military establishment.[4]

[1] M. Francès au Duc de Choiseul à Londres le 2 Septembre, 1768.

[2] Second protest of the House of Lords, on the repeal of the stamp act.

[3] Knox, i. 23, Extra-official Papers, ii. 23.

[4] Secretary Lord Egremont to the Lords of Trade, 5 May, 1763: "North America naturally offers itself as the principal object of your lordship's consideration upon this occasion, with regard to which I shall first obey his majesty's commands in proposing to your lordships some general questions, before I proceed to desire you will furnish that information which his majesty expects from your lordships with regard to the North American and Southern parts of this continent, considered separately.

"The questions which relate to North America in general, are—

"1st. What new governments should be established, and what form should be adopted for such new governments? And where the

CHAP. VI. 1763. May.

The head of the Board of Trade was the Earl of Shelburne. He was at that time not quite six and twenty years old, had served creditably in the seven years' war, as a volunteer, and, on his return, was appointed aide-de-camp to George the Third. He had supported the peace[1] of 1763, as became a humane and

capital or residence of each governor should be fixed?

"2dly. What military establishment will be sufficient? What new forts should be erected? And which, if any, may it be expedient to demolish?

"3dly. In what mode, least burdensome and most palatable to the colonies, can they contribute towards the support of the additional expense which must attend this civil and military establishment, upon the arrangement which your lordships shall propose?"

*   *   *   *

It is noticeable, that the question as to taxing America by parliament, implied in the third interrogatory, does not relate to the expediency of doing it, but the mode. On the right or propriety of the measure, the Board of Trade is not invited to express an opinion.

[1] Walpole, in Memoirs of the Reign of King George III. i. 257, 258, says of Shelburne: "The probability was, that he (Shelburne) intended to slip into the pay-office himself." Again; he insinuates that Shelburne, in negotiating with Fox to support the peace, practised "the pious fraud" of concealing Lord Bute's intention of retiring. Similar anecdotes were told me by one of the worthiest men in England. Having read a vast deal of Lord Shelburne's correspondence, I observed how unlike these imputations were to the character imprinted on his writings. I was advised to inquire if in the papers of the first Lord Holland these charges are preserved; and having opportunity to do so, I was answered with courtesy and frankness, that they are not to be found in the unpublished memoirs, nor, I believe, in any of the papers of Lord Holland.

As to the first surmise, that Shelburne desired to slip into the pay-office himself, there exists no evidence to justify it; while every letter that has since come to light, goes to show such a readiness on the part of Bute, and, for a time, of Grenville, to gratify Fox, that he himself was satisfied and avowed his purpose to give every support to the new ministry. The whole tone of their intercourse is inconsistent with the supposition of any difference about the paymaster's place. Grenville's Diary, in Papers ii. 207, 208. As for Shelburne, he was marked out for the higher office of a Secretary of State; but, "in the handsomest manner, wished to be omitted." Bute to Grenville, 1 April, 1763, in Grenville Papers, ii. 41.

As to the other insinuation, the concealment of Bute's purpose of resigning, whether blamable or not, was the act of Bute himself, with whom Fox negotiated directly. "I am come from Lord Bute," writes Fox to the Duke of Cumberland, on the 30 Sept. 1762, "more than ever convinced that he never has had, nor now has, a thought of retiring or treating." Albemarle's Memoirs of Rockingham, i. 132. That Fox was with Bute repeatedly before superseding Grenville in the lead of the House of Commons,

liberal man; in other respects he was an admirer of Pitt.

CHAP. VI.

1763. May.

While his report was waited for, Grenville, through Charles Jenkinson,[1] began his system of saving, by an order to the Commander-in-Chief of the Forces in America, now that the peace was made, to withdraw the allowance for victualling the regiments[2] stationed in the cultivated parts of America. This expense was to be met in future by the colonies.

appears from Albemarle, i. 127, 129 and 132. Bedford Correspondence, iii. 124 and 133. That Fox did not regard this concealment as an offence appears from his own testimony; for he himself, in December, 1763, said to Grenville, that "he believed Lord Bute to be a perfect honest man; that he respected him as such; and that in the intercourse between them Lord Bute had never broken his word with him." See G. Grenville's Diary for Wednesday, 25 Dec. 1764. Even Walpole admits that Lord Holland's own friends as well as the Bedfords, refused to find Shelburne blamable. Walpole's Geo. III. i. 262, 263.

In the very paragraph in which Walpole brings these unsubstantiated charges against Shelburne, he is entirely at fault in narrating confidently that the Treasury was offered to Fox. The Grenville Papers show that it was not.

The name of Shelburne will occur so often in American history during the next twenty years, that I was unwilling to pass over the aspersions of Walpole. It is to be remembered also, that both whig and tory were very bitter against Shelburne; some of the Rockingham whigs most of all, particularly C. J. Fox and Edmund Burke.

[2] C. Jenkinson to Sir Jeffery Amherst, 11 May, 1763. Treasury Letter Book, xxii. 392.

[3] Weyman's New-York Gazette, 3 October, 1763. No. 251, 2, 1.

CHAPTER VII.

PONTIAC'S WAR.—THE TRIUMVIRATE MINISTRY CONTINUED.

MAY—SEPTEMBER, 1763.

CHAP. VII. 1763. May

THE western territory, of which England believed itself to have come into possession, was one massive forest, interrupted only by rocks, or prairies, or waters, or an Indian cleared field for maize. The English came into the illimitable waste as conquerors, and, here and there in the solitudes, all the way from Niagara to the Falls of the St. Mary and the banks of the St. Joseph's, a log fort with a picketed inclosure was the emblem of their pretensions. In their presumptuous eagerness to supplant the French, they were blind to danger, and their posts were often left dependent on the Indians for supplies. The smaller garrisons consisted only of an ensign, a sergeant, and perhaps fourteen men; and were stationed at points so widely remote from one another, that, lost in the boundless woods, they could no more be discerned than a little fleet of canoes scattered over the whole Atlantic, too minute to be perceptible, and safe only during fair weather. Yet, feeble as they were, their presence alarmed the red man, for it implied the design to occupy the country which for ages had been his own.[1] His canoe could no longer quiver on the bosom of the St. Mary's, or pass into the clear waters of Lake Huron, or paddle through the strait that connects Huron and Erie, or cross from the waters of the St. Lawrence to those of the Ohio, without passing by the British flag. By what right was that banner unfurled in the west? What claim to the red man's forest could the English derive from victories over the French?

The French had won the affection of the savages by their pliability and their temperance, and retained it by religious influence; they seemed no more to be masters, but rather companions and friends. More formidable enemies now appeared, arrogant in their pretensions, scoffing insolently at those whom they superseded, driving away their Catholic priests, and introducing the traffic in rum, which till then had been effectually prohibited. Since the French must go, no other nation should take their place. Let the Red Men at once vindicate their right to what was their own heritage, or consent to their certain ruin.

The wide conspiracy began with the lower nations, who were the chief instigators of discontent.[2] The Iroquois, especially the Senecas,[3] who were very much enraged against the English,[4] joined with the Dela-

[1] Hutchinson to Richard Jackson, August, 1763.

[2] Sir Jeffery Amherst to Major Gladwin, New-York, 29 May, 1763. "The nations below, who seem to be the chief instigators of this mischief."

[3] Sir Jeffery Amherst to Sir William Johnson, New-York, 29 May, 1763. "The Senecas seem to have a principal hand. * * * Other tribes enter into plots against their benefactors," &c. &c.

[4] Speech of the Miami chief, 30 March, 1763.

CHAP. VII. 1763. May.

wares and Shawnees, and for two years[1] they had been soliciting the north-western nations to take up arms. "The English mean to make slaves of us, by occupying so many posts in our country," said the lower nations to the upper.[2] "We had better attempt something now, to recover our liberty, than wait till they are better established." So spoke the Senecas to the Delawares, and they to the Shawnees, and the Shawnees to the Miamis[3] and Wyandots, whose chiefs, slain in battle by the English, were still unavenged,[4] until every where, from the falls of Niagara and the piny declivities of the Alleghanies to the whitewood forests of the Mississippi[5] and the borders of Lake Superior, all the nations concerted to rise and put the English to death.[6]

A prophetic spirit was introduced among the wigwams. A chief of the Abenakis persuaded first his own tribe, and then the red men of the west, that the Great Manitou had appeared to him in a vision, saying "I am the Lord of Life; it is I who made all men; I wake for their safety. Therefore, I give you warning, that if you suffer the Englishmen to dwell among you, their diseases and their poisons shall destroy

[1] Speech of Pontiac. Harangue faite à la Nation Illinoise, et au chef Pondiak, &c. &c. 18 Avril, 1765. Aubry to the French minister, 16 May, 1765. Gayarré Histoire de la Louisiane, ii. 131. The work of Gayarré is one of great merit and authority, built firmly upon trustworthy documents.

[2] Major Gladwin, commanding officer at the Detroit, to Sir Jeffery Amherst, Detroit, 20 April, 1763. "They say we mean to make slaves of them," &c. &c.

[3] Speech made by the chief of the Miamis Indians at the delivery of the belt of wampum, sent to them from the Shawnee nation, at Fort Miamis, 30 March, 1763. "This belt we received from the Shawnees, and they received it from the Delawares, and they from the Senecas."

[4] Speech of Hudson, a Cayuga chief, to Captain Ourry, in June, 1763.

[5] Speech of Tamarois, chief of the Kaskaskias, to Fraser, in April, 1765.

[6] Speech of the Miamis Indians, of 30 March, 1763.

you utterly, and you shall all die."[1] "The Master of Life himself," said the Potawatomies, "has stirred us up to this war." CHAP. VII. 1763. May.

The plot was discovered in March by the officer in command at Miami;[2] and the Bloody Belt, which was then in the village and was to be sent forward to the tribes on the Wabash,[3] was with great difficulty, "after a long and troublesome" interview, obtained from an assembly of the chiefs of the Miamis.[4]

On receiving the news, Amherst, who had not much alertness or sagacity, while he prepared reinforcements, pleased himself with calling the acts of the Indians "unwarrantable;" hoped they would be "too sensible of their own interest" to conspire against the English; and declared that if they did, he wished them to know that, in his eyes, they would make "a contemptible figure." Yes, he repeated, "a contemptible figure." The mischief would recoil on themselves, and end in their destruction.[5]

But Pontiac, the colossal chief of the North West, "the king and lord of all that country;"[6] a Catawaba[7] prisoner, as is said, adopted into the clan of the Ottawas, and elected their chief;[8] respected, and in a manner adored, by all the nations around

[1] M. de Neyon à M. de Kerlerec, au Fort de Chartres, le 1er Décembre, 1763.

[2] Ensign Holmes, commanding officer at Miamis, to Major Gladwin, dated Fort Miamis, 30 March, 1763.

[3] Speech of the Miamis Chief, 30 March, 1763.

[4] Holmes to Gladwin, 30 March, 1763.

[5] Letter of Amherst to Major Gladwin, May, 1763.

[6] Rogers: Account of North America.

[7] William Smith to H. Gates, 22 November, 1763. Gladwin speaks of the Ottawa Nation as Pontiac's Nation. A less authority than that of Smith might not deserve to be regarded; but Smith is one of the accurate.

[8] Gladwin to Amherst, 14 May, 1763.

CHAP. VII. 1763. May. him; a man "of integrity and humanity,"[1] according to the morals of the wilderness; of a comprehensive mind, fertile in resources, and of an undaunted nature, persevered in the design of recovering the land of the Senecas, and all west of it, by a confederacy of insurgent nations. His name still hovers over the north-west, as the hero who devised and conducted their great but unavailing struggle with destiny for the independence of their race.

Of all the inland settlements, Detroit was the largest and the most esteemed. The deep, majestic river, more than a half mile broad, carrying its vast flood calmly and noiselessly between the strait and well-defined banks of its channel, imparted grandeur to a country whose rising grounds and meadows, plains festooned with prolific wild vines, woodlands, brooks and fountains, were so mingled together that nothing was left to desire.[2] The climate was mild, and the air salubrious. Good land abounded, yielding maize, wheat, and every vegetable. The forests were a natural park, stocked with buffaloes, deer, quails, partridges and wild turkeys. Water-fowl of delicious flavor hovered along its streams, which yielded to the angler an astonishing variety of fish, especially the white fish, the richest and most luscious of them all. There every luxury of the table might be enjoyed at the sole expense of labor.[3] The lovely and cheerful region attracted settlers, alike white men and savages; and the French had so occupied the two banks of the river that their num-

[1] Fraser to Gen. Gage, 15 May, 1765.

[2] Charlevoix, iii. 256. 4to edit.

[3] Mante, 524, 525.

bers were rated even so high as twenty-five hundred souls, of whom five hundred were men able to bear arms,[1] or as three or four hundred French families;[2] yet an enumeration, in 1764, proved them not numerous,[3] with only men enough to form three companies of militia;[4] and in 1768 the official census reported but five hundred and seventy-two souls,[5]—an account which is in harmony with the best traditions.[6] The French dwelt on farms, which were about three or four acres wide upon the river, and eighty acres deep; indolent in the midst of plenty, graziers as well as tillers of the soil, and enriched by Indian traffic.

The English fort, of which Gladwin was the commander, was a large stockade, about twenty-feet high and twelve hundred yards in circumference,[7] inclosing, perhaps, eighty houses.[8] It stood within the limits of the present city, on the river bank, commanding a wide prospect for nine miles above and below.[9] The garrison was composed of the shattered remains of the eightieth regiment,[10] reduced to about one hundred and twenty men and eight officers.[11] Two

[1] Rogers: Account of North America, 168. "When I took possession of the country, soon after the surrender of Canada, they were about 2500 in number, there being near 500 that bore arms, and near 300 dwelling houses."

[2] Journal of George Croghan, 17 August, 1765: "The people here consist of three or four hundred French families." Craig's Olden Times, 414.

[3] Mante's History of the War in North America, 525.

[4] Ibid, 515.

[5] State of the Settlement of Detroit, in Gage to Hillsborough, No. 2, of 15 May, 1768: "Number of souls, 572; cultivated acres, 514½; corn produced yearly, 9789 French bushels; horned cattle, 600; hogs, 567."

[6] Mss. in my possession, containing the Recollections of Madame Catharine Thibeau; "About sixty French families in all, when the English took possession of the country; not more than eighty men at the time; very few farms, not more than seven or eight farms settled." Memory is here below the truth. It usually exceeds.

[7] Rogers: Concise Account, 168.

[8] Croghan's Jour. in Craig, i. 414.

[9] Croghan's Jour. in Craig, i. 414.

[10] Mante's History, 485.

[11] Cass: Discourse before the Michigan Historical Society, from an ancient Diary. Carver, 155, says, 300.

CHAP. VII. 1763. May.

armed vessels lay in the river;[1] of artillery, there were but two six-pounders, one three-pounder, and three mortars, so badly mounted as to be of no use, except to inspire terror.[2]

The nation of the Pottawatamies dwelt at about a mile below the fort; the Wyandots a little lower down, on the eastern side of the strait; and five miles higher up, but on the same eastern side, the Ottawas.

On the first day of May, Pontiac entered the fort with about fifty[3] of his warriors, announcing his purpose in a few days to pay a more formal visit. He appeared on the seventh, with about three hundred warriors, armed with knives, tomahawks and guns, cut short and hid under their blankets.[4] He was to sit down in council, and when he should rise, was to speak with a belt white on one side and green on the other;[5] and turning the belt was to be the signal for beginning a general massacre. But luckily Gladwin had the night before been informed of his coming,[6] and took such precautions that the interview passed off without results. Pontiac was allowed, perhaps unwisely, to escape.

On the morning of the same day, an English party who were sounding the entrance of Lake Huron were seized and murdered.[7] On the eighth, Pontiac ap-

[1] Weyman's New-York Gazette, 11 July, 1763.

[2] Cass: Discourse, &c. &c.

[3] Major Gladwin to Sir J. Amherst, 14 May, 1763, enclosure No. 9 in Amherst to Egremont, 27 June, 1768.

[4] Same to same.

[5] Mante's History of the War, 486.

[6] The lover of the romantic may follow Carver, 155, 156, or the improvements upon his story, made by tradition, till the safety of the fort became a tale of love on the part of a Chippewa girl for Gladwin, the commander. Gladwin simply says, "I was luckily informed the night before that he was coming," &c.

[7] Amherst to Gladwin.

[8] Weyman's New-York Gazette, 11 July, 1763, No. 239, 3 1. Gladwin to Amherst.

peared once more with a pipe of peace, proposing to come the next day, with the whole Ottawa nation to renew his friendship. But on the afternoon of the ninth, he struck his tent, began hostilities, and strictly beleaguered the garrison, which had not on hand provisions enough for three weeks. "The first man that shall bring them provisions, or any thing else, shall suffer death." Such was Pontiac's proclamation of the blockade of Detroit. On the tenth there was a parley, and the garrison was summoned to capitulate to the Red Men as the French had done to the English. Not till after Gladwin had obtained the needed supplies did he break off the treaty, and bid the enemy defiance,[1] yet leaving in their hands the unhappy officer who had conducted the parley. The garrison was in high spirits, though consisting of no more than one hundred and twenty men,[2] against six or seven hundred besiegers.[3]

And now ensued an unheard of phenomenon. The rovers of the wilderness, though unused to enterprises requiring time and assiduity, blockaded the place closely. The French inhabitants were divided in their sympathies. Pontiac made one of them his secretary,[4] and supplied his wants by requisitions upon them all. Emissaries were sent even to Illinois to ask for an officer who should assume the conduct of the siege.[5] The savages of the west took part in the general hatred of the English, and would not be reconciled to their dominion. "Be of good cheer, my fathers;"

[1] Gladwin to Amherst, 14 May, 1763. Letter from Detroit of 9 July, 1763, in Weyman's New-York Gazette of 15 August, 1763.

[2] Weyman's New-York Gazette of 15 August, 1763.

[3] Gladwin to Amherst: "I believe the enemy may amount to six or seven hundred." His own number he does not give.

[4] Mante: History, &c. 486.

[5] See the N. B. to the account of the loss of the post of Miamis.

CHAP. VII. 1763. May.

such were the words of one tribe after another to the commander at Fort Chartres;—"do not desert thy children: the English shall never come here so long as a red man lives." "Our hearts," they repeated, "are with the French; we hate the English, and wish to kill them all. We are all united: the war is our war, and we will continue it for seven years. The English shall never come into the west."[1] But the French officers in Illinois, though their efforts were for a long time unavailing, sincerely desired to execute the treaty of Paris with loyalty.

On the sixteenth of May, a party of Indians appeared at the gate of the fort of Sandusky. Ensign Paulli, the commander, ordered seven of them—four Hurons and three Ottawas—to be admitted as old acquaintances and friends. They sat smoking, till one of them raised his head as a signal, on which the two that were next Paulli seized and tied him fast without uttering a word. As they carried him out of the room, he saw the dead body of his sentry. The rest of the garrison lay one here and one there; the sergeant in his garden, where he had been planting—all massacred. The traders, also, were killed, and their stores plundered. Paulli was taken as a trophy to Detroit.[2]

At the mouth of the St. Joseph's the Jesuit missionaries, for nearly sixty years, had toiled among the heathen, till, at the conquest of Canada, they made way for an English ensign, a garrison of fourteen soldiers, and English traders, stationed on a spot more than a thousand miles from the sea, and inaccessible

[1] Neyon to Kerlerec, December 1, 1763.

[2] Particulars regarding the loss of Sandusky, as furnished by Ensign Paulli after his escape, in the abstract made by General Gage.

except by canoes or boats round the promontory of Michigan. On the morning of the twenty-fifth of May, a party of Pottawatamies from Detroit appeared near the fort. "We are come," said they, "to see our relatives and wish the garrison a good morning." A cry was suddenly heard in the barracks; "in about two minutes," Schlosser, the commanding officer, was seized, and all the garrison, excepting three men,[1] were massacred.[2]

Fort Pitt was the most important station west of the Alleghanies. Twenty boats[3] had already been launched upon the Ohio, to bear the English in triumph to the country of the Illinois. For three or four weeks bands of Mingoes and Delawares had been seen hovering round the place. On the twenty-seventh of May, these bitterest enemies of the English exchanged with English traders three hundred pounds worth of skins for powder and lead, and then suddenly went away, as if to intercept any attempt to descend the river. On the same day, an hour before midnight, the chiefs of the Delawares having received intelligence from the west, sent their message to Fort Pitt, recounting the attacks on the English posts. "We are sure," they added, giving their first summons, "a party is coming to cut you and your people off; make the best of your way to some place of safety, as we would not desire to see you killed in our town. What goods and other effects you have, we assure you we will take care of, and keep them safe."[4]

[1] The number of the garrison appears from Edward Jenkins to Major Gladwin, 1 June, 1763. "Eleven men killed and three taken prisoners with the officer."

[2] Particulars regarding the loss of St. Joseph's, &c. "They massacred all the garrison except three men, in about two minutes, and plundered the fort."

[3] Captain Ecuyer, Commanding Officer at Fort Pitt, to Colonel Bouquet, at Philadelphia. Fort Pitt, 29 May, 1763.

[4] Intelligence delivered, with a string of wampum, by King Beaver,

CHAP. VII. 1763. May.

The next day Indians massacred and scalped a whole family,[1] sparing neither woman nor child, and left behind them a tomahawk,[2] as their declaration of war. Fort Ligonier was threatened, and the passes to the eastward were so watched, that it was very difficult to keep up any intercourse while the woods resounded with the wild death halloos,[3] which announced successive murders.

Near Fort Wayne, just where the great canal which unites the waters of Lake Erie and the Wabash leaves the waters of the Maumee, stood Fort Miami, garrisoned also by an ensign and a few soldiers. Those who were on the lakes saw at least the water course which would take them to Niagara. Fort Miami was deep in the forest, out of sight and hearing of civilized man. On the twenty-seventh of May, Holmes, its commander, was informed that the fort at Detroit had been attacked, and put his men on their guard; but an Indian woman came to him, saying that the squaw in a cabin, but three hundred yards off, was ill, and wished him to bleed her. He went on the errand of mercy, and two shots that were heard told how he fell. The sergeant following, was taken prisoner; and the soldiers, nine only in number, and left without a commander, capitulated.[4]

with Shingas, Weindohela, &c. &c., Delaware chiefs, at Tuskarawa's, 27 May, 1763, 11 o'clock at night. Bouquet to Amherst, 10 June, 1763. Amherst to Secretary of State, 27 June, 1763.

[1] Ecuyer to Bouquet, 29 May, 1753. Letter from Fort Pitt, of 2 June, in Weyman's New-York Gazette, 20 June, 1763. Ecuyer's Message to the chiefs of the Delawares.

[2] Ecuyer to Bouquet, 30 May, 1763.

[3] Declaration of Daniel Collet, horse driver, 30 May, 1763.

[4] Account of the Loss of the Post of Miamis, by a soldier of the 60th Regiment, who was one of the garrison.

CHAP. VII. 1763. May.

On the thirtieth of May the besieged garrison of Detroit caught a hope of relief, as they saw a fleet of boats sweeping round the point. They flocked to the bastions to welcome their friends; but the death-cry of the Indians announced that the English party, sent from Niagara to rëinforce Detroit, had, two nights previously, just before midnight, been attacked in their camp, on the beach, near the mouth of Detroit River, and utterly defeated, a part turning back to Niagara, the larger part falling into the hands of the savages.[1]

June.

At eight o'clock in the night of the last day of May, the war belt reached the Indian village near Fort Ouatanon, just below Lafayette, in Indiana; the next morning the commander was lured into an Indian cabin and bound, and his garrison surrendered. The French, moving the victors to clemency by gifts of wampum,[2] received the prisoners into their houses.

At Michilimackinac, a spot of two acres on the main land, west of the strait, was inclosed with pickets, and gave room for the cabins of a few traders, and a fort with a garrison of about forty[3] souls. Savages had arrived near it, as if to trade and beg for presents. From day to day, the Chippewas, who dwelt in a plain near the fort, assembled to play ball. On the second day of June,[4] they again engaged in

[1] Lieutenant Cuyler's Report of his being attacked and routed by a party of Indians on Lake Erie. Major Wilkins to Sir Jeffery Amherst, Niagara, 6 June, 1763.

[2] Lieutenant Jenkins to Major Gladwin, Ouatanon, 1 June, 1763.

[3] Captain Etherington to Major Gladwin, Michilimackinac, 12 June, 1763. Etherington's account, contemporary and official, reports but thirty-five privates.

[4] "Yet, on the second instant"—Capt. Etherington.—Henry's Travels and Adventures in Canada and the Indian Territories, between the years 1760 and 1776. The author in his old age prepared this interesting work for press, and gave it to the public in October 1809. He makes the garrison consist of ninety; he gives the game of ball as on the king's birth-day; and makes it a trial of skill between the

CHAP. VII. 1763. June.

the game, which is the most exciting sport of the red men. Each one has a bat curved like a crosier, and ending in a racket. Posts are planted apart on the open prairie. At the beginning of the game, the ball is placed midway between the goals. The eyes of the players flash; their cheeks glow; their whole nature kindles. A blow is struck; all crowd with violence and merry yells to renew it; the fleetest in advance now driving the ball home, now sending it sideways, with one unceasing passionate pursuit. On that day the squaws entered the fort, and remained there. Etherington, the commander, with one of his lieutenants, stood outside of the gate watching the game, fearing nothing. The Indians had played from morning till noon; when, throwing the ball close to the gate, they came behind the two officers, and seized and carried them into the woods; while the rest rushed into the fort, snatched their hatchets, which their squaws had kept hidden under their blankets, and in an instant killed an officer, a trader and fifteen men. The rest of the garrison, and all the English traders, were made prisoners, and robbed of every thing they had; but the French traders were left at liberty and unharmed. Thus fell the old post of Mackinaw on the main.

The fort at Presque Isle, now Erie, was the point of communication between Pittsburg and Niagara and Detroit. It was in itself one of the most tenable, and had a garrison of four and twenty men,[1] and could

Sacs and Chippewas. These incidents heighten the romance of the story; but I think it better "to stoop to truth," and follow the authentic contemporary account. The letter of Etherington, as published in Parkman's Pontiac War, 596, reads, "Yet, on the 4th instant."

[1] "I left Ensign Christy six men to strengthen his party, as he had but eighteen men. Lieut. Cuyler's Report, &c., 6 June, 1763.

most easily be relieved. On the twenty-second of June, after a two days' defence, the commander, out of his senses[1] with terror, capitulated;[2] giving up the sole chance of saving his men from the scalping-knife.[3] He himself, with a few others, were carried in triumph by the Indians to Detroit.[4]

CHAP. VII. 1763. June.

The capitulation at Erie left Le Bœuf without hope. Attacked on the eighteenth, its gallant officer kept off the enemy till midnight. The Indians then succeeded in setting the blockhouse on fire; but he escaped secretly, with his garrison, into the woods,[5] while the enemy believed them all buried in the flames.[6]

As the fugitives, on their way to Fort Pitt, passed Venango, they saw nothing but ruins. The fort at that place was consumed, never to be rebuilt; and not one of its garrison was left alive to tell the story of its destruction.[7]

Nor was it the garrisoned stockades only that encountered the fury of the savages. They roamed the wilderness, massacring all whom they met. They struck down more than a hundred[8] traders in the woods, scalping every one of them; quaffing their gushing life-blood, horribly mutilating their bodies.

[1] "I am surprised any officer in his senses would enter into terms with such barbarians." Amherst to Bouquet, 7 July, 1763.

[2] Particulars regarding the loss of the post at Presqu' Isle. See also the account of the soldier, Benjamin Grey, in Ecuyer to Bouquet, 26 June, 1763.

[3] Mante's History of the War, 483.

[4] Particulars regarding the loss of the post at Presqu' Isle.

[5] Ensign Price to Col. Bouquet, 26 June, 1763.

[6] Weyman's New-York Gazette, 11 July, 239, 3, 1.

[7] Captain Ecuyer to Colonel Bouquet, Fort Pitt, 26 June, 1763. Ensign Price to Bouquet, 26 June, 1763.

[8] Letter from Fort Pitt of 16 June, 1763, in Weyman's New-York Gazette of 4 July, 1763, No. 238, 3, 2.

CHAP. VII. 1763. June.

They prowled round the the cabins of the husbandmen on the frontier; and their tomahawks struck alike the laborer in the field or the child in the cradle. They menaced Fort Ligonier, at the western foot of the Alleghanies, the outpost of Fort Pitt. They passed the mountains, and spread death even to Bedford. The unhappy emigrant knew not if to brave danger, or to leave his home and his planted fields, for wretchedness and poverty. Nearly five hundred families, from the frontiers of Maryland and Virginia, fled to Winchester, unable to find so much as a hovel to shelter them from the weather, bare of every comfort, and forced to lie scattered among the woods.[1]

To the horrors of Indian warfare were added new dangers to colonial liberty. In Virginia nearly a thousand volunteers, at the call of the Lieutenant Governor, hastened to Fort Cumberland and to the borders; and the Lieutenant Governor of Maryland was able to offer aid.[2] The undecided strife between the proprietaries and the assembly of Pennsylvania checked the activity of that province. Its legislature sanctioned the equipment of seven hundred men, but refused to place them under the orders of the British general. Its design was rather to arm and pay the farmers and reapers on the frontier as a resident force for the protection of the country. This policy, from which it would not swerve, excited the utmost anger in the officers of the army.[3] Their in-

[1] Letter from Winchester of 22 June, 1763, in Weyman, 238, 3, 2, of 4 July, 1763. Correspondence of Lieut. Governor Fauquier of Virginia with the Board of Trade.

[2] Amherst to Bouquet, 25 August, 1763.

[3] Lieut. Governor Hamilton of Pennsylvania to Gen. Amherst, 7 July, 1763. Amherst to Hamilton in reply, 9 July, 1763. Hamilton to Amherst, 11 July. Amherst to Hamilton, 16 July. Lieut. Colonel Robertson's Report on his return from Philadelphia.

vectives[1] against Pennsylvania brought upon it once more the censure of the king[2] for its "supine and neglectful conduct;" but the censure was no longer addressed to its government; for the ministry was firm in the purpose of keeping up an army in America, and substituting taxes by parliament for requisitions by the crown.

So the general, with little aid from Pennsylvania, took measures for the relief of the West. The fortifications of Fort Pitt had never been finished, and the floods had opened it on three sides. But the brave Ecuyer, its commander, without any engineer, or any artificers but a few shipwrights, raised a rampart of logs round the fort, above the old one, palisaded the interior of the area, constructed a fire-engine, and in short took all precautions which art and judgment could suggest for the preservation of his post.[3] The garrison consisted of three hundred and thirty men,[4] officers and all included, and was in no immediate danger;[5] but it was weakened by being the asylum of more than two hundred women and children.[6]

On the twenty-first of June, a large party of Indians made a vigorous though fruitless assault on Fort Ligonier;[7] the next day, before the issue of this

1 Amherst to Bouquet, 6 June, 1763: "I wish the Assembly would as effectually lend their assistance; but as I have no sort of dependence on them," &c. &c. Compare Bouquet to Amherst, 11 August, 1763: "Had the Provinces assisted us, this would have been the favorable moment to have crushed the barbarians, a service we cannot effect with our forces alone."

2 Secretary of State to Amherst, October, 1763.

3 Col. Bouquet to Sir Jeffery Amherst, 11 August, 1763.

4 Capt. Ecuyer to Col. Bouquet 26 June, 1763.

5 Col. Bouquet to Gen. Amherst, 3 July, 1763.

6 Ecuyer to Bouquet, 26 June, 1763.

7 Lieutenant Blane to Col. Bouquet, Ligonier, 28 June, 1763.

CHAP. VII. 1763. June. attempt could have been heard, other savages appeared on the clear ground before Fort Pitt, and attacked it on every side, killing one man and wounding another. The night of the twenty-third, they strolled round the fort to reconnoitre it, and after midnight sought a conference.[1]

"Brother, the commanding officer," said Turtle's Heart, a principal warrior of the Delawares, "all your posts and strong places, from this backwards, are burnt and cut off. Your fort, fifty miles down (meaning Ligonier), is likewise destroyed before now. This is the only one you have left in our country. We have prevailed with six different nations of Indians, that are ready to attack you, to forbear till we came and warned you to go home. They have further agreed to permit you and your people to pass safe to the inhabitants. Therefore, brother, we desire that you may set off to-morrow, as great numbers of Indians are coming here, and after two days we shall not be able to do any thing with them for you."[2]

The brave commander, in his reply to this second summons, warned the Indians of their danger from three English armies, on their march to the frontier of Virginia, to Fort Pitt and to the north-west.[3]

July. A schooner, with a reinforcement of sixty men, had reached the Detroit in June; at daybreak of the twenty-ninth of July the garrison was surprised[4] by the appearance of Dalyell, an aide-de-camp to Am-

[1] Ecuyer to Bouquet, 26 June, 1763.

[2] Speech of The Turtle's Heart, a principal warrior of the Delawares, to Capt. Ecuyer, 24 June, 1763, at nine in the morning.

[3] Answer of S. Ecuyer, captain commanding.

[4] Major Gladwin, to Sir J. Amherst, Detroit, 18 August, 1763.

herst, with a detachment of two hundred and sixty men.[1] They had entered the river in the evening, and came up under cover of the night, or so small a command would have been intercepted, for the enemy were numerous, brave, and full of confidence from success.

CHAP. VII. 1763. July.

At once, after but one day's rest, Dalyell proposed a midnight sally against the besiegers. He was warned that they were on their guard; but the opinions and express instructions of Amherst were on his side. "The enemy," said he, "may be surprised in their camp and driven out of the settlement." Gladwin expressed a very different judgment. "You may do as you please," said Dalyell, "but there is no difficulty in giving the enemy an irrecoverable blow."[2] Gladwin reluctantly yielded, and, half an hour before three o'clock on the last morning of July, Dalyell marched out with two hundred and forty-seven chosen men, while two boats followed along shore to protect the party and bring off the wounded and dead. They proceeded in double file, along the great road by the river side, for a mile and a half, then forming into platoons, they advanced a half mile further, when they suddenly received, from the breastworks of the Indians, a very heavy and destructive fire, which staggered the main body and put the whole into confusion. As the savages outnumbered the English, the party which made the sally could escape being surrounded only by an inglorious retreat. Twenty of the English were killed, and forty-two

[1] Dalyell to Amherst, 15 July, 1763, quoted in Amherst to Gladwin, 10 August, 1763.

[2] Detail of the action of the 31 July, 1763, commanded by Captain Dalyell, against the Indian nations, near Fort Detroit, inclosed in Gladwin to Amherst, 8 August, 1763.

CHAP. VII. 1763. July.

wounded; leaving to a peaceful rivulet the name of The Bloody Run, in memory of that day. Dalyell himself fell while attempting to bring off the wounded;[1] his body remained to the victors; his scalp became one more ornament to the red man's wigwam.

The victory encouraged the confederates. The wavering began to fear no longer to be found on the side of Pontiac; two hundred recruits joined his forces, and the siege of Detroit was continued by bands exceeding a thousand men.[2]

The vigor and courage that pervaded the whole wilderness was without example. Once more the Delawares gathered around Fort Pitt, accompanied by the Shawnees. The chiefs, in the name of their tribes and of the north-western Indians, for a third time, summoned the garrison to retire. "You sent us word," said they, "that you were not to be removed. Brothers, you have towns and places of your own. You know this is our country, and that your having possession of it must be offensive to all nations. You yourselves are the people that have disturbed the chain of friendship. You have nobody to blame but yourselves for what has happened. All the nations over the lakes are soon to be on their way to the Forks of the Ohio. Here is the wampum. If you return quietly home to your wise men, this is the furthest they will go. If not, see what will be the consequence; so we desire that you do remove off."[3]

The next day Ecuyer gave his answer. "You suf-

[1] Amherst to Secretary of State, 3 Sept. 1753.

[2] Major Gladwin to Amherst, Detroit, 11 Aug. 1763.

[3] Speech of Shingas, with the principal warriors of the Delawares, and Big Wolf, with Shawnees, to Captain Ecuyer, 26 July, 1763.

fered the French," said he, "to settle in the heart of your country; why would you turn us out of it now? I will not abandon this post; I have warriors, provisions, and ammunition in plenty to defend it three years against all the Indians in the woods. Go home to your towns, and take care of your women and children."[1]

CHAP. VII. 1763. July.

No sooner was this answer received than the united forces of the Delawares, Shawnees, Wyandots, and Mingoes closely beset and attacked the fort. With incredible boldness they took post under the banks of both rivers, close to the fort, where, digging holes, they kept up an incessant discharge of musketry and threw fire arrows. They were good marksmen, and, though the English were under cover, they killed one and wounded seven. Ecuyer himself was struck on the leg by an arrow.[2] This continued through the last day of July, when they vanished from sight.

Bouquet was at that time making his way to relieve Fort Pitt and reinforce Detroit. His little army consisted chiefly of the remains of two regiments of Highlanders,[3] who, having been wasted by the enfeebling service of the West Indies, were now to brave the danger of mountain passes and a slow and painful journey through the wilderness. He moved onwards with but about five hundred men, driving a hundred beeves and twice that number of sheep, with powder,

[1] Captain Ecuyer's Answer, 27 July, 1763.

[2] Col. Bouquet to Amherst, 11 August, 1763. Weyman's New-York Gazette, 29 August, 1763, 246, 2, 3.

[3] "I have therefore ordered the remains of the 42d and 77th regiment, the first consisting of 214 men, including officers, and the latter of 133, officers included, which will march this evening." Amherst to Bouquet, 23 June, 1763.

CHAP. VII. 1763. July. flour, and provisions on pack-horses and in wagons drawn by oxen. Between Carlisle and Bedford they passed the ruins of mills, deserted cabins, fields waving with the harvest, but without a reaper, and all the signs of a savage and ruthless enemy.

On the twenty-eighth of July the party left Bedford, to wind its way, under the parching suns of midsummer, over the Alleghanies, along the narrow road, which was walled in by the dense forest on either side.

Aug. On the second day of August the troops and convoy arrived at Ligonier, but the commander could give no intelligence of the enemy. All the expresses for the previous month had been killed or forced to return.

Leaving the wagons at Ligonier, Bouquet, on the fourth of August, proceeded with the troops and about three hundred and fifty pack-horses. At one o'clock on the fifth, the savages, who had been besieging Fort Pitt, suddenly attacked the advanced guard; but two companies of Highlanders drove them from their ambuscade. When the pursuit ceased, the savages returned. The Western Nations, as if at the crisis of their destiny, fought like men contending for their homes, and forests, and hunting grounds, and all that they loved most. Again the Highlanders charged with fixed bayonets; but as soon as the savages were driven from one post they appeared in another, and at last were in such numbers as to surround the English, who would have been utterly routed and cut to pieces but for the cool behavior of the troops and the excellent conduct of the officers[1]

[1] Col. Bouquet to Sir Jeffery Amherst: Camp at Edge Hill, 5 Aug. 1763.

Night intervened, during which the English remained on Edge Hill, a ridge a mile to the east of Bushy Run, commodious for a camp except for the total want of water.

CHAP. VII.

1763. Aug.

All that night hope cheered the Red Men. Morning dawned only to show the English party that they were leaguered round on every side. They could not advance to give battle; for then their convoy and their wounded men would have fallen a prey to the enemy: if they remained quiet, they would be picked off one by one, and crumble away miserably and unavenged; yet the savages pressed upon them furiously, and grew more and more audacious. With happy sagacity, Bouquet took advantage of their resolute intrepidity, and feigned a retreat. The red men hurried to charge with the utmost daring, when two companies, that had been purposely concealed, fell upon their flank; others turned and met them in front; and the Indians, yielding to the irresistible shock, were utterly routed and put to flight.

But Bouquet in the two actions lost, in killed and wounded, about one-fourth of his men,[1] and almost all his horses; so that he was obliged to destroy his stores, and was hardly able to carry his wounded. That night the English encamped at Bushy Run, and in four days more they arrived at Pittsburg. From that hour the Ohio valley remained securely to the white man.

Before the news of the last disaster could reach New-York, the anger of Amherst against "the bloody

[1] Return of killed and wounded in the two actions at Edge Hill, near Bushy Run, the 5th and 6th August, 1763: total killed, 50; wounded, 60; missing, 5. Total of the whole, 115.

CHAP. VII. 1763. Aug.

villains" knew no bounds; and he became himself a man of blood. "As to accommodation with the savages, I will have none," said he, "until they have felt our just revenge. I would have every measure that can be fallen upon for their destruction taken." Pontiac he declared to be "the chief ringleader of mischief." "Whoever kills Pontiac," he continued, "shall receive from me a reward of one hundred pounds;"[1] and he bade the commander at Detroit make public proclamation for an assassin. He deemed the Indians not only unfit to be allies, and unworthy of being respected as enemies, "but as the vilest race of beings that ever infested the earth, and whose riddance from it must be esteemed a meritorious act, for the good of mankind. You will, therefore," such were his instructions to the officers engaged in the war, "take no prisoners, but put to death all that fall into your hands."[2]

Had this spirit prevailed, the war would have for ever continued in an endless series of alternate murders, in which the more experienced Indian excelled the white man. The Senecas, against whom Amherst had specially directed unsparing hostilities, lay in

[1] Sir J. Amherst to Major Gladwin, 10 August, 1763: "You will make known to the troops under your command, that whoever kills Pontiac, who seems to have been the chief ringleader of the mischief, shall receive from me a reward of one hundred pounds."

[2] Sir Jeffery Amherst's instructions to Captain Lieutenant Gardiner, to be shown to Major Gladwin, &c. New-York, 10 August, 1763: "The Senecas, * * with all the other nations on the lakes, * * must be deemed our enemies, and used as such; not as a generous enemy, but as the vilest race of beings that ever infested the earth, and whose riddance from it must be esteemed a meritorious act, for the good of mankind. You will, therefore, take no prisoners, but put to death all that fall into your hands of the nations who have so unjustly and cruelly committed depredations. * * I have thought proper to promise a reward of one hundred pounds to the man who shall kill Pontiac, the chief of the Ottawas—a cowardly villain," &c. &c. Signed Jeff. Amherst.

CHAP. VII. 1763 Sept.

ambush for one of his convoys about three miles below Niagara Falls; and on its return down the carrying-place, fell upon it with such suddenness and vigor that but eight wounded men escaped with their lives, while seventy-two were victims to the scalping-knife.

The first effective measures towards a general pacification proceeded from the French in Illinois. De Neyon, the French officer at Fort Chartres, sent belts and messages, and peace-pipes to all parts of the continent, exhorting the many nations of savages to bury the hatchet, and take the English by the hand, for they would never see him more.[2]

[1] Return of the killed, wounded and missing in the action on the carrying-place, at Niagara, 14 Sept. 1763.

[2] Neyon et Bobé à Kerlerec, Dec. 1763. Neyon à Kerlerec, 1 Dec. 1763.

CHAPTER VIII.

THE TREASURY ENTER A MINUTE FOR AN AMERICAN STAMP TAX—MINISTRY OF GRENVILLE AND BEDFORD.

MAY—SEPTEMBER, 1763.

CHAP. VIII. 1763. May. THE savage warfare was relentlessly raging when the young statesman to whom the forms of office had referred the subject of the colonies, was devising plans for organizing governments in the newly acquired territories. Of an Irish family, and an Irish as well as an English peer, Shelburne naturally inclined to limit the legislative authority of the parliament of Great Britain over the outlying dominions of the crown. The world already gave him credit for great abilities: he had just been proposed to supersede Egremont in the department of state, and, except the lawyers who had been raised to the peerage, he was the best speaker in the House of Lords. For a moment the destinies of America hung upon his judgment.

June. For the eastern boundary of New England, Shelburne hesitated between the Penobscot and the St. Croix; on the north-east he adopted the crest of the water shed dividing the streams tributary to the St. Lawrence river from those flowing into the Bay of Fundy, or the Atlantic Ocean, or the Gulf of the St.

Lawrence, south of Cape Rosieres, designating the line with precision on a map, which is still preserved.[1] At the south, the boundary of Georgia was extended to its present line.

Of Canada, General Murray advised[2] to make a military colony, and to include the west within its jurisdiction, in order to overawe the older colonies, and keep them in fear and submission. Against this project Shelburne desired to restrict[3] the government of Canada within narrower limits, and to bound it on the west by a line drawn from the intersection of the parallel of forty-five degrees north with the St. Lawrence to the east end of Lake Nipising. This advice was promptly rejected by the imperative Earl of Egremont,[4] who insisted on including in the new province all the great lakes and all the Ohio valley to the Mississippi; but Shelburne[5] resolutely enforced his opinion, which, for the time, prevailed,[6] and the plan of intimidating America by a military colony at its north and west was deferred.

With regard to "the mode of revenue least burthensome and most palatable to the colonies, whereby they were to contribute to the additional expense which must attend the civil and military establishments adopted on the present occasion," Shelburne

[1] "With regard to the limits of these governments, as described in the report, and marked out in the chart thereunto annexed," &c. Earl of Egremont to the Board of Trade, 14 July, 1763 (E. and A., 278).

[2] General Murray's opinion, given by himself to Francès, as contained in M. Francès au Duc de Choiseul, à Londres le 2 Septembre, 1768.

[3] Lords of Trade to the Secretary of State, 8 June, 1763.

[4] Secretary of State to Lords of Trade, 14 July, 1763.

[5] Lords of Trade to the Secretary of State, 5 August, 1763.

[6] Secretary of State to the Lords of Trade, 19 September, 1763: "His Majesty is pleased to lay aside the idea of including within the government of Canada the lands which are to be reserved, for the present, for the use of the Indians."

CHAP. VIII. 1763. July.

gave warning that it was a "point of the highest importance,"[1] and declined to implicate himself in the plans for taxing America.[2]

This refusal on the part of Shelburne neither diminished the stubborn eagerness of Egremont nor delayed the action of the treasury department; and, as it had been decided that America was to be taxed by parliament to defray the additional expense of its military establishment, it belonged to Jenkinson, the principal Secretary of the Treasury, from the nature of his office, to prepare the business for consideration.[3] Grenville would have esteemed himself unpardonable if he could have even thought of such a measure as the stamp act, without previously making every possible inquiry into the condition of America.[4] In addition to the numerous public reports and correspondence, information was sought from men who were esteemed in England as worthy of trust in all situations, and the exaggerated accounts given by the officers who had been employed in America, dispelled every

[1] Lords of Trade to Egremont, 8 June (E. and A., 275), 1763.

[2] Grenville Diary, Tuesday, 13 Dec., 1763; Grenville Papers, ii. 238: "He (Henley) told him (G. G.) that the king had told his lordship, in the summer, that upon occasion of some disputes between Lord Egremont and Lord Shelburne, relating to the Board of Trade, Lord Mansfield had given it as his advice to his Majesty, to show favor to Lord Shelburne, in order to play them one against the other, and by that means to keep the power in his own hands."

This, as far as it proves any thing, tends to show that the king was not the author of the high American measures, though he approved them and wished them to be adopted.

[3] See the note to Grenville Papers, by their editor, ii. 373, and compare Jenkinson to Grenville, 2 July, 1764.

[4] G. Grenville, in Cavendish, i. 494, Debate of fifth of March, 1770: "I should have been unpardonable, if I had thought of such a measure (as the stamp act) without having previously made every possible inquiry into the condition of America. Sir, I had information from men of the first respectability, of the first trust; men who, in all situations, and upon every occasion, are worthy of credit."

doubt of its ability to bear a part in the national expenses.[1] Halifax, one of the triumvirate, had had the experience of nine years in administering the affairs of the colonies, and for nearly as long had been fixed in his opinions, that parliament must intervene to raise a revenue. Egremont, his colleague, selected, as his confidential friend, Ellis, a favorite of Halifax, and for several years Governor of Georgia; a statesman and man of letters, esteemed as one of the ablest men that had been employed in America, of whose interests he made pretensions to a thorough knowledge. He had no small share in introducing the new system, and bore away sinecure offices for his reward.

McCulloh, a crown officer in North Carolina, and agent for an English company concerned in a purchase of more than a million acres of land in that province, a man who had influence enough to gain an office from the crown for his son, with seats in the council for his son and nephew, furnished Jenkinson with a brief state of the taxes usually raised in the old settled colonies, and assured him that a stamp tax on the continental colonies would, at a moderate computation, produce sixty thousand pounds per annum, and twice that sum if extended to the West Indies.[3]

[1] Reed's Reed, i. 32.

[2] Wm. Knox, Extra Official Papers: "The newly appointed governor, my earliest and most intimate friend, Mr. Ellis, a gentleman whose transcendent talents had then (1756) raised him to that high office, and afterwards made him the confidential friend of the Earl of Egremont, when Secretary of State." This is in harmony with the letter of Joseph Reed to Charles Pettit. London, 11 June, 1764: "Ellis, late Governor of Georgia, * * * has had no small share in the late events." Reed's Reed, i. 32, 33. Add to this, that, immediately on the peace in 1762, Knox, who looked up to Ellis, put into Bute's hands a plan for reducing America.

[3] Henry McCulloh to Charles Jenkinson, Turnham Green, 5 July,

CHAP. VIII. 1763. July. He also renewed the proposition which he had made eight years before to Halifax, for gaining an imperial revenue by issuing exchequer bills for the general use of America. But before the bill for the American tax was ordered to be prepared, Egremont was no longer Secretary of State, nor Shelburne at the head of the Board of Trade.

The triumvirate ministry, "the three Horatii,"

1763, in a note of the editor of the Grenville Papers, ii. 374: Henry McCulloh had for many years been a speculator in land in North Carolina, and acted as the land agent of George A. Selwyn as well as others. He obtained a patent for 1,200,000 acres in the time of George II. for himself and his associates. At the time of his correspondence with Jenkinson, in 1763, he appears to have been a crown officer, probably in the revenue department, as may be inferred from one of his own letters respecting "arrears of salary." [Henry McCulloh to Secretary of the Board of Trade, 2 June, 1764.] He was not at that time, nor was he himself ever, agent for North Carolina. His son, Henry Eustace McCulloh, like his father, a zealous royalist, was collector of the port of Roanoke, as well as a member of the Council of North Carolina. [Tryon to Board of Trade, 28 April, 1767. Board of Trade, N. C., vol. 15.] On the second of December, 1768, H. E. McCulloh was appointed agent to the province of North Carolina by the Assembly [see America and West Indies, vol. 198], but the resolve, to which Governor Tryon had no objection, dropped in the Council. [Tryon to Hillsborough, 25 Feb. 1769.] He therefore acted for a time as agent of the Assembly. [Henry Eustace McCulloh to Hillsborough, 5 June, 1768.] In the session of 1769 he was appointed agent for the province of North Carolina by an act of the Legislature. [1769, Nov. 27, Carolina Acts, 351.] This appointment was renewed 2 Dec. 1771. Henry McCulloh, the father, died, at a great age, in 1779. [Letter from D. L. Swain, late Governor of North Carolina.] Alexander McCulloh, the nephew of Henry, became also a member of the Council of North Carolina.

On reading the note in Grenville Papers, ii. 373, 374, I made inquiries respecting Henry McCulloh. The records of North Carolina, at Raleigh, have been thoroughly searched on the occasion, as well as the papers of the Board of Trade.

For the honor of precedence, in favoring the second proposal of McCulloh, we shall by and by see Charles Townshend, in the House of Commons, dispute with Grenville. I attribute to McCulloh no other influence in these affairs than that of a convenient subordinate, courting his superiors by serving their views. Grenville says of himself, "that he made every possible inquiry into the condition of America." But it does not appear from the note of the editor of the Grenville Papers, whether the communication from Henry McCulloh was volunteered or prepared at the request of Jenkinson.

CHAP. VIII. 1763 Aug.

"the ministerial Cerberus,"[1] as they were called, although too fond of office to perceive their own weakness, had neither popularity, nor weight in parliament, nor the favor of the court. To strengthen his government, the king, conforming to the views sketched by Bute in the previous April,[2] but against the positive and repeated advice[3] of his three ministers, directed Egremont to invite Lord Hardwicke to enter the cabinet, as President of the Council.

"It is impossible for me," said Hardwicke, at an interview on the first day of August,[4] "to accept an employment, whilst all my friends are out of court."[5] "The king," said Egremont, "cannot bring himself to submit to take in a party in gross, or an opposition party." "A king of England," answered Hardwicke, "at the head of a popular government, especially as of late the popular scale has grown heavier, will sometimes find it necessary to bend and ply a little; not as being forced, but as submitting to the stronger reason, for the sake of himself and his government. King William, hero as he was, found himself obliged to this conduct; so had other princes before him, and so did his majesty's grandfather, King George the Second, who thanked me for advising him to it."[6]

The wise answer of the illustrious jurist was re-

[1] Wilkes to Temple, 26 July. Grenville Papers, ii. 81.

[2] Bute to Bedford, 2 April, 1763: "I once gone, it will be very hard for me to believe that the Duke of Newcastle will, with Lord Hardwicke, &c. continue a violent or peevish opposition," &c. &c. Bedford Cor. iii. 226.

[3] Grenville's Diary, in Grenville Papers, ii. 191.

[4] The date of Newcastle's letter, in Albemarle's Memoirs of Rockingham, i. 169, is given as of June 30, 1763, a mistake, for the letter refers to the conversation held in August.

[5] Hardwicke to his son, 5 August, 1763, in Harris, 370.

[6] Grenville's Diary, in Grenville Papers, 191. Hardwicke, in Harris, iii. 372. Walpole, in his Reign of George III., i. 285, mixing fiction with fact.

CHAP. VIII. 1763. Aug.

ported to the king, who, disregarding the most earnest dissuasions of Grenville, desired ten days for reflection, on which Grenville went into the country to await the decision. But on Wednesday, the third, Halifax, with Egremont at his side, harangued the king for half an hour, pressing him, on the instant, to resolve either to support his administration or to form another from their adversaries. Halifax turned this in all the ways that eloquence could dictate or invent, yet without extorting any answer whatever; and when he said, that surely the king could not mean to take into his service the whole body of the opposition and yield to the invasion of those he had detested, the usual disclaiming of such a purpose was also suppressed.[1] The angry Egremont spoke to the same effect, and the king still preserved absolute silence. "Behavior so insulting and uncivil," said Egremont to Grenville, "I never knew nor conceive could be held to two gentlemen." Yet the king had only remained silent on a subject on which he had reserved to himself ten days before coming to a decision; and it was his ministers, whose questions were insulting, uncivil, and impertinent. Instead of hastily resigning,[2] Egremont was ready to concert with Grenville how to maintain themselves in office in spite of the king's wishes, by employing "absolute necessity and fear."[3]

It is not strange that the discerning king wished to be rid of Egremont. To that end Shelburne, who was opposed to Egremont's schemes of colonial government, was commissioned to propose a coalition be-

[1] Egremont to Geo. Grenville, 3 August, 1763, in Grenville Papers, ii. 83, 84.

[2] Geo. Grenville to Egremont, 4 August, 1763, in Grenville Papers, ii. 85–87.

[3] Egremont to Grenville, 6 Aug. 1763, in Grenville Papers, ii. 88.

CHAP. VIII. 1763. Aug.

tween Pitt and Temple[1] on the one side, and the Duke of Bedford[2] on the other.

The anger of Bedford towards Bute, for having communicated to the French minister the instructions given him during his embassy, had ripened into a stiff, irrevocable hatred. He was therefore willing to enter the ministry[3] on condition of Bute's absence from the king's counsels and presence, and Pitt's concurrence in a coalition of parties and the maintenance of the present relations with France.[4] Pitt was willing to treat,[5] had no objection to a coalition of parties, and could not but acquiesce in the peace, now that it was once made; but Bedford had been his strongest opponent in the cabinet, had contributed to force him into retirement, and had negotiated the treaty which he had so earnestly arraigned. For Pitt to have accepted office with Bedford would have been a marked adoption of the peace, alike glaringly inconsistent with his declared opinions and his engagements with the great Whig families[6] in opposition. So ended the attempt to supersede Egremont by Pitt, with Bedford in the vacant chair of President of the Council.

For a day or two the king hesitated, and had to endure the very long and tedious speeches of Grenville

[1] Calcraft to Lord Temple, 10 August, and Temple to Calcraft, 12 August, 1763, in the Grenville Papers, ii. 90, 91.

[2] Geo. Grenville's Diary, in Grenville Papers, ii. 204.

[3] Note by Grenville to his Diary, in Grenville Papers, ii. 204.

[4] Bedford Papers in Wiffen's Memoirs of the House of Russell, ii. 526, 527. The paper here cited by Wiffen seems not to be printed in the Bedford Correspondence.

[5] Grenville's Diary, in Grenville Papers, ii. 204.

[6] Rigby to the Duke of Bedford, 15 August, 1763, in Wiffen, ii. 527, and Bedford Cor., ii. 236.

CHAP. VIII. 1763. Aug.

on the inconvenience of sacrificing his ministry.[1] "I have fully considered upon your long discourse on the Friday," said he to his minister on Sunday the twenty-first; "by your advice I mean to conduct myself. It is necessary to restrain the licentiousness of the times; if I suffer force to be put upon me by the opposition, the mob will try to govern me next;"[2] and he decided to stand by the ministry.

But, just at that moment, news came that Egremont was dying of a stroke of apoplexy. The place of secretary now seemed to await Pitt's acceptance. "Your majesty has three options," said Grenville and Halifax; "to strengthen the hands of the present ministry, or to mingle them with a coalition, or to throw the government entirely into the hands of Pitt and his friends." "To the last," said the king, "I never will consent."[3]

The Duke of Bedford, who hated and despised[4] George Grenville, came to town. "Your government," said he to the king, "cannot stand; you must send to Mr. Pitt and his friends." When Grenville heard this, he was overwhelmed with consternation and rage. His anger towards the Duke of Bedford[5] became unappeasable; and he never forgave him the advice.

It was the interest of Bute to see Pitt at the head of affairs, for Pitt alone had opposed him as a minister without animosity towards him as a man. They who had sided with him when in power, now so dreaded

[1] Grenville's Diary, 19 August, Grenville Papers, ii. 193.

[2] Geo. Grenville's Diary, Sunday, 21 August, in Grenville Papers, ii. 193.

[3] Grenville's Diary. 22 and 23 August, in Grenville Papers, ii. 194.

[4] C. Townshend to Temple, 11 Sept. 1763, in Gr. P. ii. 121.

[5] Sir Denis Le Marchant's note to Walpole's Memoirs, i. 287.

to share his unpopularity, that they made a parade of proscribing him, and wished not only to deprive him of influence, but to exile him from the court and from Westminster. He, therefore desired, and long continued to desire, to see Pitt in office, of whose personal magnanimity he was sure. The wish was inconsistent with the politics of the times; but the moment was one when parties in England, though soon to be consolidated, were as yet in a nebulous state, and very many of the time-serving public men, even Charles Townshend himself, were entirely at fault. The real option lay between a government by the more liberal aristocracy under popular influence as its guide, and an administration on new principles independent of both.

The king appeared on that occasion as the moderator between factions; and informed Grenville of his intention to call Pitt to the management of his affairs, yet with as few changes as possible.[1]

On Saturday the twenty-seventh, Grenville went to the king and found Pitt's servants waiting in the court. He passed two long hours of agony and bitterness in the antechamber, incensed and humiliated, on finding himself at the mercy of the brother-in-law whom he had betrayed.

The king, in his interview with Pitt, proceeded upon the plan of defeating faction by a coalition of parties; and offered the Great Commoner his old place of Secretary of State. "I cannot abandon the friends who have stood by me," said Pitt, and he declined to accept office without them. "Do you think it possible for me," answered the king, "to give up

[1] Grenville's Diary for Friday 26 August, 1763.

CHAP. VIII. 1763. Aug.

those who have served me faithfully and devoted themselves to me?" "The reproach," answered Pitt, "will light on your ministers, and not on yourself. It is fit to break the present government, which is not founded on true revolution principles;" and he showed the principles which he wished should rule, by insisting on excluding Lord Mansfield from the cabinet, and proposing Pratt for a peerage. Nor did he fail to comment on the infirmities of the peace as "dishonorable, dangerous and criminal;" and to declare that "the Duke of Bedford should have no efficient office whatever." He would restore to the king's council the men of the great Whig families, who, like himself, had been driven from power, yet not as a party to triumph over the prerogative. The king preserved his self-possession, combated several of these demands, said now and then that his honor must be consulted,[1] and reserved his decision till a second interview.[2]

[1] For the king's account of this interview to Grenville, in Grenville's Diary, 197, 199; to Hertford in Walpole's George III. i. 291; to Sandwich, in Sandwich to Bedford, and in Bedford to Neville, in Bedford Cor. iii. 238, 241. For Pitt's account to Wood, see Wood's Letter, in the Chatham Correspondence; to Hardwicke, in Hardwicke to Royston, Harris iii. 377, 380; to the House of Commons, in Walpole, i. 318, 319, and in several contemporary letters, containing the accounts of the debates.

[2] Charles Townshend to Temple, 11 Sept. 1763, in Grenville Papers, ii. 121. "The general idea of Mr. Pitt's establishment, is asserted to have been never accepted or approved in any one meeting."

That Pitt had no good reason to think the king intended to accept his terms, appears also from his own account of it, as reported by Hardwicke. Bute, in his interview, wished at first to keep it a secret one. Then openness was pushed to an extreme. Pitt's summons to court was an unsealed note, as little confidential as a Lord Chamberlain's card of invitation. When Pitt named names, the king asked him to write them down, which Pitt declined to do. Some of Pitt's suggestions were so offensive to the king, that while he said he liked to hear him, and bade him go on, he yet said "now and then" that is repeatedly that his honor must be consulted. Surely to describe the acceptance of a proposition as inconsistent with honor, would seem not to be an encouragement that it would be accepted.

When Grenville, after his long and anxious suspense, was called in, he could think only of his griefs, pleading his adhesion to the king, on Pitt's leaving the cabinet in 1761; the barbarous usage he had in consequence received from his family; the assurances given at that time by Bute, that his honor should be the king's honor, his disgrace the king's disgrace. The king bowing to him, stopped his complaints by observing, "It is late;" and as the afflicted minister was leaving him, said only "Good morrow, Mr. Greenville, good morrow, Mr. Greenville," for he never called him by his right name.

Whether Pitt, who had himself attained a kind of royalty, and was ever mindful to support his own majesty,[1] pleased himself with seeing the great Whig families at his heels; or, which is more probable, aware that the actual ministry could not go on, was himself deceived by his own presumptuously hopeful nature into a belief that those who made the overture must carry it through, he summoned Newcastle, Devonshire, Rockingham, and Hardwicke[2] to come to London as his council.

From his own point of view, there was no unreasonableness[3] in his demands. But to the court it seemed otherwise. On Sunday evening Grenville found the king in the greatest agitation. "Rather than submit to the hard terms proposed by Pitt," said he, "I would die in the room I now stand in."[4]

Early in the morning of the twenty-ninth, Bute, through Beckford, urged Pitt to be content with filling up the places of the two Secretaries of State, and put-

[1] Lyttelton to Royston, in Phillimore, ii. 646.

[2] Hardwicke in Harris, iii. 379.

[3] W. Gerard Hamilton in Chatham Cor. ii. 378.

[4] Grenville Papers, ii. 197.

CHAP. VIII. 1763. Aug.

ting a neutral person at the head of the Treasury, instead of Lord Temple.[1] The message was an announcement to Pitt that his system was rejected; and the great commoner stood forewarned in the presence of his sovereign. The audience lasted nearly two hours. The king proposed Halifax for the Treasury: Pitt was willing he should have the Paymaster's place. "But I had designed that," said the king, "for poor George Grenville; "he is your own relation, and you once loved him." To this the only answer was a low bow. The king as a lure named Temple to be at the head of the Treasury. "That," said Pitt, "is essential;" but he still insisted on a thorough change of administration. "Well, Mr. Pitt," said the king, "I see this won't do. My honor is concerned, and I must support it."[2] A government formed out of the minority who had opposed the peace, seemed to the king an offence to his conscience and a wound to his honor.[3] "The House of Commons," said Pitt, on taking leave, "will not force me upon your majesty, and I will never come into your service against your consent."[4]

Events now shaped themselves. First of all, Bute, having disobliged all sides, went to the country with the avowed purpose of absolute retirement. His retreat was his own act;[5] and not a condition to be made the basis of a new ministry. As his only protection against the Duke of Bedford, he desired

[1] Grenville's Diary, in Grenville Papers, ii. 202.

[2] Hardwicke in Harris.

[3] Grenville to Strange, 3 Sept. 1763, in Grenville Papers, ii. 105. "The consideration of his honor, &c., and of his conscience, &c."

[4] King's account to Hertford in Walpole, i. 292.

[5] Grenville's Diary, in Papers, ii. 203. Compare too Grenville to Stuart Mackenzie, 16 Sept. 1763; and Grenville to Lord Strange, and to Lord Granby, 3 Sept. 1763.

that Grenville might be armed with every degree of power.[1] Next Lord Shelburne withdrew from office, and remained ever the firmest friend of Pitt, giving an example of the utmost fidelity of attachment. At the same time Bedford doubly irritated at being proscribed[2] by the very statesman whom he had proposed to the king as minister, promised for himself and, as a consequence, for his numerous and powerful connection, to support the present system in all its parts.[3] The king entreated him to take a place in the administration. Grenville, too, smothering alike his hatred and his fears, urged him to preside in the council. And Bedford, though personally indifferent to office, now that Bute had gone into retreat, under the influence of his friends, especially of Sandwich who became Secretary of State, accepted the post which was pressed upon him.

The union of the Bedford party and of Grenville, was, said Pitt, "a treaty of connivance;" Lord Melcombe said, "It is all for quarter day;" but it was more. From seemingly accidental causes, there arose within ten days out of a state of great uncertainty, a compact and well cemented ministry. The king, in forming it, stood on the solid ground of the constitution. The last great question in parliament was on the peace; and was carried in its favor by an overwhelming majority. The present ministers had made or supported that peace, and so were in harmony with

[1] Gilbert Elliot to Geo. Grenville, 31 August, 1763.

[2] Sandwich to Bedford, 5 Sept. 1763, in Bedford Cor. iii. 238. Walpole's George III. i. 293.

[3] Sandwich to Grenville, 3 Sept. 1763. Grenville's Diary, Grenville Papers, ii. 108, 203. Compare, also, Bedford to Neville, 5 Sept. 1763. Bedford Cor. iii. 240, 241; and Sandwich to Bedford 5 Sept. 1763. Bedford Cor. iii. 238.

CHAP. VIII. 1763. Sept.

parliament. There was a coincidence of opinion between them and the king; but there was not one of them all whom the king could claim as his own personal friend. If the ministry was too little favorable to liberty, the fault lay in the system on which parliament was organized; it was undoubtedly a fair and adequate representation of the British constitution, and needed nothing but cordial personal union among themselves and with the king to last for a generation.

Of the Secretaries of State, Halifax, as the elder, had his choice of departments, and took for himself the Southern, "on account of the Colonies;"[1] and the Earl of Hillsborough, like Shelburne an Irish as well as an English Peer, was placed at the head of the Board of Trade.

One and the same spirit was at work on each side of the Atlantic. From Boston Bernard urged anew the establishment of a sufficient and independent civil list—out of which enlarged salaries were to be paid to the crown officers. And while he acknowledged that "the compact between the king and the people was in no colony better observed than in that of the Massachusetts Bay," that "its people in general were well satisfied with their subordination to Great Britain," that "their former prejudices which made them otherwise disposed, were wholly or almost wholly worn off," he nevertheless railed at "the unfortunate error in framing the government, to leave the council to be elected annually." He advised rather a council "resembling as near as possible the House of Lords;" its members to be appointed for life, with some title,

[1] Lord Chesterfield to his Son, September, 1763. Letter cclxxii.

CHAP. VIII. 1763. Sept.

as Baronet or Baron, composed of people of consequence, willing to look up to the king for honor and authority. A permanent civil list, independent of colonial appropriations, an aristocratic middle legislative power, and a Court of Chancery—these were the subjects of the very earnest recommendation of Bernard to the British government.[1]

On the extension of the British frontier by the cession of Canada, and the consequent security of the interior, New-England towns, under grants from Wentworth, the Governor of New-Hampshire, rose up on both sides of the Connecticut, and extended to the borders of Lake Champlain. But New-York coveted the lands, and under its old charter to the Duke of York, had long disputed with New-Hampshire the jurisdiction of the country west of Connecticut River. The British government had hitherto regarded the contest with indifference; but Colden now urged the Board of Trade to annex to New-York all of Massachusetts and of New-Hampshire west of the Connecticut River. "The New-England Governments," he reasoned, "are all formed on republican principles, and those principles are zealously inculcated in the minds of their youth. The government of New-York, on the contrary, is established as nearly as may be after the model of the English Constitution. Can it, then, be good policy to diminish the extent of jurisdiction in his majesty's province of New-York, to extend the power and influence of the

[1] Answer of Francis Bernard, Esq., Governor of Massachusetts Bay, to the queries proposed by the Lords Commissioners for Trade and Plantations; dated 5 September, 1763. King's Library, Mss. ccv. 423. Compare on the loyalty of Massachusetts, Bernard to Sec. of State, 16 Feb. 1763, and same to same, 25 Oct. 1763.

CHAP. VIII. others?"[1] Little was the issue of this fatal advice foreseen.

1763. Sept. While Massachusetts was in danger of an essential violation of its charter with regard to one branch of its legislature, the Assembly of South Carolina was engaged in a long contest for "that most essential privilege, solely to judge and finally determine the validity of the election of their own members;" for Boone, the governor, claimed exclusive authority to administer the required oaths, and on occasion of administering them, assumed the power to reject members whom the House declared duly elected and returned, "thereby taking upon himself to be the sole judge of elections."[2]

The "arbitrary and imperious" governor was too clearly in the wrong to be sustained;[3] but the controversy which had already continued for a twelvemonth, and was now at its height, lasted long enough to train the statesmen of South Carolina to systematical opinions on the rights of their legislature, and of the king's power in matters of their privilege.

The details of the colonial administration belonged to Halifax. No sooner was the ministry definitively established, than Grenville, as the head of the treasury, proceeded to redeem the promise made to the House of Commons of an American revenue.

The revenue from the customs in America could by no means produce a sufficient fund to meet the expenses of its military establishment.

[1] Colden to the Board of Trade, New-York, 26 Sept., 1763.

[2] Gov. Thomas Boone to Lords of Trade, 15 Sept. 1763. Petition to the king of the Commons House of Assembly of the Province of South Carolina, in Boone's letter of 10 Sept. 1763.

[3] South Carolina to Garth, their agent, 2 July, 1766.

CHAP. VIII. 1763 Sept.

On the morning of the twenty-second day of September, three lords of the treasury, George Grenville, Lord North, and one Hunter who completed the number requisite for the transaction of business, held a board in the room set apart for their use in Downing-street, and, without any hesitancy or discussion, they adopted a minute directing Jenkinson, the First Secretary of the Treasury, to "write to the Commissioners of the Stamp Duties to prepare the draft of a bill to be presented to parliament for extending the stamp duties to the colonies."[1] The very next day, Jenkinson accordingly wrote to the commissioners, desiring them "to transmit to him the draft of an act for imposing proper stamp duties upon his majesty's subjects in America and the West Indies."[2]

Who was the author of the American stamp tax? At a later day, Jenkinson assured the House of Commons that, "if the stamp act was a good measure, the merit of it was not due to Grenville; if it was a bad one, the ill policy did not belong to him;" but he never confessed to the house where the blame or the merit could rest more justly. In his late old age he delighted to converse freely, with the son he loved best, on every topic connected with his long career, save only on the one subject, of the contest

[1] Treasury Minute, 22 September, 1763: "Present, Mr. Grenville, Lord North, Mr. Hunter."

"Write to the Commissioners of the Stamp Duties to prepare the draft of a bill, to be presented to parliament, for extending the stamp duties to the colonies."

[2] C. Jenkinson to the Commissioners of Stamps. Letter Book, xxii. p. 432:

"Treasury Chambers. Gentlemen, The Lords Commissioners of His Majesty's Treasury are pleased to direct me to desire that you would forthwith prepare and transmit to me, for their Lordships' consideration, a draught of an Act for imposing proper Stamp Duties upon His Majesty's Subjects in America and the West Indies. I am, &c. C. Jenkinson.—23 Sept. 1763."

CHAP. VIII. with America. On that, and on that alone, he maintained an inflexible and total silence. He never was heard even to allude to it. But, though Jenkinson proposed the American tax, while private secretary to Bute, and brought it with him into the treasury for adoption by Bute's successor, he was but a subordinate without power of direction or a seat in council, and cannot bear the responsibility of the measure. Nor does the final responsibility attach to Bute;[1] for the ministry had forced him into absolute retirement, and would not have listened to his advice in the smallest matter; nor to the king, for though the king approved the stamp tax and wished it to be adopted, he exerted no influence to control his ministry on the occasion; and besides, the ministry boasted of being free from sycophancy to the court. Hunter, one of the lords of the treasury, who ordered the minute, was but a cipher; and Lord North, who supported the stamp act, himself told the House of Commons that he took the propriety of passing it very much upon the authority of Grenville.[2]

1763. Sept.

From the days of King William there was a steady line of precedents of opinion that America should, like Ireland, provide in whole, or at least in part, for the support of its military establishment. It was one of the first subjects of consideration on the organization of the Board of Trade.[3] It again employed the attention of the servants of Queen Anne. It was still more seriously considered in the days of George the First; and when, in the reign of

[1] Benjamin Franklin to Deborah Franklin, 6 April, 1765. Works, vii. 309.

[2] Lord North's Speech, 2 March, 1769. Cavendish, i. 299.

[3] Representation of the Board of Trade to the Lords Justices, September 30, 1696. Compare Penn's Brief and Plain Scheme, 8 February, 169$\frac{6}{7}$.

George the Second, the Duke of Cumberland was at the head of American military affairs, it was laid down as a principle, that a revenue sufficient for the purpose must be provided. The ministry of Bute resolved to provide such a revenue; for which Charles Townshend pledged the government. Parliament wished it.[1] The king wished it.[2] Almost all sorts and conditions of men repeatedly wished it.[3]

CHAP. VIII.

1763. Sept.

How America was to be compelled to contribute this revenue remained a question. For half a century or more, the king had sent executive orders or requisitions. But if requisitions were made, the colonial legislature claimed a right of freely deliberating upon them; and as the colonies were divided into nearly twenty different governments, it was held that they never would come to a common result. The need of some principle of union, of some central power was asserted. To give the military chief a dictatorial authority to require subsistence for the army, was suggested by the Board of Trade in 1696, in the days of King William and of Locke; was more deliberately planned in 1721; was apparently favored by Cumberland, and was one of the arbitrary proposals put aside by Pitt. To claim the revenue through a congress of the colonies, was at one time the plan of Halifax; but if the congress was of governors, their decision would be only consultatory, and have no more weight than royal instructions; and if the congress was a representative

[1] Speech of Grenville, December 1765.

[2] Speech of Grenville:—"His majesty, ever desirous of dividing equally the burdens of his people, wished to see them so divided in this instance."—Wright's Cavendish.

[3] Ibid. "It was in consequence of the repeated wish of almost all sorts and conditions of men, that I took the step which I did."

CHAP. VIII. 1763. Sept.

body, it would claim and exercise the right of free discussion. To demand a revenue by instructions from the king, and to enforce them by stringent coercive measures, was beyond the power of the prerogative, under the system established at the revolution. When New-York had failed to make appropriations for the civil service, a bill was prepared to be laid before parliament, giving the usual revenue; and this bill having received the approbation of the great whig lawyers, Northey and Raymond, was the precedent which overcame Grenville's scruples about taxing the colonies without first allowing them representatives.[1] It was settled then that there must be a military establishment in America of twenty regiments; that after the first year its expenses must be defrayed by America; that the American colonies themselves, with their various charters, never would agree to vote such a revenue, and that parliament must do it.

It remained to consider what tax parliament should impose. And here all agreed that the first object of taxation was foreign and intercolonial commerce. But that, under the navigation acts, would not produce enough. A poll tax was common in America; but, applied by parliament, would fall unequally upon the colonies holding slaves. The difficulty in collecting quit-rents, proved that a land tax would meet with formidable obstacles. An excise was thought of, but kept in reserve. An issue of exchequer bills to be kept in circulation as the currency of the continent, was urged on the ministry, but conflicted with the policy of acts of parliament against the use of paper money in the colonies.

[1] Knox, in a pamphlet, of which George Grenville was part author.

CHAP. VIII. 1763. Sept.

Every body[1] who reasoned on the subject, decided for a stamp tax, as certain of collection; and in America, where lawsuits were frequent, as likely to be very productive. A stamp act had been proposed to Sir Robert Walpole; it had been thought of by Pelham; it had been almost resolved upon in 1755; it had been pressed upon Pitt; it seems beyond a doubt to have been a part of the system adopted in the ministry of Bute, and was sure of the support of Charles Townshend.

Knox, the agent of Georgia, stood ready to defend the stamp act, as least liable to objection. The agent of Massachusetts, through his brother, Israel Mauduit, who had Jenkinson for his fast friend and often saw Grenville, favored raising the wanted money in that way, because it would occasion less expense of officers, and would include the West India Islands;[2] and speaking for his constituents, he made a merit of cheerful "submission" to the ministerial policy.

One man in Grenville's office, and one man only, did indeed give him sound advice; Richard Jackson,[3] his Secretary as Chancellor of the Exchequer, advised him to lay the project aside, and refused to take any part in preparing or supporting it. But Jenkinson, his Secretary of the Treasury, was ready to render

[1] Cornwall in Cavendish.

[2] Grenville, in the House of Commons, in the debate of 5 March, 1770: "Far from thinking the tax impracticable, some of the assemblies applied to me, by their agents, to collect this very tax." Compare Whately's Considerations, 71. "Mr. Mauduit, the Massachusetts agent, favored the raising of the wanted money by a stamp duty, as it would occasion less expense of officers, and would include the West India islands." Gordon's History of the American Revolution, i. 158.

[3] Richard Jackson to Jared Ingersoll, 22 March, 1766, in Letters of Ingersoll, 43: "I was never myself privy to any measures taken with respect to the stamp act, after having formally declined giving any other advice on the subject, excepting that I had always given, to lay the project aside."

CHAP VIII. every assistance, and weighed more than the honest and independent Jackson.

1763. Sept. Grenville therefore adopted[1] the measure which was "devolved upon him," and his memory must consent, as he himself consented, that it should be "christened by his name."[2] It was certainly Grenville, "who first brought this scheme into form."[3] He doubted the propriety of taxing colonies, without allowing them representatives;[4] but he loved power, and placed his chief hopes on the favor of parliament; and the parliament of that day contemplated the increased debt of England with terror, knew not that the resources of the country were increasing in a still greater proportion, and insisted on throwing a part of the public burdens upon America.

[1] Walpole's Geo. III., iii. 32: "Grenville adopted, from Lord Bute, a plan of taxation formed by Jenkinson."

[2] Grenville, in Cavendish.

[3] Burke's Speech on American taxation, Works, i. 460.

[4] Knox: Extra-official State Papers, ii. 31; and Grenville to Knox, 4 Sept. 1768; and Grenville to T. Pownall.

CHAPTER IX.

ENFORCEMENT OF THE ACTS OF NAVIGATION.—GRENVILLE'S ADMINISTRATION CONTINUED.

OCTOBER, 1763—APRIL, 1764.

CHAP. IX. 1763. Oct.

THE stamp act was to be the close of a system of colonial "measures," founded, as Grenville believed, "on the true principles of policy, of commerce, and of finance."[1] He, said those who paid him court, is not such a minister as his predecessors; he is neither ignorant like some of them of the importance of the colonies; nor like others, impotently neglectful of their concerns; or diverted by meaner pursuits from attending to them. England is now happy in a minister who sees that the greatest wealth and maritime power of Great Britain depend on the use of its colonies, and who will make it his highest object to form "a well digested, consistent, wise and salutary plan of colonization and government."[2]

The extent of the American illicit trade was very great; in particular, it was thought that of a million

[1] The Regulations lately made concerning the Colonies, and the Taxes imposed upon them Considered, 1765, 114. This ministerial pamphlet was professedly the exposition of Grenville's opinions and policy, and, as such, was circulated in America; its reputed author was Campbell, crown agent for Georgia.

[2] The Regulations, 5.

CHAP. IX. 1763. Oct. and a half pounds of tea consumed annually in the colonies, not more than one tenth part was sent from England.[1] Grenville held that the contraband was all stolen from the commerce and part of it from the manufactures of Great Britain, against the fundamental principles of colonization, and the express provisions of the law. Custom had established in the American ports a compromise between the American claim to as free trade as the English, and the British acts of restriction. Grenville did what none of his predecessors had done: he read the Statute Book of Great Britain; and the integrity of his mind revolted at this connivance. It pleased his austere vanity to be the first and only minister to insist on enforcing the laws,[2] which usage and corruption[3] had invalidated; and this brought him in conflict with the spirit which

[1] Campbell, 93.

[2] Hutchinson to Richard Jackson, Grenville's Secretary in the Exchequer, Sept. 1763: "The real cause of the illicit trade in this province has been the indulgence of the officers of the customs; and we are told that the cause of this indulgence has been, that they are quartered upon for more than their legal fees, and that without bribery and corruption they must starve. If the venality of the present age will not admit of a reform in this respect, perhaps the provision now made may be the next best expedient."

[3] "I, Sampson Toovey, clerk to James Cockle, Esq., Collector of His Majesty's Customs for the port of Salem, do declare on oath, that ever since I have been in the office, it hath been customary for said Cockle to receive of the masters of vessels entering from Lisbon, casks of wine, boxes of fruit, &c., which was a gratuity for suffering their vessels to be entered with salt or ballast only, and passing over unnoticed such cargoes of wine, fruit, &c., which are prohibited to be imported into his majesty's plantations. Part of which wine, fruit, &c., he the said James Cockle used to share with Governor Bernard. And I further declare that I used to be the negotiator of this business, and receive the wine, fruit, &c., and dispose of them agreeable to Mr. Cockle's orders. Witness my hand, Sampson Toovey.

Essex Co. Salem, Sept. 27, 1764. Then Mr. Francis Toovey made oath to the truth of the above, before Benjamin Pickman, J. Peace.

Boston Gazette, 12 June, 1769. No. 741, 3, 2. Same in the London Daily Advertiser and Morning Chronicle of July 22, 1769, and in Boston Gazette of 9 Oct., 1796, 757. 2. 1. Compare what Lieut.-Governor Sharpe, of Maryland, and Temple, the Surveyor-General of the Customs say of Bernard's integrity in revenue affairs.

Otis had aroused in Boston, and which equally prevailed among the descendants of the Dutch of New-York. The island of Manhattan lay convenient to the sea, sheltered by other islands from the ocean; having safe anchorage in deep water for many miles along its shores, inviting the commerce of continents, of the near tropical islands, and of the world. To-day its ships, fleet, safe, and beautiful in their forms, exceed in amount of tonnage nearly twice over all the commercial marine of Great Britain at the moment of Grenville's schemes. Between its wharves and the British harbors, its packets run to and fro, swiftly and regularly, like the weaver's shuttle, weaving the band that joins nations together in friendship. Its imports of foreign produce are in value equal twice-told to all that was imported into the whole island of Great Britain in 1763. Nor does a narrow restrictive policy shut out the foreigner; its port is lively with the display at the mast-head of the flag of every civilized nation of the earth. People of all countries have free access, so that it seems the representative city of all Europe, in whose streets may be heard every language that is spoken from the steppes of the Ukraine to the Atlantic. Grenville would have interdicted direct foreign commerce and excluded every foreign vessel. American independence, like the great rivers of the country, had many sources; but the head-spring which colored all the stream was the Navigation Act.

Reverence for the colonial mercantile system was branded into Grenville's mind as deeply and ineffaceably as ever the superstition of witchcraft into a credulous and child-like nature. It was his "idol;"[1] and

[1] Burke.

CHAP. IX. 1763. Oct. he adored it as "sacred."[1] He held that "Colonies are only settlements made in distant parts of the world for the improvement of trade; that they would be intolerable except on the conditions contained in the Act of Navigation; that those who, from the increase of contraband, had apprehensions that they may break off their connection with the mother country, saw not half the evil; that wherever the Acts of Navigation are disregarded, the connection is actually broken already.[2] Nor did this monopoly seem to him a wrong; he claimed for England the exclusive trade with its colonies as the exercise of an indisputable right which every state, in exclusion of all others, has to the services of its own subjects.[3] His indefatigable zeal could never be satisfied.

All officers of the customs in the colonies were ordered to their posts; their numbers were increased; they were provided with "new and ample instructions enforcing in the strongest manner the strictest attention to their duty;" every officer that failed or faltered was instantly to be dismissed.

Nor did Grenville fail to perceive that "the restraint and suppression of practices which had long prevailed, would certainly encounter great difficulties in such distant parts of the king's dominions;" the whole force of the royal authority was therefore invoked in aid.[4] The Governors were to make the suppression of the forbidden trade with foreign nations the constant and immediate object of their care. All officers, both civil, and military, and naval, in America and the West Indies, were to give their co-

1 Walpole.
2 Campbell.
3 Whately's Considerations.
4 Memorial from the Right Honorable the Commissioners of his majesty's Treasury, 4 Oct., 1763.

operation. "We depend," said a memorial from the treasury, "upon the sea-guard as the likeliest means for accomplishing these great purposes," and that sea-guard was to be extended and strengthened as far as the naval establishments would allow. To complete the whole, and this was a favorite part of Grenville's scheme, a new and uniform system of Courts of Admiralty was to be established. On the very next day after this memorial was presented, the king himself in council gave his sanction to the whole system.[1]

Forthwith orders were issued directly to the Commander-in-chief in America that the troops under his command should give their assistance to the officers of the revenue for the effectual suppression of contraband trade.[2]

Nor was there delay in following up the new law to employ the navy to enforce the Navigation Acts. To this end Admiral Colville,[3] the naval Commander-in-chief on the coasts of North America, from the river St. Lawrence to Cape Florida and the Bahama Islands, became the head of a new corps of revenue officers. Each captain of his squadron had custom-house commissions and a set of instructions from the Lords Commissioners of the Admiralty for his guidance; and other instructions were given them by the Admiral to enter the harbors or lie off the coasts of America; to qualify themselves by taking the usual custom-house oaths to do the office of custom-

[1] Order in Council of 5 October, 1763. S. P. O. Am. and W. I. vol. lxxvii.

[2] Halifax to the Commander-in-chief of his Majesty's Forces in North America, 11 October, 1763.

[3] Admiral Colville to Lieutenant-Governor of New-York. Bernard to Egremont, 25 October, 1763.

CHAP. IX. 1763. Oct. house officers; to seize such persons as were suspected by them to be engaged in illicit trade.

The promise of large emoluments in case of forfeitures stimulated their natural and irregular vivacity[1] to enforce laws which had become obsolete, and they pounced upon American property as they would have gone in war in quest of prize-money. Even at first their acts were equivocal, and they soon came to be as illegal as they were oppressive. There was no redress. An appeal to the Privy Council was costly and difficult, and besides, when as happened before the end of the year,[2] an officer had to defend himself on an appeal, the suffering colonists were exhausted by the delay and expenses, while the treasury took care to indemnify their agent.

The rule adopted for colonizing America, was founded on the uniform principle of grants of lands from the crown, subject to quit-rent; so that the new settlements would consist entirely of the king's tenants,[3] and would owe their landlord a large annual rental. In the small West India islands, an agrarian law set bounds to the cupidity for land. Egmont, the new head of the admiralty, an upright and able, but eccentric man, preferred the feudal system to every form of government, and made a plan for establishing it in the isle of St. John. This reverie of a visionary he desired to apply to all the conquered countries, to Acadia and Canada on the north; and to the two Floridas on the south, which were to be divided into great baronies, each composed of a hundred vassals. In each pro-

[1] Edmund Burke, in Annual Register viii. 18, 19.

[2] Governor Bernard to the Secretary of State, 24 December, 1763. Thomas Whately, Secretary of the Treasury, to Commissioners of the Customs, 17 April, 1764. Treasury Letter Book, xxiv. 3.

[3] Campbell, 7.

vince there were to be castles, fortified, casemated, and armed with cannon, placed near enough to preserve a connection. The contemptuous neglect of his project[1] inclined him to think lightly of Grenville's ability, and to hate him,[2] nor did he forgive Hillsborough for his opposition.

In forming the new territory into provinces, the fear of danger from large states led to the division of Florida; for it was held to be good policy to enhance the difficulties of union among the colonies by increasing the number of independent governments.[3]

The boundary of Massachusetts, both on the east and on the north, was clearly defined; extending on the east to the St. Croix, and on the north leaving to the province of Quebec the narrow strip only, from which the water flows into the St. Lawrence.[4]

For Canada, or the province of Quebec, as it was called, the narrower boundaries, on which Shelburne had insisted, were adopted. All that lay to the west of Lake Nepising, and all the country beyond the Alleghanies, were, by a solemn proclamation, shut against the emigrant, from the fear that remote colonies would claim the independence which their position would favor.

England had conquered the west and dared not make use of it. She went to war for the Ohio valley, and having got possession of it, set it apart to be kept as a desert. A puny policy would have pulled down

[1] M. Francès au Duc de Choiseul, à Londres le 21 8bre. 1768. "Il méprise les talens de M. Grenville et hait sa personne."

[2] Francès to the Duke de Choiseul, Oct. 1768. Il (Egmont) n'a pas pardonné à my Lord Hillsborough, qui étoit alors à la tête du bureau des plantations, de s'être opposé à son exécution.

[3] Campbell, 17, 18.

[4] Halifax to the Lords of Trade, 27 September, 1763. Representation of the Lords of Trade to the King, 5 October, 1763.

CHAP. IX. 1763. Oct. the monument to Pitt's name at the head of the Ohio, and have brought all the settlers to this side the mountains. "The country to the westward of our frontiers, quite to the Mississippi, was intended to be a desert for the Indians to hunt in and inhabit."[1]

Such a policy was impossible; already there was at Detroit the seed of a commonwealth. The long protracted siege drew near its end. The belts sent in all directions by the French, reached the nations on the Ohio and Lake Erie. The Indians were assured[2] that their old allies would depart; the garrison in the Peorias was withdrawn; the fort Massiac was dismantled; its cannon sent to St. Genevieve, the oldest settlement of Europeans in Missouri. The missionary, Forget, retired. At Vincennes[3] the message to all the nations on the Ohio was explained to the Piankishaws, who accepted the belts and the calumets.

The courier who took the belt to the north, offered peace to all the tribes wherever he passed;[4] and to Detroit, where he arrived on the last day of October, he bore a letter of the nature of a proclamation, informing the inhabitants of the cession of Canada to England; another, addressed to twenty-five nations by name, to all the Red Men, and particularly to Pontiac, chief of the Ottawas; a third to the commander, expressing a readiness to surrender to the English all the forts on the Ohio, and east of the Mississippi. The next morning Pontiac sent to Gladwin, that he accepted the peace which his father, the

[1] Lord Barrington's Narrative.

[2] Neyon de Villiere à toutes les nations de la Belle Rivière, et du lac, et notamment à ceux de Detroit, à Pondiac, chef des Couata souas au Detroit.

[3] Letter of M. de St. Ange, of 24 Octobre, in Lettre de M. de Neyon à M. de Kerlérec, 1er, Xbre. 1763.

[4] De Neyon a Kerlérec, 1 Dec. 1763.

French, had sent him, and desired all that had passed might be forgot on both sides.[1] CHAP. IX.

Friendly words were exchanged, though the formation of a definitive treaty of peace was referred to the Commander-in-Chief. The savages dispersed to their hunting grounds. 1763. Oct.

Nothing could restrain the Americans from peopling the wilderness. To be a freeholder was the ruling passion of the New England man. Marriages were early and very fruitful. The sons, as they grew up, skilled in the use of the axe and the rifle, would, one after another, move from the old homestead, and with a wife, a yoke of oxen, a cow, and a few husbandry tools, build a small hut in some new plantation, and by tasking every faculty of mind and body, win for themselves plenty and independence. Such were they who began to dwell among the untenanted forests that rose between the Penobscot and the Sainte Croix, or in the New Hampshire Grants, on each side of the Green Mountains, or in the exquisitely beautiful valley of Wyoming, where on the banks of the Susquehanna, the wide and rich meadows, shut in by walls of wooded mountains, attracted emigrants from Connecticut, though their claim of right under the charter of their native colony was in conflict with the territorial jurisdiction of the proprietaries of Pennsylvania.

The mild climate of the south drew the herdsmen still further into the interior. In defiance of reiterated royal mandates, Virginian adventurers outgrew all limits of territorial parishes, and seated themselves on the New River, near the Ohio, in the forbidden valley of

[1] Major-General Gage to Secretary Halifax, 23 Dec. 1763.

CHAP. IX. 1763. Oct. the Mississippi; and not even the terrors of border wars with the savages "could stop the enthusiasm of running backwards to hunt for fresh lands,"[1] in men who loved no enjoyment like that of perfect personal freedom in the companionship of nature.

From Carolina the hunters[2] annually passed the Cumberland Gap, gave names to the streams and rocky ridges of Tennessee, and with joyous confidence chased game in the basin of the Cumberland river. On all the waters, from the Holston river to the head springs of the Kentucky and the Cumberland, there dwelt not one single human inhabitant. It was the waste forest and neutral ground that divided the Cherokees from the Five Nations and their dependents. The lovely region had been left for untold years the paradise of wild beasts, which had so filled the valley with their broods, that a thrifty hunter could, in one season, bring home peltry worth sixteen hundred dollars.[3]

So the Mississippi valley was entered at Pittsburgh, on the New River, and on the Holston and Clinch. It was only Florida, the new conquest, accepted in exchange for Havana, that civilized men left as a desert. When, in July, possession of it was taken, the whole number of its inhabitants, of every age and sex, men, wives, children, and servants, was three thousand, and of these the men were almost all in the pay of the Catholic King.[4] The possession of it had cost Spain nearly two hundred and thirty thou-

[1] Fauquier to the Lords of Trade.

[2] John Heywood's Civil and Political History of the State of Tennessee, from its earliest settlement up to the year 1796. Knoxville, 1823, page 35. Compare also, page 74.

[3] Ibid, 25, 26.

[4] Lt.-Col. Robertson's Report of the State of E. and W. Florida, 115.

sand dollars annually; and now Spain, as a compensation for Havana, made over to England the territory which occasioned this fruitless expense. Most of the people, receiving from the Spanish treasury indemnity for their losses, migrated to Cuba, taking with them the bones of their saints and the ashes of their distinguished dead; leaving, at St. Augustine, their houses of stone, in that climate imperishable, without occupants, and not so much as a grave tenanted.

1763. Oct.

The western province of Florida extended west and north to the Mississippi, in the latitude of thirty-one degrees. On the twentieth of October the French surrendered the post of Mobile, with its brick fort,[1] which was fast crumbling to ruins. A month later the slight stockade at Tombecbe,[2] in the west of the Choctaw country, was delivered up. In all this England gained nothing for the time but an unhealthy station for her troops, for whom there was long no shelter but low huts of bark. To secure peace at the south, the Secretary of State had given orders[3] to invite a congress of the southern tribes, the Catawbas, Cherokees, Creeks, Chicasaws and Choctaws; and in a convention held on the tenth of November, at Augusta, at which the governors of Virginia and the colonies south of it were present, the peace with the Indians[4] of the south and southwest was ratified. The head man and chiefs of both the upper and lower Creek nations, whose warriors were thirty-six hundred in num-

Nov.

Gayarré.

Florida, in America, and the West Indies, cxxxiv. Gayarré, ii.108.

[3] Egremont to Governor Boone, 16 March, 1763. Boone to Egremont, 1 June, 1763.

[4] Treaty with the upper and lower Creeks, 10 Nov. 1763. Fauquier to Egremont, 20 November, 1763. M'Call's History of Georgia, i. 301.

CHAP. IX. 1763. Nov. ber, agreed to extend the frontier of the settlement of Georgia. From this time dates the prosperity of that province, of which the commerce, in ten years, increased almost five fold.

For these vast regions Grenville believed he was framing a perfect system of government. If he was ignorant as to America, in England he understood his position, and proudly and confidently prepared to meet that assembly, in which English ambition contends for power. His opponents were divided, Charles Yorke, the attorney-general, had resigned, but so reluctantly, that in doing it he burst out into tears. Newcastle and his friends designed him as their candidate for the high station of Lord Chancellor, which was the great object of his ambition. But Pitt would never hear of it. "My resistance of my Lord Mansfield's influence," said he, "is not made in animosity to the man, but in opposition to his principles." Since through Charles Yorke the ways of thinking of Lord Mansfield would equally prevail in Westminster Hall, he cared not to hear the name of Yorke sound the highest among the long robe, and he dismissed from his mind the vain dream that any solid union on revolution principles was possible under the various entanglements.[1] So when parliament assembled, Yorke was with the court in principle, and yet a leader of the opposition.

On the first night of the session there were two divisions relating to Wilkes, and on both the ministers had a majority of nearly three to one.

In the debate on the king's speech and the address,

[1] Grenville Papers, ii. 149, 218, 239. Chatham Correspondence, ii. 261.

CHAP. IX. 1763. Nov.

Pitt spoke with great ability;[1] Grenville, in answering him, went through all the business of the summer, and laid before the house his plans of economy; contrasting them with the profusion which had marked the conduct of the war. He was excessively applauded during the whole course of his speech, and afterwards complimented and congratulated by numbers of people upon the firmness of his conduct and the establishment of the king's government, which now seemed thoroughly settled. The king repeated to him the praises bestowed on the superiority of talent and judgment with which he had spoken.[2]

In the ensuing debate on the question, whether the privilege of parliament preserved a member from being taken up for writing and publishing a libel, Charles Yorke, the great lawyer of the Rockingham whigs, spoke against the claim of privilege, and the house decided by a great majority, that a member of parliament, breaking the laws, is not privileged against arrest. Nor would Grenville or the king brook opposition; Barre, the gallant associate of Wolfe, was dismissed from the army for his votes, and the brave and candid Conway from the army and from his place in the bed-chamber. Shelburne also was not to remain the king's aid-de-camp.

The House of Commons entering upon the consideration of supplies with entire confidence in the minister, readily voted those necessary for the military establishment in the colonies; and this was followed

[1] Barrington to Mitchell, quoted in Chat. Corr. ii. 262.

[2] Grenville in Diary, 16 Nov. ii. 224, 225.

CHAP. IX. 1763. Dec. by a renewed grant of the land-tax, which, at four shillings in the pound, produced a little more than two million pounds sterling. Grenville promised that the tax should be continued at that rate for only two years after the peace; and then should be reduced to three shillings in the pound, an easement to the landed interest of five hundred thousand pounds. Huske, the new member for Malden, once subservient to Charles Townshend, a native of New-Hampshire, educated at Boston, the same who nearly nine years before had in 1755 foreshadowed the stamp-tax,[1] and had publicly pledged himself to propose[2] a plan for defraying all the expenses of the military service in America by a fund on the colonies, a man who was allowed to understand the colonies very well, seized an opportunity[3] to renew his proposal, boasting that taxes might be laid on the colonies to yield £500,000, which would secure the promised relief to the country gentlemen. This sum, he insisted, the Americans were well able to pay, and he was heard by the House with great joy and atten-

[1] Huske's Present State of North America, &c., 1755. Of this work there were two English editions in that year, and one in Boston, 82, 83.

[2] "I shall humbly propose a plan in my last chapter," &c.: Huske, 83. His last chapter was not printed.

[3] "What is most unlucky for us is, there is one Mr. Huske, who understands America very well, and has lately got a seat in the House of Commons; but, instead of standing an advocate for his injured country (for he is an American born, and educated in Boston), he has officiously proposed, in the House of Commons, to lay a tax on the colonies which will amount to £500,000 per annum, sterling; which he says they are well able to pay; and he was heard by the house with great joy and attention."

Those who report Huske's speech do not specify the day on which it was pronounced. It seems to me it must have been spoken either on the vote of supply for maintaining the forces and garrisons in the plantations, in committee on the 5th Dec., in the house, on the 6th; or on the vote of the land tax, in committee on the 7th, in the house on the 8th of Dec. These are the only occasions on which, as it would appear, the speech would not have been out of order. Journal of the House of Commons, xxix. 695, 698. Annual Register, for 1764. Appendix to Chronicle, 157, 163. A reduction of a shilling in

tion,[1] betraying his native land for the momentary pleasure of being cheered by the aristocracy, which was soon to laugh at him.[2]

In England the force of opposition was broken. Charles Yorke came penitently and regretfully to Grenville to mourn over his mistake in resigning office, and make complaint of the exigency of the times which had whirled him out of so eminent and advantageous a post in the law; and Grenville felt himself so strong as to dare to slight him. Even Charles Townshend was ready to renounce the friendship of Pitt, and his manifest desire of taking office passed unheeded. Nothing was feared from the opposition in England. Who could look, then, for resistance from America? or forbode danger from a cause on trial in a county court in Virginia?

Tobacco was the legalized currency of Virginia. In 1755,[3] a year of war and consequent interruption of agricultural pursuits, and again in 1758,[4] a year of the utmost distress, the legislature indulged the people in the alternative of paying their public dues, including the dues to the established clergy, in money at the fixed rate of two pence for the pound of tobacco. All but the clergy acquiesced in the law. At their

the pound on the land tax would have been a reduction of £508,732.

[1] For an account of Huske's speech, see extract of a letter from a gentleman in London to his friend in New-York, in Weyman's New-York Gazette of 5 April, 1764. Gordon, in History of American Revolution, i. 157, quotes the letter as from Stephen Sayre to Capt. Isaac Sears, of New-York. See, also, Joseph Reed to Charles Pettit, London, 11 June, 1764, in Reed's Life and Correspondence of Reed, i. 33. The date of Sayre's letter shows the speech must have been made before the 7th of Feb., 1764; probably in December, 1763.

[2] Reed's Reed, i. 33.

[3] Rev. James Maury to John Fontaine, 15 June, 1756, from the collections of Peter Force.

[4] Rev. James Maury, in 1763: "The act of 1758." Wirt's Life of Patrick Henry, 39.

CHAP. IX. 1763. Dec.

instance its ratification was opposed by the Bishop of London, who remarked on "the great change in the temper of the people of Virginia in the compass of a few years, and the diminution of the prerogative of the crown." "The rights of the clergy and the authority of the king," said he, "must stand or fall together."[1] And the Act was negatived by the king in council. The "Two-penny Act" became, therefore, null and void from the beginning; and in the Virginia courts of law it remained only to inquire by a jury into the amount of damages which the complainants had sustained.[2]

Patrick Henry was one of those engaged to plead against "the parsons," whose cause was become a contest between the prerogative and the people of Virginia. When a boy, he had learned something of Latin; of Greek the letters; but nothing methodically. It had been his delight to wander alone with the gun or the angling-rod; or by some sequestered stream to enjoy the ecstasy of meditative idleness. He married at eighteen; attempted trade; toiled unsuccessfully as a farmer; then with buoyant mind resolved on becoming a lawyer; and answering questions successfully by the aid of six weeks' study of Coke upon Littleton and the Statutes of Virginia, he gained a license as a barrister. For three years the novice dwelt under the roof of his father-in-law, an inn-keeper near Hanover Court-house, ignorant of the science of law, and slowly learning its forms.

On the first day of December, as Patrick Henry

[1] Bishop of London to Board of Trade, January, 1759.

[2] Compare Lieutenant-Governor Fauquier to Board of Trade, 30 June, 1760.

entered the court, before which he had never spoken, he saw on the bench more than twenty clergymen, the most learned men in the colony; and the house was filled and surrounded by an overwhelming multitude. To the select jury which had been summoned, Maury, "the parson" whose cause was on trial, made objections; for he thought them of "the vulgar herd," and three or four of them dissenters of the sect called "New Lights." "They are honest men," said Henry, "and therefore unexceptionable;" and the court being satisfied, "they were immediately called to the book and sworn."

The course of the trial was simple. The contract was, that Maury should be paid sixteen thousand pounds of tobacco: the act of 1758 fixed the value at two pence a pound; in 1759 it had been worth thrice that sum. The council for the clergy briefly explained the standard of their damages, and gave a high-wrought eulogium on their benevolence.

The forest-born orator, of whose powers none yet were conscious, rose awkwardly to reply, but faltered only as he began. He built his argument on the natural right of Virginia to self-direction in her affairs, pleading against the prerogative of the crown, and the civil establishment of the church, against monarchy and priestcraft.

The act of 1758, having every characteristic of a good law, and being of general utility, could not, consistently with the original compact between king and people, be annulled. "A king," he added, "who annuls or disallows laws of so salutary a nature, from being the father of his people, degenerates into a tyrant, and forfeits all right to obedience." At this assertion, the opposing counsel cried out aloud to the

CHAP. IX. 1763. Dec.

bench, "The gentleman has spoken treason." Royalists too, in the crowd, raised a confused murmur of "treason, treason, treason." "The harangue" thought one of the hearers, "exceeds the most seditious and inflammatory of the most seditious tribunes in Rome." Some seemed struck with horror; some said afterwards, their blood ran cold, and their hair stood on end. The multitude, wrapt in silence, filling every spot in the house, and every window, bent forward to catch the words of the patriot, as he proceeded. He defined the use of an established church and of the clergy in society: "When they fail to answer those ends," said he, "the community have no further need of their ministry, and may justly strip them of their appointments. In this particular instance, by obtaining the negative of the law in question, instead of acquiescing in it, they ceased to be useful members of the state, and ought to be considered as enemies of the community." "Instead of countenance they very justly deserve to be punished with signal severity." "Except you are disposed," thus he addressed the jury, "yourselves to rivet the chains of bondage on your own necks, do not let slip the opportunity now offered of making such an example of the reverend plaintiff, as shall hereafter be a warning to himself and his brothers, not to have the temerity to dispute the validity of laws authenticated by the only sanction which can give force to laws for the government of this colony, the authority of its own legal representatives, with its council and governor." Thus he pleaded for the liberty of the continent, and its independence of all control from England over its legislature; treating the negative of the king in council as itself in equity a nullity. The cause seemed to involve only the interests of the clergy, and Henry made it the cause of the people of America. The jury promptly rendered a verdict of a penny damages. A motion for a new trial was refused: an appeal was granted. But the verdict being received, there was no redress. The vast throng gathered in triumph round their champion, child of the yeomanry, who on that day had taught them to aspire to religious liberty and legislative independence. "The crime of which Henry is guilty," wrote one of the clergy, "is little, if any, inferior to that which brought Simon Lord Lovat to the block." For "the vindication of the king's injured honor and authority," they urged the punishment of the young Virginian, and a list was furnished of witnesses against him. CHAP. IX. 1763. Dec.

But Patrick Henry knew not fear; nor did his success conquer his aversion to the old black letter of the law books. Though he removed to the county of Louisa, in quest of business, he loved the green wood better even than before, and would hunt deer for days together, taking his only rest under the trees; and as he strolled through the forest, with his ever ready musket in his hand, his serene mind was ripening for duty, he knew not how, by silent communion with nature.

The movement in Virginia was directed against the prerogative. Vague rumors prevailed of new commercial and fiscal regulations, to be made by act of parliament;[1] and yet Americans refused to believe it possible that the British legislature would wilfully subvert their liberty. No remonstrance was prepared 1764. Jan.

[1] Letter to Lord George Germaine, 6, 7.

CHAP. IX. 1764. Jan.

against the impending measures, of which the extent was kept secret. Massachusetts, in January, 1764, with a view to effect the greatest possible reduction of the duty on foreign West Indian products, elected Hutchinson as its joint agent with Mauduit. But before he could leave the province, the house began to distrust him, and by a majority of two, excused him from the service.[1]

The designs of government were confided to the crown officers in America. For generations they, and their predecessors, had been urging the establishment of a parliamentary revenue for their support. They sought office in America for its emoluments; the increase and security of those emoluments formed their whole political system. When they learned that the taxes which they had so long and so earnestly recommended, were to be applied exclusively to the support of the army, they shrunk from upholding obnoxious measures, which to them were to bring no profit. They were disheartened, and began to fear that provision for the civil list, the only object they cared for, was indefinitely postponed. In their view, the regulation and the reformation of the American government was become a necessary work, and should take precedence of all other business. They would have a parliamentary regulation of colonial charters, and a certain and sufficient civil list,[2] laid upon perpetual funds. But Grenville, accepting the opinions of his secretary, Jackson, refused to become the attorney for American office-holders, or the founder of a stupendous system of colonial patronage and corruption. His policy looked mainly to the improvement

[1] Hutchinson's MS. Letter Book, ii. 76, 77. Novanglus, 283.

[2] Bernard's Letters, passim, from 1763 to 1767.

of the finances, and the alleviation of the burdens which pressed upon the country gentlemen of England. When Halifax urged the payment of the salaries of the crown officers in the colonies, directly from England, in accordance with the system which he had been maturing since 1748, Grenville would not consent to it; and though Halifax, at a formal interview with him, at which Hillsborough and Jenkinson were present, became extremely heated and eager,[1] Grenville remained inflexible.

Nor would he listen to the suggestion, that the revenue to be raised in America should constitute a fund to be disposed of under the sign manual of the king; he insisted that it should be paid into the receipt of the Exchequer, to be regularly appropriated by parliament.[2] Nor did Grenville ever take part in the schemes which were on foot to subvert the charters of the colonies, and control their domestic government. Nor did he contribute to confer paramount authority on the military officers in America.[3] On the contrary, he desired to keep the army subordinate to the law. He did not, indeed, insist that his colleagues should yield to his opinions, but, in parliament and elsewhere, he refrained from favoring the system which would have made the crown officers in America, wholly independent of American legislatures; and have raised the military power in America above the civil. When, therefore, he came to propose

[1] Grenville's Diary for Friday, 6 January, 1764, in Grenville Papers, i. 48.

[2] Hartley, in his published letters, dwells on this distinction. But compare the acts prepared by Grenville, with those of Townshend and Lord North.

[3] Pownall's Administration of the Colonies. Second Edition, 69, and compare the edition of 1776, i. 101. Grenville's speeches in Cavendish, for April, 1770.

CHAP. IX. 1764. Jan. taxes on America, he was at variance with his colleagues, whose rashness he moderated, and whose plan of government he opposed, and with the whole body of colonial office holders, to whose selfishness he refused to minister. So the plans of Halifax and Charles Townshend, for the time, fell to the ground. Grenville had but one object, to win the support or the landed gentry, whose favor secured majorities in parliament, and gave a firm tenure of office. He was narrow-minded and obstinate; but it was no part of his intention to introduce despotic government into the New World.

For a moment the existence of the ministry itself was endangered. All parties joined in condemning the writings of Wilkes; and even the extreme measure of his expulsion from his seat in parliament, was carried with only one dissentient vote.[1] The opposition, Feb. with great address, proceeded to an abstract question on the legality of general warrants. They were undoubtedly illegal. Grenville himself was sure of it. He sought, therefore, to change the issue and evade the question by delay; and insisted that a single branch of the legislature ought not to declare law; that to do so would be an encroachment on the power of parliament, and on the functions of the judiciary, before which the question was pending. Norton, the attorney-general, said, harshly, that in a court of law the opinion of the House of Commons was worth no more attention than that of so many drunken porters; but Grenville defended his well-chosen position with exceeding ability, and was said to have outdone him-

[1] Grenville Papers, ii. 258.

self.[1] In a house of four hundred and fifty he escaped, but only by a majority of fourteen. The king felt the vote of the opposition as a personal offence. "My nature," said he, firmly, "ever inclines me to be acquainted with who are my true, and who false friends; the latter I think worse than open enemies. I am not to be neglected unpunished."[2] In the account Grenville sent him of the division, marks of being dispirited were obvious, and the king instantly answered, "that if he would but hide his feelings, and speak with firmness, the first occasion that offered, he would find his numbers return." The minister followed his sovereign's advice, and the event exceeded the most sanguine expectations of both.[3]

Mar

The occasion was offered on presenting the budget. There were still reasons enough to make Grenville reluctant to propose a stamp-tax for America. But the wish for it was repeated to him from all classes of men; and was so general, that had he not proposed it, he would not have satisfied the expectations of his colleagues, or the public, or parliament, or the king.

The Americans in London unanimously denied either the justice or the right of the British Parliament, in which America was not represented, to grant their property to the crown; and this questioning of the power of parliament irritated[4] the minister. It was an impeachment of his declared belief and of his acts, and his conscience easily condemned opinions which thwarted his ambition. Besides; as a tho-

[1] Grenville Papers, ii. 493.

[2] King to Grenville, 18 February, 1764. Grenville Papers, ii. 267.

[3] In a letter from the king to Lord North, 22 February, 1780.

[4] John Huske's Letter, printed in Boston Gazette of 4 Nov. 1764.

CHAP. IX. 1764. Mar.

rough whig, he regarded the parliament of England as in all cases supreme; he knew "no other law, no other rule."[1]

The later reports of the military commanders[2] in America, accused the colonies of reluctance to furnish the men and money which the commander-in-chief had required.[3] The free exercise of deliberative powers by the colonial assemblies, seemed to show a tendency for self-direction and legislative independence, which might even reach the Acts of Navigation. Forged letters of Montcalm, too, were exhibited to Grenville,[4] in which American independence at an early day was predicted as the consequence of the conquest of Canada. Lord Mansfield, who believed the letters genuine,[5] was persuaded, as were others, that the dependence of the colonies was endangered.

Further: Grenville had been "made to believe" that the Americans were able to contribute to the revenue, and he had little reason to think them so stubborn as to refuse the payment of a tax. There was not "the least disposition in the agents of the colonies to oppose it;"[6] and the agent of Massachusetts made a merit of his submission.[7] The Secretary of

[1] George Grenville, in Cavendish i. 496.

[2] Letters of Amherst and his subordinates.

[3] Calvert to Lieutenant-Governor Sharpe, February 29 to April 3.

[4] That these letters, of which I have a copy, were shown to Grenville, is averred by Almon, Biographical Anecdotes, ii. 99. On matters which were known to Lord Temple, Almon's evidence merits consideration. That they are forgeries, appears from their style, from their exaggeration, from their want of all authentication, from the comparison, freely and repeatedly allowed by successive ministries in France, of all the papers relating to the conquest of Canada, or to Montcalm. The fabrication and sale of political papers and secrets was, in the last century, quite a traffic.

[5] Debate in the House of Lords.

[6] J. Mauduit, 11 February, 1764.

[7] Jasper Mauduit's letter to the Speaker of the House of Representatives of the province of Massachusetts Bay. London, 11 Feb. 1764.

Maryland had for years watched the ripening of the measure, and could not conceal his joy at its adoption.[1] CHAP. IX.

Thomas Pownall, "the fribble,"[2] who had been Governor of Massachusetts, and is remembered as one who grew more and more liberal as he grew old, openly contended for an American revenue to "be raised by customs on trade, a stamp-duty, a moderate land-tax in lieu of quit rents, and an excise."[3] 1764. Mar.

But on the other hand, Jackson, Grenville's able secretary, so well acquainted with the colonies, would never himself be privy to any measures taken with respect to the Stamp-Act, after having formally declined giving any other advice on the subject, excepting that which he had always given, to lay the project aside.[4] Lord Hillsborough,[5] too, then first Lord of the Board of Trade, as yet retained enough of the spirit of an Irishman to disapprove a direct taxation of a dependency of the British empire by a British Act of Parliament. He gave his advice against the stamp-tax, and to the last withheld from it his support; so that Grenville, in proposing it, was sustained neither by the civil office-holders in America, who had been and were still so clamorous for parliamentary interference, nor by the Board of Trade, which was the very author of the system.

The traditions of the whig party, too, whose principles Grenville claimed to represent, retained the

[1] Calvert to Sharpe, in many letters.

[2] Samuel Adams's opinion of Thomas Pownall.

[3] See First and Second Editions of his Administrations of the Colonies. In the later editions this is effaced. See, too, New York Gazette for Monday, 11 June, 1764.

[4] R. Jackson to Jared Ingersoll, 22 March, 1766.

[5] Hillsborough's own statement, made to W. S. Johnson, of Connecticut.

CHAP. IX. 1764. Mar. opinions[1] of Sir Robert Walpole, and questioned the wisdom of deriving a direct parliamentary revenue from America. "Many members of the House of Commons declared against the stamp-duty, while it was mere matter of conversation."[2] Nor could Grenville have been ignorant that Pitt had in vain been urged to propose an American Stamp-Tax.

The force of the objection derived from the want of representation on the part of America did not escape the consideration of Grenville. He accepted the theory of the British Constitution, which regarded the House of Commons as a representative body. In his inner mind he recognised, and to one friend he confessed, the propriety of allowing America representation in the body by which it should be taxed, and at least wished that parliament would couple the two measures. But he shunned the responsibility of proposing such a representation; and chose to risk offending the colonies, rather than forfeit the favor of parliament. He looked about him, therefore, as was always his method, for palliatives, that he might soothe the colonies, and yet gratify the landed gentry.

It was under such circumstances that Thomas Penn, one of the proprietaries of Pennsylvania, with Allen, a loyal American, then Chief Justice of Pennsylvania under a proprietary appointment, and Richard Jackson, sought an interview with Grenville. They seem to have offered no objection to the intended new act of trade; but reasoned against entering on a system of direct taxation. The stamp-duty, they said, was an internal regulation; and they entreated that it might be postponed till some sort of consent

[1] Opinion of Sir Robert Walpole in the Annual Register.

[2] Hutchinson, iii. 116.

to it should be given by the Assemblies, to prevent a tax of that nature from being laid without the consent of the colonies.[1]

Huske, too, repenting of his eager zeal in promising a revenue from America, joined in entreating delay, that opportunity might be given for America to be heard.

Grenville's colleagues did not share his scruples; but his mind was accustomed to balance opinions; and he desired to please all parties. He persisted, therefore, in the purpose of proposing a stamp-tax, but also resolved to show what he called "tenderness" to the colonies, and at the risk of being scoffed at by the whole Bedford party for his feebleness and hesitancy, he consented to postpone the tax for a year.

He also attempted to reconcile America to his new regulations. In doing this he still continued within the narrow limits of protection. The British consumption of foreign hemp amounted in value to three hundred thousand pounds a year. Grenville was willing to shake off the precarious dependence upon other countries. The bounties on hemp and flax, first given in the time of Queen Anne,[2] had been suffered to drop; for, having never been

[1] "With regard to money bills, I believe the parliament will render those not necessary, as several duties are to be laid on goods imported into the plantations, and it is proposed also to lay a stamp-duty on the colonies and islands as is done here, in order to defray all expenses of troops, necessary for their defence. We have endeavored to get this last postponed, as it is an internal tax, and wait till some sort of consent to it shall be given by the several Assemblies, to prevent a tax of that nature from being laid without the consent of the colonies; but whether we shall succeed is not certain. However, a few days will determine."—Thomas Penn, one of the proprietaries of Pennsylvania, to James Hamilton, the Lieutenant-Governor. London, 9 March, 1764. The original is in the possession of our American Philosophical Society at Philadelphia.

[2] 3 & 4 Ann. c. x., and 8 Ann. c. xiii. § 30. 12 Ann. c. ix. § 2. 8 Geo. i. c. xii. § 1. 2 Geo. ii. c. xxxv.

CHAP. IX. 1764. April. called for, they had fallen into oblivion. The experiment was again renewed; and a bounty of eight pounds per ton for seven years, then of six pounds for seven years, then of four pounds for as many more, was granted on hemp or undressed flax imported from America.[1]

But as to manufactures, it was expected that no American would be "so unreasonable or so rash" as to engage in the establishment of linen manufactories there, even of "the coarser kinds" of linens; for in that case "not prohibitory laws, but laws to which no American could form an objection, would effectually thwart all their endeavors,"[2] as the exigencies of the state required that Great Britain should disappoint American establishments of manufactures as "contrary to the general good."[3]

To South Carolina and Georgia special indulgence was shown; following the line of precedent,[4] rice, though an enumerated commodity, was, on the payment of a half subsidy, allowed to be carried directly to any part of America, to the southward of those colonies; that is, to the foreign West India islands;[5] so that the broken and mowburnt rice might be sold as food for negroes, and good rice made cheaper for the British market.

The boon that was to mollify New England was concerted with Israel Mauduit, acting for his brother, the agent of Massachusetts, and was nothing less than

[1] Report of Privy Council, 7 March, 1764. Order in Council, 9 March. Geo. iii. c. xxvi. § 1. Compare the regulations lately made, 53, 55.

[2] Regulations lately made, &c. 68, 69.

[3] Ibid., 69.

[4] 3 Geo. ii. c. xxviii., and 27 Geo. ii. c. xviii.

[5] 4 Geo. iii. c. xxvii. Regulations, &c. 52, 53.

CHAP IX. 1764. April.

the whale fishery.[1] Great Britain had sought to compete with the Dutch in that branch of industry; had fostered it by bounties; had relaxed the act of navigation, so as to invite even the Dutch to engage in it from British ports in British shipping. But it was all in vain. Grenville gave up the unsuccessful attempt, and sought a rival for Holland in British America, which had hitherto lain under the double discouragement, of being excluded from the benefit of a bounty, and of having the products of its whale fishing taxed unequally. He now adopted the plan of gradually giving up the bounty to the British whale fishery, which would be a saving of thirty thousand pounds[2] a year to the Treasury, and of relieving the American fishery from the inequality of the discriminating duty, except the old subsidy, which was scarcely one per cent.[3] This is the most liberal act of Grenville's administration, of which the merit is not diminished by the fact, that the American whale fishery was superseding the English under every discouragement. It required liberality to accept this result as inevitable, and to favor it. It was done too, with a distinct conviction that "the American whale fishery, freed from its burthen, would soon totally overpower the British." So this valuable branch of trade, which produced annually three hundred thousand pounds, and which would give employment to many shipwrights and other artificers, and to three thousand seamen,[4] was resigned to America. The gain would, in the first instance, be the gain of

[1] Jasper Mauduit, the Agent of Massachusetts. Report of Privy Council, 7 March. Order in Council, 9 March, 1764.

[2] Regulations lately made, 60.

[3] 4 Geo. iii. c. xxix.

[4] Regulations lately made, &c., 49–51.

CHAP. IX. 1764. April. New England, but the mother country, reasoned Grenville, feels herself benefited by the welfare of every particular colony; and the colonies must much more contribute interchangeably to the advantage of each other.

Such was the system of regulations for the colonies, prepared under the direction of Grenville, with minute and indefatigable care.

It was after these preparations, that on the memorable ninth day of March, 1764, George Grenville made his first appearance in the House of Commons as Chancellor of the Exchequer, to unfold the budget. He did it with art and ability.[1] He boasted that the revenue was managed with more frugality than in the preceding reign. He explained his method of funding the debt. He received great praise for having reduced the demands from Germany. The whole sum of these claims amounted to nearly nine millions of pounds, and were settled for about thirteen hundred thousand pounds. The demands from the Landgrave of Hesse still exceeded seventeen hundred thousand pounds, and he was put off with a payment of one hundred and fifty thousand pounds. The taxes of Great Britain exceeded, by three millions of pounds, what they were in 1754, before the war; yet the present object was only to make the colonies maintain their own army. Till the last war, they had never contributed to the support of an army at all. Besides the taxes on trade, which were immediately to be imposed, Grenville gave notice in the house,[2] that it was his

[1] Walpole's Memoirs of George III. i, 389. Thomas Whately's Considerations.

[2] "Mr. Grenville gave notice to the house, that it was his intention in the next session, to bring in a bill imposing stamp-duties in America, and the reasons for giving such notice were, because he understood some people entertained doubts of

intention, in the next session, to bring in a bill imposing stamp-duties in America, and the reasons for giving such notice were, because he understood some people entertained doubts of the power of parliament to impose internal taxes in the colonies; and because that, although of all the schemes which had fallen under his consideration, he thought a stamp-act was the best, he was not so wedded to it as to be unwilling to give it up for any one that might appear more eligible; or if the colonies themselves thought any other mode would be more expedient, he should have no objections to come into it, by act of parliament. At that time the merits of the question were opened at large. The opposition were publicly called upon to deny, if they thought it fitting, the right of the legislature to impose any tax, internal or external, on the colonies; and not a single person ventured to controvert that right. Upon a solemn question, asked in a full house,[1] there was not one negative. "As we are stout," said Beckford, "I hope we shall be merciful;" and no other made a reply.

On the fourteenth of March, Charles Jenkinson,[2] from a committee, on which he had for his associates, Grenville and Lord North, reported a bill modifying and perpetuating the act of 1733, with some changes to the disadvantage of the colonies; an extension of the navigation acts, making England the

the power of parliament to impose internal taxes in the colonies; and because that although of all the schemes which had fallen under his consideration, he thought a stamp-act was the best; he was not so wedded to it as not to give it up for any one that might appear more eligible; or if the colonies themselves thought any other mode would be more expedient, he should have no objection to come into it." Letter of Garth, Agent of South Carolina, a member of parliament to South Carolina.

[1] Cavendish, i. 494.

[2] Journal 8 of Commons, xxix. 949, 978, 987, 1015, &c.

CHAP. IX. 1764. April. storehouse of Asiatic as well as of European supplies; a diminution of drawbacks on foreign articles exported to America; imposts in America, especially on wines; a revenue duty instead of a prohibitory duty on foreign molasses; an increased duty on sugar; various regulations to sustain English manufactures, as well as to enforce more diligently the acts of trade; a prohibition of all trade between America and St. Pierre and Miquelon.

The only opposition came from Huske,[1] who observed, that the colonies ought first to have notice and an opportunity of laying before the House, by their agents, any objections they may have to such a measure. The bill was rapidly carried through its several stages, was slightly amended, on the fourth of April was agreed to by the lords, and on the next day was approved by the king. England had avowedly undertaken to give and grant imposts on the American trade. The preamble declared that this was a contribution "towards" the requisite revenue which was said to be fixed at £330,000.[2] "These new taxes," wrote Whately, the joint Secretary of the Treasury, "will certainly not be sufficient to defray that share of the American expense, which America ought and is able to bear. Others must be added."[3] That this was intended appeared also from the bill itself. This act had for the first time the title of "granting duties in the colonies and plantations of America; for the first time it was asserted in the preamble, that it was just and necessary that a revenue should be raised there;" and the Commons expressed them-

[1] Secretary Caecilius Calvert to Lieut.-Governor Sharpe. London, Feb. 29 to April 1, 1764.

[2] Hutchinson to Williams.

[3] Whately to Jared Ingersoll, 3, 4.

selves "desirous to make some provision in the present session of parliament toward raising the said revenue."[1]

Grenville, who put on the appearance of candor, endeavored to gain acquiescence in the proposed stamp act; and when the agents waited upon him, to know what could be done to avert it, he answered: "I have proposed the resolution in the terms that parliament has adopted, from a real regard and tenderness for the subjects in the colonies. It is highly reasonable they should contribute something towards the charge of protecting themselves, and in aid of the great expense Great Britain put herself to on their account. No tax appears to me so easy and equitable as a stamp duty.[2] It will fall only upon property, will be collected by the fewest officers, and will be equally spread over America and the West Indies.[3] What ought particularly to recommend it is the mode of collecting it, which does not require any number of officers vested with extraordinary powers of entering houses, or extend a sort of influence which I never wished to increase.

"The colonists now have it in their power, by agreeing to this tax, to establish a precedent for their being consulted before any tax is imposed on them by parliament;[4] for their approbation of it being signified to parliament next year, when the tax comes to be imposed, will afford a forcible argument for the like proceeding in all such cases. If they think any

[1] Burke on American Taxation.

[2] W. Knox.

[3] Israel Mauduit, in Mass. Hist. Collections, ix. 270.

[4] William Knox, agent for Georgia: The Claim of the Colonies to an Exemption from Internal Taxes imposed by authority of Parliament Examined; in a Letter from a Gentleman in London to his Friend in America, 33, 34.

CHAP. IX. 1764. April. other mode of taxation more convenient to them, and make any proposition of equal efficacy with the stamp-duty, I will give it all due consideration."[1]

Grenville did not propose a requisition on the colonies, or invite them to tax themselves;[2] the delay granted was only for form's sake,[3] and with the hope of winning from them some expression of assent,[4] and was in itself a subject of censure and discontent among the more thorough reformers of colonial governments.

No hope was given that parliament would forego taxing America. On the contrary, it was held to be its bounden duty to do so. To a considerate and most respectable merchant, a member of the House of Commons, who was making a representation against proceeding with the stamp act, Grenville answered, "If the stamp duty is disliked, I am willing to change it for any other equally productive. If you object to the Americans being taxed by parliament, save your-

[1] Ibid, p 35.

[2] Edmund Burke's Speech on American Taxation: "I have disposed of this falsehood:" and it was a falsehood. Whoever wishes to see a most artful attempt to mislead, may look at Israel Mauduit's reply to Burke, or as he called him, "The Agent for New-York." He seems to say, that Grenville had given the colonies the option to tax themselves. But he does not say it; he only proves that the Massachusetts Assembly so understood the letter from his brother Jasper, communicating the account of the interview of the agents with Grenville.

[3] Cecilius Calvert, Secretary of Maryland, to the Lieutenant-Governor of Maryland, Feb. 29 to April 3, 1764: "The resolution on stamp duties left out, to apprise the colonies, if any they have, they make objections, only given, I am told, *pro forma tantum*, before it is fixed next year, which the agents are to expect, unless very good reasons are produced to the House *per contra*."

[4] "When Mr. Grenville first hesitated a doubt of the unlimited supremacy of the British legislature, if he did not moot a point, that, perhaps, would not otherwise have been called in question, he conveyed to the discontented certain information, that they might depend upon the support of a party so considerable as to deserve the attention of the British ministry." Letter to Lord Geo. Germaine on the Rise, &c., of Rebellion in the Southern Colonies, pp. 9 and 10. Compare Dean Tucker's Fourth Tract.

self the trouble of the discussion, for I am determined on the measure."[1] CHAP. IX.

1764 April

The whole weight of the British Legislature, too, was brought to intimidate the colonists. They were apprised that not a single member of either house doubted of the right of parliament to impose a stamp-duty or any other tax upon the colonies;"[2] and that every influence might be moved to induce them to yield, the king, in April, at the prorogation, gave to what he called "the wise regulations" of Grenville his "hearty approbation."[3]

Out of doors the measures were greatly applauded. It seemed as if the vast external possessions of England were about to be united indissolubly with the mother country by one comprehensive commercial system. Even Thomas Pownall, once governor of Massachusetts, who, not destitute of liberal feelings, had repeatedly predicted the nearness of American Independence, was lost in admiration of "the great minister," who was taking "pains to understand the commerce and interests" of the plantations, and with "firmness and candor" entering seriously upon regulating their affairs;[4] and he prayed that Grenville might live to see the power, prosperity and honor that must be given to his country, by so great and important an event as his interweaving the administration of the colonies into the British administration."

[1] Edmund Burke's Speech on American Taxation, in Works. Am. ed. i. 456.

[2] William Knox, 33.

Speech in Adolphus, i. 142.

[4] T. Pownall's Administration of the Colonies. First edition, March or April, 1764. Dedication to George Grenville.

CHAPTER X.

HOW AMERICA RECEIVED THE PLAN OF A STAMP TAX.—GRENVILLE'S ADMINISTRATION CONTINUED.

APRIL—DECEMBER, 1764.

CHAP. X. 1764. April.

No sooner was parliament up, than Jenkinson pressed on Grenville to forward the American stamp-act, by seeking that further information, the want of which he had assigned as a reason for not going on with it. But the treasury had no mode of direct communication with the colonies, and the Secretary of State had no mind to consult them. For the moment nothing was done, though Jackson wrote to Hutchinson of Massachusetts for his opinion on the rights of the colonists and the late proceedings respecting them.

Meantime the officers of France, as they made their last journey through Canada, and down the valley of the Mississippi, as they gazed on the magnificence of the country, and on every side received the expressions of passionate attachment from the many tribes of red men, cast a wistful and lingering look upon the empire which they were ceding.[1] But Choiseul himself saw futurity better. He who would

[1] Aubry au Ministre, Duc de Choiseul, le 7 Avril, 1764.

CHAP. X. 1764. April.

not set his name to the treaty of peace with Great Britain, issued the order[1] in April, 1764, for the transfer of the island of New-Orleans and all Louisiana to Spain. And he did it without mental reserve. He knew that the time was coming when the whole colonial system would be changed; and in the same year,[2] while he was still minister of the marine, he sent de Pontleroy, a lieutenant in the navy of the Department of Rochefort, to travel through America, under the name of Beaulieu, in the guise of an Acadian wanderer; and while England was taxing America by act of parliament, France was already counting its steps towards independence.[3]

The world was making progress; restrictive laws and the oppression of industry were passing away, not less than the inquisition and the oppression of free thought. "Every thing that I see," wrote Voltaire, in April; "every thing is scattering the seeds of a revolution, which will come inevitably. Light has so spread from neighbor to neighbor, that on the first occasion it will kindle and burst forth. Happy are the young, for their eyes shall see it."

The impulse to the revolution was to proceed from the new world, which was roused by the rumor of the bill for the impending regulations. "My heart bleeds for America," said Whitefield, at Portsmouth, in New Hampshire. "O poor New-England, there is a deep-laid plot against both your civil and religious liberties; and they will be lost. Your golden days are at an end."

[1] Le Duc de Choiseul à M. d'Abbadie, à Versailles le 21 Avril, 1764.

[2] Choiseul to Durand, 15 Sept. 1766. Les idées sur l'Amerique, soit militaires, soit politiques, sont infiniment changés depuis 30 ans.

[3] Dépêche de M. le Cte. de Guerchy à M. le Duc de Choiseul, 19 Oct. 1766.

CHAP. X. 1764. May. But in this case, as so often, evil designs created their own remedy. "If the colonist is taxed without his consent," said the press[1] of New-York, "he will, perhaps, seek a change." "The ways of Heaven are inscrutable," wrote Richard Henry Lee, of Virginia, privately to a friend;[2] "this step of the mother country, though intended to secure our dependence, may produce a fatal resentment, and be subversive of that end." "If the colonies do not now unite," was the message received from Dyer of Connecticut, who was then in England; "if they do not unite, they may bid farewell to liberty, burn their charters, and make the best of thraldom."[3]

Even while it was not yet known that the bill had passed, alarm pervaded New-England. In Boston, at the town meeting in May, there stood up Samuel Adams, a native citizen of the place, trained at Harvard College, a provincial statesman, of the most clear and logical mind, which, throughout a long life, imparted to his public conduct the most exact consistency. His vigorous and manly will resembled in its tenacity well-tempered steel, which may ply a little but will not break. In his religious faith he had from childhood been instituted a Calvinist of the straitest sect; and his riper judgment and acuteness in dialectics confirmed him in its creed. In his views on church government he adhered to the congregational forms, as most friendly to civil and religious liberty. He was a member of the Church, and in a rigid community was an example in severity of morals and the scrupulous observance of every ordinance. Evening and morning his house was a

[1] Holt's New-York Gazette, No. 116, Thursday, 24 May, 1764.

[2] Letter of R. H. Lee, of 31 May, 1764.

[3] Letter of Eliphalet Dyer, written in March, in London, received, probably, in May, and printed in Boston Gazette of 23 Sept. 1765.

CHAP. X. 1764. May.

house of prayer; and no one more revered the Christian Sabbath. The austere purity of his life witnessed the sincerity of his profession. He was a tender husband, an affectionate parent, and relaxing from severer cares, he could vividly enjoy the delights of conversation with friends; but the walls of his modest mansion never witnessed dissipation, or levity, or frivolous amusements, or any thing inconsistent with the discipline of the man whose incessant prayer for his birthplace was, that "Boston might become a Christian Sparta."[1]

For his political creed, he received and held fast the opinions of the Fathers of New-England, that the colonies and England had a common king, but separate and independent legislatures. When he commenced Master of Arts at Cambridge, he affirmed that "it is lawful to resist the Chief Magistrate, if the Commonwealth cannot otherwise be preserved;" and when, in consequence of an act of the British Parliament, overruling the laws of the colony, his father's estate had been unjustly seized, he appeared in defence of colonial supremacy within colonial limits, and by his success gratified alike his filial piety and his love of country.[2]

He was at this time near two and forty years of age; poor, and so contented with poverty, that men censured him as "wanting wisdom to estimate riches at their just value." But he was frugal and temper-

[1] Letter of Samuel Adams in my possession.

[2] The account of this act of Adams is variously colored by his contemporaries, according to their political connections. The elder Samuel Dexter, his intimate friend, used to narrate the incident as most honorable to him. The great abilities and integrity of Dexter sanction his judgment. See Thacher's Discourse on the Death of Samuel Adams. The Colonial Legislature sustained the views of Adams, and the British authorities acquiesced in them.

CHAP. X. 1764. May. ate; and his prudent and industrious wife, endowed with the best qualities of a New-England woman, knew how to work with her own hands, so that the small resources, which men of the least opulent class would have deemed a very imperfect support, were sufficient for his simple wants. Yet such was the union of dignity with economy, that whoever visited him saw around him every circumstance of propriety.[1] Above all, he combined with poverty a stern and incorruptible integrity.

His nature was keenly sensitive, yet he bore with magnanimity the neglect of friends and the malignity of enemies. Already famed as a political writer, employing wit and sarcasm, as well as energy of language and earnestness, no one had equal influence over the popular mind. No blandishments of flattery could lull his vigilance, no sophistry deceive his penetration. Difficulties could not discourage his decision, nor danger appal his fortitude. He had also an affable and persuasive address, which could reconcile conflicting interests and promote harmony in action. He never, from jealousy, checked the advancement of others; and in accomplishing great deeds he took to himself no praise. Seeking fame as little as fortune, and office less than either, he aimed steadily at the good of his country and the best interests of mankind. Of despondency he knew nothing; trials only nerved him for severer struggles; his sublime and unfaltering hope had a cast of solemnity, and was as much a part of his nature as if his confidence sprung from insight into the divine decrees, and was as firm as a sincere

[1] The late Lord Ashburton gave me an account of his dining with Samuel Adams, in Boston, and it coincided exactly with the account in the text.

Calvinist's assurance of his election. For himself and for others, he held that all sorrows and all losses were to be encountered, rather than that liberty should perish. Such was his deep devotion, such his inflexibility and courage, he may be called the last of the Puritans, and seemed destined to win for his country

The victory of endurance born.

On his motion and in his words, Boston, while it still set forth its acknowledged dependence upon Great Britain, and the ready submission of its merchants to all just and necessary regulations of trade, asserted its rights and privileges, whether held by charter or by birth. "There is no room for delay," said the town to its representatives. "Those unexpected proceedings may be preparatory to more extensive taxation; for if our trade may be taxed why not our lands and every thing we possess? If taxes are laid upon us in any shape, without our having a legal representation where they are laid, are we not reduced from the character of free subjects to the miserable state of tributary slaves? This annihilates our charter right to govern and tax ourselves. We claim British rights, not by charter only; we are born to them. Use your endeavors that the weight of the other North American colonies may be added to that of this province, that by united application all may happily obtain redress."

Thus the town of Boston denied the right of the British parliament to tax America, and looked for redress to a union of all the colonies.

At New-York the arrival of the English packet was awaited with unusual interest. When it came

CHAP. X. 1764. June. tardily along in June, it was not easy to describe the manner in which people were affected. "I will wear nothing but homespun,"[1] exclaimed one citizen; "I will drink no wine," echoed another, angry that wine must pay a new duty. "I propose," cried a third, "that we dress in sheepskins with the wool on." All expressed their resentment in the strongest manner. It was thought a French army of three thousand men might land in America without opposition from its inhabitants. "It appears plainly," said the gentle Robert R. Livingston, "that these duties are only the beginning of evils. The stamp duty, they tell us, is deferred, till they see whether the colonies will take the yoke upon themselves, and offer something else as certain. They talk, too, of a land tax, and to us the ministry appears to have run mad;" and looking forward to measures of resistance, "we in New-York," he added, "shall do as well as our neighbors: the God of Heaven, whom we serve, will sanctify all things to those who love Him and strive to serve Him."

The legislature of Massachusetts was then in session. The Boston Instructions, drawn by Samuel Adams, formed the corner-stone of its policy. In pursuance of them, James Otis prepared "a state" of the case.[2] By the laws of nature and of nations, the voice of universal reason, and of God, by statute law and the common law, this memorial claimed for the colonists the absolute rights of Englishmen—personal security and liberty, the rights of property, the power of local legislation, subject only to the king's negative as in Ireland, and the sole power of taxing them-

[1] Letter of R. R. Livingston. The text is derived from letters written at the moment, which, with other invaluable papers, were communicated to me by my friend, the present Bishop of Pennsylvania.

[2] Substance of a memorial presented to the House.

CHAP. X.

1764. June.

selves.[1] "The authority of the parliament of Great Britain," such were the words of this paper, "is circumscribed by bounds, which, if exceeded, their acts become mere power without right, and consequently void." "Acts of parliament against natural equity are void. Acts against the fundamental principles of the British institutions are void."[2] "The wild wastes of America have been turned into pleasant habitations; little villages in Great Britain into manufacturing towns and opulent cities; and London itself bids fair to become the metropolis of the world.[3] These are the fruits of the spirit of commerce and liberty. The British empire to be perpetuated must be built on the principles of justice."[4] Such were the views of Otis, sent by Massachusetts to its agent in London, "to be improved as he might judge proper."

The Assembly formally repudiated the concessions of their agent. Their silence had rather been the silence of "despair." They protested against "the burdensome scheme of obliging the colonies to maintain a standing army," as against the constitution, and against reason. They rehearsed their services during the last war. Still incredulous, they demand: "Can it be possible that duties and taxes shall be assessed without the voice or consent of an American parliament. If we are not represented, we are slaves." "Ireland," said they, connecting the questions of American and Irish liberty, "was a conquered country, yet no duties have been levied by the British parliament on Ireland." "The resolutions for a stamp act naturally and directly tend to enervate the good

1 Ibid., 70, 71.
2 Ibid., 72.
3 Ibid., 77.
4 Ibid., 80.

CHAP. X. 1764. June. will of America towards Great Britain. Prohibitions of trade are neither equitable nor just; but the power of taxing is the grand barrier of British liberty. If this is once broken down, all is lost." "In a word," say they, representing truly the point of resistance at which America was that year ready to halt, "a people may be free, and tolerably happy, without a particular branch of trade; but without the privilege of assessing their own taxes they can be neither."[1]

At the same time, Otis, Cushing, Thacher, Gray, and Sheafe, as the committee for corresponding with the other colonies, sent a circular letter to them all, exposing the danger that menaced their "most essential rights," and desiring "their united assistance." Thus the legislature adopted the principles and the line of conduct which the town of Boston, at the impulse of Samuel Adams, had recommended.[2]

On the other hand, Bernard sought to ingratiate himself in England, by sending over for the consideration of his superiors a scheme of American polity which he had employed years in maturing. He urged on the cabinet, that a general reformation of the American governments was not only desirable, but necessary; that the colonies enjoyed their separate legislatures, not as a right, but as a contingent privilege; that parliament could modify their governments as it should see fit; that its power to impose port duties, and levy internal taxes in the colonies, was not to be disputed;

[1] Letter of the House to Jasper Mauduit.

[2] In the Rights of the Colonists, by Otis, the Instructions of the town of Boston are printed; and the Memorial is declared to have been drawn up by Otis, and to have been presented to the House "in pursuance of the above instructions."

and if requisitions were neglected the power ought to be exercised; that there should be for the colonies a certain, sufficient, and independent civil list; that there should be an American nobility for life, to mediate between the king and the people; that the American charters were suited only to the infancy of states, and should be abolished, and one form of government established for all America by parliament.[1]

CHAP. X.

1764. June.

Of the paper containing this advice, Bernard sent several copies to the ministry, carefully concealing from America his treacherous solicitations, and he darkly hinted at arguments which should make his scheme acceptable, but which were "fit" only for the consideration of the cabinet.[2]

July.

While Bernard thus secretly and stealthily laid before the cabinet his views on America, Otis spoke through the press to the world of mankind; and his voice was powerful enough to reach England, and to be considered in parliament. He saw around him men who "had built much upon the fine salaries they should receive from the plantation branch of the revenue;" and "he knew that with similar views several officers of the crown in some of the colonies had been pushing for such an act for many years;" but his singularly constituted mind, which was for ever in collision with them in daily life, in its moments of exaltation, scorned all personal jealousies. He did not want affection for England. "The British constitution," said he, "comes nearest the idea of perfection of any that has been reduced to practice."

[1] Bernard's Principles of Law and Polity.

[2] Bernard's Select Letters on Trade and Government, 25.

CHAP. X. 1764. July "Let parliament lay what burthens they please on us," he even added, "it is our duty to submit and patiently bear them till they will be pleased to relieve us. If any thing fall from my pen that bears the least aspect but that of obedience, duty, and loyalty to the king and parliament, the candid will impute it to the agony of my heart." It was his purpose not to enter into war with British institutions, or the British parliament, but to treat of the first principles of free government and human rights.

"Government," such was his argument, which I shall state as nearly as possible in his own words—"government is founded, not on force, as was the theory of Hobbs, nor on compact, as was the theory of Locke and the revolution of 1688; nor on property, as had been asserted by Harrington. It springs from the necessities of our nature, and has an everlasting foundation in the unchangeable will of God. Man came into the world and into society at the same instant. There must exist in every earthly society a supreme sovereign, from whose final decision there can be no appeal, but directly to Heaven. This supreme power is originally and ultimately in the people; and the people never did in fact freely, nor can rightfully make an unlimited renunciation of this divine right. Kingcraft and priestcraft are a trick to gull the vulgar. The happiness of mankind demands that this grand and ancient alliance should be broken off for ever.

"The omniscient and omnipotent Monarch of the universe has, by the grand charter given to the human race, placed the end of government in the good of the whole. The form of government is left to the individuals of each society; and its whole super-

CHAP X. 1764. July

structure and administration should be conformed to the law of universal reason. There can be no prescription old enough to supersede the law of nature and the grant of God Almighty, who has given all men a right to be free. If every prince since Nimrod had been a tyrant, it would not prove a right to tyrannize. The administrators of legislative and executive authority, when they verge towards tyranny, are to be resisted; if they prove incorrigible, are to be deposed.

"The first principle and great end of government being to provide for the best good of all the people; this can be done only by a supreme legislative and executive ultimately in the people, or whole community, where God has placed it; but the difficulties attending a universal congress gave rise to a right of representation. Such a transfer of the power of the whole to a few was necessary; but to bring the powers of all into the hands of one, or some few, and to make them hereditary, is the interested work of the weak and the wicked. Nothing but life and liberty are actually hereditable. The grand political problem is to invent the best combination of the powers of legislation and execution: they must exist in the state, just as in the revolution of the planets; one power would fix them to a centre, and another carry them off indefinitely; but the first and simple principle is EQUALITY and THE POWER OF THE WHOLE.

"The best writers on public law contain nothing that is satisfactory on the natural rights of colonies. Even Grotius and Puffendorf establish the matter of right on the matter of fact. Their researches are often but the history of ancient abuses; and the American Admiralty courts learn of them to determine con-

CHAP. X. 1764. July.

troversies by the rules of civil and feudal law. To be too fond of studying them is a ridiculous infatuation. The British colonists do not hold their liberties or their lands by so slippery a tenure as the will of the prince. Colonists are men; the common children of the same Creator with their brethren of Great Britain.

"The colonists are men; the colonists are therefore free born; for, by the law of nature, all men are free born, white or black. No good reason can be given for enslaving those of any color. Is it right to enslave a man because his color is black, or his hair short, and curled like wool, instead of Christian hair? Can any logical inference in favor of slavery be drawn from a flat nose or a long or a short face? The riches of the West Indies, or the luxury of the metropolis, should not have weight to break the balance of truth and justice. Liberty is the gift of God, and cannot be annihilated.

"Nor do the political and civil rights of the British colonists rest on a charter from the Crown. Old Magna Charta was not the beginning of all things; nor did it rise on the borders of chaos out of the unformed mass. A time may come when parliament shall declare every American charter void; but the natural, inherent, and inseparable rights of the colonists as men and as citizens, would remain, and whatever became of charters, can never be abolished till the general conflagration.

"There is no foundation for distinction between external and internal taxes: if parliament may tax our trade, they may lay stamps, land taxes, tithes, and so indefinitely; there are no bounds. But such an imposition of taxes, whether on trade, or on land, on houses,

CHAP. X. 1764. July.

or ships, on real or personal, fixed or floating property, in the colonies, is absolutely irreconcilable with the rights of the colonists as British subjects and as men. Acts of parliament against the fundamental principles of the British constitution are void.

"Yet the colonists know the blood and treasure independence would cost. They will never think of it, till driven to it as the last fatal resort against ministerial oppression, which will make the wisest mad, and the weakest strong. The world is at the eve of the highest scene of earthly power and grandeur that has ever yet been displayed to the view of mankind. Who will win the prize is with God. But human nature must and will be rescued from the general slavery that has so long triumphed over the species."

Thus, "in the agony of his heart," Otis reasoned for his country and for the race, bringing into the living intelligence of the people the first principles of free government and human rights; ignorant of the beauty of the edifice which he was rearing.

> He wrought in sad sincerity;
> Himself from God he could not free;
> He builded better than he knew.

The book of Otis was reprinted in England. Lord Mansfield, who had read it, rebuked those who spoke of it with contempt. But they rejoined, "The man is mad." "What then?" answered Mansfield. "One madman often makes many. Massaniello was mad: nobody doubted it; yet for all that he overturned the government of Naples."

But Otis was a prophet, not the leader of a party; full of sagacity in his inspirations, but wanting stead-

CHAP. X. 1764. July. fast consistency of conduct. His colleague, Oxenbridge Thacher, was less enthusiastic and less variable. Connection with Great Britain was to him no blessing, if Great Britain would impose burdens unconstitutionally. He vindicated the right of resisting arbitrary taxation by the frequent example of the British parliament; and he dwelt on the danger to the inhabitants of England if the ministers could disfranchise a million and a half of subjects in America.[1]

"Here," said Mayhew,[2] as he lamented the cold adhesion of "the timid good,"[3] and for himself, trod the thorny path of resistance to the grandeurs of the world—"here there are many who 'see the right, and yet the wrong pursue.' But it is my fixed resolution, notwithstanding many discouragements, in my little sphere to do all I can for the service of my country, that neither the republic nor the churches of New England may sustain any injury."

And every where men began to enter into a solemn agreement not to use a single article of British manufacture; not even to wear black clothes for mourning. To encourage the growth and manufacture of wool, nearly all Boston signed a covenant to eat no lamb.

While the people encouraged one another in the conviction that taxation by parliament was tyranny, Hutchinson addressed his thoughts to the Secretary of the Chancellor of the Exchequer.

"The colonists," said he, "claim a power of making laws, and a privilege of exemption from taxes, unless

[1] Thacher's Sentiments of a British American.

[2] Mayhew to Hollis, received by Hollis, 23 Aug. 1764.

[3] Bryant.

voted by their own representatives. In Rome, not only the colonies when first planted, but the provinces when changed into colonies, were freed from taxes for the Roman exchequer of every sort. It can be of no purpose to mention modern colonies. In Europe, the inhabitants of Britain only are free, and the inhabitants of British colonies only feel the loss of freedom—and they feel it more sensibly because they thought it doubly secured as their natural right, and their possession by virtue of the most solemn engagements. Nor are the privileges of the people less affected by duties laid for the sake of the money arising from them than by an internal tax.

"Not one-tenth part of the people of Great Britain have a voice in elections to parliament; and, therefore, the colonies can have no claim to it; but every man of property in England may have his voice, if he will. Besides; acts of parliament do not generally affect individuals, and every interest is represented. But the colonies have an interest distinct from the interest of the nation; and shall the parliament be at once party and judge? Is it not a continual question, What can be done to make the colonies further beneficial to the nation? And nobody adds, consistently with their rights. You consider us as your property, to improve in the best way you can for your advantage.

"The nation treats her colonies as a father who should sell the services of his sons to reimburse him what they had cost him, but without the same reason; for none of the colonies, except Georgia and Halifax, occasioned any charge to the crown or kingdom in the settlement of them. The people of New England fled for the sake of civil and religious liberty; multitudes flocked to America with this dependence, that their

CHAP. X. 1764. July. liberties should be safe. They and their posterity have enjoyed them to their content, and therefore have endured with greater cheerfulness all the hardships of settling new countries. No ill use has been made of these privileges; but the dominion and wealth of Great Britain have received amazing addition. Surely the services we have rendered the nation have not subjected us to any forfeitures.

"I know it is said, the colonies are a charge to the nation, and they should contribute to their own defence and protection. But during the last war they annually contributed so largely that the parliament was convinced the burden would be insupportable, and from year to year made them compensation; in several of the colonies for several years together more men were raised, in proportion, than by the nation. In the trading towns, one-fourth part of the profit of trade, besides imposts and excise, was annually paid to the support of the war and public charges; in the country towns, a farm which would hardly rent for twenty pounds a year, paid ten pounds in taxes. If the inhabitants of Britain had paid in the same proportion, there would have been no great increase of the national debt.

"Nor is there occasion for any national expense in America. For one hundred years together the New England colonies received no aid in their wars with the Indians, assisted by the French. Those governments now molested, are as able to defend their respective frontiers; and had rather do the whole of it by a tax of their own raising, than pay their proportion in any other way.

"Moreover, it must be prejudicial to the national interest to impose parliamentary taxes. The advantages promised by an increase of the revenue are all fallacious and delusive. You will lose more than you gain. Britain already reaps the profit of all their trade, and of the increase of their substance. By cherishing their present turn of mind, you will serve your interest more than by your present schemes."[1]

The remonstrance of Hutchinson reflected the opinion of all candid royalists in the colonies; but the pusillanimous man entreated his correspondent to conceal his confession from those whom it would displease. Yet to his friends in America, he used to say, that there was no ground for the distinction between the duties on trade and internal taxes; that if the Parliament intended to go on, there would be a necessity to dispute the distinction; "for," said he, "they may find duties on trade enough to drain us thoroughly."[2] And it is affirmed, that to members of the legislature of Massachusetts, from whom he had ends to gain, Hutchinson denied utterly the right of parliament to tax America.[3]

The appeals of the Colonies were made in the spirit of loyalty. The wilderness was still ringing with the war-whoop of the savage;[4] and the frontiers were red with blood; while the colonies themselves, at the solicitations of Amherst and of Gage, his successor, were lavishing their treasure to secure the west to Great Britain. In July, the little army of eleven hundred men, composed chiefly of provincial battalions from New Jersey, New-York, and Connecticut, that of

[1] Abridged from Hutchinson's draft.

[2] Hutchinson to Ebenezer Silliman, 1764. Compare Hutchinson to Bollan, 7 Nov. 1764.

[3] Novanglus, printed in 1774–5.

[4] M. de St. Ange to M. d'Abadie, 15 July, 1764.

CHAP. X. Connecticut led by Colonel Israel Putnam,[1] the whole under the command of Bradstreet, reached Niagara.

1764. Aug. There was found a vast concourse of Indians, of various nations, willing to renew friendship, and expecting presents. The Senecas, to save their settlements from imminent destruction, brought in prisoners, and ratified a peace.

Bradstreet had been ordered by General Gage to give peace to all such nations of Indians as would sue for it, and to chastise those that continued in arms; but none remained in arms. Half way from Buffalo to Erie, he was met by deputations from the Shawnees, the Delawares, the Hurons of Sandusky, and the Five Nations of the Scioto valley, desiring that the chain of friendship might be brightened; and he settled a treaty with the nations dwelling between Lake Erie and the Ohio.

Sept. At Detroit, Bradstreet was welcomed by the Hurons with every expression of joy and respect. A detachment was sent to take possession of Michilimackinac, and a vessel found its way into Lake Huron.

On the seventh of September, great numbers of Indians, especially Ottawas and Chippewas, assembled at Bradstreet's tent, and seated themselves on the ground for a Congress. The Ottawas and Chippewas on that day cashiered all their old chiefs, and the young warriors shook hands with the English as with brothers.[2] The Miamis disclosed their

[1] The uncommonly meritorious work of Parkman on the Pontiac war, adopts too easily the cavils of the British officers at Bradstreet and at the American battalions. Bradstreet was an excellent officer, and the troops of Connecticut were not "scum and refuse," but good New England men, and they did their work well. Mante is an able and well-informed historian, distinguished for his accuracy and his general impartiality.

[2] Mante, 517–524.

desire that all resentment should be laid aside, and asked for peace, in the names of their wives and children. A treaty was then made, and the arms of the Chippewas and Ottawas, the Hurons and Miamis, the Pottawattamies and Sacs, were attached to it. Two days afterward, the Missisagas drew an eagle with a medal round its neck, as the signature for their nation. Pontiac did not appear, but was included in the covenant. By its conditions the Indian country was made a part of the royal dominions; its tribes were bound to render aid to the English troops; and in return were promised protection and assistance. Indian murderers and plunderers, as well as British deserters, were to be delivered up; all captives were to be set free and restored. The families of English settlers were assured of a welcome.

1764. Sept.

After securing repose to the Northwest, Bradstreet encamped near the carrying-place at Sandusky. Neither he nor those whom he deputed took possession of the country on the Mississippi.

While provincial American troops were confirming to England the possession of its conquests, the British ministry was pursuing its new methods of government. The king, "by virtue of his prerogative royal, appointed an impost of four and a half per cent., in specie, on produce shipped from Grenada, from and after the twenty-ninth day of September, 1764;"[1] and this illegal[2] order was justified on the ground that Grenada was a conquered island, in which customs

[1] Letters Patent, 20 July, 1764.

[2] For Lord Mansfield's opinion, see Judgment of Court of King's Bench, 20 Nov. 1774.

CHAP. X. 1764. Sept.

had been collected by the most Christian king. A small return to the exchequer blinded Grenville to the principles of British law.[1]

The same reasoning was applied to the Canadians; and the Attorney and Solicitor-Generals of Great Britain gave their opinion, that the duties payable in Canada to its former government at the time of the conquest, might be legally collected by the authority of the British king.[2] But arbitrary taxation was the only relic of French usages which was retained. All the laws, customs, and forms of judicature[3] of a populous and long-established colony were in one hour[4] overturned by the ordinance of the seventeenth of September; and English laws, even the penal statutes against Catholics, all unknown to the Canadians, and unpublished, were introduced in their stead.

The improper choice and the number of the civil officers sent over from England, increased the disquietude of the colony. The ignorant, the greedy, and the factious, were appointed to offices which required integrity, knowledge, and abilities.[5] The judge pitched upon to conciliate the minds of seventy thousand foreigners to the laws and government of Great Britain, was taken from a jail, and was entirely unacquainted with the civil law and the language of the people. The Attorney-General, with regard to the language,

[1] Opinion of Attorney and Solicitor General, 6 Aug. 1764. Representation of the Lords of the Treasury, 14 June, 1765. Opinion of the Attorney and Solicitor-Generals, 2 Nov. 1766, &c.

[2] Mansfield to Grenville, 24 Dec. 1764.

[3] Gov. Carlton to Sec. of State, 24 Dec. 1767.

[4] Murray to Shelburne, 30 Aug. 1766. Carlton to Shelburne, 20 Jan. 1768.

[5] Murray to Shelburne, 30 Aug. 1766. Mansfield to Grenville, 24 Dec. 1764.

CHAP. X. 1764. Sept.

was not better qualified. The offices of Secretary of the Province, Registrar, Clerk of the Council, Commissary of Stores and Provisions, Provost Marshal, and others, were given by patent to men of interest in England, who let them out to the best bidders, and so little considered the capacity of their representatives, that none of them understood the language of the natives, but all, in their turn, hired such servants as would work at the cheapest rate, without much inquiry how the work was done.[1] As no salary was annexed to these patent places, the value of them depended upon the fees, which the governor was ordered to establish equal to those in the richest ancient colonies. Nor could he restrain those officers who lived by fees from running them up to extortion. When he checked them in their views of profit, he was regarded as their enemy, nor was there any chance for harmony in the government, unless all should become equally corrupt.[2]

The Supreme Court of Judicature took to itself all causes, civil and criminal. The chicanery and expensiveness of Westminster Hall were introduced into the impoverished province; and English justice and English offices seemed to the poor Canadians an ingenious device to drain them of the little substance which was still left to them.[3] In the one hundred and ten rural parishes there were but nineteen Protestant families. The rest of the Protestants were a few half-pay officers, disbanded soldiers, traders, mechanics, and publicans, who re-

[1] Carlton to Secretary of State, 12 April, 1768.

[2] Carlton to Shelburne, 20 Jan. 1768.

[3] Carlton to Shelburne, 24 Dec. 1767.

CHAP. X. 1764. Sept. sided in Quebec and Montreal, most of them followers of the army, of low education, all with their fortunes to make, and little solicitous about the means;[1] so that, as the Catholics were disfranchised, magistrates were to be made, and juries composed from about four hundred and fifty suttlers and traders—men of narrow ideas, ignorant, and intoxicated with unexpected power.

Disorder and division ensued in attempting to introduce the civil administration. The troops that had conquered, and for four years had ruled the country, remained in it, commanded by an officer, who by the new establishment was deprived of the government of half the province, and who remained in every respect independent of the civil authority. As there were no barracks in the country, the quartering the troops furnished perpetual opportunities of displaying their importance and rancor. The meek and unresisting province was given over submissively to hopeless oppression, as cold iron suffers blows on the anvil, but neither takes shape nor sparkles. The history of the world furnishes no instance of so rash injustice.[2]

The British ministers were still more zealous to restrain and circumscribe the republican spirit of New England. In September, letters were received in New-York, announcing that the king in council had, at the instance of Halifax, dismembered New Hampshire, and annexed to New-York the country north of

[1] Murray to Shelburne, 30 August, 1766: "I report them to be, in general, the most immoral collection of men I ever knew."

[2] Grenville Papers, ii. 477.

CHAP. X. 1764. Sept.

Massachusetts and west of Connecticut river.[1] The decision was declaratory of the boundary; and it was therefore held by the royalists that the grants made under the sanction of the royal governor of New Hampshire were annulled. Many of the lands for which the king had received the price, and which were already occupied and cultivated, were granted in the king's name anew, and the former purchasers were compelled to redeem them, or menaced with eviction.

This decision was based upon the belief of the superior loyalty of New-York; and yet at that moment the spirit of resistance was nowhere so strong. "History," it was said, "does not furnish an instance of a revolt begun by the people which did not take its rise from oppression. Nothing but this, sensibly felt, can unite the several governments in such a design; and without union they can do nothing."[2] But the passions of New-York were too vehement to wait for concert. Its assembly contained merchants, and owners of large tracts of land, and "common farmers, which last," wrote the lieutenant governor, "are men easily deluded and led astray with popular amusements of liberty and privileges."[3] On coming together in September, their address[4] claimed for their constituents "that great badge of English liberty, the being taxed only with their own con-

[1] Board of Trade to Lieut.-Gov. Colden, 13 July, 1764. Order in Council, 20 July, 1764. Lieut.-Gov. Colden to Board of Trade, Sept. 26, 1763.

[2] Boston Gazette of 10 Sept. 1764, from New-York Mercury of 27 Aug. 1764.

[3] Lieut.-Gov. Colden to the Board of Trade, 20 Sept. 1764.

[4] Address of the General Assembly of New-York to the Lieut.-Gov. 11 Sept. 1764.

CHAP. X. 1764. Oct.

sent." This "exclusive right," the loss of which would bring "basest vassalage," they, in October, represented to the king, as a right which "had received the royal sanction;" and they enumerated as their grievances, "involuntary taxes," the "acts of trade," the substitution of the discretion of a judge of a vice-admiralty court for the trial by jury, the restraint on the use of the credit of the colony by act of parliament. These they repeated in a manifesto to the House of Lords, to whom they further "showed," that "the supreme power lodged in a single person" is less fearful than a constitution in which one part of the community holds the right for ever to tax and legislate for the other. If the constitution of Great Britain gives to parliament that right, then, they say, "it is the most unequal constitution that ever existed; and no human foresight or contrivance can prevent its final consummation in the most intolerable oppression."[1]

The same complaints were enforced in a petition and representation to the House of Commons. They pleaded that they had never refused, and promised that they never would refuse to hearken to a just requisition from the crown. They appealed to their records, as evidence before the whole world of their fidelity and steady affection to the mother country; their untainted loyalty and cheerful obedience; their exercise of their political privileges unabused.

"An exemption from the burden of ungranted and involuntary taxes"—such were the words of the General Assembly of New-York—"must be the grand principle of every free state. Without such a right vested in themselves, exclusive of all others,

[1] General Assembly of the Colony of New-York to the Lords, 18 Oct. 1764.

there can be no liberty, no happiness, no security, nor even the idea of property. Life itself would become intolerable. We proceed with propriety and boldness to inform the Commons of Great Britain, who, to their infinite honor, in all ages asserted the liberties of mankind, that the people of this colony nobly disdain the thought of claiming that exemption as a privilege. They found it on a basis more honorable, solid, and stable; they challenge it, and glory in it as their right. * * The thought of independency upon the supreme power of the parliament we reject with the utmost abhorrence. * * The authority of the parliament of Great Britain to model the trade of the whole empire, so as to subserve the interest of her own, we are ready to recognise in the most extensive and positive terms; but the freedom to drive all kinds of traffic, in subordination to, and not inconsistent with the British trade, and an exemption from all duties in such a course of commerce, is humbly claimed by the colonies, as the most essential of all the rights to which they are entitled as colonists, and connected in the common bond of liberty with the free sons of Great Britain. For, with submission, since all impositions, whether they be internal taxes, or duties paid for what we consume, equally diminish the estates upon which they are charged, what avails it to any people by which of them they are impoverished?" And they deprecated the loss of their rights as likely "to shake the power and independence of Great Britain."

The people of Rhode Island, headed by Stephen Hopkins, the governor of their own choice, proceeded more calmly and on a better foundation. They would

CHAP. X. 1764. Oct.

not recognise any just authority in parliament to enact even the laws of trade. Like Massachusetts, they elected a committee of correspondence. The colony was ready "to exert its utmost efforts to preserve its privileges inviolate." It saw that the "critical conjunction" was come "when they must be defended or finally lost;" and they invited all other colonies to maintain their liberties with spirit, and devise a method of union.

The proposition of Rhode Island was received with joy by the assembly of Pennsylvania. The complaints of the English ministry had been specially directed against that opulent and prosperous colony, though it had been ready to make liberal grants for the public service, and had failed to do so only because the proprietaries had interposed their negative, unless their own estates were wholly or partially exempted from taxation. They were, moreover, the landlords of all the inhabitants; and yet to the judges, who were of their own appointment and were to decide all questions between them and their tenants, they gave no other tenure of office than their own good pleasure. The government, having no support in the affections of the people, was so weak, that during the previous winter it had suffered the murder of twenty Indians to pass unpunished; and could not restrain armed mobs who went about threatening the lives of more. To escape from the perpetual intervention of private interest in public affairs, Franklin, with the great body of the Quakers, as well as royalists, desired that the province should become a royal government.

One man in the assembly, the pure-minded and ingenuous John Dickinson, though ever the opponent of the scandalous selfishness of the proprietaries, had in May spoken earnestly against the proposal; for he saw that "the province must stake on the event liberties that ought to be immortal;" and desired to see an olive leaf, at least, brought to them before they should quit their ark.[1] On the other side, Joseph Galloway urged with vigor the just complaints against the proprietaries. All royalist at heart, he had even applauded the ministry of Grenville for its disposition to mild and equitable measures, and was tolerant of a military establishment,[2] of which all the inconveniency to the colonies was to "be a proportionable part of the aids to support the troops." And Franklin, with undaunted courage supporting popular rights against every danger, was willing to transfer to the king the executive power then held by the proprietaries, believing it could be done without detriment to the established privileges of Pennsylvania.

A petition for the change was adopted by a large majority; but when in summer the policy of Grenville with regard to the American Stamp Act was better understood, a new debate arose, in which Franklin took the lead. It was argued, that, during the war the people of Pennsylvania had granted more than their proportion, and were ever ready to grant sums suitable to their abilities and zeal for the service; that, therefore, the proposition of taxing them in parliament was both cruel and unjust; that by the constitution of the colonies, their business was with the king, and never, in any way, with the chan-

[1] John Dickinson's Speech on the 24 May, 1764. 17.

[2] The Speech of Joseph Galloway, 5. 40.

CHAP. X. 1764. Oct. cellor of the exchequer; that they could not make any proposition to Grenville about taxing their constituents by parliament, since parliament had no right to tax them at all; that the notice which they had received bore no marks of being the king's order, or made with his knowledge; that the king had always accompanied his requisition with good words, but that the financier, instead of making a decent demand, had sent a menace, that they should certainly be taxed, and only left them the choice of the manner; and they accordingly "resolved, that as they always had, so they always should think it their duty to grant aid to the crown, according to their abilities, whenever required of them in the usual constitutional manner."[1]

At the elections in Autumn, the proprietary party representing that "the king's little finger would be found heavier than the proprietaries' whole loins," succeeded, by about twenty votes among near four thousand, in defeating Franklin's return as the representative of Philadelphia. But the majority of the new assembly placed in him unabated confidence, and conforming to the happy suggestions of Rhode Island, they proceeded to an act which in its consequences was to influence the world. On the twenty-sixth day of October, they elected Benjamin Franklin their agent, and in spite of the bitter protest of his opponents, he sailed for England with the sacred charge of the liberties of his country in his custody.

At that time Pennsylvania was employing her men and her treasure to defend the West. To secure

[1] Franklin to Alexander, 12 March, 1778.

a firm peace with the Indians on the Ohio it was desirable to show a strong force in the midst of their settlements. The regular army was feeble, and could furnish scarcely five hundred men, most of them Highlanders. Pennsylvania, at her own charge, added a thousand, and Virginia contributed a corps of volunteers. These took up the march, under Bouquet, for the heart of Ohio.

Virginia volunteers formed the advance guard, the axemen followed to clear three paths. At the sides, the soldiers marched in single file; in the centre, two deep, followed by the convoy of well-laden pack horses and droves of sheep and oxen; a party of light horsemen came next; again, Virginia volunteers brought up the rear. With the little army went many who had lost children, or friends, and came to search the wilderness for the captives.

At the fork in the Indian path, where it branches to the lower towns of the Muskingum, blazed forest-trees were found marked with emblematic records of deeds of war—the number of scalps taken in battle, and of prisoners that had been saved.

A little below the mouth of Sandy Creek, beneath a bower erected on the banks of the Tuscarawas, chiefs and warriors of the Senecas, the Delawares, and the Shawnees, came to light the council-fire, to smoke the calumet, and to entreat for peace. At the close of the speech, the Delaware chiefs delivered up eighteen white prisoners and eighty-three small sticks, as pledges for the return of so many more.

To insure the performance of their promises, Bouquet marched farther into their country, till, at the junction of the White Woman and the Tuscarawas, in

CHAP. X. the centre of the Indian villages, he made an encampment that had the appearance of an English town.

1764. Oct. There the Shawnees, the most violent and warlike of all the tribes, accepting the terms of peace with dejected sullenness, promised by their orator, Red Hawk, to collect all captives from the lower towns, and restore them in the spring; and there the nearer villages brought their white prisoners to the English. The arrival of the lost ones formed the loveliest scene ever witnessed in the wilderness. Mothers recognised their once lost babes; sisters and brothers, scarcely able to recover the accent of their native tongue, learned to know that they were children of the same parents.

How does humanity abound in affections! Whom the Indians spared they loved! They had not taken the little ones and the captives into their wigwams without receiving them into their hearts, and adopting them into their tribes and families. To part with them now was anguish to the red men; they shed torrents of tears; they entreated of the white men to show kindness to those whom they restored. From day to day they visited them in the camp; they gave them corn and skins. As the English returned to Pittsburg, they followed to hunt for them, and bring them provisions. A young Mingo would not be torn from a young woman of Virginia, whom he had taken as his wife. Some of the children who had been carried away young had learned to love their savage friends, and wept at leaving them. Some of the captives would not come of themselves, and were not brought away but in bonds. Who can fathom the mysteries of woman's love? Some, who were not permitted to remain, clung to their dusky lovers at parting; others, more faithful still, invented means to escape, and fly back to their places in the wigwams of their chosen warriors.

CHAP. X. 1764. Oct.

With the wilderness pacified, with the French removed, an unbounded career of happiness and tranquillity seemed opening upon the British empire. Never was there a moment when the affections of the colonists struggled more strongly toward England, or when it would have been easier for the mother country to have secured to herself all the benefits of their trade, as well as their good will. Had the officers in the public employ been wise, had the ministry possessed that moderation which is the test of greatness, independence would not have been seriously thought of. Virginia, appealing to the king, to the house of lords, and to the house of commons, declared the taxation of America by the British parliament to be "subversive of the fundamental principles of the constitution," and dangerous in its example to the empire at home. But if the people could enjoy "their undoubted rights," "their connection with Britain, the seat of liberty, would be their greatest happiness."

The people of North Carolina, in an address of the assembly, claimed the inherent right and exclusive privilege of imposing their own taxes. But they went no further than to appoint a committee to express their concurrence with the province of Massachusetts.[1]

At that time, the Assembly of Massachusetts, in the vain hope of being heard by the House of Com-

[1] Martin's History of North Carolina, ii. 188.

CHAP. X. 1764. Oct.

mons, yielded to the persuasions of Hutchinson, and consented to plead for the liberties and privileges long enjoyed without making the claim of right; and invited England to be content with the advantages of confining their trade. So strong was the desire to put aside, if it were possible, the approaching conflict. Connecticut, in a methodical statement, with divisions and subdivisions, and a just enumeration of its services in the war, demonstrated, that charging stamp duties, or other internal duties, by authority of parliament, would be such an infringement of the rights, privileges, and authorities of the colonies, that it might be humbly and firmly trusted, and even relied upon, that the supreme guardians of the liberties of the subject would not suffer the same to be done."

In the midst of the strife about taxation, Colden planned the prostration of the influence of the lawyers, and great landholders, by insisting that in all cases, even in the common law courts, from the verdict of a jury and without a writ of error, there lay the right to appeal to the king. The judges refused to admit of such appeals. "I stand singly," said Colden, "in support of the king's prerogative. All that the owners of the great patents can do will only serve to irritate the ministry; for the king's prerogative will be zealously supported, whatever they may foolishly think of intimidating ministers." To the Earl of Halifax, he signalized the lawyer, John Morin Scott, as an incendiary; and entreated the removal of Justice Robert R. Livingston, who had firmly maintained the validity of the verdict of juries. In this way the liberal party in New-York acquired its strength. The merchants opposed the government from hostility to restrictions on trade; the lawyers, from re-

CHAP. X. 1764. Nov.

spect to the due course of justice; the large land-holders, from fear of the diminution of their estates by the arbitrary exertion of the prerogative.

In Massachusetts, Bernard was eager to carry into effect a "new arrangement of New England," believing that "the proper time for this business was now come."

The two republics of Connecticut and Rhode Island were to be dissolved; the government of New-York extended as far as Connecticut river; and Massachusetts was to embrace the country from the Connecticut river to the Piscataqua. Another colony, with Falmouth—now Portland—as its capital, might extend to the Penobscot, and yet another to the St. John's. "Massachusetts," he continued, "would then afford a fine opportunity for trying the experiment of the most perfect form of government for a mature American province." A modification of its charter, a certain civil list, an order of nobility for life, and places of profit with sure emoluments, would place the king's authority "upon a rock."[1]

If the new arrangement were to be conducted by the king in parliament, the consent of the colonies would not be necessary, and the business might soon be brought to a conclusion. Nor did Bernard forget to remind Lord Halifax, that once Massachusetts had for a season established a stamp act.[2]

In Connecticut, the aged Johnson, then enjoying "sweet retirement" in the lovely village of Stratford, familiar with the royalists of New-York, and the acknowledged organ of the Episcopalians of the north,

[1] Bernard to Halifax, 8 November, 1764.

[2] Bernard to Halifax, 12 November, 1764.

CHAP. X. 1764. Dec. thought it no sin to pray to God that "the monstrously popular constitution" of Connecticut might be changed; that the government at home might make but "one work" of bringing "all the colonies under one form of government,"[1] confidently hoping that the first news in the spring would be, bishops for America, and all charter governments dependent immediately on the king.[2]

In Rhode Island also, the few royalists made known in England their wish for a change of government.[3]

The ministry, in December, were deliberating how to present the affairs of America to parliament. It was certain that the commons would be all but unanimous in their assertion of the power of parliament; and that the lords would be excited to insolent scorn by the opposite doctrine. The Board of Trade,[4] therefore, represented to the king, that the legislature of Massachusetts, by its votes in June—of New-York, by its address to Colden, in September, had been guilty "of the most indecent disrespect to the legislature of Great Britain."[5] This the privy council[6] reported "as a matter of the highest consequence to the kingdom;" and Halifax[7] was ordered to "receive the king's pleasure with respect to the time and manner of laying the papers before parliament." Having thus made sure in advance of the

[1] Rev. Dr. S. Johnson to Benjamin Franklin, November, 1764.

[2] Rev. Dr. S. Johnson to Archbishop Secker, 20 Sept. 1764.

[3] Letter from Newport, of Feb. 19, 1765, in Providence Gazette of 23 Feb. 1765. Compare Hutchinson to a friend in Rhode Island, 16 March, 1765, in Hutchinson's Letter Book, ii. 132.

[4] Representation of the Board of Trade, 11 Dec. 1765.

[5] Council Register, Geo. III., No. 4, p. 48, 12 Dec. 1765.

[6] Council Register, Geo. III., No. 4, p. 54, 14 Dec. 1765.

[7] Council Register, Geo. III., No. 4, p. 62, 19 Dec. 1765.

support of vast majorities, the ministry retired to enjoy the Christmas holidays in the country-houses, where wealth, and intelligence, and tradition, combined to give to aristocratic hospitality its greatest grace, abundance, and refinement.

CHAPTER XI.

THE TWELFTH PARLIAMENT OF GREAT BRITAIN PASSES THE AMERICAN STAMP TAX. — GRENVILLE'S ADMINISTRATION CONTINUED.

JANUARY—APRIL, 1765.

CHAP. XI. 1765. Jan.

AT the opening of the year 1765, the people of New England were reading the history of the first sixty years of the Colony of Massachusetts, by Hutchinson. This work is so ably executed that as yet it remains without a rival; and his knowledge was so extensive, that, with the exception of a few concealments, it exhausts the subject. Nothing so much revived the ancestral spirit, which a weariness of the gloomy superstitions, mixed with Puritanism, had, for a long time, overshadowed. But now all hearts ran together in the study of the character of New England's fathers; and liberty became the dearer as men read at large through what sorrow, and self-denial, and cost of life it had been purchased.

New England seemed summoned to play a great part in the history of the world. "I always," said John Adams, "consider the settlement of America with reverence and wonder, as the opening of a grand scene and design in Providence for the illumination of

CHAP. XI. 1765. Jan.

the ignorant, and the emancipation of the slavish part of mankind all over the earth."[1]

This vision was drawing near its fulfilment. Afraid to meet parliament on the naked proposal of the expediency of taxing America, Grenville, with consummate art, resolved to place it "upon the most general and acknowledged grounds of whig policy."[2] The king, therefore, on opening the session on the tenth of January, most wisely for the immediate gain of great majorities by his ministry, most unwisely for his own peace and the welfare of his realm, presented the American question as one of "obedience to the laws and respect for the legislative authority of the kingdom." The raising such a question was dangerous in the extreme; if passed by undecided, it must leave the administration of the colonies in confusion; if denied, it must heighten their daring; if asserted, it must wound their affections beyond remedy.

The words of the king were echoed by the Lords and by the Commons, with the promise of that "temper and firmness which would best conciliate due submission and reverence."[3] The ministry were confident of a triumphant session and confirmed power. The impending measure drew attention from all quarters. In private, the arguments of America were urged with persuasive earnestness. The London merchants[4] found that America was in their debt to the amount of four millions of pounds sterling. Grenville sought to relieve their fears by the profuse offer of

[1] MS. Diary of John Adams, communicated to me by the late John Quincy Adams.

[2] Lloyd's Conduct, &c. 119.

[3] King's Speech, 10 Jan., 1765. Lords' Address of Thanks. Commons' Address of Thanks.

[4] Unpublished letter of Benjamin Franklin to John Ross.

CHAP. XI. 1765. Jan. bounties to the Americans, as offsets to the intended taxation. "If one bounty," said he to them, "will not do, I will add two; if two will not do, I will add three.[1]" He wished to act smoothly in the matter; but he was firmly resolved "to establish as undoubted the authority of the British legislature in all cases whatsoever."

The purpose found its warmest advocate in Charles Townshend. In the debates on the forces to be kept up in the navy and the army, he spoke for the largest numbers; "for the colonies," said he, "are not to be emancipated."[2]

Feb. Grenville was more obstinate and more cool, abounding in gentle words. The agents of the colonies had several meetings among themselves; and on Saturday, the second of February, Franklin, with Ingersoll, Jackson and Garth, as agents for Pennsylvania, Connecticut, and South Carolina, waited on the minister, to remonstrate in behalf of America, against taxation of the colonies by parliament, and to propose, that if they were to be taxed, they might be invited to tax themselves. "I take no pleasure," replied he, "in bringing upon myself their resentments: it is the duty of my office to manage the revenue. I have really been made to believe that, considering the whole circumstances of the mother country and the colonies, the latter can and ought to pay something to the common cause. I know of no better way than that now pursuing to lay such tax. If you can tell of a better, I will adopt it." Franklin pleaded for the usual

[1] Grenville, in Cavendish Debates, i. 404.

[2] Walpole to Hertford, 27 Jan. 1765. Walpole's Geo. III., ii. 46, 47.

method, by the king's requisition, through the Secretary of State; and he put into his hands the pledge of Pennsylvania to respect the demand when so made. "Can you agree," rejoined Grenville, "on the proportions each colony should raise?" To this they could only answer, no; on which he remarked, that the stamp act would adapt itself to the number and increase of the colonies. Jackson pointed out the danger to the liberties of the colonies, when the crown should have a civil list and support for a standing army from their money, independent of their assemblies. The assemblies, he thought, would soon cease to be called together. "No such thing is intended," replied Grenville warmly, addressing himself to the Americans. "I have pledged my word for offering the stamp bill to the House, and I cannot forego it: they will hear all objections, and do as they please. I wish you may preserve moderation in America. Resentments indecently expressed on one side of the water will naturally produce resentments on the other. You cannot hope to get any good by a controversy with the mother country. With respect to this bill, her ears will always be open to every remonstrance expressed in a becoming manner."

While the Americans in London were unwearied in offering objections to the stamp tax, Soame Jenyns, the oldest member of the Board of Trade, published authoritatively the views of his patrons. He mocked at the "absurdity" of Otis, and "the insolence" of New-York and Massachusetts.

"The arguments of America," said he, "mixed up with patriotic words, such as liberty, property,

CHAP. XI. 1765. Feb.

and Englishmen, are addressed to the more numerous part of mankind, who have ears but no understanding.

"The great capital argument, the elephant at the head of this nabob's army, is this: that no Englishman is or can be taxed but by his own consent, or the persons whom he has chosen to represent him. But this is the very reverse of truth; for no man that I know of is taxed by his own consent, least of all an Englishman. The unfortunate counties which produce cider were taxed without the consent of their representatives; and while every Englishman is taxed, not one in twenty is represented. Are not the people of Manchester and Birmingham Englishmen? And are they not taxed?

"If every Englishman is represented in parliament, why does not this imaginary representation extend to America? If it can travel three hundred miles, why not three thousand? If it can jump over rivers and mountains, why cannot it sail over the ocean? If Manchester and Birmingham are there represented, why not Albany and Boston? Are they not Englishmen?

"But it is urged, if the privilege of being taxed by the legislative power within itself alone is once given up, that liberty, which every Englishman has a right to, is torn from them; they are all slaves, and all is lost. But the liberty of an Englishman cannot mean an exemption from taxes imposed by the authority of the parliament of Great Britain. No charters grant such a privilege to any colony in America; and had they granted it, the grant could have had no force: no charter derived from the crown can possibly supersede the right of the whole legislature. The charters of the colonies are no more than those of all corporations. They can no more plead an exemption from parliamentary authority than any other corporation in England.

"If it be said, that though parliament may have power to impose taxes on the colonies, they have no right to use it, I shall only make this short reply: that if parliament can impose no taxes but what are equitable—and the persons taxed are to be the judges of that equity, they will in effect have no power to lay any tax at all.

"And can any time be more proper to require some assistance from our colonies than when this country is almost undone by procuring their present safety? Can any time be more proper to impose some tax on their trade, than when they are enabled to rival us in their manufactures by the protection we have given them? Can any time be more proper to oblige them to settle handsome incomes on their governors, than when we find them unable to procure a subsistence on any other terms than those of breaking all their instructions? Can there be a more proper time to compel them to fix certain salaries on their judges, than when we see them so dependent on the humors of their assemblies that they can obtain a livelihood no longer than during their bad behavior? Can there be a more proper time to force them to maintain an army at their expense, than when that army is necessary for their own protection, and we are utterly unable to support it? Lastly; can there be a more proper time for this mother country to leave off feeding out of her own vitals these children whom she has nursed up, than when they are arrived at such strength and maturity as to be well able to

CHAP. XI. provide for themselves, and ought rather with filial duty to give some assistance to her distress?

1765. Feb. "If parliament has a right to tax the colonies, why should this right be exercised with more delicacy in America than it has ever been even in Great Britain itself?

"One method, indeed, has been hinted at, and but one, that might render the exercise of this power in a British parliament just and legal, which is the introduction of representatives from the several colonies into that body. But I have lately seen so many specimens of the great powers of speech of which these American gentlemen are possessed, that I should be afraid the sudden importation of so much eloquence at once would endanger the safety of England. It will be much cheaper for us to pay their army than their orators.

"The right of the legislature of Great Britain to impose taxes on her colonies, and not only the expediency but the absolute necessity of exercising that right, have been so clearly, though concisely, proved, that it is to be hoped all parties and factions, all connections, every member of the British parliament, will most cordially unite to support this measure, which every man who has any property or common sense must approve, and which every English subject ought to require of an English administration."

Thus did the old subordinate of Halifax with supercilious frankness publish the views which the majority of the cabinet and Charles Townshend boldly advocated, and which Grenville dared not openly resist and could never heartily approve.

While his colleagues in the ministry scoffed at the

CHAP. XI. 1765. Feb.

idea of an American representation, he was resolved on proposing it indirectly through his subordinate Jackson; and he refused to take part in raising the army in America above the civil power.[1] But the two branches of the ministry pursued their course, independent of each other, and without discord.

A dispute had arisen in West Florida between the fiery and half frantic governor, Johnstone[2], and the commanding officer. Johnstone insisted on the subordination of the military. The occasion was seized to proclaim its supremacy in America. The continent was divided into a northern and southern district, each with its brigadier, beside a commander-in chief for the whole; and on the morning of Wednesday, the sixth of February, Welbore Ellis,[3] Secretary of War, who, at the request of Halifax, had taken the king's pleasure on the subject, made known his intention, "that the orders of his commander-in-chief, and under him of the brigadiers general commanding in the northern and southern departments, in all military matters, should be supreme, and be obeyed by the troops as such in all the civil governments of America." In the absence, and only in the absence, of the general and of the brigadiers, the civil governor might give the word. And these instructions, which concentrated undefined power in the hands of the Commander-in-Chief, rested, as was pretended, on the words of the commission which Hardwicke had prepared for governing the troops in time of war.

[1] Compare Grenville's speech in the debate of 25 April, 1770, in Cavendish, i. 551; also the first editions of Pownall's Administration of the Colonies oppose the keeping up a military force; and these editions were but a ministerial pamphlet.

[2] State Paper Office. America and West Indies, ccxxiv.

[3] Ellis to Halifax, War Office, 7 Feb. 1765. A. and W. I. 251. Halifax to the Governor of East Florida, 9 Feb. 1765.

CHAP. XI. 1765. Feb.

Such was the sad condition of America: the king, the ministry, the crown officers in the colony, all conspiring against her liberties, while she was overflowing with affection for the parent country. There was no help unless from parliament. For centuries that body had shone on the world as the star of freedom. Was it weary of its honors and willing to abdicate its guardianship of human liberty?

At a few hours later, on the same day with the interview of Welbore Ellis and the king, George Grenville, in the British House of Commons, proposed to the Committee of Ways and Means of the whole house, fifty-five resolutions, embracing the details of a stamp act for America, and making all offences against it cognizable in the Courts of Admiralty; so that the Americans were not only to be taxed by the British parliament, but to have the taxes collected arbitrarily under the decrees of British judges, without any trial by jury.

To prove the fitness of the tax, Grenville argued, that the colonies had a right to demand protection from parliament, and parliament, in return, a right to enforce a revenue from the colonies; that protection implied an army, an army must receive pay, and pay required taxes; that, on the peace, it was found necessary to maintain a body of ten thousand men, at a cost exceeding three hundred thousand pounds, most of which was a new expense; that the duties and taxes already imposed or designed would not yield more than one hundred thousand pounds; so that England would still have to advance two-thirds of the new expense; that it was reasonable for the colonies to contribute this one-third part of the expense necessary for their own security; that the debt of England

CHAP. XI. 1765. Feb.

was one hundred and forty millions sterling, of America but eight hundred thousand pounds; that the increase of annual taxes in England, within ten years, was three millions, while all the establishments of America, according to accounts which were produced, cost the Americans but seventy-five thousand pounds.[1]

The charters of the colonies were referred to, and Grenville interpreted their meaning. The clause under which a special exemption was claimed for Maryland was read, and he argued, that that province, upon a public emergency, is subject to taxation, in like manner with the rest of the colonies, or the sovereignty over it would cease; and, if it were otherwise, why is there a duty on its staple of tobacco? and why is it bound at present, by several acts affecting all America, and passed since the grant of its charter? Besides, all charters, he insisted, were under the control of the legislature.[2]

"The colonies claim, it is true," he continued, "the privilege which is common to all British subjects, of being taxed only with their own consent, given by their representatives, and may they ever enjoy the privilege in all its extent: may this sacred pledge of liberty be preserved inviolate to the utmost verge of our dominions, and to the latest pages of our history."[3] "But the remonstrances of the Americans," he insisted, "failed in the great point of the colonies not being represented in parliament."[4] It was the com-

[1] J. Ingersoll to Fitch, Feb. 11 and March 6. Letters of Israel Mauduit, Jasper Mauduit, and Garth, the last a member of parliament.

[2] Calvert to Sharpe, 9 Feb. 1765.

[3] Campbell's Regulations. Report of Grenville's Speech, in New-York Gaz., 16 May, 1765. 1167, 3, 1.

[4] Letters from London to a friend in Connecticut. Calvert to Lieut.-Gov. H. Sharpe, 9 Feb. 1765. Letter from a gentleman in London, to a gentleman in Charlestown, 8 Feb. 1765.

CHAP. XI. 1765. Feb.

mon council of the whole empire, and as such was as capable of imposing internal taxes as impost duties, or taxes on intercolonial trade, or laws of navigation.

The house was full, and all present seemed to acquiesce in silence. Yet Beckford, a member for London, a friend of Pitt, and himself a large owner of West India estates, without disputing the supreme authority of parliament, openly declared his opinion, that "taxing America for the sake of raising a revenue would never do."[1]

Jackson, who had concerted with Grenville to propose an American representation in parliament, spoke and voted against the resolutions.

"The parliament," he argued, "may choose whether they will tax America or not; they have a right to tax Ireland, yet do not exercise that right. Still stronger objections may be urged against their taxing America. Other ways of raising the moneys there requisite for the public service exist, and have not yet failed; but the colonies in general have with alacrity contributed to the common cause. It is hard all should suffer for the fault of two or three. Parliament is undoubtedly the universal, unlimited legislature of the British dominions; but it should voluntarily set bounds to the exercise of its power; and if the majority of parliament think they ought not to set these bounds, then they should give a share of the election of the legislature to the American colonies, otherwise the liberties of America, I do not say will be lost, but will be in danger; and they cannot be injured without danger to the liberties of Great Britain."[2]

[1] Cavendish Debates, i. 41.

[2] R. Jackson's Letter of 7 June, 1765, in Connecticut Gazette, of 9 Aug. 1765. Knox's Extra-official State Papers, ii. 31. R. Jackson to William Johnson, 5 April, 1774, and 30 November, 1784.

CHAP. XI. 1765. Feb.

Thus calmly reasoned Jackson. Grenville urged the house not to suffer themselves to be moved by resentment. One member, however, referred with asperity to the votes of New-York and Massachusetts, and the house generally seemed to hold that America was as virtually represented in parliament as the great majority of the inhabitants of Great Britain.

Isaac Barrē, the companion and friend of Wolfe, sharer of the dangers and glories of Louisburg and Quebec, seemed to admit the power of parliament to tax America,[1] yet derided the idea of virtual representation. "Who of you, reasoning upon this subject, feels warmly from the heart," he cried, putting his hand to his breast, "who of you feels for the Americans as you would for yourselves, or as you would for the people of your own native country?" and he taunted the house with its ignorance of American affairs, charging "those who should hold up their hands for the bill as acting very much in the dark;" "but, perhaps," he added, "as well in the dark as any way."

The charge of ignorance called upon his feet Charles Townshend, the reputed great master of American affairs. He confirmed the equity of the taxation, and insisted that the colonies had borne but a small proportion of the expenses of the last war, and had yet obtained by it immense advantages at a vast expense to the mother country.[2] "And now," said he, "will these American children, planted by our care, nourished up by our indulgence to a degree

[1] Jared Ingersoll's Correspondence.

[2] Massachusetts Gazette of 9 May, 1765.

CHAP. XI. 1765. Feb.

of strength and opulence, and protected by our arms, grudge to contribute their mite to relieve us from the heavy burden under which we lie?"[1]

As he sat down, Barrē rose, and with eyes darting fire and outstretched arm, uttered an unpremeditated reply:

"*They planted by* YOUR *care!* No; your oppressions planted them in America. They fled from your tyranny to a then uncultivated, unhospitable country; where they exposed themselves to almost all the hardships to which human nature is liable; and among others to the cruelties of a savage foe, the most subtle, and I will take upon me to say, the most formidable of any people upon the face of God's earth; and yet, actuated by principles of true English liberty, they met all hardships with pleasure, compared with those they suffered in their own country, from the hands of those who should have been their friends. *They nourished up by* YOUR *indulgence!* They grew by your neglect of them. As soon as you began to care about them, that care was exercised in sending persons to rule them in one department and another, who were, perhaps, the deputies of deputies to some members of this house, sent to spy out their liberties, to misrepresent their actions, and to prey upon them; men whose behavior on many occasions has caused the blood of those SONS OF LIBERTY to recoil within them; men promoted to the highest seats of justice, some who, to my knowledge, were glad, by going to a foreign country, to escape being brought to the bar of a court of justice in their own. *They protected by*

[1] Parliamentary History, xv. 38, and Adolphus, i. 71, erroneously attribute this speech to Grenville.

YOUR *arms!* They have nobly taken up arms in your defence; have exerted a valor amidst their constant and laborious industry, for the defence of a country whose frontier was drenched in blood, while its interior parts yielded all its little savings to your emolument. And believe me—remember I this day told you so—the same spirit of freedom which actuated that people at first will accompany them still. But prudence forbids me to explain myself further. God knows I do not at this time speak from motives of party heat; what I deliver are the genuine sentiments of my heart. However superior to me in general knowledge and experience the respectable body of this house may be, yet I claim to know more of America than most of you, having seen and been conversant in that country. The people, I believe, are as truly loyal as any subjects the king has; but a people jealous of their liberties, and who will vindicate them, if ever they should be violated. But the subject is too delicate; I will say no more."

As Barré spoke, there sat in the gallery Ingersoll, of Connecticut, a semi-royalist, yet joint agent for Connecticut. Delighted with the speech, he made a report of it, which the next packet carried across the Atlantic. The lazy posts of that day brought it in nearly three months to New London, in Connecticut, and it was printed in the newspapers of that village. May had not shed its blossoms, before the words of Barré were as household words in every New England town. Midsummer saw it distributed through Canada, in French; and the continent rung from end to end with the cheering name of the SONS OF LIBERTY. But at St. Stephen's, the members only observed that Townshend had received a heavy blow, and the rest

CHAP. XI. 1765. Feb.

of the debate seemed languid. The opponents of the measure dared not risk a division on the merits of the question, but, about midnight, after a debate of seven hours, Beckford moved an adjournment, which Sir William Meredith seconded; and, with all the aid of those interested in West Indian estates, it was carried against America, by two hundred and forty-five to forty-nine. Conway and Beckford alone were said to have denied the power of Parliament; and it is doubtful how far it was questioned even by them.

Even while this debate was proceeding, faith in the continuance of English liberty was conquering friends for England, and advancing her banners into new regions. The people of Louisiana, impatient of being transferred from France to Spain, longed to come over to the English side—save only a band of poor Acadians, two hundred in number, wanderers of ten years, doomed ever to disappointment. Hearing of one open territory, where the flag they loved still waved, they came through St. Domingo to New Orleans, pining away of want and wretchedness. Touched with compassion at the sight, Aubry at first assigned them homes on the right bank of the Mississippi, near New Orleans; but there the lands were flooded at high water, so that levees would have been needed They were, therefore, encouraged to go to the Attacapas, about forty-five leagues west of the river, where they became herdsmen. But for the charity of the French governor, they must all have perished.[1]

No sentiment of attachment for England, could rise in the breast of the Acadians; but, for many

[1] Gayarré Hist. de la Louisiane, ii. 131. Aubry au ministre. Nouvelle Orléans, 1er Mars, 1765, & 16 Mai, 1765.

CHAP. XI. 1765. Feb.

years, the French of New Orleans would gladly have exchanged the dominion of Spain for a dependency on England. The Americans, too, were every where intent on extending the boundaries of the English empire. A plan was formed to connect Mobile and Illinois.[1] Officers from West Florida reached Fort Chartres,[2] preparatory to taking possession of the country, which was still delayed by the discontent of the Indians. With the same object, Croghan and a party descended the Ohio from Pittsburg. The governor of North Carolina believed that, by pushing trade up the Missouri, a way to the great Western ocean would be discovered, and an open trade to it be established.[3] So wide was the territory—so vast the interests for which the British Parliament was legislating!

On the day after the debate on American affairs, Grenville, Lord North, and Jenkinson, with others, were ordered to bring in a Stamp-bill for America, which on the thirteenth was introduced by Grenville himself, and read the first time without a syllable of debate.[4] Among the papers that were to be stamped, it contained an enumeration of the several instruments of ecclesiastical law used in the courts of episcopal jurisdiction; for Grenville reasoned, that one day such courts might be established in America.[5] On the fifteenth of February, merchants trading to Jamaica presented a petition against it,

[1] Gov. Johnstone to Sec. of State, Mobile, 12 Dec. 1764; 7 Jan. 1765; 9 Feb. 1765.

[2] Lieut. Ross to Major Farmar, Fort Chartres, 21 Feb. 1765.

[3] Dobbs to Halifax, 26 Feb. 1765.

[4] Journals of the House of Commons. Letter to New-York of 16 Feb. 1765, in Boston Gazette of 3 June, 1765.

[5] F. Maseres, 25, 26.

CHAP. XI. 1765. Feb.

and prayed to be heard by counsel. "No counsellor of this kingdom," said Fuller, formerly chief justice of Jamaica, "would come to the bar of this house, and question its authority to tax America. Were he to do so, he would not remain there long." It was the rule of the house "to receive no petition against a money bill;" and the petition was withdrawn.[1]

Next, Sir William Meredith, rising in behalf of Virginia, presented a paper, in which Montague, its agent, interweaving expressions from the votes of the Assembly of the Old Dominion, prayed that its House of Burgesses might be continued in the possession of the rights and privileges they had so long and uninterruptedly enjoyed, and might be heard. Against this, too, the same objection existed. But Virginia found an advocate in the amiable Conway—a man always anxious to do right, of a cold temperament and little vigor of will, yet so warmed to opposition by indignation at his recent dismissal from the army, that as he rose in the House of Commons in opposition to Grenville, his cheeks were flushed, and he was tremulous with anger.[2]

"Shall we shut our ears," he argued, "against the representations which have come from the colonies, and for receiving which we, with an affectation of candor, allotted sufficient time? For my own part, I must declare myself just as much in the dark as I was the last year. My way of life does not engage me in intercourse with commercial gentlemen, or those who have any knowledge of the colonies. I declare, upon my honor, I expected, as a member sitting in this

[1] Jared Ingersoll's Letters on the Stamp Act, 1765, 21–30.

[2] Journals of the House. J. Ingersoll to the General Assembly convened by special order at Hartford, 19 Sept. 1765.

CHAP. XI. 1765. Feb.

house, in consequence of the notice given, to receive from the colonies information by which my judgment might be directed and my conduct regulated. The question regards two millions of unrepresented people. The light which I desire, the colonists themselves alone can give. The practice of receiving no petitions against money bills is but one of convenience, from which, in this instance, if in no other, we ought to vary. For from whom, unless from themselves, are we tc learn the circumstances of the colonies, and the fatal consequences that may follow the imposing of this tax? None of them are represented in parliament. Gentlemen cannot be serious when they insist even on their being virtually represented. Will any man in this house get up and say, he is one of the representatives of the colonies?"

"The Commons," said Gilbert Elliot, "have maintained against the crown and against the Lords their right of solely voting money without the control of either, any otherwise than by a negative; and will you suffer your colonies to impede the exercise of those rights, untouched as they now are by the other branches of the legislature?"[1]

"This," retorted Conway," is the strangest argument I ever heard. Can there be a more declared avowal of your power than a petition submitting this case to your wisdom, and praying to be heard before your tribunal against a tax that will affect them in their privileges, which you at least have suffered, and in their property, which they have acquired under your protection? From a principle of lenity, of policy, and of justice, I am for receiving the petition

[1] Letter from London, of 16 Feb. 1765, in New-York Gazette 1169, 2, 3, of 3? May, 1765.

CHAP. XI. 1765. Feb.

of a people from whom this country derives its greatest commerce, wealth, and consideration."[1]

In reply, Charles Yorke entered into a very long and most elaborate defence of the bill, resting his argument on the supreme and sovereign authority of parliament. The colonies, he insisted, with a vast display of legal erudition, were but corporations; their power of legislation was but the power of making by-laws, subject to parliamentary control. Their charters could not convey the legislative power of Great Britain, because the prerogative could not grant that power. The charters of the proprietary governments were but the king's standing commissions: the proprietaries were but his hereditary governors. The people of America could not be taken out of the general and supreme jurisdiction of parliament.

The authority of Yorke seemed conclusive: less than forty were willing to receive the petition of Virginia. A third from South Carolina, a fourth from Connecticut, though expressed in the most moderate language; a fifth from Massachusetts, though silent even about the question of "right," all shared the same refusal.[2] That from New-York no one could be prevailed upon to offer.[3] That from Rhode Island, offered by Sherwood, its faithful agent, claimed by their charter, under a royal promise, equal rights with their fellow-subjects in great Britain; and insisted that the colony had faithfully kept their part of the compact; but it was as little heeded as the rest. The House of

[1] Letter from London to New-York, 16 Feb. 1765, in Boston Gazette of 3 June.

[2] J. Mauduit's letter, 19 Feb. 1765. Journals of the House.

[3] Ingersoll's Letters, 21. Letter of Charles, the agent for New-York, to the New-York Committee, 9 Feb. 1765. MS. Memorandum of Geo. Chalmers.

CHAP. XI. 1765. Feb.

Commons would neither receive petitions nor hear counsel.

All the efforts of the agents of the colonies were fruitless. Within doors less resistance was made to the act than to a common turnpike bill.[1] "We might," said Franklin, "as well have hindered the sun's setting." The tide against the Americans was irresistible. "We have power to tax them," said one of the ministry, "and we will tax them."[2] "The nation was provoked by American claims of independence (of parliament), and all parties joined in resolving by this act tc settle the point."[3]

On the twenty-seventh of February, the Stamp Act passed the House of Commons. Rockingham had freely expressed his opinion at Sir George Saville's as to the manner in which the colonies could best resist it.[4] In public he was silent. Lord Temple[5] had much private conversation with Lord Lyttelton on the subject; and both approved the principle of the measure, and the right asserted in it. Had there existed any doubt concerning that right, they were of opinion it should then be debated, before the honor of the legislature was engaged to its support. But on the eighth of March the bill was agreed to by the Lords without having encountered an amendment, debate, protest, division, or single dissentient vote. The royal assent was long waited for.

The king was too ill to ratify the act in person.

[1] Letter to New-York, 16 Feb. 765, in Boston Gazette of 3 June.

[2] Letter from London, of Oct. 1765, quoted in R. H. Lee's of 2 Feb. 1766.

[3] Franklin to Charles Thompson, MS.

[4] Letter from London, by William Bollan.

[5] Phillimore's Lyttelton, ii. 690.

CHAP. XI. 1765. Mar.

The character of his disease was concealed; it was believed that the malady was "no trifling one;"[1] that he was "very seriously ill, and in great danger."[2] At one time pains were taken "to secrete him from all intercourse with his court." His physician hinted the propriety of his retiring "to one of his palaces in the country."[3] To a few only was the nature of his illness known. Be every sentiment of anger towards the king absorbed in pity. At the moment of passing the Stamp Act, George the Third was crazed.[4] So, on the twenty-second of March, it received the royal assent by a commission. The sovereign of Great Britain, whose soul was wholly bent on exalting the prerogative, taught the world that a bit of parchment bearing the sign of his hand, scrawled in the flickering light of clouded reason, could, under the British constitution, do the full legislative office of the king. Had he been a private man, his commission could have given validity to no instrument whatever.

It was Grenville's purpose to exercise the assumed right of taxing the colonies with great tenderness; supposing it "prudent to begin with small duties and taxes, and to advance in proportion as it should be found the colonies would bear." For the present he attempted nothing more than to increase the revenue from the colonial post-office by reducing the rate of postage in America.[5]

Lord Chesterfield, 22 April.

[2] Walpole to Hertford, 26 March, 1765.

[3] Walpole's George III., 83.

[4] Adolphus's History of England, i. 175. London Quarterly Review for June, 1840.

[5] Hutchinson to a friend, 9 April, 1765: "I have a letter from a member of parliament, who, although

CHAP XI. 1765. Mar.

There he paused. His colleagues desired to extend the Mutiny Act to America, with power to billet troops on private houses. Clauses for that purpose, drafted by Robertson, the Deputy Quartermaster General,[1] were sent home by Gage, and recommended strongly to be enacted.[2] They had neither the entire conviction nor the cordial support of Grenville;[3] so that they were referred by Halifax[4] to Welbore Ellis, the Secretary at War, by whom they were introduced and carried through. In their progress, provincial barracks, inns, alehouses, barns, and empty houses were substituted by the merchants and agents for private houses; but there remained the clause to compel the colonies to furnish the troops, at the expense of the colony, with fire, candles, vinegar, salt, bedding, utensils for cooking, beer, or cider, or rum; and the sums needed for the purpose were "required to be raised in such manner as the public charges for the province are raised."[5] Thus the bill contained, what had never before been heard of, a parliamentary requisition on the colonies; it enjoined things "different from the general principles of the constitution," and passed without at-

he says this right of taxing the colonies is to be exercised with great tenderness, yet, in another place, supposes it prudent to begin with small duties and taxes, and to advance in proportion or degree as it shall be found the colonies will bear." This is excellent authority. Take, also, Calvert to Sharpe: "Last year the first stone was laid, this year another, and will be succeeded by every ministerial builder, until the whole American structure of their folly is, by the mother country, completed on them." "The Commons was full, but not a member against taxation of them, nor an advocate that could or did offer a better lenitive scheme."

[1] Lieut. Col. Robertson's Memorial, and Regulations proposed to be made in the Mutiny Act.

[2] Gage to Halifax, 23 January, 1765.

[3] Shelburne to Chatham, 1767, in Chatham Correspondence, iii. 192 and 208.

[4] Endorsement on the Memorial, and on the Regulations.

[5] 5 Geo. III. c. xxxiii. § 8.

CHAP. XI. tentive examination[1] on the part of the government.

1765. April.

To soothe America, bounties[2] were at the same time granted on the importation of deals, planks, boards, and timber from the plantations. Coffee of their growth was exempted from an additional duty; their iron might be borne to Ireland; their lumber to Ireland, Madeira, the Azores, and Europe, south of Cape Finisterre; the prohibition on exporting their bar iron from England was removed; the rice of North Carolina was as much liberated as that of South Carolina; and rice might be warehoused in England for re-exportation without advancing the duties. In executing the Stamp Act, it was further provided, that the revenue to be derived from it should not be remitted to England, but constitute a part of the sum to be expended in America.[3]

Grenville also resolved to select the stamp officers for America from among the Americans themselves; and the friends and agents of the colonies were invited to make the nominations; and they did so, Franklin[4] among the rest.

"You tell me," said the minister, "you are poor, and unable to bear the tax; others tell me you are able. Now, take the business into your own hands; you will see how and where it pinches, and will certainly let us know it; in which case it shall be eased."[5]

[1] Shelburne to Chatham, in Chatham Corr. iii. 208.

[2] 5 Geo. III. c. xlv. C. Jenkinson to Secretary Pownall, 19 March, 1765.

[3] T. Whately to Commissioners of Stamps, 20 April, 1765. Treasury minute, 26 April, 1765.

[4] Franklin to Dean Tucker, 26 Feb. 1774. Tucker to Franklin.

[5] Ingersoll to Assembly of Connecticut, Sept. 1765.

CHAP. XI. 1765. April.

Every agent in England believed the stamp tax would be peacefully levied.[1] Not one "imagined the colonies would think of disputing the matter with parliament at the point of the sword." "It is our duty to submit," had been the words of Otis.[2] "We yield obedience to the act granting duties,"[3] had been uttered solemnly by the legislature of Massachusetts. "If parliament, in their superior wisdom, shall pass the act, we must submit," wrote Fitch, the governor[4] of Connecticut, elected by the people, to Jackson. "It can be of no purpose to claim a right of exemption," thought Hutchinson. "It will fall particularly hard on us lawyers and printers," wrote Franklin[5] to a friend in Philadelphia, never doubting it would go into effect, and looking for relief to the rapid increase of the people of America.

The agent for Massachusetts had recommended the tax. Knox,[6] the agent for Georgia, wrote publicly in its favor. The honest but eccentric Thomas Pownall, who had been so much in the colonies, and really had an affection for them, congratulated Grenville in advance, "on the good effects he would see derived to Great Britain and to the colonies from his firmness and candor in conducting the American business."[7]

Still less did the statesmen of England doubt the result. No tax was ever laid with more general approbation.[8] The act seemed sure to enforce itself.

[1] Grenville's Speech, 5 March, 1770, in Cavendish, i. 494.

[2] Otis's Rights of the Colonies, 40.

[3] Answer of the Council and House, 3 Nov. 1764.

[4] Governor Thomas Fitch to Richard Jackson. Norwalk, 23 Feb. 1765.

[5] Franklin to Ross, 14 Feb. 1765.

[6] The Claim of the Colonies to Exemption from Taxes Imposed by Parliament Examined, 1765.

[7] Pownall's Dedication to George Grenville of the second edition of his Administration of the Colonies.

[8] Considerations, &c., 109.

CHAP. XI. 1765. April. Unless stamps were used, marriages would be null, notes of hand valueless, ships at sea prizes to the first captors, suits at law impossible, transfers of real estate invalid, inheritances irreclaimable. Of all who acted with Grenville in the government, he never heard one prophesy that the tax would be resisted.[1] "He did not foresee the opposition to the measure, and would have staked his life for obedience."[2]

[1] Grenville's Speech of 26 Jan. 1769, in Cavendish, i. 202.

[2] Grenville's Speech, 5 March, 1770, in Cavendish, i. 496.

CHAPTER XII.

THE MINISTRY OFFEND THE KING AS WELL AS THE COLONIES—ADMINISTRATION OF GRENVILLE CONTINUED.

April—May, 1765.

CHAP. XII. 1765. April.

Events within the palace delayed the conflict with America. The king, in his zeal to give the law to his ministers and to govern as well as reign, lost his opportunity of enforcing the stamp act. No sooner had he recovered from the illness, of which the true nature was kept secret even from the members of his cabinet, than, bearing in mind that the heir to the throne was an infant of but two years old, he fearlessly contemplated the contingency of his own incapacity or death; and though his nerves were still tremulous from mental disease, he, with the aid of Lord Holland, framed a plan for a regency.

The manifest want. of confidence in his ministers roused their jealousy, and when they received his orders to prepare a bill for carrying his design into effect, they thought to fix in the public mind their hostility to Bute and win popularity by disqualifying the princess dowager. To this end, in the choice of the regent, the king was to be "restrained to the queen or any other person of the royal family." He approved the minute entirely, not knowing that, in the opinion of Bedford, Grenville, Halifax and Sandwich, his own

CHAP. XII. 1765. April. family did not include his mother. At the request of the duke of Cumberland, the king, again without consulting his four ministers, gave directions, that his uncle and his brothers, five in all, should be specially designated as fixed members of the council. This they refused to approve; and yielded to his wishes only on condition that he should renounce the priv ilege which he had reserved of appointing four others To Grenville he refused this concession; but afterwards accepted it in concert with Northington.

Grenville had certainly just cause of complaint, and on Sunday, the twenty-eighth of April, "with a firm and steady countenance," and at very great length, he expostulated with the king on his withholding confidence from his ministers. The king at first started and professed surprise; and as the conversation proceeded, grew "exceedingly agitated and disturbed, changed countenance, and flushed so much that the water stood in his eyes from the excessive heat of his face;" but he neither denied nor admitted the charge; used no words of anger, of excuse, or of softening; and only put on a smile, when, at a "late hour," the tedious minister "made his bow."

The bill for the regency was committed to Halifax, to be presented to the House of Lords. On the May. second reading, they consented, by a large majority, to leave to the king the naming of the regent. "But who are the royal family to whom the selection is restrained?" asked the duke of Richmond, in the debate of the first of May. "Does it include the princess Amelia and the princess dowager?" Talbot, one of the king's friends, answered, that it included both, and such was the opinion of the chancellor. "The royal family are those who are in the order of succession, one after another," answered Bedford, unmasking the malice in which the bill had been conceived. Richmond wished that, in the doubt, the judges should be consulted. On this, Sandwich moved the adjournment.

The king, who had never intended to appoint his mother, was anxious to save her name from disagreeable discussion in parliament. When, therefore, he received the report of the occurrence, Halifax was authorized to use words whose meaning would admit of no dispute. But before he could deliver his message, Richmond proposed to include among those eligible to the regency, "the princess dowager, and others descended from the late king." The motion was rejected by the ministers; after which Halifax, using the king's authority, renewed the same motion, except that he omitted the princess dowager. In this way the bill passed the House of Lords. The ministry had not intended so much; they had circumvented the king, and used his name to put a brand upon his mother. Bute's friends were thunderstruck, while the duke of Bedford almost danced for joy.

May 2.

The king's natural affection was very strong; he suffered the utmost agitation, even to tears; and declared that Halifax "had surprised him into the message." When on the fifth of May, he admitted Grenville, he colored with great emotion, complained of the mark of disregard shown to his mother as an offence to her which he could not bear; and with the embarrassment of a man who begs a favor which he fears may be denied, entreated its removal. Grenville obstinately refused himself to make the neces-

May 5.

CHAP. XII. 1765. May.

sary motion; but true to his character as the man of compromises, always wishing to please everybody and always balancing one thing against another, he consented with no good grace that the name of the princess dowager should be inserted in the House of Commons by one of her own servants. This was done, and he advocated the alteration in a speech, which, however, seemed chiefly designed to shield the ministry from the charge of inconsistency.

"If Lord Halifax is even reprieved," it was said, "the king is more enslaved to a cabal than ever his grandfather was." The ministers believed themselves strong enough to compel their sovereign to conform in all things to their advice. Bedford, therefore, in defiance, tried the experiment of mentioning to him his suspicions, that Bute had been "operating mischief to overthrow the government." Grenville also was earnest that the king's ministers should be suffered to retire, or be seen manifestly to possess his favor. But they got no satisfactory answer; though Grenville was led to believe his own services indispensable, and admitted into his mind the pleasing delusion, that they would be required, even should his old enemy, the duke of Bedford, be dismissed. On the thirteenth of May, the king, in his impatience of ministers, who did not love each other and only agreed to give him the law, invoked the aid of his uncle, the duke of Cumberland, and authorized negotiations with Pitt, with Temple, and the great Whig families, for constructing a new administration, in which Charles Townshend should be one of the secretaries of state, and Northumberland, Bute's son-in-law, at the head of the treasury.

On that same day the regency bill, with the amendment, rehabilitating the princess dowager, was accepted by the House of Lords. It so happened, that in the same sitting a bill came up, raising the duties on silks, for the benefit of English weavers. In the Commons it had been countenanced by Grenville, who was always the friend of the protective policy; and it had the approval of the king. But Bedford having, like Edmund Burke, caught the more liberal views of political economy which were then beginning to prevail, especially in France and in Scotland, spoke on the side of freedom of trade; and the bill was refused a second reading. CHAP. XII. 1765. May 13.

The silk weavers were exasperated; professing to believe that Bedford had been bought by the French. On Tuesday they went in a large body to Richmond 14. to petition the king for redress. Cumberland, at that time, was explaining his commission to Rockingham and Newcastle, both of whom were zealous for the proposed change. The Earl of Albemarle, therefore, communicated, in his name, with Pitt, who terminated a conversation of four hours without an engagement, yet without a negative. Edmund Burke, as he watched the negotiation, complained of Pitt's hesitancy, and derided his "fustian."

Temple and Grafton were summoned to town. Of Grafton, Cumberland asked, if a ministry could be formed out of the minority, without Pitt; and received for answer, that "nothing so formed could be stable." "The wings of popularity were on Pitt's shoulders."

Lord Temple, who had not one personal quality 15. that fitted him to become a minister, but derived all

CHAP. XII. 1765. May 15. his importance from his rank and wealth, some popularity and his connection with Pitt, already began to be estranged from his brother-in-law, whom he envied and disliked, and reconciled to Grenville, his brother and apparent heir, whom he was now well pleased to see in office. His mind, like Bedford's, was haunted with the spectre of Bute's influence, and the whim seized him to gratify his capricious resentment to the utmost, and show his importance by creating embarrassments. He scouted the idea of placing at the head of the Treasury a man like Northumberland, whom he looked upon as Bute's lieutenant; while in his heart he was resolved to prevent the dismissal of his brother. Yet, at Cumberland's request, he agreed to hold a consultation with Pitt.

This happened on Wednesday, when the king, on his way to accept the act for a regency, found himself followed by a crowd of weavers, who beset the House of Parliament. They piqued themselves on showing him respect; but they vowed vengeance against Bedford, whom they insulted, and stoned in his chariot, so that he narrowly escaped with his life.

16. The next day, while Temple, avoiding every pledge on his own part, was concerting with Pitt preliminary questions, the mob of weavers paraded the streets of London. Bedford himself repaired with complaints to the king, and Grenville also remonstrated; but the king's emotion and disorder betrayed his settled purpose of changing the government.

The ministry had never been, and was not then, a thoroughly united body: Grenville, whom the king had originally chosen as a counterpoise to Bedford,

May 16.

transacted the business; but the secretaries of state claimed equal power, as in the months of the triumvirate; in the language of Woburn, Bedford was minister; and, in point of fact, the ministers were four. Now, however, Bedford took the undisputed lead, insisting that they all should act in perfect union; and Grenville, concealing his deep distrust of his colleagues, gave and received promises to withstand the court with inseparable fidelity.

17. On Friday, Albemarle repaired once more to Pitt, but met no success. In London, the weavers, threatening death to the duke of Bedford, assembled in the evening round his house, which they might have sacked and destroyed but for the timely presence of an armed force. The town was in commotion, and persons of all parties hastened to Bedford House to mark their abhorrence of the riot and their joy at its suppression. The dismissing Bedford at such a moment had the aspect of inviting the mob to dictate a new ministry. Public sympathy turned on the side of the duke. "To attempt changing the government," said Lord Mansfield, "is madness, infatuation, and utter ruin to the king's authority forever."

18. But the king had all the impatience of offended pride, excited by sleeplessness and nervous disease. Having received the report of the questions concerted between Pitt and Temple, he said to the duke of Cumberland, on Saturday, in the kindest terms and most explicit words: "I put myself wholly in this affair into your hands."

Early, therefore, on Sunday, the nineteenth of May, the prince hastened to visit Pitt, inviting Temple to join them at a later hour. His journey was a

CHAP. XII. 1765. May 19.

public proclamation of the king's purpose. While the royal envoy was negotiating with the Great Commoner at Hayes, Grenville, Bedford, Halifax, and Sandwich, confident that no new ministry could be formed, each by himself, went in to the king. Grenville insisted upon receiving orders relating to the change of government. "I would have you adjourn the Parliament till Monday fortnight," said the king. "I cannot do it," answered Grenville. "I trust you will put nothing upon me that is disgraceful and dishonorable. Parliament must be adjourned by the man whom your Majesty destines to be my successor."

The duke of Bedford went in next. He spoke of his personal relations from the moment of his consenting to go into France to make the peace; his resolution on his return to live in quiet retirement. He had yielded to the king's earnest solicitations to enter into the ministry; but only on the promise that Lord Bute should not be consulted on any matter. Having reminded the king "how very unfaithfully the conditions proposed by himself had been kept," he proceeded to sketch the character of the favorite, as of one who was at once very ambitious and altogether incompetent to conduct business. "For me," he continued, "I have served you well. All Europe is witness to the strength which your present ministers have restored to your authority, that was tottering under that of my adversary. The opposition is every day becoming more and more feeble. But since I can no longer be useful, I entreat you not to lose a moment in replacing us all, for the harmony which has subsisted between us does and will continue." Here the king interposed to say, "It is not yet time." Bedford intimated that the mob had been instigated to attack him by Lord Bute; for he saw the hand of Bute in every thing that he disliked. "Believe no such thing," said the king. "I shall give every order necessary for your safety." "Sir," said Bedford, "I believe it; for your honor is pledged to do so, and your authority is already but too deeply wounded by the daily attacks on one of your ministers, and a peer of the realm, for having given his opinion in parliament."

"Thus," says the duke, "I left him." Bedford was blunt, as suited his open nature, warm as one who felt himself wronged, excited, as the bravest man might have been, after the risk of having his house torn down about his family. Unabashed, he meant to be plain-spoken, but not to be insolent, and, if he had been so, he did not know it. He was more independent than his royal master. The latter must have a ministry; the former was under no necessity of being of it. He went about, vowing vengeance on the courtiers who had exposed him to such unworthy treatment, and resolved to remain in power in spite of the king. "I can depend," said he, "on all my friends as well as colleagues. There have been examples of new ministries that have not been able to last more than four-and-twenty hours."

Meantime, the royal envoy at Hayes was making the Great Commoner every offer. "I am ready to go to St. James's," said Pitt, "if I can carry the constitution along with me." Since his health was no longer equal to the post of secretary of state, he might select any station. For measures, he might balance the Bourbon alliance by any alliance that he should

CHAP. XII. 1765. May 19. judge the most valid, and direct the foreign course of England at his pleasure. His views of the course to be pursued at home implied the condemnation of general warrants, a peerage for Pratt, and the restoration of Conway and other officers, dismissed for their opinions. "The terms," said Cumberland, "are perfectly just, and must be agreed to." For the treasury Temple was declared acceptable. "Chalk out a list of such as you would wish to fill all the posts of business," thus Cumberland earnestly entreated him, "and I answer for it, the king will instantly adopt it." And it is certain, that in the conduct of this negotiation no obstacle arose from the palace. But the wayward Temple had taken part in the interview. "I did not want inducements," said he, "to accept of the great post that presented itself as a supplicant at my gate;" but, in his excessive jealousy of Bute, and his newly revived affection for his brother, he refused to royalty the small alms which it begged; and without the concurrence of Temple, Pitt could not overcome his own well-founded scruples.

20. The ministry now set no bounds to their arrogance; and resolved to brave and overcome the still obstinate resistance from the king. Exaggerating the danger from the continuance of the riots, Halifax, on Monday, obeying Bedford's directions about the disposition of the troops, wrote to the king to appoint the Marquis of Granby, their partisan, to the command in chief, insinuating against Cumberland the old and just charge of cruelty and want of popularity; while the king himself, in violation of the constitution, privately ordered Cumberland to act as captain-general. Meantime, the House of Lords

warmly took up the cause of the ministers; they cheered Halifax as he declared, that he who should dare to advise the king to dismiss Bedford, would be the detestation of every honest man in the nation and be held in abomination for ever; and under strong excitement, making Bedford's persecution their own, they voted unanimously an address to the king for a proclamation against the riots. CHAP. XII. 1765. May 20.

The king, nevertheless, sent once more a messenger to Pitt; but he perceived that the moment was not propitious to his return to power, since the old ministers were turned out for no other reason than insisting that the employments and councils of state should not be separated.

One last effort was made to form an administration, with Lyttelton at the head of the treasury, and Charles Townshend as chancellor of the exchequer. But Lyttelton was too conscious of his weakness, to listen to the offer; and Townshend, laughing it to scorn, reserved himself for the paymaster's place, which, two days after, he accepted.

On Tuesday, the twenty-first, the king was in despair; and, though the old ministry was sustained by parliament, and at that moment by public opinion, he would yet have put "in their places any mortal who could have carried on business." Cumberland hated Grenville; but he knew no remedy, and advised his nephew to submit. 21.

The king next attempted to divide the ministers. "I had a design to change my government," said he to Grenville; "but it is over now." And then artfully referring to the differences that had existed between Grenville and other members of the cabinet,

CHAP. XII. 1765. May 21. he said, "You never have displeased me; I did not mean to have removed you; I know nothing that could induce me to do it;" and he sought to draw from him separately a positive promise to remain in his service. Grenville urged the necessity of consulting his colleagues; and met them for that purpose; but he had hardly begun the conference, before the king, who was in such a state of helpless restlessness, that for many days he had not slept two hours in twenty-four, sent for him again "to come to him that moment," showed great impatience on meeting him, and again pressed for his answer. Grenville, in the name of the rest, observed, that "before they should again undertake his affairs they must lay before him some questions." "Questions!" said he, abruptly; "conditions you mean, sir; what are they?"

22. On Wednesday Grenville, in behalf of the four, communicated to their sovereign the terms offered him for his capitulation. They were, that he should renew assurances against Bute's meddling in state affairs; that Mackenzie, Bute's brother, should be dismissed from his employment and place; that Lord Holland, the adviser of the plan for the regency bill, should meet with the same treatment; that Granby should be appointed commander-in-chief, to the exclusion of Cumberland; and that the ministers should settle the government in Ireland. Terms more humiliating could not have been devised.

23. On the next day Grenville called to receive the king's submission. Of the insult to be offered to his uncle he obtained a modification; and no one was made commander-in-chief. He agreed that Bute

should never, directly or indirectly, publicly or privately, have any thing to do with his business; he consented to dismiss Mackenzie from the administration of the affairs of Scotland, but not from the office of Privy Seal. Grenville was obstinate. "But," interposed the king, "he has my promise to continue in that employment for life; I passed to him my royal word," and, falling into great agitation, he went so far as to say, "I should disgrace myself, if I dismissed him." "In that case, sir," replied Grenville, "we must decline coming in." "No," said the king, "I have desired you to stay in my service; I see, I must yield; I do it for the good of my people. But if you force me to violate my royal word, you are responsible for it, not I." Thus the king gave way; but he was so deeply moved, that his physicians were ordered to attend him; his manner became gloomy and discontented; on the following Sunday, the usual drawing-room was omitted; and his mind was still so convulsed, that he did not even choose to take the sacrament.

This is the moment when the power of the British Oligarchy, under the revolution of 1688, was at its culminating point. The ministry esteemed itself, and, through itself, the power of parliament, more firmly established than ever. It had subdued the king, and imposed a system of taxes on America for the benefit of the British exchequer. The colonists could not export the chief products of their industry; neither sugar, nor tobacco, nor cotton, nor indigo, nor ginger, nor fustic, nor other dyeing woods; nor molasses, nor rice, with some exceptions; nor beaver, nor peltry, nor copper ore, nor pitch, nor

CHAP. XII. 1765. May. tar, nor turpentine, nor masts, nor yards, nor bowsprits, nor coffee, nor pimento, nor cocoa-nuts, nor whale-fins, nor raw silk, nor hides, nor skins, nor pot and pearl ashes, to any place but Great Britain, not even to Ireland. Nor might any foreign ship enter a colonial harbor. Salt might be imported from any place into New England, New York, Pennsylvania, and Quebec; wines might be imported from the Madeiras and the Azores, but were to pay a duty in American ports for the British exchequer; and victuals, horses, and servants might be brought from Ireland. In all other respects, Great Britain was not only the sole market for the products of America, but the only storehouse for its supplies.

Lest the colonists should multiply their flocks of sheep, and weave their own cloth, they might not use a ship, nor a boat, nor a carriage, nor even a pack-horse, to carry wool or any manufacture of which wool forms a part, across the line of one province to another. They could not land wool from the nearest islands, nor ferry it across a river, nor even ship it to England. A British sailor, finding himself in want of clothes in their harbors, might not buy there more than forty shillings' worth of woollens.

Where was there a house in the colonies that did not cherish, and did not possess the English Bible? And yet to print that Bible in British America would have been a piracy; and the Bible, though printed in German, and in a native savage dialect, was never printed there in English till the land became free.[1]

[1] Thomas, History of Printing, i. 304, 305, repeats only what he heard. Himself a collector, he does not profess ever to have seen a copy of the alleged American edition of the English Bible. Search has repeatedly been made for a copy, and always without success. Six or eight hundred Bibles in quarto could hardly have been printed, bound,

CHAP. XII. 1765. May.

That the country, which was the home of the beaver, might not manufacture its own hats, no man in the plantations could be a hatter, or a journeyman at that trade, unless he had served an apprenticeship of seven years. No hatter might employ a negro, or more than two apprentices. No American hat might be sent from one plantation to another, or be loaded upon any horse, cart, or carriage for conveyance.

America abounded in iron ores of the best quality, as well as in wood and coal; slitting mills, steel furnaces, and plating forges, to work with a tilt hammer, were prohibited in the colonies as "nuisances."

While free labor was debarred of its natural rights, the slave trade was encouraged with unrelenting eagerness; and in the year that had just expired, from Liverpool alone, seventy-nine ships had borne from Africa to the West Indies and the continent more than fifteen thousand three hundred negroes, two-thirds as many as the first colonists of Massachusetts.

And now taxation, direct and indirect, was added to colonial restrictions; and henceforward both were to go together. A duty was to be collected on foreign sugar, molasses, indigo, coffee, Madeira wine, imported directly into any of the plantations in America; also a duty on Portugal and Spanish wines, on Eastern silks, on Eastern calicoes, on foreign linen cloth, on French lawn, though imported directly from Great Britain; on British colonial coffee shipped from one

and sold in Boston, then a small town, undiscovered. Nor would they all have disappeared. The most complete catalogues of English Bibles enumerate no one with the imprint, which was said to have been copied. Till a copy of the pretended American edition is produced, no credit can be given to the second-hand story, which is moreover at variance with the statement of Dr. Chauncy, the minister of the first church of Boston, at the time of the pretended publication.

CHAP. XII. 1765. May. plantation to another. Nor was henceforward any part of the old subsidy to be drawn back on the export of foreign goods of Europe or the East Indies, except on the export of white calicoes and muslins, on which a still higher duty was to be exacted and retained. And stamp duties were to be paid throughout all the British American colonies, on and after the first day of the coming November.

These laws were to be enforced, not by the regular authorities only, but by naval and military officers, irresponsible to the civil power in the colonies. The penalties and forfeitures for breach of the revenue laws were to be decided in courts of vice-admiralty, without the interposition of a jury, by a single judge, who had no support whatever but from his share in the profits of his own condemnations.

Such was the system which Grenville had carried far towards its complete development. The bounties which he had introduced, and the appointment of Americans to offices under the stamp act, were to pacify complaints; and that nothing might be wanting to produce contentment, pamphlets were sent over with the acts, one recommending the new regulations to the good opinion of the colonists, and another wishing them joy that Britain at this time had "the most vigilant, upright, and able chancellor of the exchequer that ever served her since the days of Sir Robert Walpole."

It was held that the power of parliament, according to the purest whig principles, was established alike over the king and over the colonies; but, in truth, the stamp act was the harbinger of American Independence, and the knell of the unreformed House of Commons.

CHAPTER XIII.

THE DAY-STAR OF THE AMERICAN UNION.

April—May, 1765.

If the British Parliament can tax America, it may tax Ireland and India, and hold the wealth of the East and of the West at the service of its own septennial oligarchy. As the relation of the government to its outlying dominions would become one of power and not of right, it could not but employ its accumulated resources to make itself the master of the ocean and the oppressor of mankind. "This system, if it is suffered to prevail," said Oxenbridge Thacher, of Boston, "will extinguish the flame of liberty all over the world." CHAP. XIII. 1765. April.

On the discovery of the new hemisphere, the tradition was widely spread through the old, that it conceals a fountain whose ever-flowing waters have power to reanimate age and restore its prime. The tradition was true; but the youth to be renewed was the youth of society; the life to bloom afresh was the life of the race.

CHAP. XIII. 1765. April.

Freedom, thy brow
Glorious in beauty though it be, is scarred
With tokens of old wars; thy massive limbs
Are strong with struggling. Power at thee has launched
His bolts, and with his lightnings smitten thee;
They could not quench the life thou hast from heaven.

Here in the Western World, the ancient warrior, "twin-born with man," counselled by the ripened wisdom of thousands of years, shall renovate his being, and guide every people of every tongue through the assured self-direction of the individual mind to the harmonious exercise of the collective reason of the State.

"The Colonies," said the press of New-York, just before the Stamp Act became a law, "may from present weakness submit to the impositions of ministerial power, but they will certainly hate that power as tyrannical; and, as soon as they are able, will throw it off." Colonial opposition confidently appealed from acts of authority to the sanctity of law; from the bar, weekly papers came forth, which loyalists denounced as "most licentious." "Associations of lawyers," said Colden, in the impotence of despair, "are the most dangerous of any next to the military," and he "lamented" that, as yet, "the faction" could not be "crushed."[1]

Still New-York continued tranquil. New England, where the chief writer against the impending Stamp Act had admitted the jurisdiction of the British parliament, was slow to anger. The child of Old England, she was loth to impute to the parent country a fixed design to subvert her rights. The patriot Hopkins

[1] Colden to Halifax, 22 Feb. and 27 April, 1765.

of Rhode Island, had written, and that colony had authoritatively published their common belief, that "the glorious constitution of Great Britain is the best that ever existed among men." Such was the universal opinion. Massachusetts had been led to rely on the inviolability of English freedom, and on the equity of parliament; and, when the blow fell, which, though visibly foreshown, had not been certainly expected, "the people looked upon their liberties as gone," giving way for a time to listless agony. "Tears," said Otis, "relieve me a moment;" and repelling the imputation, "that the continent of America was about to become insurgent," "it is the duty of all," he added, "humbly and silently to acquiesce in all the decisions of the supreme legislature. Nine hundred and ninety-nine in a thousand of the colonists, will never once entertain a thought but of submission to our sovereign, and to the authority of parliament in all possible contingencies."[1] "They undoubtedly have the right to levy internal taxes on the colonies."[2] "From my soul," said he, "I detest and abhor the thought of making a question of jurisdiction."[3]

CHAP. XIII. 1765. April.

May.

No person appeared to wish for national self-existence. In North Carolina, where Tryon[4] acted as Governor, the majority of the legislature were even persuaded by him to make provision for the support of the Church of England, so that dissenters themselves, who more and more abounded in that colony, should not be exempted from sharing the cost of the

[1] Brief Remarks on the Defence of the Halifax Libel on the British American Colonies. Boston: printed by Edmund Gill in Queen-street.

[2] Vindication of the British Colonies, 21, 26.

[3] Otis: Vindication, 26.

[4] Tryon's Speech to the General Assembly of North Carolina, 2 May, 1765.

CHAP. XIII. 1765. May. established religion. In Georgia, the stamp duty seemed as equal as any that could be generally imposed on the colonies;[1] though the manner of imposing it greatly inspired alarm.

While the act was in abeyance, Hutchinson had, in letters to England, pleaded for the ancient privilege of the colonies with regard to internal taxes; but, on learning the decision of parliament, he made haste to say, that "it could be to no purpose to claim a right of exemption, when the whole body of the people of England were against it." He was only "waiting to know what more parliament would do towards raising the sums which the colonies were to pay," and which as yet were not half provided for.[2] Openly espousing the defence of the act as legally right,[3] in his charges, as Chief Justice, he admonished "the jurors and people" of the several counties to obey.[4] Nor did the result seem doubtful. There could be no danger but from union; and "no two colonies," said he, "think alike; there is no uniformity of measures; the bundle of sticks thus separated will be easily broken." "The Stamp Act," he assured the ministry, five weeks after the news of its passage, "is received among us with as much decency as could be expected;" it leaves no room for evasion, and will execute itself."[5]

Yet the opposition to its execution was preparing, and in theory it was at once rejected.

"Should Great Britain tax Ireland," inquired a

[1] Georgia Committee to Knox, 15 April, 1765.

[2] Hutchinson to I. Williams, 26 April 1775.

[3] Hutchinson to Richard Jackson, 30 Aug. 1765.

[4] Hutchinson to Secretary of State, 10 Oct. 1765.

[5] Hutchinson to a friend, 4 March, 1765: to R. Jackson, 5 May, 4 and 5 June, 1765.

CHAP. XIII. 1765. May.

plain New England yeoman early in May, through the Providence Gazette, "would it be thought a project of independence for that people to remonstrate? The northern colonies fall but little short of Ireland for numbers. Their inhabitants are not dependent on the people of Britain, nor the people of Britain on them, only that they are subjects of the same king."[1]

In Boston, the annual election of representatives in May excited the passions of the people. Men called to mind the noble sentiments which had been interwoven into the body of the remonstrances of New-York; and compared them with the diffidence and want of spirit in the petition which the arts of Hutchinson had prevailed on the legislature of Massachusetts Bay to accept. They were embittered at the thought that they had been cajoled into forbearing to claim exemption from taxation as a right; and that yet their prayer had been suppressed by the ministry with haughty and impartial disdain. While the patriots on the one side censured the fatal acquiescence of Otis,[2] as a surrender of their liberties, the friends of government jeered at the vacillations and strange moods into which his irritability betrayed him, and called him a Massaniello and a madman. Keenly sensitive, and in the gloom that was thickening around him, conscious of his own sincerity, he repelled the insult with scorn. "The divine Brutus," said he, "once wore the cloak of a fool and a madman; the only cloak a man of true honor and spirit condescends to put on." And to merited reproaches he answered like one who was broken-hearted and could find no consolation: "Tell me, my once dear friends,

[1] Providence Gazette, 11 May. [2] J. Adams: Novanglus, 238.

CHAP. XIII. 1765. May.

what I have got by all this, besides the curse causeless of thousands, for whose welfare my heart has bled yearly, and is now ready to burst?[1] Were it lawful to get at the cause of all your calamities, I would leap like the roe to purchase your ransom with my life or his."

The town of Boston remained faithful to the most genial of its patriots; and though his conduct was often wild, and wayward, and contradictory, never failed to show him honor, so long as he retained enough of the light of reason to be sensible of its confidence.

Thus opinion was fermenting at the North, but as yet without a declared purpose in action.

Virginia received the plan to tax America by parliament with consternation. At first the planters foreboded universal ruin; but soon they resolved that the act should recoil on England, and began to be proud of frugality; articles of luxury of English manufacture were banished; and thread-bare coats were most in fashion. A large and embarrassing provincial debt enforced the policy of thrift.

Happily, the legislature of Virginia was then assembled; and the electors of Louisa county had just filled a sudden vacancy in their representation by making choice of Patrick Henry. He had resided among them scarcely a year, but his benignity of temper, pure life, and simplicity of habits, had already won their love. Devoted from his heart to their interest, he never flattered the people, and was never forsaken by them. As he took his place, not yet

[1] James Otis: To the Freeholders and other inhabitants of Boston. In Boston Gazette, 13 May.

acquainted with the forms of business in the house, or with its members, he saw the time for the enforcement of the stamp-tax drawing near, while all the other colonies, through timid hesitation, or the want of opportunity, still remained silent, and cautious loyalty hushed the experienced statesmen of his own. More than half the assembly had made the approaching close of the session an excuse for returning home. But Patrick Henry disdained submission. Alone, a burgess of but a few days, unadvised and unassisted, in an auspicious moment, of which the recollection cheered him to his latest day, he came forward in the committee of the whole house, and while Thomas Jefferson, a young collegian, from the mountain frontier, stood outside of the closed hall, eager to catch the first tidings of resistance, and George Washington, as is believed, was in his place as a member, he maintained by resolutions,[1] that the inhabitants of Virginia inherited from the first adventurers and settlers of that Dominion, equal franchises with the people of Great Britain; that royal charters had declared this equality; that taxation by themselves, or by persons chosen by themselves to represent them, was the distinguishing characteristic of British freedom and of the constitution; that the people of that most ancient colony had uninterruptedly enjoyed the right of being thus governed by their own laws respecting their internal polity and taxation; that this right had never been forfeited, nor in any other way given up,

CHAP. XIII.

1765. May.

[1] For the authentic copy of Henry's Resolutions as first proposed, see Wirt's Patrick Henry, Section Second.

CHAP. XIII. but had been constantly recognised by the king and people of Great Britain.

1765. May. Such was the declaration of colonial rights, adopted at his instance by the Assembly of Virginia. It followed from these resolutions, and Patrick Henry so expressed it in a fifth supplementary one, that the General Assembly of the whole colony have the sole right and power to lay taxes on the inhabitants of the colony, and that any attempt to vest such power in any other persons whatever tended to destroy British as well as American freedom. It was still further set forth, yet not by Henry, in two resolutions, which, though they were not officially produced, equally embodied the mind of the younger part of the Assembly, that the inhabitants of Virginia were not bound to yield obedience to any law designed to impose taxation upon them, other than the laws of their own General Assembly, and that any one who should, either by speaking or writing, maintain the contrary, should be deemed an enemy to the colony.

A stormy debate arose, and many threats were uttered.[1] Robinson, the Speaker, already a defaulter, Peyton Randolph, the king's attorney, and the frank, honest, and independent George Wythe, a lover of classic learning, accustomed to guide the house by his strong understanding and single-minded integrity, exerted all their powers to moderate the tone of "the hot and virulent resolutions;"[2] while John Randolph, the best lawyer in the colony, "singly"[3] resisted the whole proceeding. But, on the other side, George Johnston, of Fairfax, reasoned with solidity and firmness, and Henry flamed with impassioned zeal. Lifted

[1] Patrick Henry, in Wirt.

[2] Fauquier to Lords of Trade, 5 June, 1765, and 11 May, 1776.

[3] Dunmore to Dartmouth, 25 June, 1775.

CHAP XIII. 1765 May.

beyond himself, "Tarquin," he cried, "and Cæsar, had each his Brutus; Charles the First, his Cromwell; and George the Third——" "Treason!" shouted the Speaker; "treason, treason!" was echoed round the house, while Henry, fixing his eye on the first interrupter, continued without faltering, "may profit by their example!"[1]

Swayed by his words, the committee of the whole showed its good will to the spirit of all the resolutions enumerated; but the five offered by Patrick Henry were alone reported to the house, and on Thursday, the thirtieth of May, having been adopted by small majorities, the fifth by a vote of twenty to nineteen, they became a part of the public record. "I would have given five hundred guineas for a single vote,"[2] exclaimed the Attorney-General, aloud, as he came out past young Jefferson, into whose youthful soul the proceedings of that day sunk so deeply, that resistance to tyranny became a part of his nature. But Henry "carried all the young members with him."[3] That night, thinking his work done, he rode home; but the next day, in his absence, an attempt was made to strike all the resolutions off the journals, and the fifth, and the fifth only, was blotted out. The Lieutenant Governor, though he did not believe new elections would fall on what he esteemed cool, reasonable men, dissolved the assembly; but the four resolutions which remained on the journals, and the two others, on which no vote had been taken, were published in the newspapers throughout

[1] Letter from Virginia, 14 June, 1765. In the London Gazetteer of 13 Aug. 1765; and in General Advertiser to New-York Thursday's Gazette, 31 Oct. 1765.

[2] Jefferson to Wirt.

[3] Fauquier to Lords of Trade, 5 June, 1765.

CHAP. XIII. 1765. May. America, and by men of all parties, by royalists in office, not less than by public bodies in the colonies, were received without dispute as the avowed sentiment of the Old Dominion.

This is the "way the fire began in Virginia."[1] Of the American colonies, "Virginia rang the alarum bell."[2] "Virginia gave the signal for the continent."[3]

At the opening of the legislature of Massachusetts, Oliver, who had been appointed stamp-distributor, was, on the joint ballot of both branches, re-elected councillor, by a majority of but three out of about one hundred and twenty votes.[4] More than half the representatives voted against him.

On the very day on which the resolves of Virginia were adopted, and just as the publication of the speech of Barre in the New England papers acquainted all the people, that within parliament itself they had been hailed as the "Sons of Liberty," a message from Governor Bernard, who believed the fulfilment of his hopes and counsels near at hand, informed the new legislature of Massachusetts, that "they should not vainly make the difficult or impracticable attempt to transfer manufactures from their established abode; that the general settlement of the American provinces, though it might necessarily produce some regulations disagreeable from their novelty, had been long ago proposed, and would now be prosecuted to its utmost completion; that submission to the decrees of the supreme legislature, to which all

[1] John Hughes's Letter, in Boston Gazette of 22 Sept. 1766.

[2] Bernard to Halifax, Aug. 1765.

[3] Gage to Conway, 23 Sept. 1765.

[4] Bernard to Lords of Trade. Representation of Lords of Trade, 1 Oct. 1765.

other powers in the British empire were subordinate, was the duty and the interest of the colonies; that this supreme legislature, the parliament of Great Britain, was happily the sanctuary of liberty and justice; and that the prince who presided over it realized the idea of a patriot king." CHAP. XIII. 1765. May.

Contrary to usage, the house made no reply; but on the sixth of June, James Otis,[1] of Boston, in single-minded wisdom, advised the calling of an American Congress, which should come together without asking the consent of the king, and should consist of committees from each of the thirteen colonies, to be appointed respectively by the delegates of the people, without regard to the other branches of the legislature. Such an assembly had never existed; and the purpose of deliberating upon the acts of parliament was equally novel. The tories sneered[2] at the proposal, as visionary and impracticable; Grenville himself had circulated through the colonies the opinion that "from jealousy of neighborhood and clashing interests, they could never form a dangerous alliance among themselves, but must permanently preserve entire their common connection with the mother country." But heedless alike of the derision of those about them, and of the prophecy of the minister, the representatives of Massachusetts shared the creative instinct of Otis. Avoiding every expression of a final judgment, and insuring unanimity by even refusing[3] to consider the question of their exclusive right to originate mea-

[1] Diary of Ezra Stiles. Tenth Toast at Liberty Tree, 14 Aug. 1766. The late Alden Bradford informed me, that Mrs. Warren, of Plymouth, who was the sister of Otis, told him the proposal was planned at her house, on the return of Otis from a visit to Barnstable. The impulse was given in the Boston Instructions of 1764.

[2] Letter from Boston in New-York Gazette of 3 Feb. 1766.

[3] Brigadier Ruggle's Reasons, &c.

CHAP. XIII. 1765. May. sures of internal taxation, they sent letters to every assembly on the continent, proposing that committees of the several assemblies should meet at New-York, on the first Tuesday of the following October, "to consult together," and "consider of a united representation to implore relief." They also elected Otis and two others of their own members to repair to New York accordingly.

At the same time the province increased its strength by perseverance in appropriating annually fifty thousand pounds towards discharging its debt; and so good was its credit, and so affluent its people, that the interest on the remaining debt was reduced from six to five per cent. by a public subscription among themselves.[1]

Simultaneously, in the very first days of June, and before the proceedings in Virginia and Massachusetts were known in New-York, where the re-print of the Stamp Act was hawked about the streets as the "Folly of England and the ruin of America," a Freeman of that town, discussing the policy of Grenville, and the arguments on which it rested, demonstrated that they were leading alike to the reform of the British parliament and the independence of America.

"It is not the tax," said he, "it is the unconstitutional manner of imposing it, that is the great subject of uneasiness to the colonies. The minister admitted in parliament, that they had in the fullest sense the right to be taxed only by their own consent, given by their representatives; and grounds his pretence of the

[1] Bernard to Lords of Trade, 15 July, 1765.

right to tax them entirely upon this, that they are virtually represented in parliament. CHAP. XIII.

"It is said that they are in the same situation as the inhabitants of Leeds, Halifax, Birmingham, Manchester, and several other corporate towns; and that the right of electing does not comprehend above one-tenth part of the people of England. 1765. May.

"And in this land of liberty, for so it WAS our glory to call it, are there really men so insensible to shame, as before the awful tribunal of reason, to mention the hardships which, through their practices, some places in England are obliged to bear without redress, as precedents for imposing still greater hardships and wrongs upon America?

"It has long been the complaint of the most judicious in England, as the greatest misfortune to the nation, that its people are so unequally represented. Time and change of circumstances have occasioned defects in the rules or forms of choosing representatives for parliament. Some large towns send none to represent them; while several insignificant places, of only a few indigent persons, whose chief support is the sale of their votes, send many members. Seats are purchased with the nation's money; and a corrupt administration, by bribing others with places and pensions, can command a majority in the House of Commons that will pass what laws they please. These evils are too notorious to escape general observation, and too atrocious to be palliated. Why are not these crying grievances redressed? Only because they afford the greatest opportunities for bribery and corruption.

"The fundamental principle of the English constitution is reason and natural right. It has within itself the principle of self-preservation, correction, and

CHAP. XIII. 1765. May. improvement. That there are several towns, corporations, and bodies of people in England in similar circumstances as the colonies, shows that some of the people in England, as well as those in America, are injured and oppressed; but shows no sort of right for the oppression. Those places ought to join with the Americans in remonstrances to obtain redress of grievances.

"The absurdity of our being represented in parliament is so glaring, that it is almost an affront to common sense to use arguments to expose it; and yet it has been so much insisted upon, that it seems as if the free use of common sense was to be prohibited as well as our other common rights.

"But the cases in England, cited to justify the taxation of America, are in no way similar. The taxation of America is arbitrary and tyrannical, and what the parliament of England have no right to impose. The colonies are not only unconnected in interest with any members of parliament, but, in many respects, entirely opposite; indeed, I believe, in all respects where their affairs would come before that house; for when has it meddled with any matter relating to them, except to lay some imposition upon them?

"As to the towns in England which send no members to parliament, there are many persons in parliament deeply interested in them; all the counties where they stand, do send members; and many of their inhabitants are voters for the county members. As to the moneyed interest, there are in the house a sufficient number of those who have considerable property in money to take due care of that interest. Those persons who have no votes have yet the opportunity of influence in elections. Nor is it difficult for any man of fortune to procure a right of voting. So that the mention of these cases, as parallel with that of the colonies, is wonderfully trifling and impertinent.

CHAP. XIII. 1765. May.

"Our adherence to the English Constitution is on account of its real excellence. * * It is not the mere name of English rights that can satisfy us. It is the reality that we claim as our inheritance, and would defend with our lives. * * Can any man be represented without his own consent? * * Where is the advantage of it, if persons are appointed to represent us without our choice? * * Would not our greatest enemies be the most likely to endeavor to be chosen for that office? * * Could such a right of representation be ever desired by any reasonable man? Is English liberty such a chimera as this?

"The great fundamental principles of a government should be common to all its parts and members, else the whole will be endangered. If, then, the interest of the mother country and her colonies cannot be made to coincide, if the same constitution may not take place in both, if the welfare of the mother country necessarily requires a sacrifice of the most valuable natural rights of the colonies,—their right of making their own laws, and disposing of their own property by representatives of their own choosing,—if such is really the case between Great Britain and her colonies, then the connection between them ought to cease; and sooner or later it must inevitably cease. The English government cannot long act towards a part of its dominions upon principles diametrically opposed to its own, without losing itself in the slavery

CHAP. XIII. it would impose upon the colonies, or learning them to throw it off and assert their freedom.

1765. May. "There never can be a disposition in the colonies to break off their connection with the mother country, so long as they are permitted to have the full enjoyment of those rights to which the English constitution entitles them. * * They desire no more; nor can they be satisfied with less." * *

Such were the words in which the sober judgment of New-York embodied its convictions.[1] They were caught up by the impatient colonies; were reprinted in nearly all their newspapers; were approved of by the most learned and judicious on this continent; and even formed part of the instructions of South Carolina[2] to its agent in England.

Thus revolution proceeded. Virginia marshalled resistance; Massachusetts entreated union; New-York pointed to independence.

[1] Was John Morin Scott the author of the piece signed "Freeman?" Colden and Gage attribute the political papers to the lawyers; and Scott seems most likely to have written this. But the opinion is only inferential. I know of no direct evidence.

[2] South Carolina to Garth, 16 Dec. 1765.

CHAPTER XIV.

SOUTH CAROLINA FOUNDS THE AMERICAN UNION.

JUNE—JULY, 1765.

CHAP. XIV. 1765. June.

THE essays of Freeman had appeared, and the summons for the Congress had gone forth from Massachusetts, when the resolves of Virginia were published to the world. "They have spoken treason," said the royalists. "Is it treason," retorted others, "for the deputies of the people to assert their rights, or to give them away?" "Oh! those Virginians," cried Oxenbridge Thacher, from his deathbed, where, overplied by public exertions, he was wasting away with a hectic, "those Virginians are men; they are noble spirits. I long to be out—to speak in court against tyranny, words that shall be read after my death." "Why," said one of his friends, "are not our rights and liberties as boldly asserted by every government in America as by Virginia?" * * * "Behold," cried another, "a whole continent awakened, alarmed, restless, and disaffected."[1] Every where, from North to South—through the press, in letters, or as they met

[1] Letter of J. Adams. Boston Gazette. Hutchinson. Hist. iii.

CHAP. XIV. 1765. June. in private, for counsel, or in groups in the street, the "Sons of Liberty" told their griefs to one another, and planned retaliation or redress.

"No good reason can be given," observed the more calm among them, "why the colonies should not modestly and soberly inquire, what right the parliament of Great Britain has to tax them." "We were not sent out to be slaves," they continued, citing the example of ancient Greece, and the words of Thucydides; "we are the equals of those who remained behind. Americans hold equal rights with those in Britain, not as conceded privileges, but as inherent and indefeasible rights." "We have the rights of Englishmen," was the common voice, "and as such we are to be ruled by laws of our own making, and tried by men of our own condition."[1]

"If we are Englishmen," said one, "on what footing is our property?" "The great Mr. Locke," said another, "lays it down that no man has a right to that which another may take from him." And a third, proud of his respect for the law, sheltered himself under the words of the far-famed Coke: "The Lord may tax his villain, high or low, but it is against the franchises of the land for freemen to be taxed but by their own consent in parliament." "If the people in America are to be taxed by the representatives of the people in England, their malady," said Hopkins, of Rhode Island, "is an increasing evil, that must always grow greater by time." "When the parliament once begins," such was the discourse at Boston, "there is no drawing a line." "And it is only the first step," repeated the New-York owners of large

[1] Hopkins, Bland, and others. Providence Gazette.

estates; "a land tax for all America will be thought of next."[1] CHAP. XIV.

"It is plain," said even the calmest, "Englishmen do not regard Americans as members of the same family, brothers, and equals, but as subordinates, bound to submit to oppression at their pleasure." "A bill was even prepared," thus men warned each other against new dangers, "that authorized quartering British soldiers upon American private families." "And is not our property seized," they further exclaimed, "by men who cry, 'give, give,' and never say, 'enough,' and thrown into a prerogative court to be forfeited without a jury?"[2] 1765. June

"There is not silver enough in the colonies to pay for the stamps," computed patriot financiers, "and the trade by which we could get more is prohibited." "And yet," declared the eager merchants of New-York, "we have a natural right to every freedom of trade of the English." "To tax us, and bind our commerce and restrain manufactures," reasoned even the most patient, "is to bid us make brick without straw." "The northern colonies will be absolutely restricted from using any articles of clothing of their own fabric," predicted one colony to another. And men laughed as they added: "catching a mouse within his majesty's colonies with a trap of our own making will be deemed, in the ministerial cant, an infamous, atrocious, and nefarious crime." "A colonist," murmured a Boston man who had dipped into Grenville's pamphlet, "a colonist cannot make a horse-shoe

[1] Boston Gazette. N. Y. Gazette. Hopkins's Grievances. Hutchinson's Correspondence. R. R. Livingston's Correspondence.

[2] Hutchinson's Correspondence. Boston Gazette.

CHAP. XIV. 1765. June.

or a hob-nail, but some ironmonger of Britain shall bawl that he is robbed by the 'American republican.'" "Yes, they are even stupid enough," it was said in the town of Providence, "to judge it criminal for us to become our own manufacturers."[1]

"We will eat no lamb," promised the multitude, seeking to retaliate; "we will wear no mourning at funerals." "We will none of us import British goods," said the traders in the towns. The inhabitants of North Carolina set up looms for weaving their own clothes, and South Carolina was ready to follow the example. "The people," wrote the Lieutenant-Governor Sharpe, of Maryland, "will go on upon manufactures." "We will have homespun markets of linens and woollens," passed from mouth to mouth, till it found its way across the Atlantic, and alarmed the king in council; "the ladies of the first fortune shall set the example of wearing homespun." "It will be accounted a virtue in them to wear a garment of their own spinning." "A little attention to manufactures will make us ample amends for the distresses of the present day, and render us a great, rich, and happy people."[2]

When the churchmen of New-York preached loyalty to the king as the Lord's anointed, "The people," retorted William Livingston, "are the Lord's anointed. Though named 'mob' and 'rabble,' the people are the darling of Providence." Was the Bible quoted as demanding deference to all in authority? "This,"

[1] Colden's Corr. Boston Gazette. N. Y. Gazette. Providence Gaz. Lloyd's Conduct, &c. Newport Mercury.

[2] Hutchinson's History. Pa. Gaz. N. Y. Gaz. Boston Gaz. Sharpe to Calvert, 10 July. Letter from Charleston, S. C.

it was insisted, "is to add dulness to impiety." For "tyranny," they cried, "is no government; the gospel promises liberty, glorious liberty." "The gospel," so preached Mayhew, of Boston, always, "the gospel permits resistance."[1]

CHAP. XIV. 1765. June.

And then patriots would become maddened with remembering, that "some high or low American had had a hand in procuring every grievance." "England," it was said, "is deceived and deluded by placemen and office-seekers." "Yes," exclaimed the multitude; "it all comes of the horse-leeches." When "the friends to government" sought to hush opposition by terror of the power of parliament and its jealousy of its own supremacy, "you are cowards," was the answer; "you are fools; you are parasites; or, rather, you are parricides."[2]

"Power is a sad thing," said the Presbyterians of Philadelphia; "our mother should remember we are children and not slaves."[3] "When all Israel saw that the king hearkened not unto them," such was the response of the Calvinists of the North, "the people answered the king, saying: 'What portion have we in David? what inheritance in the son of Jesse? To your tents, O Israel! Now see to thine own house, David!'"[4] "Who cares," said the more hardy, "whether George or Louis is the sovereign, if both are alike?"[5] "The beast of burden," continued others, "asks not whose pack it carries."[6] "I would bear allegiance to King George," said one who called himself a lover of truth, "but not be a slave to his British subjects."[7]

[1] Sentinel, in N. Y. Gaz. Mayhew to Hollis.

[2] Boston Gaz. Otis's Considerations. N. Y. Gaz. Hutchinson's Correspondence.

[3] F. Alison to E. Stiles, 13 June.

[4] Boston Gaz. 15 July.

[5] Otis, and many others.

[6] O. Thacher, and many others.

[7] Philalethes, in N. Y. Gaz.

CHAP. XIV. 1765. June.

"But the members of parliament," argued the royalists, "are men of the highest character for wisdom, justice, and integrity, and incapable of dealing unjustly." "Admitting this to be true," retorted Hopkins, "one who is bound to obey the will of another is as really a slave, though he may have a good master, as if he had a bad one; and this is stronger in politic bodies than in natural ones."

The plea recurred, that the British parliament virtually represented the whole British empire. "It is an insult on the most common understanding," thought James Habersham of Georgia, and every American from the banks of the Savannah to the frontier of Maine, "to talk of our being virtually represented in parliament." "It is an insult on common sense to say it," repeated the Presbyterian ministers of the middle states to the Calvinist ministers of New England. "Are persons chosen for the representatives of London and Bristol, in like manner chosen to be the representatives of Philadelphia or Boston? Have two men chosen to represent a poor borough in England, that has sold its votes to the highest bidder, any pretence to say that they represent Virginia or Pennsylvania? And have four hundred such fellows a right to take our liberties?"[1]

But it was argued again and again: "Manchester, Birmingham, and Sheffield, like America, return no members." "Why," rejoined Otis, and his answer won immediate applause in England,[2] "why ring everlasting changes to the colonists on them? If they are not represented, they ought to be." "Every man of a sound mind," he continued, "should have his vote." "Ah, but," replied the royalists, holding

[1] F. Alison to E. Stiles. [2] Monthly Review.

Otis to his repeated concessions, "you own that parliament is the supreme legislature; will you question its jurisdiction?" And his answer was on the lips of all patriots, learned and unlearned: "Lord Coke declares, that it is against Magna Charta and against the franchises of the land, for freemen to be taxed but by their own consent; Lord Coke rules, that an act of parliament against common law is void."[1]

CHAP. XIV. 1765. June.

Thus opinion was echoed from mind to mind, as the sun's rays beam from many clouds, all differing in tints, but every hue an emanation from the same fires.

In the midst of the gloom, light broke from the excitement of a whole people. Associations were formed in Virginia, as well as in New England, to resist the Stamp Act by all lawful means. Hope began to rise, that American rights and liberties might safely be trusted "to the watchfulness of a united continent."

The insolence of the royal officers provoked to insulated acts of resistance The people of Rhode Island, angry with the commander of a ship of war, who had boarded their vessels and impressed their seamen, seized his boat, and burned it on Newport[2] Common.

Men of New England, "of a superior sort," had obtained of the government of New Hampshire a warrant for land down the western slope of the Green Mountains, on a branch of the Hoosic, twenty miles east of the Hudson river; formed already a community of sixty-seven families, in as many houses, with an ordained minister; had elected their own municipal officers; founded three several public schools; set their meeting-house among the primeval forests

[1] Hutchinson's Correspondence. [2] Letter from Newport, June, 1765.

CHAP. XIV. 1765. June.

of beech and maple; and, in a word, enjoyed the flourishing state which springs from rural industry, intelligence, and unaffected piety. They called their village Bennington. The royal officers at New-York disposed anew of that town, as well as of others near it, so that the king was known to the settlers near the Green Mountains, chiefly by his agents, who had knowingly sold his lands twice over.[1] In this way, the soil of Bennington became a fit battle-ground for independence.

Events like these sowed the seeds of discontent; but still there was no present relief for America, unless union could be perfected. Union was the hope of Otis—union that "should knit and work into the very blood and bones of the original system every region, as fast as settled." Yet how comprehensive and how daring the idea! The traditions of the Board of Trade branded it as "mutinous."[2] Massachusetts had proceeded cautiously and almost timidly, naming for its delegates to the proposed Congress, with the patriot Otis, two others who were "friends to government."[3]

Virginia was ready to convince the world that her people were firm and unanimous in the cause of liberty,[4] but its newly-elected assembly was not suffered by Fauquier to come together.

New Jersey received the circular letter of Massachusetts on the twentieth of June, the last day of the session of its legislature. The Speaker, a friend to the British government, at first inclined to urge sending delegates to the proposed Congress; but, on

[1] Hutchinson to Gov. Pownall, 10 July, 1765.

[2] Bladen, in Hutchinson, iii. 109.

[3] Bernard to Lords of Trade, 8 July.

[4] R. H. Lee to L. Carter.

some "advice" from the governor, changed his mind, and the house, in the hurry preceding the adjournment, rather from uncertainty than the want of goodwill, unanimously declined the invitation. The Assembly of New Hampshire seemed to approve but did not adopt it.

CHAP. XIV. 1765. June.

The great measure was in peril; and its failure would make of American resistance a mockery. "Nothing will be done in consequence of this intended Congress," wrote Bernard, in July; and he seized the opportunity to press "more and more" upon the government at home "the necessity of taking into their hands the appointment of the American civil list," as well as changing the council of the province.

July.

Even the liberal Governor of Maryland reported "that the resentment of the colonists would probably die out; and that, in spite of the violent outcries of the lawyers, the Stamp Act would be carried into execution."

But far away towards the lands of the sun, the Assembly of South Carolina was in session; and on the twenty-fifth day of July, the circular from Massachusetts was debated. Many objections were made to the legality, the expediency, and most of all to the efficiency of the proposed measure; and many eloquent words were uttered, especially by the youthful John Rutledge, when the subject, on the deliberate resolve of a small majority, was referred to a committee, of which Gadsden was the chairman. He was a man of deep and clear convictions; thoroughly sincere; of an unbending will, and a sturdy, impetuous integrity, which drove those about him, like a mountain torrent dashing resistlessly on an over-shot

CHAP. XIV. 1765 July.

wheel, though sometimes clogging with back water from its own violence. He possessed not only that courage which defies danger, but that persistence which neither peril, nor imprisonment, nor the threat of death can shake. Full of religious faith, and at the same time inquisitive and tolerant, methodical, yet lavish of his fortune for public ends, he had in his nature nothing vacillating or low, and knew not how to hesitate or feign. After two legislatures had held back, South Carolina, by "his achievement," pronounced for union. "Our state," he used to say, "particularly attentive to the interest and feelings of America, was the first, though at the extreme end, and one of the weakest, as well internally as externally, to listen to the call of our northern brethren in their distresses. Massachusetts sounded the trumpet, but to Carolina is it owing that it was attended to. Had it not been for South Carolina, no Congress would then have happened."

As the united American people spread through the vast expanse over which their jurisdiction now extends, be it remembered that the blessing of union is due to the warm-heartedness of South Carolina. "She was all alive, and felt at every pore." And when we count up those who, above others, contributed to the great result, we are to name the inspired "madman," James Otis, and the magnanimous, unwavering lover of his country, Christopher Gadsden.

Otis now seemed to himself to hear the prophetic song of the "Sibyls," chanting the spring-time of a "new empire."

CHAPTER XV.

THE DUKE OF CUMBERLAND FORMS A MINISTRY—THE ROCKINGHAM WHIGS.

JUNE—JULY, 1765.

CHAP. XV. 1765. June.

WHILE America was giving force to its resistance by union, divisions that could not be healed, planted confusion in the councils of its oppressors. We left the king quivering with wounded pride at the affront from his ministers. But far from giving way, he thwarted their suggestions about appointments to office, frowned on those whom they promoted, and publicly showed regard to his friends whom they displaced.

Grenville, in apparently confident security, continued his schemes of colonial revenue, and by the fourteenth of June, represented to the king, "that the Canadians were subject to taxation by virtue of his prerogative." But the duke of Bedford had already filled the palace with more rankling cares. The plain-spoken man, exasperated by the sense of his own unpopularity and by the coldness of the court, was growing weary of public life and wished to retire. On the twelfth of June, being resolved once more on an explanation, he recapitulated to his sovereign in person what had passed between him and his ministers on their resuming their functions, when

CHAP. XV. 1765. June. he had promised them his countenance and support. "Has this promise," he demanded, "been kept? On the contrary, are not almost all our bitter enemies countenanced in public? Has not the earl of Bute, as the favorite, interfered, at least indirectly, in public councils, with the utmost hazard to himself, and risk to the king's quiet and the safety of the public? I hope your majesty will be pleased to give your countenance to your ministers, and for the future let your support and your authority go together; or else that you will give your authority where you are pleased to give your favor." The king only answered, "that he was much hurt at being told of consulting Lord Bute." That "his silence was a symptom of amendment," was Rigby's comment; for, said he, "to hold one's tongue is honester than to falsify all one says." At the same time the king was resolved to interpret the discourse of Bedford as a resignation; though the colleagues of the duke were by no means disposed to retire, or to push matters so far as to provoke their dismissal. "The thoroughly wise Grenville" was expected to counterwork the king with Temple; for their reconciliation had been attended with the mutual engagement to act together in future; and if Temple and Pitt would only be neuter, a removal of the ministry appeared impossible.

The king, who was resolved at all hazards to make a change, again appealed to Cumberland, and through him summoned Pitt to an audience. On Wednesday, the nineteenth of June, in an interview which continued for three hours, the conversation turned not only on a Prussian alliance, an explanation of general warrants, and a repeal of the cider tax; but

Pitt declared himself against the measures that had been adopted to restrain the American colonies from trade with the Spanish islands, and against the taxation of the colonies by act of parliament, which nothing but extreme illness had prevented him from opposing in the House of Commons, and of which his mind foreboded the fatal consequences. The discussion was renewed on the following Saturday, when Pitt, having obtained satisfaction as to measures and as to men, entered most thoroughly and most heartily upon the work of forming an administration. On receiving the news by an express from Pitt, Temple broke confidence so far as privately to communicate its substance to Grenville, who, before returning to London, hastened to Woburn, and received from Bedford full powers to dispose of him entirely as he should think fit. Meantime, Temple, with a predetermined mind, repaired on Monday to Pitt at Hayes. The two statesmen were at variance on no important measure except the policy of the stamp act, which Pitt was resolved to abrogate as inconsistent with right, and which Temple, in common with the great body of the landed aristocracy, desired to confirm. Here was an irreconcilable antagonism of opinion which was to divide them for the rest of their lives. On account of their difference on the American question, or from a perfidious concert with Grenville and Bedford, or for reasons that have remained unrevealed, Temple refused to take office. Pitt was alike surprised, wounded, and embarrassed. Lord Temple was his brother-in-law; had, in the time of his retiring from the office of paymaster, helped him with his purse; had twice gone into a ministry

CHAP. XV. 1765. June. with him; and twice faithfully retired with him. The long discussion that ensued deeply affected both; but Temple inflexibly resisted Pitt's judgment, declaration, and most earnest remonstrance; he would not consent to supplant the brother whose present measures he applauded, and with whom he had just been reconciled; and Pitt felt himself disabled by this refusal. As they parted, he said pathetically, in the words of a Roman poet: "You, brother, bring ruin on me, and on yourself, and on the people, and the peers, and your country."

When Temple, on the morning of Tuesday, the twenty-second, received the visit of Grenville, he appeared "under great agitation." He was still "nervous and trembling" when he went in to the king, and declined "entering his service in any office," assigning reasons of the most tender and delicate nature, which he did not explain. "I am afraid," he added —and it was the king himself who repeated the remark—"I foresee more misfortunes in your majesty's reign than in any former period of history."

Deserted in this wise by the connection in whom he had trusted, Pitt immediately sought an interview with the king, who accepted his excuses, and "parted from him very civilly." Thus passed what seemed to him the most difficult and painful crisis of his life. "All is now over with me," said he despondingly, "and by a fatality I did not expect;" and with grief and disappointment in his heart, he retired into Somersetshire.

"Let us see," said the ministers, "if the duke of Cumberland will be desperate enough to form an administration without Pitt and Temple." Northington assured them, that they might remain in office if they chose. The most wary gave in their adhesion; even Charles Yorke went to Grenville and declared his support, and Gilbert Elliott did the like. "Our cause is in your hands," said the Bedfords to Grenville, "and you will do it justice." This was the moment of his greatest pride and political importance; he was at the head of the Treasury; he had defeated his sovereign's efforts to change the ministry; he was looked up to and owned by the Bedfords as their savior and protector. His ambition, his vanity, and his self-will were gratified. CHAP. XV. 1765. June.

The king had been complaining in strong terms of the little business done, and especially of "the neglect of the colonies and new conquests;" and the indefatigable Grenville applied himself earnestly to American measures. Bishops were to be engrafted on a plan which he favored for an ecclesiastical establishment in Canada. On the fourth of July, he proposed a reform in the courts of admiralty; in the following days, he, with Lord North, settled the emoluments of the officers charged with carrying into execution the American stamp act; made an enumeration of the several districts for inspection; provided for supplying vacant places among the stamp distributors; and on the ninth, his very last day in office, consulted about removing incidental objections to the measure, in which he gloried as his own. July.

Meantime Cumberland had succeeded in forming an administration out of the remnants of the old whig aristocracy and their successors; and on the tenth Grenville was summoned to St. James's to surrender the seals of his office. "By what means have I drawn

CHAP. XV. 1765. July. down your Majesty's displeasure?" asked the discarded minister. "I have found myself too much constrained," answered the king; "and when I have had any thing proposed to me, it was no longer as counsel, but what I was to obey." Grenville then told him, that "he understood the plan of his new administration was a total subversion of every act of the former; that nothing having been undertaken as a measure without his Majesty's approbation, he knew not how he could let himself be persuaded to see it in so different a light, and most particularly the regulations concerning the colonies. "I beseech your Majesty," he continued, "as you value your own safety not to suffer any one to advise you to separate or draw the line between your British and American dominions. Your colonies are the richest jewel of your Crown. For my own part I must uniformly maintain my former opinions both in Parliament and out of it. Whatever is proposed in Parliament must abide the sentence passed upon it there; but if any man should venture to defeat the regulations laid down for the colonies, by a slackness in the execution, I shall look upon him as a criminal and the betrayer of his country."

The conditions on which the new ministry took office, were agreed upon at the house of the duke of Newcastle, and did not extend beyond the disposal of offices. They introduced no system adapted to the age, no projects of reform; they gave no pledges in behalf of liberty, except such as might be found in the traditions of their party and their own personal characters. The old duke of Newcastle was the type of the administration, though he took only the post of privy seal, with the patronage of the church. The law adviser of its choice, as attorney general, was Charles Yorke, whose political principles coincided with those of Mansfield. Its mediator with the king was the duke of Cumberland, who had a seat in the cabinet as its protector.

But younger men also came into power, giving hope for the future. In place of Grenville, the able debater, the learned jurist, the post of head of the treasury was assigned to the marquis of Rockingham. He was an inexperienced man of five and thirty, possessing no great natural abilities, of a feeble constitution, and a nervous timidity which made him almost incapable of speaking in public; acquainted with race-courses, and the pedigree of horses; unskilled in the finances of his country, and never before proposed for high office. But he had clear and sagacious sense and good feeling, unshaken fortitude, integrity, kindness of nature, and an honest and hearty attachment to liberty within established limits. His virtues were his arts, and they were his talents also. Had he been untitled and less opulent, he never would have been heard of; but being high in rank, of vast wealth, and generous without wastefulness, he was selected at the moment when the power of the oligarchy was passing its culmination, to lead its more liberal branch; and such was his own ambition of being first in place, such his sincerity, such his fidelity to his political connections, that from this time till the day of his death he remained their acknowledged standard-bearer.

His deficiencies in knowledge and in rhetoric, the minister compensated by selecting as his secretary and

CHAP. XV. 1765. July.

intimate friend Edmund Burke, who had recently escaped from the service of one of the opposite party, and from a pension bestowed by Halifax. It was characteristic of that period for a man like Rockingham to hold for life a retainer like Edmund Burke; and never did a true-hearted, kindly and generous patron find a more faithful adherent. He brought to his employer, and gave up to his party, all that he had—boundless stores of knowledge, especially respecting the colonies, wit, philosophy, imagination, gorgeous eloquence, unwearied industry, mastery of the English tongue, and, as some think, the most accomplished intellect which the nation had produced for centuries. His ambition was fervid, yet content with the applause of the aristocracy. His political training had brought him in contact with the Board of Trade, and afterwards with the government of Ireland, the country of his birth. His writings are a brilliant picture of the British constitution, as it existed in the best days of the eighteenth century; and his genius threw lustre over the decline of the party which he served. No man had a better heart, or more thoroughly hated oppression; but he possessed neither experience in affairs, nor tranquil judgment, nor the rule over his own spirit; so that his genius, under the impulse of his bewildering passions, wrought much evil to his country and to Europe, even while he rendered noble service to the cause of commercial freedom, to Ireland, and to America.

The seals of the Northern department of state were conferred on the duke of Grafton, a young man of respectable abilities, yet impaired by fondness for pleasure, a ready speaker, honest and upright, naturally inclining to the liberal side. He had little sagacity, but he meant well; and, in after years, preferred himself to record and to explain his errors of judgment rather than to leave in doubt the sincerity of his character. This is he to whom the poet Gray, in verses splendid but not venal, flung praise as to one who kept the steady course of honor through the wild waves of public life. In his college vacations, he had seen Pitt at Stowe, and been fascinated by his powers; he took office, in the hope that the ministry might adopt the Great Commoner as its chief.

Conway, who had been arbitrarily dismissed from military office, was suggested, as Grafton's associate. But "thinking men foresaw" peril to the stamp act, in "intrusting its execution to one of the very few persons who had opposed the passing of it;" and the king wished to consign that office to Charles Townshend, by whom it had so long been coveted. Who can tell how America would have fared under him, in an administration whose patron and adviser was the victor at Culloden? But though the king, in person, used every argument to prevail with him, yet he declined to join in a system which he compared to "lutestring, fit only for summer wear." Even so late as on the ninth of July, the king, who had reserved the place of secretary at war for Conway, renewed his entreaties; but the decisive refusal of Townshend, who held fast to his lucrative office of paymaster, threw the seals of the southern department and America, at the very last moment, into the hands of Conway.

The new secretary, like Shelburne and Edmund Burke, was an Irishman, and, therefore, disposed to

CHAP. XV. 1765. July. have "very just notions" of the colonies. His temper was mild and moderate; in his inquiries he was reasonable and accurate; and it was his desire to unite both countries in affection, as well as interest. But he was diffident and hesitating. He seemed to be inflexibly proud, and was not firm—to be candid, and was only scrupulous. His honesty, instead of nerving his will, kept him for ever a sceptic. He would in battle walk up to the cannon's mouth with imperturbable courage; but in the cabinet his mind was in a perpetual see-saw, balancing arguments, and never reaching fixed conclusions, unless his sense of honor was touched, or his gentle disposition was invigorated by his humanity. The necessity of immediate action was sure to find him still wavering. He was so fond of doing right, that the time for doing it passed before he could settle what it was; and the man who was now appointed to guide the mind of the House of Commons, never knew how to make up his own.

The ministry would have restored Shelburne to the Presidency of the Board of Trade; but he excused himself, because Rockingham, on taking office, had given no pledges but as to "men." "Measures, not men," said Shelburne, "will be the rule of my conduct;" and thus the two branches of the liberal aristocracy gained their watchwords. The one was bound to provide for its connection; the other to promote reform. There could be no progress of liberty in England, but from the union of the aristocratic power of the one with the popular principle of the other. The refusal of Shelburne leaves the important office to the earl of Dartmouth, a young man, utterly inexperienced in business, distinguished only for his piety;

The one who wears a coronet and prays.

A peerage was conferred on Pratt, who took the name of Camden; though Rockingham was averse to his advancement. But it was through Rockingham himself, that Lord George Sackville, who had been degraded while Pitt was minister, was restored to a seat at the Council Board, and raised to one of the lucrative vicetreasurerships of Ireland.

Thus was an administration, whose policy had been sanctioned by large and increasing majorities in parliament, and by the most cordial approbation of the king, avowedly turned out, to gratify his personal disgust at its exercising its constitutional right to control him in the use of the court favor. The new cabinet did not include one man of commanding ability, nor had it a single measure to propose to the crown, to the nation, or to the colonies; nor did it possess the confidence of parliament, in which its want of debating talent stamped its character with weakness. Grenville, in revenge, sullenly predicted to his friends, that every day would produce difficulties in the colonies, and with foreign powers.

"Within the last twelve years," wrote Voltaire at that time, "there has been a marked revolution in the public mind. Light is certainly spreading on all sides." George the Third, without intending it, promoted the revolution which Voltaire anxiously awaited, and hastened results affecting America and the world, of which neither Voltaire nor himself had any preconception.

The new ministry did not enter upon their career with any purpose of repealing or changing the stamp act. Many of those whose support was essential to them, among others, Northington, who remained in

CHAP. XV. 1765. July.

the cabinet as chancellor, Yorke, and Charles Townshend, were among its earliest and most strenuous supporters; and the duke of Cumberland was the last man in England to temporize with what he might think to be rebellion. The agents of the colonies seeing among the ministry some who had been their friends, took courage to solicit relief; but for many weeks Franklin* admitted no hope of success. An order in council,[1] sanctioned by the name, and apparently, by the advice of Lord Dartmouth—perhaps the worst order ever proposed by the Board of Trade, so bad that it was explained away by the crown lawyers as impossible to have been intended—permitted appeals to the privy council from any verdict given by any jury in the courts of New-York; while the Treasury Board, with Rockingham at its head, directed the attorney and solicitor general to prepare instruments for collecting in Canada, by the king's authority, the same revenue which had been collected there under the government of Louis XV.; and without any apparent misgiving, proceeded to complete the arrangements for executing the stamp act.

[1] Report of the Lords in Council, 26 July, 1765.

* That Franklin believed the Stamp Act would be carried into effect appears from the verbal remark to Ingersoll, attributed to him; from his conduct; and from his correspondence. Take, for example, this extract from his letter to Charles Thompson, never before correctly published:

LONDON, July 11th, 1765.

* * * —— "Depend upon it, my good neighbor, I took every step in my power to prevent the passing of the Stamp Act. Nobody could be more concerned in interest than myself to oppose it, sincerely and heartily. But the tide was too strong against us. The nation was provoked by American claims of Independence; and all parties joined in

resolving by this act to settle the point. We might as well have hindered the sun's setting: that we could not do. But since 'tis down, my friend, and it may be long before it rises again, let us make as good a night of it as we can. We may still light candles. Frugality and industry will go a great way towards indemnifying us. Idleness and pride tax with a heavier hand than kings and parliaments; if we can get rid of the former, we may easily bear the latter."

CHAP XV. 1765. July.

For the opportunity of printing the above paragraph correctly, in Franklin's own words, I am indebted to Mrs. Chamberlain, of Newark, Delaware, who has the original in her possession. The copy was made for me, with the utmost exactness, by Mr. A. H. Grimshaw, of Wilmington, and carefully compared with the original by Mr. Grimshaw and one of his friends.

There is another version in circulation, which makes Franklin say: "Idleness and pride tax with a heavier hand than kings and parliaments. If we can get rid of the former, we can get rid of the latter."

This is not what Franklin wrote. To "*bear*" with kings and parliaments and to "*get rid of*" kings and parliaments, are very different things. Franklin was long-suffering, and waited some years yet before he advised to get rid of kings. He himself printed a part of this letter, but with amplifications, in the London Chronicle of Nov. 14 to 16, 1765, from which it was copied into Weyman's New-York Gazette of Feb. 3, and other papers. In all of them, as well as in the letter itself, the words are, "*bear* the latter," and not, "*get rid* of the latter."

CHAPTER XVI.

HOW THE STAMP OFFICERS WERE HANDLED IN AMERICA—ADMINISTRATION OF ROCKINGHAM.

AUGUST—SEPTEMBER, 1765.

CHAP. XVI. 1765. Aug. SIX weeks and more before the news of the change of ministry was received in Boston, and while the passions of the public mind throughout the continent were still rising, Jared Ingersoll, of Connecticut, late agent for that province, now its stamp-master, arrived from England at Boston; and the names of the stamp distributors were published on the eighth of August. But Grenville's craftily devised policy of employing Americans failed from the beginning. "It will be as in the West Indies," clamored the people; "there the negro overseers are the most cruel."

"Had you not rather," said a friend of Ingersoll, "these duties should be collected by your brethren than by foreigners?" "No, vile miscreant! indeed we had not," answered Dagget,[1] of New Haven. "If your father must die, is there no defect in filial duty in becoming his executioner, that the hangman's part of the estate may be retained in the family? If the ruin of your country is decreed, are you free from

[1] Connecticut Gaz. 9 August.

CHAP. XVI. 1765. Aug.

blame for taking part in the plunder?" "North American liberty is dead," wrote another, who had a clear view of the issue. "She is dead, but happily she has left one son, the child of her bosom, prophetically named Independence,[1] now the hope of all when he shall come of age." "But why wait?" asked the impatient. "Why should any stamp officers be allowed in America at all?" "I am clear in this point," declared Mayhew,[2] "that no people are under a religious obligation to be slaves, if they are able to set themselves at liberty."

"The Stamp Act," it was said universally in Boston, "is arbitrary, unconstitutional, and a breach of charter. Let it be of short duration. There are two hundred thousand inhabitants in this province, and by computation about two millions in America. It is too late for us to be dragooned out of our rights. We may refuse submission, or at least the stamp officers will be afraid to stab their country."[3] If every one of them could be forced to resign, the statute which was to execute itself, would perish from the beginning. Spontaneously, the decree seemed to go forth, that Boston should lead the way in the work of compulsion.[4]

It was already known there, that the king, desirous of changing his ministry, had sent for William Pitt; and the crowd that kindled the bonfire in King-street on the birthday of the Prince of Wales, rent the air with "God bless our true British king! Heaven preserve the Prince of Wales! Pitt and liberty for ever!" And high and low, rich and poor, joined in the chorus, "Pitt and liberty!"

[1] Boston Evening Post, and other papers.
[2] Mayhew to Hollis, 8 August.
[3] Letter from Boston, 5 August.
[4] Gage to Conway, Sept.

CHAP. XVI. 1765. Aug.

The daybreak of Wednesday, the fourteenth of August, saw the effigy of Oliver tricked out with emblems of Bute and Grenville, swinging on the bough of a stately elm, the pride of the neighborhood, known as the Great Tree, standing near what was then the entrance to the town. The pageant had been secretly prepared by Boston mechanics,[1] true-born SONS OF LIBERTY, Benjamin Edes, the printer; Thomas Crafts, the painter; John Smith and Stephen Cleverly, the braziers; and the younger Avery; Thomas Chase, a fiery hater of kings;[2] Henry Bass, and Henry Welles. The passers-by stopped to gaze on the grotesque spectacle, and their report collected thousands. Hutchinson, as chief justice, ordered the sheriff to remove the image. "We will take them down ourselves at evening," said the people.

Bernard summoned his council. "The country, whatever may be the consequence," said some of them, "will never submit to the execution of the Stamp Act." The majority spoke against interfering with the people. The day passed, and evening came, and Bernard and Hutchinson were still engaged in impotent altercations with their advisers, when, just after dark, an "amazing" multitude, moving in the greatest order and following the images borne on a bier, after passing down the main street, marched directly through the old State House and under the council-chamber itself, shouting at the top of their voices: "Liberty, Property, and no Stamps." Giving three huzzas of defiance, they next, in Kilby-street, demolished a frame which they thought Oliver was building for a Stamp-Office, and with the wooden trophies made a funeral pyre for his effigy in front of his house on Fort Hill.

[1] Gordon, i. 175. J. Adams, ii.175. [2] Affidavit of R. Silvester.

"The Stamp Act shall not be executed here," exclaimed one who spoke the general sentiment. "Death to the man who offers a piece of stamped paper to sell!" cried others. "All the power of Great Britain," said a third, shall not oblige us to submit to the Stamp Act." "We will die," declared even the sober-minded, "we will die upon the place first."[1] "We have sixty thousand fighting-men in this colony alone," wrote Mayhew.[2] "And we will spend our last blood in the cause," repeated his townsmen.

Hutchinson directed the colonel of the militia to beat an alarm. "My drummers," said he, "are in the mob." With the sheriff, Hutchinson went up to disperse the crowd. "Stand by, my boys," cried a ringleader; "let no man give way;" and Hutchinson, as he fled, was obliged to run the gauntlet, yet escaping with one or two blows. At eleven, the multitude repaired to the Province House, where Bernard lived, and after three cheers, they dispersed quietly.

"We have a dismal prospect before us," said Hutchinson, the next morning, anticipating tragical events in some of the colonies." "The people of Connecticut," reported one whose name is not given, "have threatened to hang their distributor on the first tree after he enters the colony." "If Oliver," said Bernard, with rueful gravity, "had been found last night, he would certainly have been murthered." "If he does not resign," thought many, "there will be another riot to-night, and his house will be pulled down about his ears." So the considerate self-seeker,

[1] Hutchinson's MS. Narrative. Bernard to Lords of Trade, 15 Aug. 1765.

[2] Mayhew to Hollis, August.

CHAP. XVI.

1765. Aug.

with the bitterness of enduring anger and disappointed avarice in his heart, seasonably in the day-time, "gave it under his own hand," that he would not serve as Stamp Officer, while Bernard, deserting his post as guardian of the public peace, hurried trembling to the castle, and could not recover from his fears, though immured within the walls of a fortress. At night, a bonfire on Fort Hill celebrated the people's victory Several hundred men were likewise gathered round the house of Hutchinson. "Let us but hear from his own mouth," said their leader, "that he is not in favor of the Stamp Act, and we will be easy." But Hutchinson evaded a reply.

The governor, just before his retreat, ordered a proclamation for the discovery and arrest of the rioters. "If discovery were made," said Hutchinson, "it would not be possible to commit them." "The prisons," said Mayhew, "would not hold them many hours. In this town, and within twenty miles of it, ten thousand men would soon be collected together on such an occasion." And on the next Lord's Day but one, before a crowded audience, choosing as his text,—"I would they were even cut off which trouble you; for, brethren, ye have been called unto liberty,"—he preached fervidly in behalf of civil and religious freedom. "I hope," said he, "no persons among ourselves have encouraged the bringing such a burden as the Stamp Act on the country."

The distrust of the people fell more and more upon Hutchinson.—"He is a prerogative man," they cried. "He grasps at all the important offices in the state."—"He himself holds four, and his relations six or seven more."—"He wiped out of the petition of Massachusetts every spirited expression."

—"He prevailed to get a friend of Grenville made agent for the colony."—"He had a principal hand in projecting the Stamp Act."—"He advised Oliver against resigning."—"To enforce the acts of trade, he granted writs of assistance, which are no better than general warrants."—"He took depositions against the merchants as smugglers."

CHAP. XVI. 1765. Aug.

Thus the rougher spirits wrought one another into a frenzy. On the twenty-sixth of August, a bonfire in front of the Old State House collected at nightfall a mixed crowd. They first burned all the records of the hated Vice-Admiralty Court; they next ravaged the house of the Comptroller of the Customs; and then, giving Hutchinson and his family barely time to escape, split open his doors with broadaxes, broke his furniture, scattered his plate and ready money, his books and manuscripts, and at daybreak left his house a ruin.

The coming morning, the citizens of Boston, in town-meeting, expressed their "detestation of these violent proceedings," and pledged themselves to one another to "suppress the like disorders for the future." "I had rather lose my hand," said Mayhew, "than encourage such outrages;" and Samuel Adams agreed with him; but they, and nearly all the townsmen, and the whole continent, applauded the proceedings of the fourteenth of August; and the elm, beneath which the people had on that day assembled, was solemnly named "the Tree of Liberty."

The officers of the crown were terror-stricken.[1] The Attorney-General did not dare to sleep in his own house, nor two nights together in the same place;

[1] Hutchinson to R. Jackson, 30 Aug. 1765.

CHAP. XVI. 1765. Aug.

and for ten days could not be got sight of. Several persons who thought themselves obnoxious, left their houses and removed their goods. Hutchinson fled to the castle, wretched from anxiety and constant agitation of mind. His despair dates from that moment. He saw that England had placed itself towards the colonies in the dilemma, that, "if parliament should make concessions, their authority would be lost; if they used external force, affection was alienated for ever."

"We are not bound to yield obedience," voted the freemen of Providence, echoing the resolves of Virginia. The patriots of Rhode Island, remembering the renowned founders of the colonies, thanked God, that their pleasant homes in the western world abounded in the means of "defence."[1] "That little turbulent colony," reported Gage,[2] "raised their mob likewise." And on the twenty-eighth day of August, after destroying the house and furniture of one Howard, who had written, and of one Moffat, who had spoken in favor of the power of parliament to tax America, they gathered round the house of their stamp officer, and, after a parley, compelled him to resign.

At New-York, the Lieutenant-Governor expressed a wish to the General for aid from the army. "You shall have as many troops as you shall demand, and can find quarters for," replied Gage; and at the same time, he urged Colden to the severe exertion of the civil power. "The public papers," he continued, "are crammed with treason, and the people excited to revolt."[3] But mean time, McEvers, the stamp officer of New-York resigned; "for," said he, "if I attempt

[1] Providence Gaz. Ex., 24 August, 1765. Lloyd's Conduct, 90, 91.

[2] Gage to Lee, Sept. 1765.

[3] Gage to Colden, 31 Aug. 1765.

to receive the stamps, my house will be pillaged."[1]—"McEvers is terrified," said Colden to a friend;[2] "but I shall not be intimidated; and the stamps shall be delivered in proper time;" intending himself to appoint a stamp distributor. 1765. Aug.

Yet dismay was spreading on every side among the crown officers. On the third of September, Coxe, the stamp officer for New Jersey, renounced his place. Sept.

On the previous night,[3] a party of four or five hundred, at Annapolis, pulled down a house, which Zachariah Hood, the stamp master for Maryland, was repairing, to be occupied, it was believed, for the sale of the stamps; and, shaking with terror, yet not willing to part with the unpopular office, which had promised to be worth many hundreds[4] a year, he fled from the colony to lodgings in the fort of New-York, as the only safe asylum.[5] The Maryland lawyers were of opinion, that the Stamp Tax must be declared invalid by the courts of Maryland, as a breach of chartered rights. One man published his card, refusing to pay taxes to which he had not consented. All resolved to burn the stamp paper, on its arrival in Annapolis; and the Governor had no power to prevent it, or to suppress any insurrection that might happen.[6]

On the fifth, Bernard, at Boston, gave way, without dignity or courage. After the resignation of Oliver, it became his duty to take possession of the stamped paper that might arrive. He had adopted measures

[1] J. McEvers to Colden, August.

[2] Colden to Sir W. Johnson, 31 August.

[3] Sharpe to Halifax, 15 Sept.

[4] Sharpe to Calvert, 16 Aug., 1765.

[5] Petition of Z. Hood to Colden, 16 Sept. 1765. Colden to Conway, 23 Sept.

[6] Sharpe to Gage 5 Sept. 1765.

CHAP. XVI. to increase the garrison at the castle, from fear of the people of Boston. He countermanded the levy; and,
1765. in an official declaration, he voluntarily set forth to a
Sept. very full council, "the absurdity of such a supposition, as that he should cause the stamped papers to be lodged in the Castle, there to be unpacked and distributed; he had no warrant whatsoever to unpack a bale of them, or to order any one else to do so; and it could not be conceived, that he should be so imprudent as to undertake the business."

On the ninth of September, a ship entered Boston, bringing news of the change of ministry, which created great joy, and the sanguine expectation of the speedy repeal of the Stamp Act. "If Astraea were not fled," said Mayhew, "there might be grounds for the hope;" and the colonies, mingling doubt with confidence, persevered in the purpose of making parliament plainly see that the act would prove pernicious to Great Britain itself. George Meserve,[1] the stamp distributor for New Hampshire, arriving in the same vessel, resigned his office before stepping on land; and afterwards, on his return to Portsmouth, repeated his resignation on the parade, in the presence of a great multitude.

Connecticut, which from its compact population and wealth, was, in military resources, second only to Massachusetts, loved its charter, of which it dreaded to risk the forfeiture by involving its legislature. The people, therefore, systematically assumed the direction of opinion. Assured of the protection of Fitch, the governor, who at heart was a lukewarm royalist, Ingersoll sought to reason the people into for-

[1] Meserve to Conway, 31 July, 1766.

CHAP. XVI. 1765. Sept.

bearance. "The act is so contrived," said he, "as to make it your interest to buy the stamps. When I undertook the office I meant a service to you."[1] "Stop advertising your wares," he was answered, "till they arrive safe at market." "The two first letters of his name," said another, "are those of that traitor of old. It was decreed our Saviour should suffer; but was it better for Judas Iscariot to betray him, so that the price of his blood might be saved by his friends?" The multitude, surrounding his house, demanded if he would resign. "I know not," he replied, "if I have power to resign." But he promised, if stamps came to him, to re-ship them, or leave his doors open to the people to do with them as they would.

New Haven, his own town, spoke out with authority in town-meeting. On Tuesday, the seventeenth of September, they elected as one of their representatives Roger Sherman, one of the great men of his time, a farmer's son, who had been educated at the common school, after the custom of New England, and having begun life as a shoemaker by trade, developed high capacity as a jurist and a statesman. They next, by public vote, "earnestly desired Ingersoll to resign his stamp office immediately." "The vote is needless," interposed a friend. "I shall await," said Ingersoll, "to see how the General Assembly is inclined." But the cautious people were anxious to save their representatives from a direct conflict with the British parliament; and already several hundreds of them, particularly three divisions from Norwich, from New London, and from Windham, and adjacent towns, had

[1] J. I., in Conn. Gaz.

CHAP. XVI. come out on horseback, with eight days' provisions, resolved to scour the colony through, till their stamp

1765 Sept. officer should be unearthed and reckoned with.

To save his house from the peril of an attack, Ingersoll rode out from New Haven, in company with the governor, intending to place himself under the protection of the legislature, which was to convene on Thursday. Meeting two men on horseback, with newly barked cudgels in their hands, Fitch charged them to go and tell their companions to return back. "We look upon this," they answered, "as the cause of the people; we will not take directions about it from any one;" and Ingersoll sent word by them that he would meet the concourse at Hartford.

On Thursday morning Ingersoll set forward alone. Two or three miles below Wethersfield, he met an advanced party of four or five; half a mile further, another of thirty; and soon the main body of about five hundred men, farmers and freeholders, all bearing long and large staves, white from being freshly rinded, all on horseback, two abreast, preceded by three trumpeters, and led by two militia officers in full uniform. They opened and received Ingersoll, and then, to the sound of trumpets, rode forward through the alluvial farms that grace the banks of the "lovely" Connecticut, till they came into Wethersfield. There in the broad main street, twenty rods wide, in the midst of neat dwelling-houses, and of a people that owned the soil and themselves held the plough, in the very heart of New England culture, where the old Puritan spirit, as it had existed among "the Best" in the days of Milton, had been preserved with the least admixture, the cavalcade halted, saying, "We cannot all hear and see so well in a house; we

1765. Sept.

had as good have the business done here;" and they bade Ingersoll resign. "Is it fair," said he, "that the counties of New London and Windham should dictate to all the rest of the colony?" "It don't signify to parley," they answered; "here are a great many people waiting, and you must resign." "I wait," said he, "to know the sense of the government. Besides, were I to resign, the governor has power to put in another." "Here," said they, "is the sense of the government; and no man shall exercise your office." "What will follow if I won't resign?" "Your fate." "I can die," said Ingersoll, "and, perhaps, as well now as at any time; I can die but once." "Don't irritate the people," said the leader, who knew that the selfish man ever clings to life, seeking only to multiply its comforts. Ingersoll asked leave to go to Hartford. "You shall not," it was answered, "go two rods till you have resigned." Entering a house with a committee, he sent word to the governor and assembly of his situation; and for three hours kept the people at bay by evasive proposals. "Get the matter over before the assembly has time to do any thing about it," said several of the members. "This delay," said others, enraged at his trifling, "is his artifice to wheedle the matter along till the assembly shall get ensnared in it." "I can keep the people off no longer," said the leader, coming up from below, with a crowd following in the passage. "It is time to submit," thought Ingersoll; and saying, "the cause is not worth dying for," he publicly resigned, making a written declaration, that it was his own free act, without any equivocation or mental reservation. "Swear to it," said the crowd. But from that he excused himself. "Then," said they, "shout Liberty

CHAP. XVI. 1765. Sept. and Property three times;" and throwing his hat into the air, he shouted, "Liberty and Property, Liberty and Property, Liberty and Property;" on which the multitude gave three loud huzzas.

After dinner, a cavalcade, which by this time had increased to the number of near one thousand men, escorted him along the road, studded with farm houses, from Wethersfield into Hartford, and dismounted within twenty yards of the house where the Assembly was sitting. The main body, led by Durkee,[1] with their white cudgels in their hands, marched in ranks, four abreast, to the sound of trumpets, round the court-house, and formed into a semicircle. Ingersoll was then directed to read the paper which he had signed, and he did so, within the hearing and presence of the Legislature.[2] This was succeeded by the cry of Liberty and Property, and three cheers; soon after which the people, than whom better men never "walked in glory behind the plough," having done their work thoroughly, rode home to their several villages.

There the Calvinist ministers nursed the flame of piety and the love of civil freedom. Of that venerable band, none did better service than the American-born Stephen Johnson, the sincere and fervid pastor of the first church of Lyme. "Bute, Bedford, and Grenville," said he to the people, "will be had in remembrance by Americans as an abomination, execration, and curse. As the result of all, these measures tend to a very fatal civil war; and France and

[1] The name is Durgie in my copy of Hutchinson's Letter to Governor Pownall, October, 1765. Ingersoll, in his account, is careful to name no one. Connecticut Courant, 27 Sept, 1765.

[2] Connecticut Courant, No. 483.

CHAP. XVI. 1765. Sept.

Spain would make advantage of the crisis. If they are pursued, the dear patrimony of our fathers must pass to taskmasters here, or the men of ease and wealth in Great Britain, who have schemed them away for nought. This people cannot bear it till they have lost the memory of their dear fathers, and their affection to their posterity. The Americans will call to mind revolution principles, such as, 'where there is a right there is a remedy.' Their uneasiness is not the sudden heat of passion, from the novelty of the tax, but is the more deep rooted, the more attentively it is considered.

"The advocates for these measures seem to be counsellors of Rehoboam's stamp. Instead of hearing the cries, and redressing the grievances of a most loyal and injured people, they are for adding burden upon burden, till they make the little finger of his present majesty a thousand times heavier than the loins of his good grandfather; and would bind all fast with a military chain. Such counsels ended in Israel in such a revolt and wide breach as could never be healed. That this may end in a similar event is not impossible to the providence of God, nor more improbable to Britons than five years ago this Stamp Tax was to Americans."[1]

[1] New London Gaz. No. 90.

CHAPTER XVII.

AMERICA REASONS AGAINST THE STAMP ACT—MINISTRY OF ROCKINGHAM CONTINUED.

September, 1765.

CHAP. XVI. 1765 Sept. During these acts of compulsory submission, and while Boston, in a full town-meeting unanimously asked the pictures of Conway and Barre for Faneuil Hall, the Lords of the Treasury in England, Rockingham, Dowdeswell, and Lord John Cavendish being present, held meetings almost daily, to carry the Stamp Act into effect; and without any apparent reluctance, completed the lists of stamp officers; provided for the instant filling of vacancies that might result from death or neglect; signed warrants for the expense of preparing the American stamps; and enjoined the Governor to superintend and assist their distribution.[1] These minutes might have had their excuse in the principle, that there existed no power to dispense with the law of the land; but Dartmouth, from the Board of Trade, adopting the worst measure of corruption, which Grenville had firmly resisted, proposed to make the government of a province independent of the provincial legislature for its sup-

[1] Treasury Minute Book, xxxvii. 120, 123, 133. Treasury Letter, Book, xxiii. 205, 214.

port.[1] Every thing implied confidence in the obedience of the colonies. CHAP. XVII.

And yet the tide of opinion in America was swelling and becoming irresistible. "To the north and to the southward," said Hutchinson, "the people are absolutely without the use of reason." A majority in every colony was resolved to run all hazards rather than submit. When they were asked, "What will you do after the first of November?" "Do?" they replied, "do as we did before." "Will you violate the law of parliament?" "The Stamp Act," repeated every one over and over, "is against Magna Charta, and Lord Coke says, an act of parliament against Magna Charta is for that reason void." 1765. Sept.

In a more solemn tone, the convictions and purposes of America found utterance through the press. John Adams, of Massachusetts, a fiery Protestant, claiming intellectual freedom as the birthright of man, at once didactic and impetuous, obeying the impulses of "a heart that burned for his country's welfare," summoned the whole experience of the human race and human nature herself, to bear witness, that through the increase and diffusion of intelligence, the world was advancing towards the establishment of popular power. Full of hope, he set liberty and knowledge over against authority and ignorance; America over against Europe; the modern principle of popular freedom over against the Middle Age and its tyrannies; the New World over against the Old.

"The people," thus he continued, "the populace, as they are contemptuously called, have rights antecedent to all earthly government—rights that cannot

[1] Representation of Lords of Trade to the king, 27 Sept. 1765.

CHAP. XVII. 1765. Sept.

be repealed or restrained by human laws—rights derived from the Great Legislator of the Universe." Tracing the gradual improvement of human society from the absolute monarchy of the earliest ages, and from the more recent tyrannies of the canon and the feudal law, he saw in the Reformation the uprising of the people, under the benign providence of God, against the confederacy of priestcraft and feudalism—of spiritual and temporal despotism.

"This great struggle"—these are his words—"peopled America. Not religion alone, a love of universal liberty projected, conducted, and accomplished its settlement. After their arrival here, the Puritans formed their plan, both of ecclesiastical and civil government, in direct opposition to the canon and feudal systems. They demolished the whole system of diocesan episcopacy. To render the popular power in their new government as great and wise as their principles of theory, they endeavored to remove from it feudal inequalities, and establish a government of the state, more agreeable to the dignity of human nature than any they had seen in Europe.

"Convinced that nothing could preserve their posterity from the encroachments of the two systems of tyranny but knowledge diffused through the whole people, they laid very early the foundations of colleges, and made provision by law, that every town should be furnished with a grammar-school. The education of all ranks of people was made the care and expense of the public, in a manner unknown to any other people, ancient or modern, so that a native American, who cannot read and write, is as rare an appearance as a comet or an earthquake.

"There seems to be a direct and formal design on

foot in Great Britain, to enslave all America. Be it remembered, Liberty must at all hazards be defended. Rulers are no more than attorneys, agents, and trustees for the people; and if the trust is insidiously betrayed, or wantonly trifled away, the people have a right to revoke the authority that they themselves have deputed, and to constitute abler and better agents. We have an indisputable right to demand our privileges against all the power and authority on earth.

"The true source of our sufferings has been our timidity. Let every order and degree among the people rouse their attention and animate their resolution. Let us study the law of nature, the spirit of the British constitution, the great examples of Greece and Rome, the conduct of our British ancestors, who have defended for us the inherent rights of mankind against kings and priests. Let us impress upon our souls the ends of our own more immediate forefathers in exchanging their native country for a wilderness. Let the pulpit delineate the noble rank man holds among the works of God. Let us hear that consenting to slavery is a sacrilegious breach of trust. Let the bar proclaim the rights delivered down from remote antiquity; not the grants of princes or parliaments, but original rights, coequal with prerogative and coeval with government, inherent and essential, established as preliminaries before a parliament existed, having their foundations in the constitution of the intellectual and moral world, in truth, liberty, justice and benevolence. Let the colleges impress on the tender mind the beauty of liberty and virtue, and the deformity and turpitude of slavery and vice, and spread far and wide the ideas of right and the sensation of freedom. No one of any feeling, born and

CHAP. XVII. 1765. Sept.

educated in this happy country, can consider the usurpations that are meditating for all our countrymen, and all their posterity, without the utmost agonies of heart, and many tears."

Such were the genuine sentiments of New England, uttered by John Adams, in words which, in part, were promptly laid before the king in council. In Maryland, Daniel Dulany, an able lawyer, not surpassed in ability by any of the crown lawyers in the House of Commons, "a patriot councillor, inclined to serve the people," discussed the propriety of the Stamp Act, not before America only, but seeking audience of England. He admitted that the colonies were subordinate to the supreme national council; that the British parliament had the unquestionable right to legislate on the trade of the colonies; that trade may frequently be most properly regulated by duties on imports and exports; that parliament is itself to determine what regulations are most proper; and that if they should produce an incidental revenue, they are not, therefore, unwarrantable.

But in reply to the arguments of the crown lawyers, and the ministerial defenders of the Stamp Act, he argued, with minute and elaborate learning, that the late regulations for the colonies were not just, because the Commons of England, in which the Americans were neither actually nor virtually represented, had no right, by the common law or the British constitution, to give and grant the property of the Commons in America; that they were rightfully void, as their validity rested only on the power of those who framed them to carry them into effect; that they were not lenient, the taxes imposed being excessive and unequal; that they were not politic, as Great

CHAP XVII. 1765. Sept.

Britain, by the acts of trade, had all from the colonies before, and could but drive them to observe the strictest maxims of frugality, and to establish manufactures of leather, cotton, wool, and flax; that they were not consistent with charters, which were the original compacts between the first emigrants to America and the crown; that they were against all precedents of the previous legislation of the British parliament; that they were equally against the precedents of legislation for Ireland, which was as subject to Great Britain as were the colonies; that they were against the judgment of former British ministers, whose requisitions for revenue were uniformly transmitted to the colonies to tax themselves.

"There may be a time," he added, "when redress may be obtained. Till then, I shall recommend a legal, orderly, and prudent resentment to be expressed in a zealous and vigorous industry. A garment of linsey-woolsey, when made the distinction of patriotism, is more honorable than the plumes and the diadem of an emperor without it. Let the manufacture of America be the symbol of dignity and the badge of virtue, and it will soon break the fetters of distress."

Thus wrote Dulany, the champion of the day, pleading, not for truths pregnant with independence, but for exemption from taxes imposed without consent; promoting repeal, but beating back revolution. His opinions were thought to have moulded those of William Pitt, by whom they were publicly[1] noticed with great honor; and they widely prevailed in America.

"This unconstitutional method of taxation," observed Washington, at Mount Vernon, of the Stamp Act,

[1] Shelburne to Chatham, 6 Feb. 1765: "The American pamphlet, to which your lordship did so much honor last session."

CHAP. XVII. 1765. Sept.

"is a direful attack upon the liberties of the colonies, will be a necessary incitement to industry, and for many cogent reasons will prove ineffectual. Our courts of judicature," he added, "must inevitably be shut up; and if so, the merchants of Great Britain will not be among the last to wish for its repeal."

Enlightened by discussions, towns, and legislatures, as opportunity offered, made their declaration of rights, following one another like a chime of bells, and preparing the public mind for the union of the continent.

In the infant colony of Georgia, all feeble as it was, the great majority of the representatives, at the instance of their speaker, against the will of the governor, came together on Monday, the second of September, and though they doubted their power, at such a voluntary meeting, to elect delegates to the Congress, they sent an express messenger to New-York to promise their adhesion to its results; "for," said they, "no people, as individuals, can more warmly espouse the common cause than do the people of this province."

Further north, on the ninth of September, the assembly of Pennsylvania, disregarding the opinions of Galloway, its speaker, who wished to see the Stamp Act executed, accepted the plan of Congress by a majority of one. At the same time it recognised the indispensable duty to grant requisite aids cheerfully and liberally, but only in a constitutional way, through its own assembly.

Next in time, but first in the explicit declaration of rights, the Assembly of Rhode Island not only joined the union, but unanimously directed all the officers of the colony to proceed in all their duties as usual, without regard to the Stamp Act, and engaged to indemnify them and save them harmless. CHAP. XVII.

In the same month, Delaware, by the spontaneous act of the representatives of each of its counties; Connecticut, with the calm approval of its assembly; Maryland, trusting in the express language of its charter, and by the earnest patriotism of its inhabitants, obtaining the consent of every branch of its legislature,—successively elected delegates to the general American Congress. 1765. Sept.

In Massachusetts, Boston, under the guidance of Samuel Adams, set the example to other towns, and in his words denounced to its representatives the Stamp Act, and its Courts of Admiralty, as contrary to the British constitution, to the charter of the province, and to the common rights of mankind; and built "the warmest expectations" on the union of the colonies in Congress. A week later, the town of Braintree, led by John Adams, declared "the most grievous innovation of all" to be, "the extension of the power of Courts of Admiralty; in which one judge presided alone, and, without juries, decided the law and the fact; holding his office during the pleasure of the king, and establishing that most mischievous of all customs, the taking of commissions on all condemnations."

To the Legislature which convened on the twenty-fifth, Bernard attempted to draw a frightful picture of the general outlawry and rising of the poor against the rich, which were to ensue, if stamps were not used, and so to draw the Assembly into adopting the distinction between the power of parliament and the expediency of the Stamp Act. "I shall not," so he

CHAP. XVII. 1765. Sept. said, "enter into any disquisition of the policy of this act; I have only to say, it is an act of the parliament of Great Britain; and I trust that the supremacy of that parliament over all the members of their wide and diffused empire, never was, and never will be, denied within these walls.

"The right of the parliament of Great Britain to make laws for her American colonies, however it has been controverted in America, remains indisputable at Westminster. If it is yet to be made a question, who shall determine it but the parliament? If the parliament declares, that their right is inherent in them, are they likely to acquiesce in an open and forcible opposition to the exercise of it? Will they not more probably maintain such right, and support their own authority?

"The gentlemen who opposed this act in the House of Commons, did not dispute the authority of parliament to make such a law, but argued upon the inexpediency of it at this time.

"The power of taxing the colonies may be admitted, and yet the expediency of exercising that power at such a time may be denied; but, if the questions are blended together, so as to admit of but one answer, the affirmative of the right of parliament will conclude for the expediency of this act.

"I would not willingly aggravate the dangers which are before you. I do not think it very easy to do it; this province seems to me to be on the brink of a precipice; it depends upon you to prevent its falling. From this time, this arduous business" of executing the Stamp Act, "will be put into your hands, and it will become a provincial concern."

"There is a snake in the grass," said the wary

CHAP. XVII. 1765. Sept.

people of Boston; "touch not the unclean thing;" and to make sure of a vigilance which could not be lulled, they elected Samuel Adams to be their representative, in the place made vacant by the death of Thacher. On the day on which Samuel Adams took his seat, he found the legislature adopting resolves, that all courts should do business without stamps; on which Bernard, in a fright, prorogued it till nine days before the first of November.

The eye of the whole continent watched with the intensest anxiety the conduct of New-York, the capital of the central province, and head-quarters of the standing forces in America; having a septennial assembly, a royal council, ships of war anchored near its wharves, and within the town itself a fort, mounting many heavy cannon.[1] There the authority of the British government was concentrated in the hands of Gage, the general, whose military powers, as ample as those of a Viceroy, extended over all the colonies, and who was "extremely exasperated"[2] at the course of events, as well in New-York as Massachusetts. But he was at a loss what to do. Besides, the officers of government had no confidence in one another. In Boston, Gage was not esteemed a man of "capacity;" and he, in his turn, thought Bernard pusillanimous. At New-York, he called upon the civil power to exert itself more efficiently. "All civil authority is at an end,"[3] answered Colden; "the presence of a battalion is the only way to prevent mischief." "It will be more safe for the government," interposed the Council[4] of the province of New-York,

[1] Journal of an Officer. King's Lib. MS. 213.

[2] N. Rogers to Hutchinson, N. Y. 16 Sept. 1765.

[3] Colden to Gage, 2 Sept. 1765.

[4] Advice of Counsel to Colden, 7 Sept.

CHAP. XVII. "to show a confidence in the people." But Colden, emboldened by the arrival of two artillery companies

1765. Sept. from England, put the fort in such a state of offence and defence, as to be able to boast alike to Conway[1] and Amherst,[2] that he had "effectually discouraged" sedition. "The people here will soon come to better temper, after taxes become more familiar to them," wrote an officer[3] who had been sent to America, on a tour of observation. "I will cram the stamps down their throats with the end of my sword,"[4] cried the braggart James, major of artillery, as he busied himself with bringing into the fort more field-pieces, as well as powder, shot, and shells.[5] "If they attempt to rise, I," he gave out, "will drive them all out of the town for a pack of rascals, with four-and-twenty men."[6] But the press of New-York continued its daring. From denying the right of parliament to tax the colonies, it proceeded to doubt its legislative authority over America altogether. On the twenty-first day of September, a paper called "The Constitutional Courant" made its appearance, and "JOIN OR DIE" was its motto. "Join or Die" was echoed from one end of the continent to the other.

[1] Colden to Conway, 23 Sept.

[2] Colden to Amherst, 10 Sept.

[3] King's Lib. MS. 213. The author seems to have been Lord Adam Gordon.

[4] James to Colden, giving an account of his examination before Parliament. Letter from N. Y. in S. C. Gazette.

[5] A. Colden to C. Colden, Sept. 1765.

[6] James's Account of his Examination.

CHAPTER XVIII.

THE COLONIES MEET IN CONGRESS.—ROCKINGHAM ADMINISTRATION.

October, 1765.

CHAP. XVIII. 1765. Oct.

The cry was the harbinger of an American Congress. The delegates of South Carolina, the fearless Gadsden, who never practised disguise, the upright, able, and eloquent Rutledge; Lynch, who combined good sense, patriotism, and honesty, with fiery energy, conciseness of speech, and dignity of manner, arrived first at its place of meeting. A little delay in its organization gave time for the representatives of New Jersey, where the lawyers were resolved to forego all business rather than purchase a stamp, to imitate the example of Delaware. "Such a Congress," said Colden to the delegates from Massachusetts, "is unconstitutional and unlawful; and I shall give them no countenance."

While they were waiting, on the third day of October, the last stamp officer north of the Potomac, the stubborn John Hughes, a quaker of Philadelphia, as he lay desperately ill, heard muffled drums beat through the city, and the State House bell ring muffled, and then the trampling feet of the people assembling to

CHAP. XVIII. 1765. Oct

demand his resignation. His illness obtained for him some forbearance; but his written promise was extorted, not to do any thing that should have the least tendency to put the Stamp Act into execution in Pennsylvania or Delaware; and he announced to the governor his "resignation." "If Great Britain can or will suffer such conduct to pass unpunished," thus he wrote to the Commissioners of Stamps, "a man need not be a prophet, nor the son of a prophet, to see clearly that her empire in North America is at an end."

On Monday, the seventh of October, delegates chosen by the House of Representatives of Massachusetts, of Rhode Island, Connecticut, Pennsylvania, Maryland, and South Carolina; delegates named by a written requisition from the individual representatives of Delaware and New Jersey, and the legislative Committee of Correspondence of New-York, met at New-York, in Congress. New Hampshire, though not present by deputy, yet agreed to abide by the result; and they were gladdened during their session by the arrival of the express messenger from Georgia, sent near a thousand miles by land to obtain a copy of their proceedings.[1]

The members of this first Union of the American people were elected by the representatives of the people of each separate colony. While they formed one body, their power was derived from independent sources. Each of the colonies existed in its individuality; and notwithstanding great differences in their respective population and extent of territory, as they met in Congress they recognised each other as equals,

[1] James Otis to Henry Shelburne, MS.

"without the least claim of pre-eminence one over the other." CHAP. XVIII.

The Congress entered directly on the consideration of the safest groundwork on which to rest the collective American liberties. Should they build on charters, or natural justice; on precedents and fact, or abstract truth; on special privileges, or universal reason? Otis was instructed by Boston to support not only the liberty of the colonies, but also chartered rights. Johnson, of Connecticut, submitted a paper, which pleaded charters from the crown. But Robert R. Livingston, of New-York, "the goodness of whose heart set him above prejudices, and equally comprehended all mankind," would not place the hope of America on that foundation;[1] and Gadsden, of South Carolina, giving utterance to the warm impulses of a brave and noble nature, spoke against it with irresistible impetuosity. "A confirmation of our essential and common rights as Englishmen," thus he himself reports his sentiments,[2] "may be pleaded from charters safely enough; but any further dependence upon them may be fatal. We should stand upon the broad common ground of those natural rights that we all feel and know as men, and as descendants of Englishmen. I wish the charters may not ensnare us at last, by drawing different colonies to act differently in this great cause. Whenever that is the case, all will be over with the whole. There ought to be no New England man, no New-Yorker, known on the continent, but all of us Americans." 1765. Oct.

These views prevailed; and in the proceedings of the Congress, the argument for American liberty

[1] R. R. Livingston, jr., to the historian, Gordon.

[2] MS. Letter of Christopher Gadsden.

CHAP. XVIII. 1765. Oct. from royal grants was avoided. This is the first great step towards independence. Dummer had pleaded for colony charters; Livingston, Gadsden, and the Congress of 1765, provided for Americans self-existence and union, by claiming rights that preceded charters, and would survive their ruin.

And how would that union extend? What nations would be included in the name of Americans? The members of that Congress believed themselves responsible for the liberties of the continent; and even while they were deliberating, the vast prairies of Illinois, the great eastern valley of the Mississippi, with all its rivers gushing from the Alleghanies, with all its boundless primeval forests, spreading from the mountain tops to the alluvial margin of the mighty stream, with all its solitudes, in which futurity would summon the eager millions of so many tongues to build happy homes, passed from the sway of France into the temporary custody of England.

The French officers had, since the peace, been ready loyally to surrender the country to the English. From Mobile, Ross had passed through the land of the Choctaws and the Chickasaws, to the Cherokee river, which he descended in a canoe of his own building, to the Ohio, and so to the Mississippi and the Illinois. But the Illinois, the Missouri, and the Osage tribes, in a council held at Fort Chartres, breathed nothing but war. In vain did St. Ange entreat them to be soothed. "My father," spoke the chief of the Kaskaskias in the name of all, "My father, the Illinois nation deliberates on what it will do, without the counsel of others; but in what we have now done, we follow the mind of all the red men. We have held many councils on this subject, and no man has been of a mind to accept this peace." And turning to the English officer, he said, "Go hence as soon as you can, and tell your chief, that the Illinois and all our brethren will make war on you, if you come upon our lands. Away, away, and tell your chief that these lands are ours; no one can claim them, not even the other red men. Why will you come here? You do not know us; we never have seen you. Tell your chief to stay on his own lands, as we do on ours. Assure him that we will have no English here, and that this is the mind of all the red men. Adieu. Go, and never return, or our wild warriors will make you fall." "We," said the chiefs of the Osages and Missouris, "think like our brethren, the Illinois; we will aid them to keep their lands. Why, O Englishman, do you not remain on your lands as the red men do on theirs. These lands are ours; we hold them from our ancestors; they dwelt upon them, and now they are ours. No one can claim them of us. Therefore depart; begone, begone, begone; and tell your chief, the Red Men will have no Englishman here. Begone, never to return. We will have among us none other than the French." Ross was obliged to go down the river to New Orleans, indebted for his safety to the circumspection of St. Ange.

But Fraser, who arrived from Pittsburg, brought proofs that the Senecas, the Delawares, and the Shawnees, had made peace with the English. "It was not the Illinois who declared war against the English," the chiefs of the Kaskaskias then said. "We took up the hatchet, solicited by our elder brothers, the Delawares, the Senecas, the Shawnees, and the Ottawas. Let them make peace: we ourselves have none

CHAP. XVIII. 1765. to make; we follow as they shall lead." "I waged this war," said Pontiac, "because, for two years together, the Delawares and Shawnees begged me to take up arms against the English. So I became their ally, and was of their mind;" and resisting no longer, he who was in a manner adored by the nations round about, plighted his word for peace, and kept[1] it with integrity and humanity.

A just curiosity may ask, how many persons of foreign lineage had gathered in the valley of the Illinois since its discovery by the missionaries. Fraser was told that there were of white men, able to bear arms, seven hundred; of white women, five hundred; of their children, eight hundred and fifty; of negroes of both sexes, nine hundred.[2] The banks of the Wabash, we learn from another source, were occupied by about one hundred and ten French families, most of which were at Vincennes.[3] Fraser sought to overawe the French traders with the menace of an English army that was to come among them. But they laughed him to scorn, pointing to the Mississippi, which they could so easily cross, and beyond which they would be safe from English jurisdiction. As he embarked for New Orleans, Pontiac again gave him assurances of continuing peace, if the Shawnees and other nations on the Ohio would recall their war-belts.

Already Croghan, an Indian agent, was on his way from Fort Pitt to Illinois, attended with Shawnese deputies. As he approached the Wabash, his party was attacked and plundered by a band of Indians of that river, who killed two of his own men

[1] Fraser to Gage, 18 May.
[2] Fraser to Gage, 15 May.
[3] Croghan, in Craig's Olden Time, and in Mann Butler's Kentucky. Gage to Halifax, 10 Aug.

and three of the Shawnees. But hearing from him that the Iroquois, the Shawnees, and the Delawares had made peace, they were terrified lest the whole of the northern Indians should join to avenge on them the death of those whom they had slain; and they sued piteously for forgiveness. The five nations that dwelt on the Wabash gave him each a calumet, and offered to guide British troops from Fort Pitt to the Illinois.

"Brother," said they all to Croghan, "have pity on us, our women and children. The Great Spirit, who made all things, made you and the French first, and us after, so that we are your youngest brethren. It is you, brother, and the French made this last war. The French and you are now all as one people. In the name of all our tribes, promote the good work of peace."

While on his way to the Illinois, Croghan met deputations from the nations dwelling there, and Pontiac himself;[1] with whom it was agreed, that the English should take possession of all the posts which the French formerly held. From the Wabash, the agent went to Detroit, where the good results were confirmed in council.

As soon as an account of the success of this negotiation reached Fort Pitt, Captain Stirling, with one hundred men of the Forty-second regiment, was detached down the Ohio, to relieve the French garrison. They arrived safely at Fort Chartres, where St. Ange gave them a friendly reception; and, in the fall of the leaf, on the morning of the tenth of October,[2] he surrendered to them the left bank of the Mississippi.

[1] Croghan to Alexander McKee, 3 Aug.

[2] Capt. Stirling to Gage. French Procès Verbal.

CHAP. XVIII. 1765. Oct. Some of the French crossed the river, so that at St. Genevieve, a place that had been occupied for several years, there were at least five-and-twenty families; while St. Louis, whose origin dates from the fifteenth of February, 1764,[1] and whose skilfully chosen site and unequalled advantages soon attracted the admiration of the British commander, already counted about twice that number, and ranked as the leading settlement on the western side of the Mississippi. In all the English portion of the valley, there remained less than two thousand inhabitants of European origin. And of these, few or none were attached to England. She had won the valley of the Mississippi, and dared not colonize it, lest colonies so remote should renounce their dependence. The government then instituted was the absolute rule of the British army, with a local judge to decide all disputes among the inhabitants according to the customs of the country, yet subject to an appeal to the military chief.

Thus France retired from the valley of the Mississippi, and cast behind no look of longing. The philosophers of that day, a name which comprehended almost every body in Paris, were full of joy at their success in effecting the exile of the Jesuits. The clergy, in their remonstrances to Louis XV., unmindful of America, uttered only their fear, that "the press would soon effect the ruin of church and state—of religion, and the fundamental laws of monarchy."[2] The king, immersed in the most scandalous voluptuousness, dreamed not of danger from afar, and cared not for losing the imperial territory that bore his

[1] Prinne's Anniversary Discourse.

[2] Bishops to Louis XV.: "Nous touchons au moment fatal, où la librairie perdra l'église et l'état."

name; but shared the alarm[1] of the church at the free-thinking and free press which late years had fostered. The Duke de Choiseul, who at that time was minister of the marine and for the colonies, revolved in his own mind the coming fortunes of the new world; repressed regrets for Louisiana, because he saw that America must soon become independent; predicted to his sovereign the nearness of the final struggle between England and its dependencies, and urged earnestly, that France should so increase its naval force,[2] as to be prepared to take advantage of the impending crisis.

The amiable, but inexperienced men who formed the active ministry of England, were less discerning. The names of Rockingham, and Grafton, and Conway, must be pronounced with respect; yet suddenly and unexpectedly brought to the administration of an empire, they knew not what to propose. Of the men on whose support they were compelled to rely, many were among the loudest and ablest supporters of the Stamp tax. So orders were given[3] to Bernard, in Massachusetts, and elsewhere to governors, in cases of a vacancy, to act as stamp-distributors; and the resolves of Virginia were reserved for the consideration of that very parliament which had passed the Stamp Act by a majority of five to one. Rockingham had promised nothing to the friends of America but relief to trade, where it was improperly curbed. To rouse the ministry from its indifference, Thomas Hollis,[4] who perceived in the "ugly squall," that had just reach-

[1] The king's answer to the clergy, 1765.

[2] Memorial of Choiseul, communicated to me verbally, by M. de Barante, who has a copy of it.

[3] Grey Cooper to Bernard, 8 Oct, 1765. Same to Shirley, 10 Oct. Treasury Letter Book.

[4] Hollis: Diary, 23 Oct.

CHAP. XVIII. 1765. Oct.

ed them from America, the forerunner of the general hurricane, waited on Rockingham, with the accounts which he had received from Mayhew,[1] that the Stamp Act, and the power given to the Admiralty courts to dispense with juries, were detested "as instances of grievous oppression, and scarce better than downright tyranny," not by Boston only, but by the people throughout the continent; that it could never be carried into execution, unless at the point of the sword, by at least one considerable army in each province at the hazard of either the destruction of the American colonies, or their entire revolt and loss. The ministry shrunk from enforcing by arms the law which a part of them in their hearts disapproved; and on the twenty-fourth of October, the last day but one of the session of the American Congress, and only seven before the time for the Stamp Act to go into effect, Conway, by advice of the Privy Council, sent orders to the American Governors, and to the General, exhorting to "persuasive methods," and "the utmost prudence and lenity."[2]

The conduct of America was regulated by the Congress, at New-York. "Those who compose it," said Gage, "are of various characters and opinions; but in general, the spirit of democracy is strong among them; supporting the independence of the provinces, as not subject to the legislative power of Great Britain. The question is not of the inexpediency of the Stamp Act; but that it is unconstitutional and contrary to their rights."[3] No colony

[1] Mayhew to Hollis, 26 Sept.

[2] Conway to Gage; to Bernard; to the Governors of North America.

[3] Gage to Conway, 12 Oct.

was better represented than South Carolina. Her delegation gave a chief to two of the three great committees, and in all that was done well, her mind visibly appeared.

The difficult task of defining the rights and "setting forth the liberty" which America "ought to enjoy," led the Assembly to debate for two weeks "on liberty, privileges, and prerogative." In these debates, Otis, of Boston, himself the father of the Congress, displayed great knowledge of the interests of America, and assisted to kindle the fires which afterwards lighted the country on its path to freedom.

It was proposed to "insist upon a repeal of all acts, laying duties on trade, as well as the Stamp Act." "If we do not make an explicit acknowledgment of the power of Britain to regulate our trade," said the too gentle Livingston, "she will never give up the point of internal taxation." But he was combated with great heat, till at last the Congress, by the hand of Rutledge, of South Carolina, erased from the declaration of rights the unguarded concession; and the restrictions on American commerce, though practically acquiesced in, were enumerated as grievances.

Still Gadsden and Lynch were not satisfied. With vigorous dialectics, they proceeded from a denial of the power of parliament in America, to deny the propriety of approaching either house with a petition. "The House of Commons," reasoned Gadsden, with the persevering earnestness of conviction, "refused to receive the addresses of the colonies, when the natter was pending; besides, we neither hold our rights from them nor from the Lords." But yielding to the majority, Gadsden suppressed his opposition; "for," said he, "union is most certainly all in all."

CHAP. XVIII. 1765. Oct.

The carefully-considered documents in which the Congress embodied the demands of America, dwell mainly on the inherent right to trial by jury, in opposition to the extension of the Admiralty jurisdiction, and the right to freedom from taxation, except through the respective colonial legislatures. These were promulgated in the declaratory resolutions, with the further assertion, that the people of the colonies not only are not, but, from their local circumstances, never can be represented in the House of Commons in Great Britain; that taxes never have been and never can be constitutionally imposed on the colonies, but by their respective legislatures; that all supplies to the crown are free gifts; and that for the people of Great Britain to grant the property of the colonists was neither reasonable nor consistent with the principles, nor with the spirit of the British constitution. The same immunities were claimed in the address to the king, as "essential principles, inherent rights and liberties;" of which the security was necessary to the "most effectual connection of America with the British empire." They also formed the theme of the memorial to the House of Lords, mingled with complaints of the "late restrictions on trade."

Having thus insisted on their rights in strong terms, the Congress purposely[1] employed a different style in the address to the House of Commons, insisting chiefly on the disadvantages the new measure might occasion, as well to the mother country as to the colonies. They disclaimed for America the "impracticable" idea of a representation in any but American Legislatures. Acknowledging "all due subordina-

[1] South Carolina to its agent, Garth, 16 Oct. 1765.

tion to the parliament of Great Britain," and extolling the "English constitution as the most perfect form of government," the source of "all their civil and religious liberties;" they argued that, in reason and sound policy, there exists a material distinction between the exercise of a parliamentary jurisdiction in general acts of legislation for the amendment of the common law or the regulation of trade through the whole empire, and the exercise of that jurisdiction by imposing taxes on the colonies; from which they, therefore, entreated to be relieved.

While the Congress were still anxiously engaged in weighing each word and phrase which they were to adopt, it was rumored that a ship laden with stamps had arrived. At once, all the vessels in the harbor lowered their colors in sign of grief. The following night, papers were posted up at the doors of every public office, and at the corners of the streets, in the name of the country, threatening the first man that should either distribute or make use of stamped paper. "Assure yourselves," thus the stamp distributors were warned, "the spirit of Brutus and Cassius is yet alive." The people grew more and more inflamed, declaring, "we will not submit to the Stamp Act upon any account, or in any instance." "In this, we will no more submit to parliament than to the Divan at Constantinople." "We will ward it off till we can get France or Spain to protect us." From mouth to mouth flew the words of John Adams, "You have rights antecedent to all earthly government; rights that cannot be repealed or restrained by human laws; rights derived from the Great Legislator of the Universe." In the midst of this intense excitement, the Congress brought its deliberations to a

CHAP. XVIII. 1765. Oct.

close. Ruggles, of Massachusetts, and Ogden, of New Jersey, pretended that the resistance to the Stamp Act through all America was treason, argued strenuously in favor of the supreme authority of parliament, and cavilling to the last at particular expressions, refused to sign the papers prepared by the Congress. Dyer, of Connecticut, had conceded that there were objections of weight; but in the night of the twenty-fourth, "union," said he, "is so necessary, disunion so fatal, in these matters, that as we cannot agree upon any alteration, they ought to be signed as they are, by those who are authorized to do so."[1] Ogden insisted that it was better for each province to petition separately for itself; and Ruggles, the presiding officer of the Congress, heedless of their indignation, still interposed his scruples and timidities.

On the morning of the twenty-fifth, the anniversary of the accession of George the Third, the Congress assembled for the last time, and the delegates of six colonies being empowered to do so, namely; all the delegates from Massachusetts, except Ruggles; all from New Jersey, except Ogden; all those of Rhode Island; all of Pennsylvania, excepting Dickinson, who was absent but adhered; all of Delaware; and all of Maryland, with the virtual assent of New Hampshire, Connecticut, New-York, South Carolina, and Georgia, set their hands to the papers, by which the colonies became, as they expressed it, "a bundle of sticks, which could neither be bent nor broken."

[1] Journal of W. S. Johnson. Dyer to Johnson, 8 Oct.

CHAPTER XIX.

AMERICA ANNULS THE STAMP ACT—ROCKINGHAM'S ADMINISTRATION CONTINUED.

OCTOBER—DECEMBER, 1765.

CHAP. XIX. 1765. Oct.

ON the day on which the Congress consummated the Union, the Legislature which first proposed it, having been reassembled at Boston, and now cheered and invigorated by the presence of Samuel Adams, embodied in their reply to Bernard, the opinion on the power of parliament, from which the colony was never to recede.

"Your Excellency tells us," they said, "that the province seems to be upon the brink of a precipice! To despair of the commonwealth is a certain presage of its fall. The representatives of the people are awake to the sense of its danger, and their utmost prudence will not be wanting to prevent its ruin.

"Of the power of parliament, there undoubtedly are boundaries. The church, in the name of the Sacred Trinity, in the presence of king Henry the Third and the estates of the realm, solemnly denounced that most grievous sentence of excommunication against all those who should make statutes, or observe them, being made contrary to the liberties of Magna Charta.

CHAP. XIX. 1765. Oct. Such acts as infringed upon the rights of that charter were always repealed. We have the same confidence in the rectitude of the present parliament. To require submission to an act as a preliminary to granting relief from the unconstitutional burdens of it, supposes such a wanton exercise of mere arbitrary power as ought never to be surmised of the patrons of liberty and justice.

"The charter of the province invests the General Assembly with the power of making laws for its internal government and taxation; and this charter has never yet been forfeited.

"There are certain original inherent rights belonging to the people, which the parliament itself cannot divest them of: among these is the right of representation in the body which exercises the power of taxation. There is a necessity that the subjects of America should exercise this power within themselves, for they are not represented in parliament, and indeed we think it impracticable.

"To suppose an indisputable right in parliament to tax the subject without their consent, includes the idea of a despotic power.

"The people of this province have a just value for their inestimable rights, which are derived to all men from nature, and are happily interwoven in the British constitution. They esteem it sacrilege ever to give them up; and rather than lose them, they would willingly part with every thing else.

"The Stamp Act wholly cancels the very conditions upon which our ancestors, with much toil and blood, and at their sole expense, settled this country, and enlarged his majesty's dominions. It tends to destroy that mutual confidence and affection, as well as that equality, which ought ever to subsist among all his majesty's subjects in this wide and extended empire; and, what is the worst of all evils, if his majesty's American subjects are not to be governed according to the known and stated rules of the constitution, their minds may, in time, become disaffected."

In addition to this state paper, which was the imprint of the mind of Samuel Adams,[1] and had the vigor and polished elegance of his style, the house adopted "the best, and the best digested series of resolves," prepared by him, "to ascertain the just rights of the province," which the preamble said "had been lately drawn into question" by the British parliament.

The answer of the house was regarded in England as the ravings of "a parcel of wild enthusiasts:" in America, nothing was so much admired through the whole course of the controversy; and John Adams, who recorded at the time the applause which it won, said also, that of all the politicians of Boston, including Otis and Cushing, Samuel Adams had the most thorough understanding of liberty and her resources in the temper and character of the people, though not in the law and the constitution; as well as the most habitual radical love of it, and the most correct, genteel, and artful pen." "He is a man," he continued, "of refined policy, steadfast integrity, exquisite humanity, genteel erudition, obliging, engaging manners, real as well as professed piety, and a universal good

[1] Not of Otis. The paper has not the style of Otis, and does not express his opinions. Besides; he was absent from Boston from the delivery of Bernard's speech till after the reply was made, performing his duty at New-York, as a member of Congress. The paper has the style of S. Adams, and expresses his sentiments exactly. Moreover, Hutchinson names him. Bernard's letters point to him, without naming him. The head of the committee was Samuel Dexter, who had the greatest regard for Samuel Adams. J. Adams: Works, ii. 163, 181.

CHAP. XIX. character, unless it should be admitted that he is too attentive to the public, and not enough so to himself

1765. Oct. or his family. He is always for softness and prudence, where they will do; but is staunch, and stiff, and strict, and rigid, and inflexible in the cause."

The firmness of the new legislator was sustained by the unwavering confidence of the people of Boston beyond what was given to any of his colleagues; and the vacillation of Otis, increasing with his infirmities, ceased to be of public importance. Massachusetts never again discussed with the British ministry the amount of a practical tax, or the inexpediency of taxation by parliament, or the propriety of an American representation in that body.

"I am resolved to have the stamps distributed," wrote Colden to the British secretary, the day after the Congress adjourned. Officers of the navy and army, with great alacrity, gave him every assistance he required; and they ridiculed the thought that the government would repeal the Stamp Act, as the most singular delusion of party spirit. His son, whom he appointed temporary distributor, wrote on the same day to the commissioners of stamps, soliciting to hold the place permanently; for, he assured them, "in a few months, the act would be quietly submitted to."[1] But the people of New-York, one and all, cried out, "Let us see who will dare put the Act into execution, upon the governor's appointment; we will take care of that."

Oct. On the thirty-first of October, Colden and all he royal governors took the oath to carry the Stamp

[1] David Colden to Commissioners of Stamp Office. Fort George, New-York, 26 Oct. 1765.

Act punctually into effect. In Connecticut, which, in its assembly, had already voted American taxation by a British parliament to be "unprecedented and unconstitutional," Dyer, of the council, entreated Fitch not to take an oath which was contrary to that of the governor, to maintain the rights of the colony. But Fitch had urged the assembly to prosecute for riot the five hundred that coerced Ingersoll at Wethersfield; had talked of the public spirit in the language of an enemy; had said that the Act must go down; that forty regulars could guard the stamp papers; and that the American conduct would bring from home violent measures and the loss of charters; and he resolved to comply;[1] on which Pitkin, Trumbull, and Dyer, truly representing the sentiments of Connecticut, rose with indignation and left the room. The governor of Rhode Island stood alone in his patriotic refusal.

CHAP. XIX. 1765. Oct.

But every where, either quietly of themselves, or at the instance of the people, amidst shouts and the ringing of bells and the firing of cannon, or as in Virginia, with rage changing into courtesy on the prompt submission of the Stamp master, or as at Charleston, with the upraising of the flag of liberty, surmounted by a branch of laurel—everywhere the officers resigned. There remained not one person duly commissioned to distribute stamps.

Something more was needed to incline England to relent; and the merchants of New-York, on the last day of October, coming together, unanimously bound themselves to send no new orders for goods or

[1] E. Stiles' Diary.

CHAP. XIX. merchandise; to countermand all former orders; and not even to receive goods on commission, unless the 1765. Oct. Stamp Act be repealed. Thus a city, built on the ocean side, the chosen home of navigation, renounced all commerce; a people, who, as yet, had no manufactures, gave up every comfort from abroad, rather than continue trade at the peril of freedom. A committee of intercolonial correspondence was raised, and while James Delancy and others hesitated, the unflinching Isaac Sears, with Lamb, Mott, Wiley, and Robinson, assumed the post of greatest danger, and sent expresses[1] to invite the people of the neighboring governments to join in the league, justly confident they would follow the example of New-York.

Nov. Friday, the first morning of November, broke upon a people unanimously resolved on nullifying the Stamp Act. From New Hampshire to the far South, the day was introduced by the tolling of muffled bells; minute-guns were fired, and pennants hoisted at half-staff; or a eulogy was pronounced on liberty, and its knell sounded; and then again the note changed, as if she were restored to life; and, while pleasure shone on every countenance, men shouted confusion to her enemies. Even the children at their games, though hardly able to speak, caught up the general chorus, and went along the streets, merrily carolling: "Liberty, Property, and no Stamps."

The publishers of newspapers which appeared on Friday, were the persons called upon to stand the brunt in braving the penalties of the Act. Honor, then, to the ingenious Benjamin Mecom, the bold-

[1] R. R. Livingston to R. Livingston, 2 Nov.

hearted editor at New Haven, who on that morning, without apology or concealment, issued the Connecticut Gazette, filled with patriotic appeals; for, said he, "the press is the test of truth, the bulwark of public safety, the guardian of freedom, and the people ought not to sacrifice it."[1]

Nor let the true lovers of their country pass unheeded the grave of Timothy Green, one of an illustrious family of printers, himself publisher of the New London Gazette, which had always modestly and fearlessly defended his country's rights; for on Friday, the first day of November, his journal came forth without stamps, and gave to the world a paper from the incomparable Stephen Johnson, of Lyme.[2]

"The liberty of free inquiry," said he, "is one of the first and most fundamental of a free people. They have an undoubted right to be heard and relieved. They may publish their grievances; the press is open and free. We may go on to enjoy our rights and liberties as usual. The American governments or inhabitants may associate for the mutual defence of their birthright liberties. A person or people collectively may enjoy and defend their own. The hearts of Americans are cut to the quick by the Act; we have reason to fear very interesting and terrible consequences, though by no means equal to tyranny or slavery. But what an enraged, despairing people will do, when they come to see and feel their ruin, time only can reveal.

"It is the joy of thousands, that there is union and concurrence in a general Congress. We trust they will also lay a foundation for another Congress. The

[1] Con. Gaz. No. 488, Friday, 1 Nov. 1765.

[2] New London Gaz. No. 103, Friday, 1 Nov. 1765.

CHAP. XIX. 1765. Nov. American colonies cannot be enslaved but by their own folly, consent, or inactivity. Truly Britons have nothing at all to hope for from this most unnatural war. My countrymen, your concern is great, universal, and most just. I am an American born, and my all in this world is embarked with yours, and am deeply touched at heart for your distress. O, my country! my dear, distressed country! For you I have wrote; for you I daily pray and mourn; and, to save your invaluable rights and freedom, I would willingly die!

"Forgive my lamenting tears. The dear Saviour himself wept over his native country, doomed to destruction. We appeal to our Supreme Judge against the hand whence these evils are coming. If we perish, we perish, being innocent, and our blood will be required at their hands. Shut not your eyes to your danger, O! my countrymen. Do nothing to destroy or betray the rights of your posterity; do nothing to sully or shade the memory of your noble ancestors. Let all the governments and all the inhabitants in them unitedly resolve to a man, with an immovable stability, to sacrifice their lives and fortunes, before they will part with their invaluable freedom. It will give you a happy peace in your own breasts, and secure you the most endeared affection, thanks, and blessing of your posterity; it will gain you the esteem of all true patriots and friends of liberty through the whole realm; yea, and as far as your case is known, it will gain you the esteem and the admiration of the whole world."

Such was the spirit of the clergy of Connecticut; and such the conduct and such the language of the New London Gazette; patriots grew up within its sphere, and he who would single out in the country the region, where at that time the fire of patriotism burned with the purest flame, can find none surpassing the county of New London. The royalists of New-York, like Bernard, at Boston, railed at all Connecticut as a land of republicans, and maligned Yale College, as "a seminary of democracy," the prolific mother of patriots.[1]

In New-York, "the whole city rose up as one man in opposition to the Stamp Act." The sailors came from their shipping; "the people flocked in," as Gage thought, "by thousands; the number seemed to be still increasing;" and the leader of the popular tumult was Isaac Sears, the self-constituted, and for ten years, the recognised head of the people of New-York. At the corners of streets, at the doors of the public offices, placards threatened all who should receive or deliver a stamp, or delay business for the want of one.

Colden himself retired within the fort, and got from the Coventry ship of war a detachment of marines. He would have fired on the people, but was menaced with being hanged like Porteus of Edinburgh,[2] upon a sign-post, if he did so. In the evening a vast torch-light procession, carrying a scaffold and two images, one of the Governor, the other of the devil, came from the Fields, now the Park, down Broadway, to within ten or eight feet of the fort, knocked at its gate, broke open the Governor's coach-house, took out his chariot, carried the images upon it round town, and returned

[1] "The pretended patriots, educated in a seminary of Democracy." Gage to Sir W. Johnson, 20 Sept. 1765.

[2] Paper delivered at the fort gate by an unknown hand, 1 Nov. 1765.

CHAP. XIX. 1765. Nov. to burn them with his own carriages and sleighs, before his eyes, on the Bowling Green, under the gaze of the garrison on the ramparts, and of all New-York gathered round about.

"He has bound himself," they cried, "by oath, to be the chief murderer of our rights." "He was a rebel in Scotland, a Jacobite." "He is an enemy to his king, to his country, and mankind." At the same time, a party of volunteers sacked the house occupied by James, and bore off the colors of the royal regiments.

On Saturday, the second of November, Colden gave way. The council questioned his authority to distribute the stamps, and unanimously advised him to declare that he would do nothing in relation to them, but await the arrival of the new governor; and his declaration to that effect, duly authenticated, was immediately published. But the confidence of the people was shaken. "We will have the stamp papers," cried Sears to the multitude, "within four-and-twenty hours;" and as he appealed to the crowd, they expressed their adherence by shouts. "Your best way," added Sears to the friends of order, "will be to advise Lieutenant-Governor Colden to send the stamp papers from the fort to the inhabitants." To appease their wrath, Colden invited Kennedy to receive them on board the Coventry. "They are already lodged in the fort," answered Kennedy, unwilling to offend the people.

The Common Council of New-York next interposed.[1] They asked that the stamped paper should be delivered into the care of the corporation, to be

[1] Minutes of the Common Council of N. Y. 5 Nov. Colden to Gage, 5 Nov.

deposited in the City Hall, offering in that case to prevent further confusion. The Common Council were a body elected by the people; they were the representatives of the people over against the king's Governor and Council, and the military Viceroy. Colden pleaded his oath, to do his utmost, that every clause of the Act should be observed; he pleaded further the still greater contempt[1] into which the government would fall by concession. But the Council, in which William Smith, the historian of New-York, acted a prudent part,[2] as the negotiator between the Lieutenant-Governor, the General, and the people, answered that his power was unequal to the protection of the inhabitants;[3] Gage, being appealed to,[4] avowed the belief, that a fire from the fort would be the signal for "an insurrection," and "the commencement of a civil war." So the head of the province of New-York, and the military chief of all America, confessing their inability to stop the anarchy, capitulated to the municipal body which represented the people. The stamps were taken to the City Hall; the city government restored order; the press continued its activity, and in all the streets was heard the shout of "Liberty, Property, and no Stamps."

The thirst for revenge rankled in Colden's breast. "The lawyers," he wrote to Conway, at a time when the government in England was still bent on enforcing the Stamp Act,[5] "the lawyers of this place are the authors and conductors of the present sedition.

[1] Colden to Maj. James, 6 Nov.

[2] Diary of John Adams.

[3] Minutes of Council.

[4] Colden to Gage, 5 Nov. Gage to Colden, 5 Nov. Gage to Conway, 8 Nov. Colden to Conway, 9 Nov.

[5] R. Jackson to Bernard, 8 Nov. 1765.

CHAP. XIX. 1765. Nov.

If judges be sent from England, with an able Attorney-General and Solicitor-General, to make examples of some very few, this colony will remain quiet." Others of his letters pointed plainly to John Morin Scott, Robert R. Livingston, and William Livingston, as suitable victims. At the same time, some of the churchmen avowed to one another their longing to see the Archbishop of Canterbury display a little more of the resolution of a Laud or a Sextus Quintus; "for what," said they, "has the church ever gained by that which the courtesy of England calls prudence?"[1]

Yet when Moore, the new governor, arrived, he could do nothing but give way to the popular impulse. He dismantled the fort, and suspended his power to execute the Stamp Act.[2] When the assembly came together, it confirmed the doings of its committee at the Congress, and prepared papers analogous to them.

In New Jersey, Ogden found himself disavowed by his constituents. The assembly, by a unanimous vote, accepted his resignation as speaker, and thanked the two faithful delegates who had signed the proceedings of the Congress. Of those proceedings, New Hampshire, by its assembly, signified its entire approbation. The voluntary[3] action of the representatives of Georgia was esteemed a valid adhesion to the design of the Congress on the part of the colony. Its governor was met by "the same rebellious spirit[4] as prevailed at the North."

The delegates of South Carolina were received by

[1] Thomas B. Chandler, 12 Nov. 1765.

[2] Sir H. Moore to Conway, 21 Nov.

[3] Letter from Gadsden, 16 Dec.

[4] Sir J. Wright to Lords of Trade, 9 Nov. 1765.

CHAP. XIX. 1765. Nov

their assembly on the twenty-sixth of November. On that morning all the papers of the Congress, the declaration of rights, and the addresses were read; in an evening session, they were all adopted without change, by a vote which wanted but one of being unanimous; they were signed by the speaker, and put on board the Charming Charlotte, a fine ship riding in the harbor with its sails bent; and the next morning, while the assembly were signifying, in the most ample and obliging manner, their satisfaction at the conduct of their agents, it stood away, with swelling canvas, for England, bearing the evidence that South Carolina gave its heart unreservedly to the cause of freedom and union.

"Nothing will save us," wrote Gadsden, "but acting together; the province that endeavors to act separately must fall with the rest, and be branded besides with everlasting infamy."

The people of North Carolina[2] would neither receive a stamp man, nor tolerate the use of a stamp, nor suffer its ports to be closed. The meeting of its legislature was so long prorogued, that it could not join in the application of the Congress; but had there been need of resorting to arms, "the whole force of North Carolina was ready to join in protecting the rights of the continent."[3] It was the same throughout the country. Wherever a jealousy was roused, that a stamp officer might exercise his functions, the people were sure to gather about him, and compel him to renew his resignation under oath, or solemnly before witnesses.

[1] Tryon to Conway, 26 Dec.
[2] Letter from South Carolina, 2 Dec. 1765.
[3] Gadsden to Garth, Dec. 1765.

CHAP. XIX.

1765. Nov.

The colonies began also to think of permanent union. "JOIN OR DIE" became more and more their motto. At Windham, in Connecticut, the freemen, in a multitudinous assembly, agreed with one another, "to keep up, establish, and maintain the spirit of union and liberty;" and for that end they recommended monthly county conventions, and also a general meeting of the colony.

Dec.

At New London, the inhabitants of the county of that name, holding a mass meeting in December, unanimously decided in carefully prepared resolves, that every form of rightful government originates from the consent of the people; that lawful authority cannot pass the boundaries set by them; that if the limits are passed, they may reassume the authority which they had delegated; and that if there is no other mode of relief against the Stamp Act and similar acts, they must reassume their natural rights and the authority with which they were invested by the laws of nature and of God. The same principles were adopted at various village gatherings, and became the political platform of Connecticut.

In New-York, the validity of the British Navigation Acts was more and more openly impugned, so that the merchants claimed a right to every freedom of trade enjoyed in England. When the General applied for the supplies, which the province was enjoined by the British Mutiny Act to contribute for the use of the troops quartered among them, the assembly would pay no heed whatever to an act of parliament to which they themselves had given no assent; and in the general tumult, their refusal passed almost unnoticed.

Everywhere the fixed purpose prevailed, that

"the unconstitutional" Stamp Act should not go into effect. Nothing less than its absolute repeal would give contentment, much as England was loved. The greatest unanimity happily existed; and all were bent on cherishing it for ever. Here was something new in the affairs of men. In the time of the crusades, and at the era of the reformation, the world was as widely convulsed; but never had the people of provinces extending over so vast a continent, and so widely sundered from one another, been thus cordially bound together in one spirit and one resolve. In all their tumults, they deprecated the necessity of declaring independence; but they yet more earnestly abhorred and rejected unconditional submission. Still satisfied with the revolution of 1688 and its theory of security to liberty and property, they repelled the name of "republican" as a slander on their loyalty, but they spurned against "passive obedience." Nothing on earth, they insisted, would deprive Great Britain of her transatlantic dominions but her harboring ungenerous suspicions, and thereupon entering into arbitrary and oppressive measures. "All eyes were turned on her with hope and unbounded affection," with apprehension and firmness of resolve. "Pray for the peace of our Jerusalem," said Otis, from his heart, fearing "the parliament would charge the colonies with presenting petitions in one hand and a dagger in the other." Others thought "England would look with favor on what was but an old English spirit of resentment at injurious treatment;" and all were strong in the consciousness of union. They trusted that "the united voice of this very extensive continent," uttering "the sober opinions of all its inhabitants," would be listened to, so that

CHAP. XIX. 1765. Dec. Great Britain and America might once more enjoy "peace, harmony, and the greatest prosperity." Delay made anxiety too intense to be endured. "Every moment is tedious," wrote South Carolina to its agent in London: "should you have to communicate the good news we wish for, send it to us, if possible, by a messenger swifter than the wind."[1]

[1] Gadsden to Garth, Dec. 1765.

CHAPTER XX.

PARLIAMENT LEARNS THAT AMERICA HAS RESISTED—ROCKINGHAM'S ADMINISTRATION CONTINUED.

DECEMBER, 1765—JANUARY, 1766.

CHAP XX. 1765. Dec.

THE Stamp Act, said George Grenville, when, emaciated, exhausted, and borne down by disappointment, he spoke in the House of Commons for the last time before sinking into the grave—"the Stamp Act was not found impracticable. Had I continued in office, I would have forfeited a thousand lives, if the Act had been found impracticable."[1] "If the administration of this country had not been changed," Richard Rigby,[2] the leader of the Bedford party, long persisted in asserting, "the stamp tax would have been collected in America with as much ease as the land-tax in Great Britain." The king had dismissed from power the only ministry bent resolutely on enforcing it; and, while America was united, his heart was divided between a morbid anxiety to execute the law, and his wish never again to employ Bedford and Grenville.

The opinion of England was as fluctuating as the mind of the king. The overbearing aristocracy desired

[1] Cavendish Debates, i. 551. [2] Force: Am. Archives, i. 76.

CHAP. XX. 1765. Dec.

some reduction of the land tax at the expense of America; and sordid politicians, accustomed to hold provincial offices by deputy, or to dispose of them to their friends, wished to increase the value of their patronage by maintaining this absolute supremacy at all hazards. The industrial classes were satisfied with the monopoly of her market. The maritime and manufacturing towns in the kingdom were alarmed at the interruption of trade, the injury to colonial credit, and the loud and distinct cry of encouragement to American industry; and letters concerted between the merchant Trecothick and Rockingham, were sent among them, to countenance applications to parliament.

The traditions of the public offices were equally at variance. Successive administrations had inquired for some system by which the revenues and expenditures in America could be determined by the central authority of the metropolis. They who wished to make thorough work of reducing the colonies, could name many ministers as having listened to schemes of coercion; but the friends of colonial freedom replied, that no minister before Grenville had consented to carry such projects into effect.

Each side confidently invoked the British constitution. Grenville declared the paramount authority of parliament throughout the British dominions to be the essence of the revolution of 1688; others insisted that that event had upheld and established principles, by which the liberty of the person was secured against arbitrary arrest, and the rights of property were recognised as sacred against every exaction without consent.

The two opinions were also represented in the

new ministry. Northington, the Lord Chancellor, and Charles Yorke, the Attorney-General, insisted on the right to tax America; while Grafton and Conway inclined to abdicate the pretended right, and the kind-hearted Rockingham declared himself ready to repeal a hundred Stamp Acts, rather than run the risk of such confusion as would be caused by enforcing one.

CHAP. XX.

1765. Dec.

History, too, when questioned, answered ambiguously. Taxation had become in Great Britain and in the colonies, a part of the general legislative power, with some reserve in favor of the popular branch of the legislature; in the Middle Age, on the contrary, when feudal liberties flourished most, the sovereign had large discretion in declaring laws to regulate civil transactions; but the service which he could demand from his vassals was fixed by capitulations and compacts, and could neither be increased, nor commuted for money, except by agreement.

The one side, not yet abandoning the field, ventured to assert, that America was virtually represented in the British parliament as much as the great majority of the British people; and while America treated the pretext as senseless, a large and growing party in England demanded for all its inhabitants a share in the national council.

Nor was the argument on which the Stamp Act rested, in harmony with the sentiments and convictions of reflecting Englishmen. Its real authors insisted that protection and obedience are correlative duties; that Great Britain protected America, and, therefore, America was bound to obedience. But this is the doctrine of absolute monarchy, not of the British Constitution.

CHAP. XX. 1765. Dec.

The colonists had a powerful ally in the public conscience and affections of the mother country. They could appeal against the acts of its government to the cherished opinions of the nation. The love of liberty was to the true Englishman a habit of mind, grafted upon a proud but generous nature. His attachment to freedom was stronger than the theory of the absolute power of a parliament, of which an oligarchy influenced the choice and controlled the deliberations. The British constitution was in its idea more popular than in its degenerate forms; it aimed at the perfection of carrying out "the genuine principles of liberty," by securing a free and unbiassed "vote to every member of the community, however poor;" but time and a loose state of national morals had tended to produce corruption. "The incurvations of practice," whether in England or the colonies, were becoming "more notorious by a comparison with the rectitude of the rule." "To elucidate the clearness of the spring conveyed the strongest satire on those who had polluted or disturbed it."[1] America divided English sympathies by appealing with steadfast confidence to the principles of English liberty in their ideal purity.

It is the glory of England, that the rightfulness of the Stamp Act was in England itself a subject of dispute. It could have been so nowhere else. The king of France taxed the French colonies as a matter of course; the king of Spain collected a revenue by his own will in Mexico and Peru, in Cuba and Porto Rico, and wherever he ruled. The States General of the Netherlands had no constitutional scruples about

[1] Blackstone's Commentaries, b. i., c. ii.

imposing duties on their outlying possessions. To England, exclusively, belongs the honor, that between her and her colonies the question of right could arise; it is still more to her glory, as well as to her happiness and freedom, that in that contest her success was not possible. Her principles, her traditions, her liberty, her constitution, all forbade that arbitrary rule should become her characteristic. The shaft aimed at her new colonial policy was tipped with a feather from her own wing.

CHAP. XX. 1765. Dec.

Had Cumberland remained alive, regiments, it was thought, would have been sent to America. The conqueror at Culloden was merciless towards those whom he deemed refractory, and willingly quenched rebellion in blood. During his lifetime, the ministry never avowed a readiness to yield to the claims of the colonists. But the night before the Stamp Act was to have gone into effect, the Duke, all weary of life, which for him had been without endearments, died suddenly, on his way to a cabinet council, and his influence, which had no foundation but in accident, perished with him.

Weakened by his death, and hopelessly divided in opinion, the ministry showed itself more and more unsettled in its policy. On the third of October they had agreed that the American question was too weighty for their decision, and required that parliament should be consulted, and yet they postponed its meeting for the transaction of business, till there had been time to see if the Stamp Act would indeed execute itself. To Franklin, who was unwearied in his efforts to promote its repeal, no hope was given of relief; and though the committee of merchants, who on the twelfth day

CHAP. XX. 1765. Dec.

of December waited on Rockingham, Dowdeswell, Conway, and Dartmouth, were received with dispassionate calmness, it was announced that the right to tax Americans could never be given up; and that a suspension was "the most that could be expected."[1]

The successive accounts from America grieved the king more and more. "Where this spirit will end," said he, "is not to be said. It is undoubtedly the most serious matter that ever came before parliament,"[2] and he urged for it "deliberation, candor, and temper." He was highly provoked[3] by the riots in New-York; and the surrender of the stamps to the municipality of the city seemed to him "greatly humiliating." He watched with extreme anxiety the preliminary meeting of the friends of the ministry; and when the day for opening parliament came, he was impatient to receive a minute report of all that should occur.[4]

The Earl of Hardwicke,[5] himself opposed to the lenity of Rockingham,[6] moved the address in the House of Lords, pledging the House "to bring to the consideration of the state of affairs in America, a resolution to do every thing which the exigency of the case might require." The Earl of Suffolk, a young man of five-and-twenty, proposed "to express indignation at the insurrections in North America, and concurrence in measures to enforce the legal obedience of the colonies, and their dependence on the sovereign authority of the kingdom." This amend-

[1] Letter from London of 14 Dec. 1765, in Boston Gazette, 24 Feb. 1766. Compare T. Pownall to Hutchinson, 3 Dec. 1765, and a letter of Franklin of 6 Jan. 1766.

[2] Geo. III. to Conway, 6 Dec.

[3] Conway to Gage, 15 Dec.

[4] Geo. III. to Conway, 17 Dec.

[5] Hugh Hammersley to Lieut. Gov. Sharpe, Dec. 1765, gives a very good report of the debate. Compare Philimore's Lyttelton, ii. 687.

[6] Albemarle, i. 284.

ment prejudged the case, and, if it had been adopted, would have pledged parliament in advance to the policy of coercion. CHAP. XX. 1765. Dec.

Grafton opposed the amendment, purposely avoiding the merits of the question till the house should be properly possessed of it by the production of papers. Of these, Dartmouth added that the most important related to New-York, and had been received within four or five days. Rockingham was dumb. Shelburne alone, unsupported by a single peer, intimated plainly his inclination for a repeal of the law. "Before we resolve upon rash measures," said he, "we should consider first the expediency of the law, and next our power to enforce it. The wisest legislators have been mistaken. The laws of Carolina, though planned by Shaftesbury and Locke, were found impracticable, and are now grown obsolete. The Romans planted colonies to increase their power; we to extend our commerce. Let the regiments in America, at Halifax, or Pensacola, embark at once upon the same destination, and no intervening accident disappoint the expedition, what could be effected against colonies so populous, and of such magnitude and extent? The colonies may be ruined first, but the distress will end with ourselves."

But Halifax, Sandwich, Gower, even Temple, Lyttelton, and Bedford, firmly supported the amendment of Suffolk.

"Protection, without dependence and obedience," they joined in saying, "is a solecism in politics. The connection between Great Britain and her colonies is that of parent and child. For the parent not to correct the undutiful child would argue weakness. The duty to enforce obedience cannot be given up, because the

CHAP. XX. 1765. Dec. relation cannot be destroyed. The king cannot separate his colonies any more than any other part of his dominions from the mother-country, nor render them independent of the British legislature. The laws and constitution of the country are prior and superior to charters, many of which were issued improvidently, and ought to be looked into.

"The colonies wish to be supported by all the military power of the country without paying for it. They have been for some time endeavoring to shake off their dependence. Pennsylvania, in 1756, refused to assist government, though the enemy was at their gates; and afterwards, in their manner of granting aid, they encroached on the king's prerogative. The next attempt of the colonies will be to rid themselves of the Navigation Act, the great bulwark of this country; and because they can thus obtain their commodities twenty-five per cent. cheaper, they will buy of the French and Dutch, rather than of their fellow subjects. They do not condescend to enter into explanations upon the Stamp Act, but object to its principle, and the power of making it; yet the law was passed very deliberately, with no opposition in this house, and very little in the other. The tax, moreover, is light, and is paid only by the rich, in proportion to their dealings. The objections for want of representation are absurd. Who are affected by the duties on hardware but the people of Manchester, Birmingham and Leeds? And how are they represented?

"But suppose the act liable to exceptions, is this a time to discuss them? When the Pretender was at Derby, did you then enter upon a tame consideration of grievances? What occasion is there for papers? The present rebellion is more unnatural, and not less notorious, than that of 1745. The king's governors have been hanged in effigy, his forts and generals besieged, and the civil power annulled or suspended. Will you remain inactive till the king's governors are hanged in person? Is the legislature always to be dictated to in riot and tumult? The weavers were at your doors last year, and this year the Americans are up in arms, because they do not like what you have passed.

"Why was not parliament called sooner? Why are we now called to do nothing? The house is on fire, and ministers, from unskilfulness, or want of will, use no endeavors to stay the flames. Shall we wait till it is burned down before we interpose? No matter whence the spark; the combustible nature of the matter creates the danger. Resist at the threshold. First repress the rebellion, and then inquire into grievances.

"Concessions are talked of, and even a repeal of the law hinted. And are not concessions always dangerous? In the struggles between the senate and people of Rome, what did the senate get by treating with the people, but a master to both? What did Charles gain by giving way to exorbitant demands and not persisting when in the right, as he sometimes was, but the loss of his crown and life? It has been said that America was conquered in Germany; but give up the law, and Great Britain will be conquered in America. It is said, though we do repeal the law, yet we will pass some declaratory act asserting our rights. But when the Americans are possessed of the substance, what regard will they pay to your paper protestations? Ministers may be afraid of going too far on their own authority; but will they refuse

CHAP. XX. 1765. Dec.

assistance when it is offered them? We serve the crown by strengthening its hands."

Northington, the Chancellor, argued from the statute book, that, as a question of law, the dependence of the colonies had been fully declared in the reign of William III.; and he "lustily roared," that "America must submit."

Lord Mansfield denied the power of the crown to emancipate the colonies from the jurisdiction of the British legislature. He cited Pennsylvania as having of all the colonies, the least pretension to the claim, since its charter expressly recognised impositions and customs by act of parliament. And he endeavored to bring the House to unanimity by recommending the ministry to assent to the amendment; "for," said he, "the question is most serious, and not one of the ordinary matters agitated between the persons in and out of office."

Failing to prevent a division, Mansfield went away without giving a vote. The opposition was thought to have shown a great deal of ability, and to have expressed the prevailing opinion in the House of Lords, as well as the sentiments of the king. But the king's friends, unwilling to open a breach through which Bedford and Grenville could take the cabinet by storm, divided against the amendment with the ministry.

In the House of Commons the new ministers were absent; for accepting office implies a resignation of a seat in the representative body, and sends a member to his constituents as a candidate for re-election; yet Grenville, enraged at seeing authority set at naught with impunity, in reference to an act of his ministry, moved to consider North America as "resisting the

CHAP. XX. 1765. Dec.

laws by open and rebellious force," and complained of the king's lenity. "What would have been thought," said he, "in 1745, if any person had called the rebellion of that day an important matter only?" Cooke, the member from Middlesex, justified the colonies, and showed the cruelty of fixing the name of rebels on all. Charles Townshend asserted with vehemence his approbation of the Stamp Act, and leaned towards the opinion of Grenville. "Sooner," said he, "than make our colonies our allies, I should wish to see them returned to their primitive deserts."[1] But he sat down, determined to vote against Grenville's amendment. Gilbert Elliot did the same; and Wedderburn displayed the basest subserviency. Norton dwelt much on the legislative authority of parliament to tax all the world under British dominion. "See," said Beckford, "how completely my prophecy about America is accomplished." Some one said that Great Britain had long arms. "Yes," it was answered, "but three thousand miles is a long way to extend them."

Especially it is observable that Lord George Sackville, just rescued from disgrace by Rockingham, manifested his desire to enforce the Stamp Act.[2]

The amendment was withdrawn, but when three days later Grenville divided the house on a question of adjourning to the ninth instead of the fourteenth of January, he had only thirty-five votes against seventy-seven. Baker, in the debate, called his motion "insolent," and chid him as the author of all the trouble in America; but he threw the blame from himself upon the parliament.

Out of doors there was a great deal of clamor,

[1] Hammersley.

[2] Letter from London of Dec. 22 and 24, 1765, in Boston Gaz. 17 Feb. 1766. Chatham Corr. ii. 352.

CHAP. XX. 1765. Dec. that repealing the Stamp Act would be a surrender of sovereignty; and that the question was, shall the Americans submit to us, or we to them? But others held the attempt at coercion to be the ruinous side of the dilemma.

While England was still in this condition of unformed opinion, the colonies were proceeding with their system of resistance. "If they do not repeal the Stamp Act," said Otis, who, nine months before had counselled submission, and who now shared and led the most excited opposition, "if they do not repeal it, we will repeal it ourselves." The first American ship that ventured to sea with a rich cargo, and without stamped papers, was owned by the Boston merchant, John Hancock. At the south, in the Savannah river, a few British ships took stamped clearances, but this continued only till a vigilant people had time to understand one another, and to interfere. In South Carolina, the Lieutenant Governor, pleading the necessity of the case, himself sanctioned opening the port of Charleston.

At New-York, the head quarters of the army, an attempt was made by the men of war to detain vessels ready for sea. The people rose in anger, and the naval commander, becoming alarmed by the danger of riots, left the road from New-York to the ocean once more free, as it was from every other harbor in the thirteen colonies.

It was next attempted to open the executive courts. In Rhode Island, all public officers, judges among the rest, continued to transact business. In New-York, the judges would willingly have held their terms, but were restrained by a menace of dismissal from office.

In Boston, this question was agitated with determined zeal; but first the people dealt with Andrew Oliver, who had received his commission as stampman. On the very day, and almost at the hour when the King was proceeding in state to the House of Lords to open parliament, the "true-born Sons of Liberty," deaf to all entreaties, placed Oliver at the head of a long procession, with Mackintosh, a leader in the August riots, at his side, and with great numbers following, on the cold wet morning, escorted him to Liberty Tree, to stand in the rain under the very bough on which he had swung in effigy. There, in the presence of two thousand men, he declared in a written paper, to which he publicly set his name, that he would never directly or indirectly take any measures to enforce the Stamp Act, and with the whole multitude for witnesses, he, upon absolute requisition, made oath to this pledge before Richard Dana, a justice of the peace. At this, the crowd gave three cheers; and when Oliver, who was the third officer in the province, with bitterest revenge in his heart, spoke to them with a smile, they gave three cheers more.[1]

On the evening of the next day, as John Adams sat ruminating in his humble mansion at Quincy, on the interruption of his career as a lawyer, a message came, that Boston, at the instance of a committee of which Samuel Adams was the chief, had joined him with Gridley and Otis, to sustain their memorial to the Governor and Council for opening the courts; and

[1] A. Oliver to Bernard, 17 Dec. Same to same, 19 Dec. Boston Gaz. J. Adams's Diary.

CHAP. XX. 1765. Dec.

he resolved to exert the utmost of his abilities in the cause. It fell to him, on the evening of the twentieth, to begin the argument before the governor and council. "The Stamp Act," he reasoned, "is invalid; it is not in any sense our act; we never consented to it. A parliament in which we are not represented, had no legal authority to impose it; and, therefore, it ought to be waived by the judges as against natural equity and the constitution." Otis reasoned with great learning and zeal on the duties and obligations of judges. Gridley dwelt on the inconveniences that would ensue on the interruption of justice.

"Many of the arguments," said Bernard, in reply, "are very good ones to be used before the judges, but there is no precedent for the interference of the governor and council. In England the judges would scorn directions from the king on points of law."

On Saturday, the town voted the answer unsatisfactory. Ever fertile in resources, Otis instantly proposed to invite the governor to call a convention of the members of both houses of the legislature; if the governor should refuse, then to call one themselves, by requesting all the members to meet; and John Adams came round to this opinion.

"The king," thus the young lawyer reasoned, on returning to his own fireside, "the king is the fountain of justice. Protection and allegiance are reciprocal. If we are out of the king's protection, we are discharged from our allegiance. The ligaments of government are dissolved, the throne abdicated." Otis, quoting Grotius and the English lawyers, of 1688, assured the public, that "If a king lets the affairs of a state run into disorder and confusion, his conduct is a real abdication;" that unless business should proceed as usual, there "would be a release of subjects from their allegiance." CHAP. XX.

1765. Dec.

If patient entreaty was to be of no avail, America must unite and prepare for resistance. In New-York, on Christmas day, the lovers of liberty pledged themselves "to march with all dispatch, at their own costs and expense, on the first proper notice, with their whole force, if required, to the relief of those who should, or might be, in danger from the Stamp Act or its abettors." Before the year was up, Mott, one of the New-York Committee of Correspondence, arrived with others at New London, bringing a letter from Isaac Sears, and charged to ascertain how far New England would adopt the same covenant.

1766 Jan.

"If the great men are determined to enforce the Act," said John Adams, on New Year's day, on some vague news from New-York, "they will find it a more obstinate war than the conquest of Canada and Louisiana." "Great Sir," said Edes and Gill through their newspaper to the king, printing the message in large letters, "Great Sir, Retreat or you are ruined."

"None," said the press of Philadelphia, in words widely diffused, "none in this day of liberty will say, that duty binds us to yield obedience to any man or body of men, forming part of the British constitution, when they exceed the limits prescribed by that constitution. The Stamp Act is unconstitutional, and no more obligatory than a decree of the Divan of Turkey."

Encouraged by public opinion, the Sons of Liberty of New-York held regular meetings, and on the seventh of January, they resolved that "there was safety for the colonies only in the firm union of the whole;" that they themselves "would go to the last extremi-

CHAP. XX. 1766. Jan.

ty, and venture their lives and fortunes, effectually to prevent the Stamp Act." On the following night the ship which arrived from London with ten more packages of stamps for New-York and Connecticut, was searched from stem to stern, and the packages were seized and carried in boats up the river to the shipyards, where, by the aid of tar barrels, they were thoroughly consumed in a bonfire.

The resolutions of New-York were carried swiftly to Connecticut. The town of Wallingford voted a fine of twenty shillings on any of its inhabitants "that should use or improve any stamped vellum or paper;" and the Sons of Liberty of that place, adopting the words of their brethren of New-York, were ready "to oppose the unconstitutional Stamp Act to the last extremity, even to take the field." The people of the county of New London, meeting at Lyme, declared "the general safety and privileges of all the colonies to depend on a firm union." They were "ready on all occasions to assist the neighboring provinces to repel all violent attempts to subvert their common liberties;" and they appointed Major John Durkee to correspond with the Sons of Liberty in the adjoining colonies. Israel Putnam, the brave patriot of Pomfret,—whose people had declared, that their connection with England was derived only from a compact, their freedom from God and nature, and to be maintained with their lives,—rode from town to town through the eastern part of Connecticut, to see what number of men could be depended upon, and gave out that he could lead forth ten thousand.

Massachusetts spoke through its House of Representatives, which convened in the middle of January. They called on impartial history to record the strong testimonies given by the people of the continent of their loyalty, and the equal testimony which they had given of their love of liberty, by a glorious stand even against an act of parliament. They proudly called to mind, that the union of all the colonies was upon a motion made in their house. And insisting that "the courts of justice must be open,—open immediately," they voted, sixty-six against four, that the shutting of them was not only "a very great grievance, requiring immediate redress," but "dangerous to his majesty's crown."

CHAP. XX. 1766. Jan.

Bernard, who consulted in secret a "select council," unknown to the law, in which the principal advisers were Hutchinson and Oliver, wished that the system of Grenville, which brought money into the British exchequer without advantage to the officers of the crown, might be abandoned for his favorite plan of the establishment of a colonial civil list by parliament; but he opposed all concession. Tranquillity, he assured the Secretary of State, could not be restored by "lenient methods." "There will be no submission," said he, "until there is a subjection. The persons who originated the mischief, and preside over and direct the opposition to Great Britain, are wicked and desperate; and the common people, whom they have poisoned, are mad and infatuated. The people here occasionally talk very high of their power to resist Great Britain; but it is all talk. They talk of revolting from Great Britain in the most familiar manner, and declare that though the British forces should possess themselves of the coast and maritime towns, they never will subdue the inland. But nothing," Bernard continued, "can be more idle. New-York and Boston would both be defenceless to

CHAP. XX. 1766. Jan.

a royal fleet; and they being possessed by the king's forces, no other town or place could stand out. A forcible subjection is unavoidable, let it cost what it will. The forces, when they come, should be respectable enough not to encourage resistance; that when the people are taught they have a superior, they may know it effectually. I hope that New-York, as well upon account of its superior rank and greater professions of resistance, and of its being the head quarters, will have the honor of being subdued first." For Bernard gave the palm to New-York, much beyond Boston, as the source of "the system of politics" which represented the colonies, as "no otherwise related to Great Britain than by having the same king."[1]

[1] Bernard to Conway, 19 Jan. and 22 Jan. 1766.

CHAPTER XXI.

HAS PARLIAMENT THE RIGHT TO TAX AMERICA?—ROCKINGHAM'S ADMINISTRATION CONTINUED.

January, 1766.

CHAP. XXI. 1766. Jan.

During the recess of parliament, Egmont, Conway, Dowdeswell, Dartmouth, and Charles Yorke, met at the house of the Marquis of Rockingham. To modify, but not to repeal the American tax, and to enact the penalty of high treason against any one who, by speaking or writing, should impeach the legislative authority of parliament, were measures proposed in this assembly; but they did not prevail. The ministry could form no plan of mutual support; and decided nothing but the words of the speech. The world looked from them to an individual in private life, unconnected and poor, vainly seeking at Bath relief from infirmities that would have crushed a less hopeful mind; and Pitt never appeared so great as now, when at a crisis in the history of liberty, the people of England bent towards him alone as the man in whose decision their safety and their glory were involved.

The cabinet, therefore, yielding to Grafton and

CHAP. XXI. 1766. Jan.

Conway, requested his advice as to the measures proper to be taken with regard to America, and expressed a desire, now or at any future time, for his reception among them as their head. This vague and indefinite offer of place, unsanctioned by the king, was but a concession from the aristocratic portion of the Whigs to a necessity of seeking support. Pitt remembered the former treachery of Newcastle, and being resolved never to accept office through him or his connections, he treated their invitation as an unmeaning compliment; declaring that he would support those and those only who acted on true revolution principles. The care of his health demanded quiet and absence from the chapel of St. Stephen's, but the excitement of his mind gave him a respite from pain. "My resolution," said he, "is taken, and if I can crawl or be carried, I will deliver my mind and heart upon the state of America."

On the fourteenth day of January, the king acquainted parliament, that "matters of importance had happened in America, and orders been issued for the support of lawful authority." "Whatever remained to be done, he committed to their wisdom."

The lords in their reply, which was moved by Dartmouth, pledged their "utmost endeavors to assert and support the king's dignity, and the legislative authority of the kingdom over its colonies." The friends of the king and of the late ministry willingly agreed to words which seemed to imply the purpose of enforcing the Stamp Act.

The meeting of the House of Commons was very full. The address proposed for their adoption was diffuse, and of no marked character, yet the speeches of the members who proposed it indicated the willingness of the administration to repeal the American tax. In the course of a long debate, Pitt entered most unexpectedly, having arrived in town that morning.

The adherents of the late ministry took great offence at the tenderness of expression respecting America. Nugent, particularly, insisted that the honor and dignity of the kingdom obliged them to compel the execution of the Stamp Act, except the right was acknowledged, and the repeal solicited as a favor. He expostulated on the ingratitude of the colonies. He computed the expense of the troops employed in America for what he called its defence, at ninepence in the pound of the British land-tax, while the Stamp Act would not raise a shilling a head on the inhabitants in America; "but," said he, "a peppercorn, in acknowledgment of the right, is of more value than millions without."

The eyes of all the house were directed towards Pitt, as the venerable man, now almost sixty years of age, rose in his place; and the Americans present in the gallery gazed at him as at the appearance of their good "angel, or their saviour." [1]

"I approve the address in answer to the king's speech, for it decides nothing, and leaves every member free to act as he will." Such was his opening sarcasm. "The notice given to parliament of the troubles was not early, and it ought to have been immediate.

"I speak not with respect to parties. I stand up in this place, single, unsolicited, and unconnected.

[1] Besides many shorter accounts of this speech of Pitt, and the account in "Political Debates," and in Walpole, I have the Précis, preserved in the French Archives, and a pretty full report by Moffat of Rhode Island, who was present.

CHAP. XXI. 1766. Jan.

As to the late ministry," and he turned scornfully towards Grenville, who sat within one of him, "every capital measure they have taken is entirely wrong. To the present ministry, to those, at least, whom I have in my eye," looking at Conway and the Lords of the Treasury,[1] "I have no objection. Their characters are fair. But pardon me, gentlemen. Youth is the season for credulity; confidence is a plant of slow growth in an aged bosom. By comparing events with each other, reasoning from effects to causes, methinks I discover the traces of overruling influences." This he said referring to the Duke of Newcastle.[2]

"It is a long time," he continued, "since I have attended in parliament. When the resolution was taken in the house to tax America, I was ill in bed. If I could have endured to have been carried in my bed, so great was the agitation of my mind for the consequences, I would have solicited some kind hand to have laid me down on this floor, to have borne my testimony against it. It is now an act that has passed. I would speak with decency of every act of this house, but I must beg indulgence to speak of it with freedom. The subject of this debate is of greater importance than ever engaged the attention of this house; that subject only excepted, when, nearly a century ago, it was a question, whether you yourselves were to be bond or free. The manner in which this affair will be terminated will decide the judgment of posterity on the glory of this kingdom, and the wisdom of its government during the present reign.[3]

"As my health and life are so very infirm and

[1] Butler's Reminiscences.

[2] Lord Charlemont to Henry Flood, Jan. 28 (by misprint in the printed copy Jan. 8) 1766.

[3] Précis in the French Archives.

precarious, that I may not be able to attend on the day that may be fixed by the house for the consideration of America, I must now, though somewhat unseasonably—leaving the expediency of the Stamp Act to another time—speak to a point of infinite moment, I mean to the right. Some seem to have considered it as a point of honor, and leave all measures of right and wrong, to follow a delusion that may lead us to destruction. On a question that may mortally wound the freedom of three millions of virtuous and brave subjects beyond the Atlantic ocean, I cannot be silent. America being neither really nor virtually represented in Westminster, cannot be held legally, or constitutionally, or reasonably subject to obedience to any money bill of this kingdom. The colonies are equally entitled with yourselves to all the natural rights of mankind and the peculiar privileges of Englishmen; equally bound by the laws, and equally participating of the constitution of this free country. The Americans are the sons, not the bastards of England. As subjects, they are entitled to the common right of representation, and cannot be bound to pay taxes without their consent.

"Taxation is no part of the governing power. The taxes are a voluntary gift and grant of the commons alone. In an American tax, what do we do? We, your majesty's Commons of Great Britain, give and grant to your majesty,—What? Our own property? No. We give and grant to your majesty the property of your majesty's Commons in America. It is an absurdity in terms.

"There is an idea in some, that the colonies are virtually represented in this house. They never have been represented at all in parliament; they were not

CHAP. XXI. 1766. Jan.

even virtually represented at the time when this law, as captious as it is iniquitous, was passed to deprive them of the most inestimable of their privileges.[1] I would fain know by whom an American is represented here? Is he represented by any knight of the shire, in any county of this kingdom? Would to God that respectable representation was augmented to a greater number. Or will you tell him, that he is represented by any representative of a borough? a borough, which, perhaps, no man ever saw. This is what is called the rotten part of the constitution. It cannot endure the century. If it does not drop, it must be amputated. The idea of a virtual representation of America in this house is the most contemptible that ever entered into the head of a man. It does not deserve a serious refutation.

"The commons of America, represented in their several assemblies, have ever been in possession of the exercise of this, their constitutional right, of giving and granting their own money. They would have been slaves if they had not enjoyed it.

"And how is the right of taxing the colonies internally compatible with that of framing regulations without number for their trade? The laws of this kind, which parliament is daily making, prove that they form a body separate from Great Britain. While you hold their manufactures in the most servile restraint, will you add a new tax to deprive them of the last remnants of their liberty? This would be to plunge them into the most odious slavery, against which their charters should protect them.[2]

"If this house suffers the Stamp Act to continue in force, France will gain more by your colonies than

[1] Précis in the French Archives. [2] Ibid.

CHAP. XXI.

1766. Jan.

she ever could have done if her arms in the last war had been victorious.[1]

"I never shall own the justice of taxing America internally until she enjoys the right of representation. In every other point of legislation, the authority of parliament is like the North star, fixed for the reciprocal benefit of the parent country and her colonies.[2] The British parliament, as the supreme governing and legislative power, has always bound them by her laws, by her regulations of their trade and manufactures, and even in a more absolute interdiction of both. The power of parliament, like the circulation from the human heart, active, vigorous, and perfect in the smallest fibre of the arterial system, may be known in the colonies by the prohibition of their carrying a hat to market over the line of one province into another; or by breaking down a loom in the most distant corner of the British empire in America;[3] and if this power were denied, I would not permit them to manufacture a lock of wool, or form a horse-shoe, or a hob-nail.[4] But I repeat, the house has no right to lay an internal tax upon America, that country not being represented.

"I know not what we may hope or fear from those now in place; but I have confidence in their good intentions. I could not refrain from expressing the reflections I have made in my retirement, which I hope long to enjoy,[5] beholding, as I do, ministries changed one after another, and passing away like shadows."[6]

A pause ensued as he ceased, when Conway rose

[1] Précis in the French Archives.
[2] Moffat.
[3] Moffat.
[4] Moffat. Compare Geo. Grenville to Knox, 15 Aug. 1768. Extra-Official State Papers, ii. Appendix, No. 3. p. 15.
[5] French Précis.
[6] Ibid, and Walpole, ii. 262.

CHAP. XXI. 1766. Jan. and spoke: "I not only adopt all that has just been said, but believe it expresses the sentiments of most, if not all the king's servants, and wish it may be the unanimous opinion of the house.[1] I have been accidentally called to the high employment I bear; I can follow no principles more safe or more enlightened than those of the perfect model before my eyes; and I should always be most happy to act by his advice, and even to serve under his orders.[2] Yet, for myself and my colleagues, I disclaim an overruling influence. The notice given to parliament of the troubles in America," he added, "was not early, because the first accounts were too vague and imperfect to be worth its attention."

"The disturbances in America," replied Grenville, who by this time had gained self-possession, "began in July, and now we are in the middle of January; lately they were only occurrences; they are now grown to tumults and riots; they border on open rebellion; and if the doctrine I have heard this day, be confirmed, nothing can tend more directly to produce a revolution. The government over them being dissolved, a revolution will take place in America.

"External and internal taxes are the same in effect, and only differ in name. That this kingdom is the sovereign, the supreme legislative power over America, cannot be denied; and taxation is a part of that sovereign power. It is one branch of the legislation. It has been, and it is exercised over those who are not, who were never represented. It is exercised over the India Company, the merchants of London, the proprietors of the stocks, and over many

[1] Moffat. Garth to South Carolina, 19 Jan. 1766.

[2] French Précis. Walpole, ii. 263 and 268.

great manufacturing towns. It was exercised over the palatinate of Chester, and the bishopric of Durham, before they sent any representatives to parliament. I appeal for proof to the preambles of the acts which gave them representatives, the one in the reign of Henry VIII., the other in that of Charles II." He then quoted the statutes exactly, and desired that they might be read; which being done he resumed

CHAP. XXI. 1766. Jan.

"To hold that the king, by the concession of a charter, can exempt a family or a colony from taxation by parliament, degrades the constitution of England. If the colonies, instead of throwing off entirely the authority of parliament, had presented a petition to send to it deputies elected among themselves, this step would have marked their attachment to the crown and their affection for the mother country, and would have merited attention.[1]

"The stamp act is but the pretext of which they make use to arrive at independence.[2] It was thoroughly considered, and not hurried at the end of a session. It passed through the different stages in full houses, with only one division on it. When I proposed to tax America, I asked the house, if any gentleman would object to the right; I repeatedly asked it, and no man would attempt to deny it. Protection and obedience are reciprocal. Great Britain protects America; America is bound to yield obedience. If not, tell me when the Americans were emancipated? When they want the protection of this kingdom, they are always ready to ask it. That protection has always been afforded them in the most

[1] French Précis. Geo. Grenville to T. Pownall, 17 July, 1768.

[2] French Précis.

CHAP. XXI. 1766. Jan.

full and ample manner. The nation has run itself into an immense debt to give it them; and now that they are called upon to contribute a small share towards an expense arising from themselves—they renounce your authority, insult your officers, and break out, I might almost say, into open rebellion.

"The seditious spirit of the colonies owes its birth to the factions in this house. We were told we trod on tender ground; we were bid to expect disobedience. What was this but telling the Americans to stand out against the law, to encourage their obstinacy with the expectation of support from hence? Let us only hold out a little, they would say, our friends will soon be in power.

"Ungrateful people of America! Bounties have been extended to them. When I had the honor to serve the crown, while you yourselves were loaded with an enormous debt of one hundred and forty millions sterling, and paid a revenue of ten millions sterling, you have given bounties on their lumber, on their iron, their hemp, and many other articles. You have relaxed, in their favor, the act of navigation, that palladium of British commerce. I offered to do every thing in my power to advance the trade of America. I discouraged no trade but what was prohibited by act of parliament. I was above giving an answer to anonymous calumnies; but in this place it becomes me to wipe off the aspersion."

As Grenville ceased, several members got up; but the house clamored for Pitt, who seemed to rise. A point of order was decided in his favor, and the walls of St. Stephens resounded with "Go on, go on."

"Gentlemen," he exclaimed in his fervor, while floods of light poured from his eyes, and the crowded assembly stilled itself into breathless silence; "Sir," he continued, remembering to address the speaker, "I have been charged with giving birth to sedition in America. They have spoken their sentiments with freedom against this unhappy act, and that freedom has become their crime. Sorry I am to hear the liberty of speech in this house imputed as a crime. But the imputation shall not discourage me. It is a liberty I mean to exercise. No gentleman ought to be afraid to exercise it. It is a liberty by which the gentleman who calumniates it might and ought to have profited. He ought to have desisted from his project. The gentleman tells us America is obstinate; America is almost in open rebellion. I rejoice that America has resisted." At the word, the whole house started as though their hands had been joined, and an electric spark had darted through them all.

CHAP. XXI. 1766. Jan.

"I rejoice that America has resisted. If its millions of inhabitants had submitted, taxes would soon have been laid on Ireland;[1] and if ever this nation should have a tyrant for its king, six[2] millions of freemen, so dead to all the feelings of liberty, as voluntarily to submit to be slaves, would be fit instruments to make slaves of the rest.

"I come not here armed at all points with law cases and acts of parliament, with the statute-book doubled down in dogs' ears, to defend the cause of liberty; if I had, I would myself have cited the two cases of Chester and Durham, to show, that even under arbitrary reigns, parliaments were ashamed of taxing a people

[1] French Précis [2] Ibid.

CHAP. XXI. 1766. Jan.

without their consent, and allowed them representatives. Why did the gentleman confine himself to Chester and Durham? He might have taken a higher example in Wales that was never taxed by parliament till it was incorporated. I would not debate a particular point of law with the gentleman, but I draw my ideas of freedom from the vital powers of the British constitution—not from the crude and fallacious notions too much relied upon, as if we were but in the morning of liberty.[1] I can acknowledge no veneration for any procedure, law, or ordinance, that is repugnant to reason, and the first elements of our constitution; and," he added, sneering at Grenville, who was once so much of a republican as to have opposed the whigs, "I shall never bend with the pliant suppleness of some who have cried aloud for freedom, only to have an occasion of renouncing or destroying it.[2]

"The gentleman tells us of many who are taxed, and are not represented—the India Company, merchants, stockholders, manufacturers. Surely, many of these are represented in other capacities. It is a misfortune that more are not actually represented. But they are all inhabitants, and as such are virtually represented. Many have it in their option to be actually represented. They have connection with those that elect, and they have influence over them.

"Not one of the ministers who have taken the lead of government since the accession of King William, ever recommended a tax like this of the Stamp Act. Lord Halifax, educated in the House of Commons, Lord Oxford, Lord Orford, a great revenue minister, never thought of this.[3] None of these ever dreamed of robbing the colonies of their constitutional rights.

[1] Moffat. [2] Ibid. [3] Walpole.

That was reserved to mark the era of the late administration. CHAP. XXI.

"The gentleman boasts of his bounties to America. 1766. Jan. Are those bounties intended finally for the benefit of this kingdom? If they are, where is his peculiar merit to America? If they are not, he has misapplied the national treasures.

"If the gentleman cannot understand the difference between internal and external taxes, I cannot help it. But there is a plain distinction between taxes levied for the purposes of raising revenue, and duties imposed for the regulation of trade for the accommodation of the subject, although in the consequences, some revenue may accidentally arise from the latter.

"The gentleman asks, when were the colonies emancipated? I desire to know when they were made slaves? But I do not dwell upon words. The profits to Great Britain from the trade of the colonies, through all its branches, is two millions a year. This is the fund that carried you triumphantly through the last war. The estates that were rented at two thousand pounds a year threescore years ago, are at three thousand pounds at present. You owe this to America. This is the price that America pays you for her protection. And shall a miserable financier come with a boast, that he can fetch a peppercorn into the exchequer to the loss of millions to the nation? I dare not say how much higher these profits may be augmented. Omitting the immense increase of people in the Northern colonies by natural population, and the migration from every part of Europe, I am convinced the whole commercial system may be altered to advantage. Improper restraints

CHAP. XXI. 1766. Jan.

have been laid on the continent in favor of the islands. Let acts of parliament in consequence of treaties remain; but let not an English minister become a custom-house officer for Spain, or for any foreign power.

"The gentleman must not wonder he was not contradicted, when, as the minister, he asserted a right of parliament to tax America. There is a modesty in this house which does not choose to contradict a minister. I wish gentlemen would get the better of it. If they do not, perhaps," he continued, glancing at the coming question of the reform of parliament, "the collective body may begin to abate of its respect for the representative. Lord Bacon has told me, that a great question will not fail of being agitated at one time or another.

"A great deal has been said without doors of the strength of America. It is a topic that ought to be cautiously meddled with. In a good cause, on a sound bottom, the force of this country can crush America to atoms. If any idea of renouncing allegiance has existed, it was but a momentary frenzy; and if the case was either probable or possible, I should think of the Atlantic sea as less than a line dividing one country from another. The will of parliament, properly signified, must for ever keep the colonies dependent upon the sovereign kingdom of Great Britain. But on this ground of the Stamp Act, when so many here will think it a crying injustice, I am one who will lift up my hands against it. In such a cause your success would be hazardous. America, IF she fell, would fall like the strong man; she would embrace the pillars of the state, and pull down the constitution along with her.

CHAP. XXI. 1766. Jan.

"Is this your boasted peace? Not to sheath the sword in its scabbard, but to sheath it in the bowels of your brothers, the Americans? Will you quarrel with yourselves, now the whole house of Bourbon is united against you? The Americans have not acted in all things with prudence and temper. They have been driven to madness by injustice. Will you punish them for the madness you have occasioned? Rather let prudence and temper come first from this side. I will undertake for America that she will follow the example.

Be to her faults a little blind;
Be to her virtues very kind.

"Upon the whole, I will beg leave to tell the house what is really my opinion. It is, that the Stamp Act be repealed, absolutely, totally, and immediately; that the reason for the repeal be assigned, because it was founded on an erroneous principle. At the same time let the sovereign authority of this country over the colonies be asserted in as strong terms as can be devised, and be made to extend to every point of legislation, that we may bind their trade, confine their manufactures, and exercise every power whatsoever, except that of taking their money out of their pockets without their consent.

"Let us be content with the advantages which Providence has bestowed upon us. We have attained the highest glory and greatness. Let us strive long to preserve them for our own happiness and that of our posterity."[1]

Thus he spoke, with fire unquenchable; "like a

[1] French Précis.

CHAP. XXI. 1766. Jan.

man inspired;"[1] greatest of orators, for his words swayed events, opening the gates of futurity to a better culture. Impassioned as was his manner, there was truth in his arguments, that were fitly joined together, so that his speech in its delivery was as a chain cable in a thunder storm, along which the lightning pours its flashes without weakening the links of iron. Men in America, for the moment, paid no heed to the assertion of parliamentary authority to bind manufactures and trade; they exulted at knowing that the Great Commoner had, in the House of Commons, taken up what Mansfield and the king called "the trumpet of sedition," and thanked God for America's resistance.

On the very next day the Duke of Grafton recommended to the king to send for Pitt, and hear his sentiments on American affairs. Had this been done, and had his opinion prevailed, who can tell into what distant age the question of American independence would have been adjourned? But at seven o'clock in the evening of the sixteenth, Grafton was suddenly summoned to the palace. The king was in that state of "extreme agitation" which so often afflicted him when he was thwarted; and avowing designs, leading to a change of ministry of a different kind, he commanded the duke to carry no declaration from him to Pitt. Two hours later he gave an audience to Charles Townshend, whom he endeavored, though ineffectually, to persuade to take a principal part in forming a new administration. The Duke of Grafton nevertheless, himself repaired to Pitt, and sought his confidence. "The differences in politics between Lord

[1] Thos. Penn to J. Hamilton, 17 Jan. 1766.

Temple and me," said the Commoner, "have never till now, made it impossible for us to act on one plan. The difference upon this American measure will, in its consequences, be felt for fifty years at least." He proposed to form a proper system, with the two present Secretaries and first Lord of the Treasury, the younger and better part of the ministry; if they would willingly co-operate with him. Honors might be offered the Duke of Newcastle, but not a place in the Cabinet. "I see with pleasure," said he, "the present administration take the places of the last. I came up upon the American affair, a point on which I feared they might be borne down."

CHAP. XXI. 1766. Jan.

Of this conversation the Duke of Grafton made so good a use, that, by the king's direction, he and Rockingham waited on Pitt, on Saturday the eighteenth, when Pitt once more expressed his readiness to act with those now in the ministry, yet with some "transposition of places." At the same time he dwelt on the disgrace brought on the nation, by the recall of Lord George Sackville to the council, declaring over and over that his lordship and he could not sit at the council board together.

But no sooner had Pitt consented to renounce his connection with Temple, and unite with the ministry, than Rockingham interposed objections, alike of a personal nature, and of principle. The speechless prime minister, having tasted the dignity of chief, did not wish to be transposed; and the principle of "giving up all right of taxation over the colonies," on which the union was to have rested, had implacable opponents in the family of Hardwicke, and in the person of his own private secretary. "If ever one man lived more zealous than another for the supremacy of par-

CHAP. XXI. 1766. Jan. liament, and the rights of the imperial crown, it was Edmund Burke." He was the advocate "of an unlimited legislative power over the colonies." "He saw not how the power of taxation could be given up, without giving up the rest." If Pitt was able to see it, Pitt "saw further than he could." His wishes were "very earnest to keep the whole body of this authority perfect and entire." He was "jealous of it;" he was "honestly of that opinion;" and Rockingham, after proceeding so far, and finding in Pitt all the encouragement that he expected, let the negotiation drop. Conway and Grafton were compelled to disregard their own avowals on the question of the right of taxation; and the ministry conformed to the opinion, which was that of Charles Yorke, the Attorney-General, and still more of Edmund Burke.

Neglected by Rockingham, hated by the aristocracy, and feared by the king, Pitt pursued his career alone. In the quiet of confidential intercourse, he inquired if fleets and armies could reduce America, and heard from a friend, that the Americans would not submit, that they would still have their woods and liberty. Thomas Hollis sent to him the "masterly" essay of John Adams on the canon and feudal law. He read it, and pronounced it "indeed masterly."

The papers which had been agreed upon by the American Congress had been received by De Berdt, the agent for Massachusetts. Conway did not scruple to present its petition to the king, and George Cooke, the member for Middlesex, was so pleased with that to the Commons, that on Monday, the twenty-seventh of January, he offered it to the house, where he read it twice over. Jenkinson opposed receiving it, as did

CHAP. XXI. 1766 Jan.

Nugent and Welbore Ellis. "The American Congress at New-York," they argued, "was a federal union, assembled without any requisition on the part of the supreme power. By receiving a petition from persons so unconstitutionally assembled, the house would give countenance to a measure pregnant with danger to his majesty's authority and government."

"The petition," said Pitt, "is innocent, dutiful, and respectful; I see no defect in it, except that the name of one of the petitioners is Oliver. Little attention was given last year to the separate petitions of particular colonies or their agents; it might well be imagined, that a general petition, prepared and signed by able gentlemen, in whom each colony reposed confidence, would be entitled to different treatment. It is the evil genius of this country that has riveted among them the union, now called dangerous and federal. The colonies should be heard. The privilege of having representatives in parliament, before they can be taxed internally, is their birthright. This question being of high concern to a vast empire rising beyond the sea, should be discussed as a question of right. If parliament cannot tax America without her consent, the original compact with the colonies is actually broken. The decrees of parliament are not infallible; they may be repealed. Let the petition be received as the first act of harmony, and remain to all posterity on the journals of this house."

Conway adhered to the opinions of Pitt on the subject of taxation, but thought the rules of the house forbade the reception of the petition.

Sir Fletcher Norton rose in great heat, and de-

[1] Lord Charlemont to Henry Flood, London, Jan. 28, 1766. The printed date is erroneously given as Jan. 8.

CHAP. XXI. 1766. Jan.

nounced the distinction between internal and external taxation, as a novelty unfounded in truth, reason, or justice, unknown to their ancestors, whether as legislators or judges—a whim that might serve to point a declamation, but abhorrent to the British constitution. "Expressions," said he, "have fallen from that member now, and on a late similar occasion, which make my blood run cold, even at my heart. I say, he sounds the trumpet to rebellion. Such language in other days, and even since the morning of freedom, would have transported that member out of this House into another, with more leisure for better reflections." Pitt, without saying one word, fixed his eye steadily on him, with an air of most marked contempt, from which Norton, abashed or chagrined, knew no escape, but by an appeal for protection to the speaker.

Edmund Burke speaking for the first time in the House of Commons, advocated the reception of the petition, as in itself an acknowledgment of the jurisdiction of the house; while Charles Townshend in a short speech treated the line drawn between external and internal taxation, as "a fiction or the ecstasy of madness."

An hour before midnight Lord John Cavendish avoided a defeat on a division, by moving the orders of the day, while Conway assured the American agents of his good will, and the Speaker caused the substance of the whole paper to be entered on the journals.

The reading of papers and examination of witnesses continued during the month, in the utmost secrecy. The evidence especially of the riots in Rhode Island and New-York, produced a very unfavorable effect. On the last day of January the weakness of the ministry appeared on a division respecting an election for some of the boroughs in Scotland; in a very full house they had only a majority of eleven. The grooms of the bedchamber, and even Lord George Sackville voted against them, whilst Charles Townshend, the paymaster, declined to vote at all. On the same day Bedford and Grenville were asked, if on Bute's opening the door, they were ready to negotiate for a change of administration, and they both sent word to the king, that his order would be attended to, with duty and respect, through "whatever channel it should come."

Had Pitt acceded to the administration, he would have made the attempt to bring the nation to the conviction of the expediency of "giving up all right of taxation over the colonies." Left to themselves, with the king against them, and the country gentlemen wavering, the ministers, not perceiving that the concession was a certain sign of expiring power, prepared a resolution to the effect, that "the king in parliament has full power to bind the colonies and people of America, in all cases whatsoever."

CHAPTER XXII.

PARLIAMENT AFFIRMS ITS RIGHT TO TAX AMERICA—ROCKINGHAM'S ADMINISTRATION CONTINUED.

The Third of February, 1766.

CHAP. XXII. 1766. Feb. It was the third day of February, when the Duke of Grafton himself offered in the House of Lords the resolution, which was in direct contradiction to his wishes. At the same time he recommended lenient measures. Shelburne proposed to repeal the Stamp Act, and avoid a decision on the question of right.

"If you exempt the American colonies from one statute or law," said Lyttelton, "you make them independent communities. If opinions of this weight are to be taken up and argued upon through mistake or timidity, we shall have Lycurguses and Solons in every coffee house, tavern, and gin shop in London. Many thousands in England who have no vote in electing representatives will follow their brethren in America in refusing submission to any taxes. The Commons will with pleasure hear the doctrine of equality being the natural right of all; but the doctrine of equality may be carried to the destruction of this monarchy."

Lord Temple treated as a jest his brother-in-law's

distinction in regard to internal taxation. Did the colonies," he continued, "when they emigrated, keep the purse only, and give up their liberties?" And he cited Shakspeare to prove that "who steals a purse steals trash;" then advising the Lords to firmness towards the colonies, he concluded with an admonition from Tacitus.

"The question before your lordships," said Camden, the youngest baron in the house, "concerns the common rights of mankind. The resolution now proposed gives the legislature an absolute power of laying any tax upon America. In my own opinion, my lords, the legislature had no right to make this law. When the people consented to be taxed, they reserved to themselves the power of giving and granting by their representatives. The colonies, when they emigrated, carried their birthright with them; and the same spirit of liberty still pervades the whole of the New Empire."[1] He proceeded to show, from the principles and precedents of English law, that none could be taxed unless by their representatives; that the clergy, the Counties Palatine, Wales, Calais, and Berwick, were never taxed till they sent members to parliament; that Guernsey and Jersey send no members, and are not taxed; and dwelling particularly on the case of Ireland, he cited the opinion of Chief Justice Hale, that Great Britain had no power to raise subsidies in Ireland. But supposing the Americans had no exclusive right to tax themselves, he maintained it would be good policy to give it them. This he argued as a question of justice; for in the clashing interests of the mother country and the colonies, every Englishman would incline against them.

[1] H. Hammersley to Sharpe.

CHAP. XXII. 1766. Feb.

This, too, he supported, as the only means of maintaining their dependence; for America felt that she could better do without England than England without America; and he reminded the house, that inflexibility lost to the Court of Vienna the dominion of the Low Countries.[1]

Thus he reasoned in a strain of eloquence, which Pitt called divine.[2] "I cannot sit silent," replied Northington, the Lord Chancellor, speaking "very shortly;" "I cannot sit silent, upon doctrines being laid down so new, so unmaintainable, and so unconstitutional. In every state there must be a supreme dominion; every government can arbitrarily impose laws on all its subjects, by which all are bound; and resistance to laws that are even contrary to the benefit and safety of the whole, is at the risk of life and fortune.

"I seek for the constitution of this kingdom no higher up than the Revolution, as this country never had one before;[3] and in the reign of King William an act passed, avowing the power of this legislature over the colonies. The king cannot suspend the Stamp Act; he is sworn by his coronation oath to do the contrary. But if you should concur as to the expediency of repeal, you will have twelve millions of your subjects of Great Britain and Ireland at your doors, not making speeches, but using club law.

"My Lords, what have these favorite Americans done? They have sent deputies to a meeting of their states, at New-York, by which" (and, as he spoke, he appealed personally to Mansfield and Camden), "I

[1] H. Hammersley to Sharpe.

[2] Chatham Correspondence, ii. 363. The editor erroneously dates the letter 15 Jan. It was of 4 February.

[3] H. Hammersley's Report MS.

CHAP. XXII. 1766. Feb.

declare, as a lawyer, they have forfeited all their charters. My Lords, the colonies are become too big to be governed by the laws they at first set out with. They have, therefore, run into confusion, and it will be the policy of this country to form a plan of laws for them. If they withdraw allegiance, you must withdraw protection; and then the petty state of Genoa, or the little kingdom of Sweden, may run away with them."

Benjamin Franklin[1] stood listening below the bar, while the highest judicial magistrate of Great Britain was asserting the absolute, unconditional dependence of the colonies on parliament, and advising radical changes in their constitutions.

Next rose Lord Mansfield, to whose authority the House of Lords paid greater deference than to that of any man living.[2] To him belonged the sad office of struggling to preserve the past, in which success is impossible; for nature flows on, and is never at rest. He performed his office earnestly and sincerely; though he entered public life as a whig, he leaned towards an arbitrary government, was jealous of popular privileges or influence, and stood ready to serve the cause of power, even without sharing it. Cautious even to timidity, his understanding was clear, but his heart was cold. The childless man had been unsuccessful in love, and formed no friendships. His vast accumulations of knowledge, which a tenacious memory stored up in its hundred cells, were ever ready to come forward at his summons. The lucid order of his arrangement assisted to bring con-

[1] Campbell's Chancellors, v. 204. [2] Newton's Life of himself, 103.

CHAP. XXII. 1766. Feb.

viction; and he would readily expound the most mysterious intricacies of law, or analyze the longest series of reasonings and evidence, with an intelligent smile on his features that spoke plainly the perfect ease with which he did it. In subtlety he had no equal; ornament seemed to flow so naturally from his subject, that while none could speak with more elegance, it seemed impossible for him to speak with less. His countenance was beautiful, inspiring reverence and regard; his eye gleaming with light; his voice acutely clear, yet varied and musical; his manner graceful and engaging. He had been a member of the cabinet when the plan of the Stamp Act was adopted; his legal opinion lay at its foundation; and now he came forward to vindicate its rightfulness, of which he saw clearly that the denial not merely invited America to independence, but also invoked changes in the British constitution.

"My Lords," said he, speaking for two hours and a half, in reply to Camden, as he himself says, without special premeditation, and showing by his superior familiarity with the subject, as well as his taking the lead in the discussion, how intimately he was connected with the policy he defended: "My Lords, I shall speak to the question strictly as a matter of right. I shall also speak to the distinctions which have been taken, without any real difference, as to the nature of the tax; and I shall point out lastly the necessity there will be of exerting the force of the superior authority of government, if opposed by the subordinate part of it.

"I am extremly sorry that the question has ever become necessary to be agitated, and that there should be a decision upon it. No one in this house will live long enough to see an end put to the mischief which will be the result of the doctrine that has been inculcated; but the arrow is shot, and the wound already given.[1]

CHAP. XXII. 1766. Feb.

"All arguments fetched from Locke, Harrington, and speculative men, who have written upon the subject of government, the law of nature, or of other nations, are little to the purpose, for we are not now settling a new constitution, but finding out and declaring the old one.[2]

"The doctrine of representation seems ill founded; there are twelve millions of people in England and Ireland who are not represented. The parliament first depended upon tenures; representation by election came by the favor of the crown, and the notion now taken up, that every subject must be represented by deputy, is purely ideal. The doctrine of representation never entered the heads of the great writers in Charles the First's time against ship money or other illegal exertions of the prerogative, nor was the right of representation claimed in the Petition of Rights at the great era of the revolution.[3]

"The colonists,"—thus he continued, after having answered one by one the writs and records quoted by Lord Camden, the arguments fetched from the Marches of Wales, from the counties palatine, from Guernsey and Jersey, from the case of the clergy, as well as those drawn from the colonies of antiquity, and from the states of Holland;—"the colonists, by the condition on which they migrated, settled and now exist,

[1] Mansfield's Own Report of his Speech, in Holliday, 242. See, too, the Abstract of the General Argument, in the Annual Register, where Mansfield's words are adopted.

[2] Letters of Hammersley.

[3] From H. Hammersley's Report.

CHAP. XXII. 1766. Feb. are more emphatically subjects of Great Britain, than those within the realm; and the British legislature have, in every instance, exercised their right of legislation over them without any dispute or question, till the fourteenth of January last.

"Our colonies emigrated under the sanction of the crown and parliament, upon the terms of being subjects of England. They were modelled gradually into their present forms, by charters, grants, and statutes; but they were never separated from the mother country, or so emancipated as to become their own masters. The very idea of a colony implies subordination and dependence, to render allegiance for protection. If they are not subjects, they ought to pay duties as aliens.[1] The charter colonies had among their directors members of the privy council and of both houses of parliament, and were under the authority of the privy council. In the nineteenth year of James I. a doubt was thrown out in the House of Commons, whether parliament had any thing to do with America, and the doubt was immediately answered by Coke.[2] The rights of Maryland were, by charter, coextensive with those of any Bishop of Durham in that county palatine, and the statute book shows that Durham was taxed by parliament before it was represented. The commonwealth parliament passed a resolution or act, and it is a question whether it is not in force now, to declare and establish the authority of England over its colonies. The charter of Pennsylvania, who have preposterously taken the lead," and Franklin was present to hear this, "is stamped with every badge of subordination;[3] and a

[1] H. Hammersley's Report.
[2] Hansard, xvi. 176.
[3] H. Hammersley.

CHAP. XXII. 1766. Feb.

particular saving as to all English acts of parliament. Could the king's bench vacate the Massachusetts charter, and yet the parliament be unable to tax them? Do they say this, when they themselves acquiesced in the judgment, and took a new charter?[1]

"In 1724, the assembly of Jamaica having refused to raise taxes for their necessary support, the late Lord Hardwicke, then Attorney-General, and Sir Clement Wearg, Solicitor-General, gave their opinion that if Jamaica is to be considered as a conquered country, the king may tax it by his own authority; if otherwise, it must be by the British legislature.

"Let the advocates for America draw their line. Let them move their exception, and say how far the sovereignty of the British parliament should go, and where it should stop? Did the Americans keep the right of the purse only, and not of their persons and their liberties?[2]

"But if there was no express law or reason founded upon any necessary inference from an express law, yet the usage alone would be sufficient to support that authority of England over its colonies; for have they not submitted, ever since their first establishment, to the jurisdiction of the mother country? In all questions of property, the appeals from them have been to the privy council here; and such causes have been determined, not by their laws, but by the law of England. They have been obliged to recur very frequently to the jurisdiction here to settle the disputes among their own governments.

"The colonies must remain dependent upon the jurisdiction of the mother country, or they must be totally dismembered from it, and form a league of

[1] Ibid. [2] Ibid.

CHAP. XXII. 1766. Feb. union among themselves against it, which could not be effected without great violences. No one ever thought the contrary, till now the trumpet of sedition has been blown. It is sufficient to turn over the index to the statute book, to show that acts of parliament have been made not only without a doubt of their legality, but with universal applause, the great object of which has been ultimately to fix the trade of the colonies, so as to centre in the bosom of that country, from which they took their original. The Navigation Act shut up their intercourse with foreign countries. Their ports have been made subject to customs and regulations, which have cramped and diminished their trade; and duties have been laid affecting the very inmost parts of their commerce. Such were the post-office acts; the act for recovering debts in the plantations; the acts for preserving timber and white pines; the paper currency act. The legislature have even gone so low as to restrain the number of hatters' apprentices in America, and have, in innumerable instances, given the forfeitures to the king. Yet all these have been submitted to peaceably, and no one ever thought till now of this doctrine, that the colonies are not to be taxed, regulated, or bound by parliament. This day is the first time we have heard of it in this house.

"There can be no doubt, my lords, but that the inhabitants of the colonies are as much represented in parliament as the greatest part of the people of England are represented; among nine millions of whom there are eight who have no votes in electing members of parliament. Every objection, therefore, to the dependency of the colonies upon parliament, which arises to it upon the ground of representation, goes to

CHAP. XXII. 1766. Feb.

the whole present constitution of Great Britain; and I suppose it is not meant to new model that too! People may form their own speculative ideas of perfection, and indulge their own fancies, or those of other men. Every man in this country has his particular notions of liberty; but perfection never did and never can exist in any human institution. For what purpose, then, are arguments drawn from a distinction in which there is no real difference, of a virtual and actual representation? A member of parliament, chosen by any borough, represents not only the constituents and inhabitants of that particular place, but he represents the inhabitants of every other borough in Great Britain. He represents the city of London and all other the commons of this land, and the inhabitants of all the colonies and dominions of Great Britain; and is in duty and in conscience bound to take care of their interests.

"The noble lord, who quoted so much law, and denied upon those grounds the right of the parliament of Great Britain to lay internal taxes upon the colonies, allowed at the same time, that restrictions upon trade and duties upon the ports were legal. But I cannot see a real difference in this distinction; for I hold it to be true, that a tax laid in any place is like a pebble falling into, and making a circle in a lake, till one circle produces and gives motion to another, and the whole circumference is agitated from the centre. A tax on tobacco, either in the ports of Virginia or London, is a duty laid upon the inland plantations of Virginia, a hundred miles from the sea, wheresoever the tobacco grows.

CHAP. XXII. 1766. Feb.

"The legislature properly interposed for the purpose of a general taxation, as the colonies would never agree to adjust their respective proportions amongst themselves.

"I do not deny but that a tax may be laid injudiciously and injuriously, and that people in such a case may have a right to complain; but the nature of the tax is not now the question: whenever it comes to be one, I am for lenity. I would have no blood drawn. There is, I am satisfied, no occasion for any to be drawn. A little time and experience of the inconveniences and miseries of anarchy may bring people to their senses. Anarchy always cures itself; but the fermentation will continue so much the longer, while hot-headed men there find that there are persons of weight and character to support and justify them here.

"Indeed, if the disturbances should continue for a great length of time, force must be the consequence, an application, adequate to the mischief, and arising out of the necessity of the case; for force is only the difference between a superior and subordinate jurisdiction. In the former, the whole force of the legislature resides collectively, and when it ceases to reside, the whole connection is dissolved. It will indeed be to very little purpose, that we sit here enacting laws or making resolutions, if the inferior will not obey them, or if we neither can nor dare enforce them; for then, of necessity, the matter comes to the sword. If the offspring are grown too big and too resolute to obey the parent, you must try which is the strongest, and exert all the powers of the mother country to decide the contest.

"Time and a wise and steady conduct may pre-

CHAP. XXII. 1766. Feb.

vent those extremities which would be fatal to both. Interest very soon divides mercantile people; and although there may be some mad, enthusiastic, or ill-designing people in the colonies, yet I am convinced that the greatest bulk, who have understanding and property, are still well affected to the mother country. The resolutions in the most of the assemblies have been carried by small majorities, and in some by one or two only. You have, my lords, many friends still in the colonies; take care that you do not, by abdicating your own authority, desert them and yourselves, and lose them for ever.

"You may abdicate your right over the colonies: take care, my lords, how you do so, for such an act will be irrevocable. Proceed, then, my lords, with spirit and firmness, and when you shall have established your authority, it will then be a time to show your lenity. The Americans, as I said before, are a very good people, and I wish them exceedingly well; but they are heated and inflamed. I cannot end better than by saying, in the words of Maurice, Prince of Orange, concerning the Hollanders, God bless this industrious, frugal, well-meaning, but easily deluded people!"

The House of Lords accepted the argument of Mansfield as unanswerable, and when the house divided, only five peers, Camden, Shelburne, and the young Cornwallis—destined to a long and chequered career,—Torrington, and Paulet, went down below the bar. With these five, stood the invisible genius of popular reform; they began a strife which the child that was unborn would rue or would bless. The rest of the peers, one hundred and twenty-five[1] in number, saw

[1] H. Hammersley. Garth to South Carolina, 9 Feb. 1766.

CHAP. XXII. 1766. Feb.

with derision the small number of the visionaries. As for Camden himself, they said Mansfield had utterly prostrated him.[2]

Even while Mansfield was explaining to the House of Lords, that the American theory of representation included in its idea a thorough reform of the British House of Commons, George the Third was led to offer a pension of a hundred guineas a year to the Genevese republican, Jean Jacques Rousseau, who had just then arrived in England, a fugitive from France, where his works were condemned to be burned by the hands of the executioner, and he himself was in peril of arrest and indefinite imprisonment. The drift of his writings was not well understood, and no one foreboded the extent of their influence. But he was come among a people very unlike himself, and the illusion that hung round the celebrated author soon gave way to disgust at his vile connections, and indifference to the sorrows of his sensitive and suspicious nature. Some, even, who should have spared the infirmities of the wretched man, ungenerously exposed him to public contempt. So he pined in neglect, no object of terror to the aristocracy or the crown. Yet the exile, then writhing under the pangs of wounded vanity, was to stand forth in the world's history more conspicuously than Mansfield. The one cherished feudalism as the most perfect form of government that had ever been devised; the other pleaded for its destruction, as an unjust and absurd system, in which the human race was degraded, and the name of man was in dishonor. Both hurried forward revolution; the counsels of the former drove America to form for the world's example

[2] De Guerchy au Duc de Praslin, 4 Février, 1766.

a government truly representing the people; the other was so to touch the French nation in Convention with the flame of his humane, but jealous, impatient, and dogmatic spirit, as to light up European wars between the New and the Old, continuously for a generation.

CHAP XXII. 1766 Feb

In the Commons, the resolution was presented by Conway, who himself at the time of passing the Stamp Act, had publicly and almost alone denied the right of parliament to impose the tax, and twice within twenty days had publicly reiterated that opinion. He now treated the question of power as a point of law, which parliament might take up. For himself, he should never be for internal taxes. He would sooner cut off his right hand than sign an order for sending out a force to maintain them. Yet he begged not to be understood to pledge himself for future measures, not even for the repeal of the Stamp Act. "When he comes to move resolutions of repeal," said Grenville's friends, "he will have in his pocket another set of resolutions of an opposite character."

Dowdeswell, the Chancellor of the Exchequer, defended the proposition in its fullest extent. Parliament might change the charters of the colonies, and much more, might tallage them; though, in point of policy, justice, or equity, it was a power that ought to be exercised in the most extraordinary cases only.[1]

Barre moved to strike out from the resolution the words, "in all cases whatsoever." He was seconded by Pitt, and sustained by Beckford. They contended that American taxation by parliament was against the spirit of the British constitution; against the authority

[1] Garth to South Carolina, 9 Feb. 1756. I have an exceedingly copious abstract of this debate, made by Garth for South Carolina.

CHAP. XXII. 1766. Feb.

of Locke, and the principles of the revolution of 1688; against the right of the colonists to enjoy English liberty; against the inherent distinction between taxation and legislation, which pervaded modern history; against the solemn compacts which parliament itself had recognised as existing between the crown and the colonies; against the rights of the American assemblies, whose duty it ever is to obtain redress of material grievances, before making grants of money, and whose essence would be destroyed by a transfer from them of the powers of taxation; against justice, for Great Britain could have interests conflicting with those of the colonies; against reason, for the assemblies of the colonists could know their own abilities and circumstances better than the Commons of England; against good policy, which could preserve America only as Rome had preserved her distant colonies, not by the number of its legions, but by lenient magnanimity.

Only three men, or rather Pitt alone, "debated strenuously the rights of America" against more than as many hundred;[1] and yet the House of Commons, half-conscious of the fatality of its decision, was so awed by the overhanging shadow of coming events that it seemed to shrink from pronouncing its opinion. Edmund Burke, eager to add glory as an orator to his just renown as an author, argued for England's right in such a manner, that the strongest friends of power declared his speech to have been "far superior to that of every other speaker;" while Grenville, Yorke, and all the lawyers, the temperate Richard Hussey, who yet was practically for humanity and justice,

[1] Garth to South Carolina: "A fuller house I don't recollect to have seen." Garth was a member.

CHAP XXII. 1766. Feb.

Blackstone, the commentator on the laws of England, who still disliked internal taxation of America by parliament, the selfish, unscrupulous, unrelenting Wedderburn, filled many hours with solemn arguments for England's unlimited supremacy. They persuaded one another and the house, that the charters which kings had granted were, by the unbroken opinions of lawyers, from 1689, subordinate to the good will of the houses of parliament; that parliament, for a stronger reason, had power to tax—a power which it had been proposed to exert in 1713, while Harley was at the head of the treasury, and again at the opening of the Seven Years' War.

It was further contended, that representation was not the basis of the authority of parliament; that its legislative power was an absolute trust; that the kingdom and colonies were one empire; that the colonies enjoyed the opportunity of taxing themselves, as an indulgence; that the exemption from taxation, when conceded to the Counties Palatine, Chester, Durham, and Lancaster, or Wales, or Ireland, or the clergy, was exceptional; that duties and impositions, taxes and subsidies were all one; and as kingdom and colonies were one body, parliament had the right to bind the colonies by taxes and impositions, alike internal and external, in all cases whatsoever.

So the watches of the long winter's night wore away, and at about four o'clock in the morning, when the question was called, less than ten voices, some said five, or four, some said but three, spoke out in the minority: "and the resolution passed for England's right to do what the treasury pleased with three millions of freemen in America." The Americans were henceforward excisable and taxable at the mercy of

CHAP. XXII. 1766. Feb. parliament. Grenville stood acquitted and sustained; the rightfulness of his policy was affirmed; and he was judged to have proceeded in conformity with the constitution.

Thus did Edmund Burke and the Rockingham ministry on that night lead Mansfield, Northington, and the gentlemen of the long robe, to found the new tory party of England, and recover legality for its position, stealing it away from the party that hitherto, under the revolution, had possessed it exclusively. It was decided as a question of law, that irresponsible taxation was not a tyranny, but a vested right; that parliament held power, not as a representative body, but in absolute trust. Under the decision, no option was left to the colonies but extreme resistance, or unconditional submission. It had grown to be a fact, that the House of Commons was no longer responsible to the people; and this night it was held to be the law, that it never had been, and was not responsible; that the doctrine of representation was not in the bill of rights. The tory party, with George the Third at its head, accepted from Burke and Rockingham the creed which Grenville claimed to be the whiggism of the revolution of 1688, and Mansfield the British constitution of his times.

In England, it was all over with the Middle Age. There was to be no more Jacobitism, no more zeal for legitimacy at home, no more union of the Catholic church and the sceptre. The new toryism was the child of modern civilization. It carried its pedigree no further back than the revolution of 1688, and was but a coalition of the king and the aristocracy upon the basis of the established law. By law the House of

Hanover held the throne; by law the English church was established, with a prayer-book and a creed as authorised by parliament, and with such bishops as the crown gave leave to choose; by law the Catholics and Dissenters were disfranchised, and none but conformers to the worship of the legal church could hold office or sit in the legislature; by law the House of Commons was lifted above responsibility to the people; by law the colonies were "bound" to be taxed at mercy. The tory party took the law as it stood, and set itself against reform. Henceforward its leaders and lights were to be found, not among the gallant descendants of ancient houses; not among the representatives of mediæval traditions. It was a new party, of which the leaders and expounders were to be new men. The moneyed interest, so firmly opposed to the legitimacy and aristocracy of the Middle Age, was to become its ally. Mansfield was its impersonation, and would transmit it, through Thurlow and Wedderburn, to Eldon.

It is the office of law to decide questions of possession. The just judge is appointed to be the conservator of society. Woe hangs over the land where the absolute principles of private law are applied to questions of public law; and the effort is made to bar the progress of the undying race by the despotic rules which ascertain the rights of property of evanescent mortals. Humanity smiled at the parchment chains which the lawyers threw around it, even though those chains were protected by a coalition of the army, the navy, the halls of justice, a corrupt parliament, and the crown. The new tory party created a new opposition. The non-electors of Great Britain were to become as little content with virtual representation

CHAP. XXII. 1766. Feb.

as the colonists. Even while Mansfield was speaking, the press of London gave to the world a very sensible production, showing the equity and practicability of a more equal representation throughout the whole British dominions;[1] and also a scheme[2] for a general parliament, to which every part of the British dominions should send one member for every twenty thousand of its inhabitants.

[1] Monthly Review for Feb. 1766, xxxiv. 155.

[2] An Account of a Conference on the Occurrences in America, in a letter to a friend, 1766, 38–40.

CHAPTER XXIII.

THE REPEAL OF THE STAMP ACT—ROCKINGHAM'S ADMINISTRATION CONTINUED.

February, 1766.

CHAP. XXIII. 1766. Feb.

On Tuesday, the fourth of February, the party of Bedford and the old ministry of Grenville coalesced with the friends of prerogative to exercise over the colonies the power, which it had just been resolved that parliament rightfully possessed. The ministry desired to recommend to them to compensate the sufferers by the American riots. The opposition, by a vote of sixty-three to sixty, changed the recommendation into a parliamentary requisition.[1] The new tory party already had a majority of votes in the House of Lords.

The next morning, Rockingham and Grafton, much irritated at this usage, went to court and proposed the removal from office of one or two of those who had appeared to be the most hostile; but the king, recently so eager to dismiss those who opposed him, refused his assent.[2]

On the night of the fifth of February, the same

[1] Chatham Corr. ii. 376. Grafton's Autobiography. De Guerchy to the Duke de Praslin, 4 Feb. and 7 Feb., 1766.

[2] Grafton's Autobiography.

CHAP. XXIII. 1766. Feb. question came up in the House of Commons, where Pitt spoke at length, with tact and gentleness. The coalition was, for the moment, thoroughly defeated; and at last the house, with considerable unanimity, contented itself with changing the proposition of the ministry into a resolution, declaratory of its opinion.[1]

It was known that the House of Lords would nevertheless persevere; and on Thursday, the sixth, it attracted the world[2] to witness its proceedings. To keep up appearances, Bute rose and declared "his most lively attachment to the person of the king, yet the interest of his country must weigh with him more than any other consideration; the king himself would not blame him or other lords for obeying the dictates of their conscience on important affairs of State."[3] Encouraged by this indirect promise of the king's good will, the new coalition, after a solemn debate, carried a majority of fifty-nine against fifty-four, in favor of executing the Stamp Act. For the House of Lords now to consent to its repeal would in some sort be an abdication of its co-ordinate authority.

Once more, on the morning of the seventh, Rockingham, forgetting alike the principles of the old whig party and of the British constitution, which forbid the interference of the king with the legislature, hurried to court, and this time asked and obtained leave to say, that the king was for the repeal of the Stamp Act; and he made haste to spread the intelligence.

The evening of that same day, Grenville resolved to test the temper of the house, and made a motion

[1] Garth to S. Carolina, 9 Feb., 1766.

[2] Chatham Corr. ii., 376. The letter is strangely misdated. Its true date is 6 Feb.

[3] De Guerchy to Praslin, 7 Feb.

tending to enforce the execution of all acts, meaning specially the Stamp Act.

With instant sagacity, Pitt, who at the time was far too ill to be in the house and yet was impelled by a sense of duty to be present, seized the advantage thus unwisely offered, and called on the house not to order the enforcement of the Stamp Act, before they had decided the question of repeal. The request was reasonable, was pressed by him with winning candor and strength of argument, and commended itself to the good sense and generous feeling of the independent members of the house.

"I shudder at the motion," cried the aged General Howard, while the crowded house listened as if awed into silence; "I hope it will not succeed, lest I should be ordered to execute it. Before I would imbrue my hands in the blood of my countrymen, who are contending for English liberty, I would, if ordered, draw my sword, but would sooner sheathe it in my own body." Nugent argued that giving way would infuse the spirit of resistance into the Irish. Charles Townshend, boasting that he had not yet declared as to whether he should vote for or against the repeal, seizing the safe opportunity of winning an advantage over Grenville, praised the general purport of his proposal, and yet censured him vehemently for anticipating the decision of the house. Grenville remained obdurate, and denounced curses on the ministers who should sacrifice the sovereignty of Great Britain over her colonies. He had expected great support. Sandwich had estimated the strength of the Bedfords at one hundred and thirty; their new allies had claimed to be eighty or ninety; and now, though Lord Granby, and all the Scotch and the king's friends, voted with

CHAP. XXIII. him, the motion was rejected, in a very full house, by more than two to one.

1766. Feb. The minority were astonished as well as overwhelmed with mortification. Some of them ungenerously blamed Grenville for his imprudence. At the palace, the king, when informed of this great majority, was so affected, that those who saw him most frequently, had never found him more so, and believed he wished for nothing so much as to be able to change his administration. His personal influence was therefore next invoked to arrest the repeal of the Stamp Act. On Monday, the tenth of February, Lord Strange, Chancellor of the Duchy of Lancaster, went in to the king on the business of his office; when he came out, he declared to some of the king's servants that "his majesty had given him authority to say, that he was for a modification of the Stamp Act, but not for a repeal of it."

Upon this the onset was renewed in the House of Commons. Trecothick was, on the eleventh, under examination at the bar of the house. "Do you think," asked Lord Strange, "the Americans will not rather submit to the Stamp Act than remain in the confusion they are in?" But this question was voted improper. "Will the Americans acquiesce, if this act is mitigated?" "No modification will reconcile them to it," answered Trecothick; "nor will any thing satisfy them less than its total repeal."

"What insolent rebels," cried the inflamed partisans of Grenville; and they redoubled their zeal to create delay, in the expectation of receiving news from America of the submission of one or more of the principal colonies to the Stamp Act. But the Sons of Liberty, acting spontaneously, were steadily advancing towards an organization, which should embrace the continent. In February, those in Boston, and in many towns in Massachusetts, acceded to the association of Connecticut and New-York; and joined in urging a continental union. They of Portsmouth in New Hampshire pledged themselves equally to the same measures.[1] In Connecticut, on the tenth of February, the patriots of Norwich welcomed the plan; while, on the next day, a convention of almost all the towns of Litchfield county resolved that the Stamp Act was unconstitutional, null, and void, and that business of all kinds should go on as usual. Then, too, the hum of domestic industry was heard more and more: young women would get together, and merrily and emulously drive the spinning wheel from sunrise till dark; and every day the humor spread for being clad in homespun.[2]

CHAP. XXIII. 1766. Feb.

Cheered by the zeal of New England, the Sons of Liberty of New-York, under the lead of Isaac Sears and John Lamb, sent circular letters as far as South Carolina, inviting to the formation of a permanent continental union.[3]

But the summons was not waited for. The people of South Carolina grew more and more hearty against the Act. "We are a very weak province," reasoned Christopher Gadsden,[4] "yet a rich growing one, and of as much importance to Great Britain as any upon the continent; and a great part of our weakness, though at the same time 'tis part of our riches, consists in having such a number of slaves amongst

[1] Gordon's Hist. of the Am. Rev. i. 198.

[2] Hutchinson's Corr. 8 March, 1766.

[3] Gordon, i. 199.

[4] From an autograph letter of Christopher Gadsden to W. S. Johnson, 16 April, 1766.

CHAP. XXIII. 1766. Feb.

us; and we find, in our case, according to the general perceptible workings of Providence, where the crime most commonly, though slowly, yet surely, draws down a similar and suitable punishment, that slavery begets slavery. Jamaica and our West India islands demonstrate this observation, which I hope will not be our case now, whatever might have been the consequence had the fatal attempt been delayed a few years longer, when we had drank deeper of the Circæan draught, and the measures of our iniquities were filled up. I am persuaded, with God's blessing, we shall not fall, or disgrace our sister colonies at this time."

Still more bold, if that were possible, was the spirit in North Carolina. The associated freeholders and inhabitants of several of its counties, mutually and solemnly plighted their faith and honor, that they would, at any risk whatever, and whenever called upon, unite, and truly and faithfully assist each other to the best of their power in preventing entirely the operation of the Stamp Act.

In the Ancient Dominion, men pledged themselves to one another for the same purpose, with equal ardor; and in case an attempt should be made to arrest an associate, they bound themselves at the utmost risk of their lives and fortunes, to restore such associate to liberty.[2] The magistrates composing the court for Northampton, unanimously decided that the Stamp Act did not bind or concern the inhabitants of Virginia, and that no penalties would be in-

[1] North Carolina Association, 18 Feb. 66.

[2] Asssociation, Virginia, 27 Feb. 1766, in Holt. 1214. 2. 1 of 10 April.

curred by those who should proceed to execute their offices.[1] CHAP. XXIII. 1766. Feb.

Trecothick then answered rightly in the House of Commons, that nothing but the repeal of the Stamp Act would satisfy America. Yet the opponents of concession claimed for their side the name of the king, whose opinions they declared that Rockingham had falsified. The irritated chief summoned the author of the rumor to meet him at the palace. There, on Wednesday, the twelfth of February, they went into the closet alternately,[2] two or three times each, to reconcile the seeming contradiction. For fear of mistakes, Rockingham wrote with a pencil these words: "Lord Rockingham was authorized by his majesty, on Friday last, to say that his majesty was for the repeal." "It is very true," said the king, as he read the paper; "but I must make an addition to it;" upon which he took a pen, and wrote at the end of it, "the conversation having been only concerning that or enforcing." He added, "I desire you would tell Lord Strange, that I am now, and have been heretofore, for modification.[3]" So Rockingham was disavowed, and the opposition declared more than ever that the ministers counterfeited as well as prostituted the sentiments of the king, whose unwritten word they would not trust,[4] and whose written word convicted them of falsehood.

On the same day, Bedford and Grenville went to

[1] Pennsylvania Journal, 13 March, 1766.

[2] From the Diary of the Earl of Dartmouth, who at that moment was in the antechamber, and received the account from Rockingham on his coming out from the king. Compare Albemarle, i. 301.

[3] King to Rockingham in Albemarle, i. 302.

[4] Lloyd's Conduct, &c., 134.

CHAP. XXIII. 1766. Feb. an interview with Bute, whom they had so hated and wronged. It was a proud moment for Bute, to find his aid solicited by his bitterest personal enemies. He desired that the past might be buried in oblivion, and that all honest men might unite; but he refused to enter upon any conference on the subject of a new administration, however much the other two wished to do so.[1]

The Duke of York interposed his offices, and bore to the king the Duke of Bedford's "readiness to receive the royal commands, should his majesty be inclined to pursue the modification, instead of the total repeal of the Stamp Act."[2] But the king, who was resolved not to receive Grenville again as his chief minister, disregarded the offer. So the measures of the ministry proceeded.

Such were the auspices, when on Thursday, the thirteenth day of February, Benjamin Franklin was summoned to the bar of the House of Commons. The occasion found him full of hope and courage, having for his interrogators, Grenville and Charles Townshend, as well as the friends of the administration; and the House of Commons for intent listeners.[3] Choiseul, too, was sure to learn and to weigh all that Franklin uttered.

In answer to questions, Franklin declared that America could not pay the Stamp Tax, for want of gold and silver, and from want of post-roads and means of sending stamps back into the country; that there were in North America about three hundred thousand white men, from sixteen to sixty years of age; that the inhabitants of all the provinces together,

[1] De Guerchy au Duc de Praslin, 3 Mars.

[2] Bedford Corr. iii. 329.

[3] Garth to South Carolina.

taken at a medium, doubled in about twenty-five years; that their demand for British manufactures increased much faster; that in 1723, the whole importation from Britain to Pennsylvania was but about fifteen thousand pounds sterling, and had already become near half a million; that the exports from the province to Britain could not exceed forty thousand pounds; that the balance was paid from remittances to England for American produce, carried to our own islands, or to the French, Spaniards, Danes, and Dutch in the West Indies, or to other colónies in North America, or to different parts of Europe, as Spain, Portugal, and Italy; that these remittances were greatly interrupted by new regulations, and by the English men-of-war and cutters stationed all along the coast in America; that the last war was really a British war, commenced for the defence of a purely British trade and of territories of the crown, and yet the colonies contributed to its expenses beyond their proportion, the House of Commons itself being the judge; that they were now imposing on themselves many and very heavy taxes, in part to discharge the debts and mortgages on all their taxes and estates then contracted; that if, among them all, Maryland, a single province, had not contributed its proportion, it was the fault of its government alone; that they had never refused giving money for the purposes of the act; that they were always willing and ready to do what could reasonably be expected from them; that the Americans, before 1763, were of the best temper in the world towards Great Britain, and were governed at the expense only of a little pen, ink, and paper; they allowed the authority of parliament in laws, except such as should lay internal duties, and never disputed it in

CHAP. XXIII. 1766. Feb.

laying duties to regulate commerce; and considered that body as the great bulwark and security of their liberties and privileges; but that now their temper was much altered, and their respect for it lessened; and if the act is not repealed, the consequence would be a total loss of the respect and affection they bore to this country, and of all the commerce that depended on that respect and affection.

Such was the form under which Franklin presented the subject to the consideration of the house. The questions of greatest interest asked of him related to the possibility of carrying the Stamp Act into effect, and to the difference laid down by so many of the Americans, and adopted by Pitt, in the House of Commons, and by Camden in the House of Lords,—between internal taxes and taxes laid as regulations of commerce. Grenville and his friends, and Charles Townshend, who had carefully considered the decisive resolutions that marked the entrance of Samuel Adams into public life, were his most earnest questioners.

"Do you think it right," asked Grenville, "that America should be protected by this country, and pay no part of the expense?" "That is not the case," answered Franklin; "the colonies raised, clothed, and paid during the last war twenty-five thousand men, and spent many millions." "Were you not reimbursed by parliament?" rejoined Grenville. "Only what, in your opinion," answered Franklin, "we had advanced beyond our proportion; and it was a very small part of what we spent. Pennsylvania, in particular, disbursed about five hundred thousand pounds, and the reimbursements, in the whole, did not exceed sixty thousand pounds."

CHAP. XXIII. 1766. Feb.

"Do you think the people of America would submit to pay the Stamp Duty if it was moderated?" "No; never. They will never submit to it." And when the subject was brought up a second and a third time, and one of Grenville's ministry asked, "May not a military force carry the Stamp Act into execution?" Franklin answered, "Suppose a military force sent into America; they will find nobody in arms; what are they then to do? They cannot force a man to take stamps who chooses to do without them. They will not find a rebellion: they may, indeed, make one."

"How would the Americans receive a future tax, imposed on the same principle with that of the Stamp Act?" "Just as they do this; they would not pay it," was the answer. "What will be the opinion of the Americans on the resolutions of this house and the House of Lords asserting the right of parliament to tax the people there?" "They will think the resolutions unconstitutional and unjust." "How would they receive an internal regulation, connected with a tax?" "It would be objected to. When aids to the crown are wanted they are, according to the old established usage to be asked of the assemblies, who will, as they always have done, grant them freely. They think it extremely hard, that a body in which they have no representatives should make a merit of giving and granting what is not its own, but theirs; and deprive them of a right which is the security of all their other rights." "The post-office," interposed Grenville to Franklin, the deputy postmaster for America, "is not the post-office, which they have long received, a tax as well as a regulation?" and Charles Townshend repeated the question. "No," replied

CHAP. XXIII. Franklin, "the money paid for the postage of letters is merely a remuneration for a service done."

1766. Feb. "But if the legislature should think fit to ascertain its right to lay taxes, by any act laying a small tax, contrary to their opinion, would they submit to pay the tax?" "An internal tax, how small soever, laid by the legislature here, on the people there, will never be submitted to. They will oppose it to the last." "The people," he answered again to the same question under many forms, "the people will pay no internal tax by parliament."

"Is there any kind of difference," continued Grenville's ministry, "between external and internal taxes to the colony on which they may be laid?" "The people," argued Franklin, "may refuse commodities, of which the duty makes a part of the price; but an internal tax is forced from them without their consent. The Stamp Act says, we shall have no commerce, make no exchange of property with each other, neither purchase, nor grant, nor recover debts; nor marry, nor make our wills, unless we pay such and such sums; and thus it is intended to extort our money from us, or ruin us by the consequences of refusing to pay it." "But suppose the external duty to be laid on the necessaries of life?" continued Grenville's ministry. And Franklin amazed them by his true answer: "I do not know a single article imported into the Northern colonies, but what they can either do without, or make themselves. The people will spin and work for themselves, in their own houses. In three years there may be wool and manufactures enough."

"Does the distinction between internal and external taxes exist in the charter of Pennsylvania?"

asked a friend of Grenville. "No," said Franklin, "I believe not."—"Then," continued the interrogator, with Charles Townshend for a listener, "may they not, by the same interpretation of their common rights, as Englishmen, as declared by Magna Charta and the Petition of Right, object to the parliament's right of external taxation?"—And Franklin answered instantly; "They never have hitherto. Many arguments have been lately used here to show them that there is no difference, and that, if you have no right to tax them internally, you have none to tax them externally, or make any other law to bind them. At present they do not reason so; but in time they may be convinced by these arguments."

CHAP XXIII.

1766. Feb.

On the twentieth of February—while the newspapers of New-York were that very morning[1] reiterating the resolves of the Sons of Liberty, that they would venture their lives and fortunes to prevent the Stamp Act from taking place, that the safety of the colonies depended on a firm union of the whole,—the ministers at a private meeting of their supporters, settled the resolutions of repeal which even Charles Townshend was present to accept, and which, as Burke believed, he intended to support by a speech.

Early the next day, every seat in the House of Commons had been taken; between four and five hundred members attended. Pitt was ill, but his zeal was above disease. "I must get up to the house as I can," said he; "when in my place, I feel I am tolerably able to remain through the debate, and cry aye to the repeal with no sickly voice;" and he hobbled into the house on crutches, swathed in flannels;

[1] New-York Gaz. 20 Feb. 1766.

CHAP. XXIII. huzzaed as he passed through the lobby, by almost all the persons there.

1766. Feb. Conway moved for leave to bring in a bill for the repeal of the American Stamp Act. It had interrupted British commerce; jeoparded debts to British merchants; stopped one-third of the manufactures of Manchester; increased the rates on land, by throwing thousands of poor out of employment. The act too breathed oppression. It annihilated juries; and gave vast power to the admiralty courts. The lawyers might decide in favor of the right to tax; but the conflict would ruin both countries. In three thousand miles of territory, the English had but five thousand troops, the Americans one hundred and fifty thousand fighting men. If they did not repeal the act, France and Spain would declare war, and protect the Americans. The colonies, too, would set up manufactories of their own. Why then risk the whole for so trifling an object as this act modified?

Jenkinson, on the other side, moved, instead of the repeal, a modification of the Stamp Act; insisting that the total repeal, demanded as it was with menaces of resistance, would be the overthrow of British authority in America. In reply to Jenkinson, Edmund Burke spoke in a manner unusual in the house; fresh, as from a full mind, connecting the argument for repeal with a new kind of political philosophy.

About eleven, Pitt rose. With suavity of manner he conciliated the wavering by allowing good ground for their apprehensions; but calmly, and with consummate and persuasive address,[1] he argued for the repeal, with eloquence which expressed conviction, and which yet could not have offended even the sensitive

[1] De Guerchy, 23 Feb.

CHAP XXIII. 1766. Feb.

self-love of the warmest friends of the act. He acknowledged his perplexity in making an option between two ineligible alternatives, pronounced, however, for repeal, as due to the liberty of unrepresented subjects, and in gratitude to their having supported England through three wars.

"The total repeal," replied Grenville, "will persuade the colonies that Great Britain confesses itself without the right to impose taxes on them, and is reduced to make this confession by their menaces. Do the merchants insist that debts to the amount of three millions will be lost, and all fresh orders be countermanded? Do not injure yourselves from fear of injury; do not die from the fear of dying;[1] the merchants may sustain a temporary loss, but they and all England would suffer much more from the weakness of parliament, and the impunity of the Americans. With a little firmness, it will be easy to compel the colonists to obedience. The last advices announce that a spirit of submission is taking the place of the spirit of revolt. America must learn that prayers are not to be brought to Cæsar through riot and sedition."[2]

Between one and two o'clock on the morning of the twenty-second of February, the division took place. Only a few days before, Bedford had confidently predicted the defeat of the ministry. The king, the queen, the princess dowager, the Duke of York, Lord Bute desired it. The scanty remains of the old tories; all the followers of Bedford and Grenville; the king's friends; every Scottish member, except Sir Alexander

[1] Junius, 19 Dec. 1767. [2] H. Hammersley to Sharpe.

CHAP. XXIII. 1766. Feb.

Gilmore and George Dempster; Lord George Sackville, whom this ministry had restored, and brought into office; Oswald, Sackville's colleague as vice-treasurer for Ireland; Barrington, the paymaster of the navy, were all known to be in the opposition.

The lobbies[1] were crammed with upwards of three hundred men, representing the trading interests of the nation, trembling and anxious, and waiting almost till the winter morning's return of light, to learn their fate from the resolution of the house. Presently it was announced that two hundred and seventy five had voted for the repeal of the act, against one hundred and sixty-seven for softening and enforcing it. The roof of St. Stephens rung with the loud shouts and long cheering of the victorious majority.

When the doors were thrown open, and Conway went forth, there was an involuntary burst of gratitude from the grave multitude, which beset the avenues; they stopped him; they gathered round him as children round a parent, as captives round a deliverer. The pure-minded man enjoyed the triumph, and while they thanked him, Edmund Burke, who stood near him, declares, that "his face was as if it had been the face of an angel." As Grenville moved along, swelling with rage and mortification, they pressed on him with hisses.[2] But when Pitt appeared, the whole crowd reverently pulled off their hats; and the applauding joy uttered around him, touched him with tender and lively delight. Many followed his chair home with benedictions.

[1] Edmund Burke.

[2] Walpole, ii. 299, is the authority. The "indignities" are again referred to, ibid, 300; and at 306 Grenville is reported as saying in the House of Commons, "I rejoice in the hiss." Walpole is not to be implicitly relied upon; but such exact references to what passed publicly, and to what was said in the House of Commons, seem worthy of credit.

CHAP. XXIII. 1766. Feb.

He felt no illness after his immense fatigue. It seemed as if what he saw and what he heard, the gratitude of a rescued people, and the gladness of thousands, now become his own, had restored him to health. But his heartfelt and solid delight was not perfect till he found himself in his own house, with the wife whom he loved, and the children, for whom his fondness knew no restraint or bounds, and who all partook of the overflowing pride of their mother. This was the first great political lesson received by his second son, then not quite seven years old, the eager and impetuous William, who, flushed with patriotic feeling, rejoiced that he was not the eldest-born, but could serve his country in the House of Commons, like his father.

At the palace, the king treated with great coolness all his servants who voted for the repeal. "We have been beaten," said Bedford to the French minister, "but we have made a gallant fight of it."

If the Scottish members, elected as they then were by a dependent tenantry, or in the boroughs by close corporations, voted to enforce the tax, the mind of Scotland was as much at variance with its pretended representatives in parliament, as the intelligence of France was in antagonism to the monarchy of Louis XV. Hutcheson, the reforming moralist of the north, had, as we have seen, declared as an axiom in ethics, the right of colonies to be independent when able to take care of themselves; David Hume confessed himself at heart a republican; Adam Smith, at Glasgow, was teaching the youth of Scotland the natural right of industry to freedom; Reid was constructing a system of philosophy, based upon the development and freedom of the active powers of man;

CHAP. XXIII. 1766. Feb.

and now, at the relenting "of the House of Commons concerning the Stamp Act," "I rejoice," said Robertson, the illustrious historian, "I rejoice, from my love of the human species, that a million of men in America have some chance of running the same great career which other free people have held before them. I do not apprehend revolution or independence sooner than these must and should come."

CHAPTER XXIV.

THE HOUSE OF LORDS GIVE WAY WITH PROTESTS.—ROCKINGHAM'S ADMINISTRATION CONTINUED.

FEBRUARY—MAY, 1766.

CHAP. XXIV. 1766. Feb.

THE heat of the battle was over. The Stamp Act was sure to be repealed; and every one felt that Pitt would soon be at the head of affairs. Rockingham still aspired to intercept his promotion, and engage his services. In its last struggle to hold place by the tenure which the king disliked, the old whig party desired to make of the rising power of the people its handmaid, rather than its oracle. But Pitt spurned to capitulate with the aristocracy. "Rockingham's tone," said he, "is that of a minister, master of the court and the public, making openings to men who are seekers of office and candidates for ministry." "I will not owe my coming into the closet to any court cabal or ministerial connection."

On Monday, the twenty-fourth of February, the committee made its report to the house. "Both England and America are now governed by the mob," said Grenville, continuing to oppose the repeal in every stage. Dyson hinted that internal taxes might be laid to ascertain the right. "To modify the act," answered Palmerston, "would be giving up the right and

CHAP. XXIV. 1766. Feb.

retaining the oppression." The motion for recommitment, was rejected by a vote of two hundred and forty to one hundred and thirty-three; and the bill for the repeal was ordered to be brought in.

Upon this, Blackstone, the commentator on the laws of England, wished clauses to be inserted, that all American resolutions against the right of the legislature of Great Britain to tax America should be expunged; but this was rejected without a division. Wedderburn would have annexed a clause enacting in substance, that it should be as high and mortal a crime to dispute the validity of the Stamp Act as to question the right of the House of Hanover to the British throne.

While he was enforcing his sanguinary amendment, the American colonies were everywhere in concert putting a denial on the pretension, and choosing the risk of civil war and independence, rather than compliance. Canada, Nova Scotia, and the Floridas, which were military governments, had submitted; the rest of the continent was firm. Massachusetts, Rhode Island, and Maryland had opened their courts. From New-York, the Governor reported that "he was left entirely to himself;" that "nothing but a superior force would bring the people to a sense of duty; that every one around him was an abettor of resistance."[1] A merchant, who had signed a stamped bond for a Mediterranean pass, was obliged to stand forth publicly, and ask forgiveness before thousands. The influence of the Sons of Liberty spread on every side Following their advice, the people of Woodbridge, in New Jersey, recommended "the union of the pro-

[1] Moore to Conway, 20 Feb., 1766.

CHAP. XXIV. 1766. Mar.

vinces throughout the continent." Stratford, in Connecticut, resolved never to be wanting, and advised "a firm and lasting union," to be fostered "by a mutual correspondence among all the true Sons of Liberty throughout the continent." Assembling at Canterbury in March, Windham county named Israel Putnam, of Pomfret, and Hugh Ledlie, of Windham, to correspond with the neighboring provinces.

Delegates from the Sons of Liberty in every town of Connecticut met at Hartford; and this solemn convention of one of the most powerful colonies, a new spectacle in the political world, demonstrating the facility with which America could organize independent governments, declared for "perpetuating the Union" as the only security for liberty; and they named in behalf of the colony, Colonel Israel Putnam, Major John Durkee, Captain Hugh Ledlie, and five others, their committee for that purpose.

"A firm union of all the colonies" was the watchword of Rhode Island, adopted in a convention of the county of Providence; and it was resolved to oppose the Stamp Act, even if it should tend to "the destruction of the union" of America with Great Britain.

At Boston, Otis declared, that "the original equality of the species was not a mere chimera."[1] Joseph Warren, a young man whom nature had adorned with grace, and manly beauty, and a courage that would have been rash audacity had it not been tempered by self-control, saw clearly that the more equal division of property among the people, tended also to equalize and diffuse their influence and authority; and he ut-

[1] Otis in Boston Gazette.

CHAP. XXIV. 1766. Mar.

tered the new war-cry of the world—"FREEDOM AND EQUALITY."[1] "Death," said he, "with all its tortures, is preferable to slavery." "The thought of independence," said Hutchinson despondingly, "has entered the heart of America."[2]

Virginia had kindled the flame; Virginia had now the honor, by the hand of one of her sons, to close the discussion, by embodying, authoritatively, in calm and dignified, though in somewhat pedantic language, the sentiments which the contest had ripened. It was Richard Bland,[3] of the Ancient Dominion, who, through the press, claimed freedom from all parliamentary legislation; and pointed to independence as the remedy for a refusal of redress.

He derived the English constitution from Anglo-Saxon principles of the most perfect equality, which invested every freeman with a right to vote at the election of members of parliament. "If," said he, "nine tenths of the people of Britain are deprived of the high privilege of being electors, it would be a work worthy of the best patriotic spirits of the nation to effectuate an alteration in this putrid part of the constitution, by restoring it to its pristine perfection." "But the gangrene," he feared, "had taken too deep hold to be eradicated in these days of venality." Discriminating between the disfranchised inhabitants of England and the colonists, and refusing to look for the rights of the colonies in former experience, whether of Great Britain, or Rome, or Greece, he appealed to "the law of nature, and those rights of mankind

[1] Joseph Warren to Edmund Dana, 19 March, 1766.

[2] Hutchinson to Thomas Pownall, March, 1766.

[3] An inquiry into the right of the British Colonies, &c. No date, but compare resolutions of the Sons of Liberty at Norfolk Court House, 31 March, 1766.

CHAP. XXIV. 1766. Mar.

which flow from it." He pleaded further, that even by charters and compacts, the people of Virginia ought to enjoy the privileges of the free people of England, as free a trade to all places and with all nations, freedom from all taxes, customs, and impositions whatever, except with the consent of the General Assembly. Far from conceding the acts of trade of Charles II. to have been a rightful exercise of power, the Virginia patriot impugned them as contrary to nature, equal freedom, and justice, nor would he admit them to be cited as valid precedents.

"The colonies," said he, "are not represented in parliament; consequently no new law made without the concurrence of their representatives can bind them; every act of parliament that imposes internal taxes upon the colonies, is an act of power and not of right; and power abstracted from right cannot give a just title to dominion. Whenever I have strength, I may renew my claim; or my son, or his son may, when able, recover the natural right of his ancestor. I am speaking of the rights of the people: rights imply equality in the instances to which they belong. The colonies are subordinate to the authority of parliament in degree, not absolutely. Every colony when treated with injury and violence, is become an alien to its mother state. Oppression has produced very great and unexpected events. The Helvetic confederacy, the states of the United Netherlands, are instances in the annals of Europe of the glorious actions a petty people, in comparison, can perform, when united in the cause of liberty."

At that time, Louis XV. was setting his heel on the parliaments of France, the courts of justice which alone offered barriers to his will. "In me," said he

CHAP. XXIV. to them solemnly, on the second day of March, "it is in me alone that the sovereign power resides. Justice
1766. Mar. is done only in my name, and the fulness of judicial authority remains always in me. To me alone belongs the legislative power, irresponsible and undivided. Public order emanates entirely from me. I am the people."[1] Against this the people could have but one rallying cry, Freedom and Equality; and America was compelled to teach the utterance of the powerful words.

For, on Tuesday, the fourth of March, 1766, came on the third reading of the bill declaratory of the absolute power of parliament to bind America, as well as that for the repeal of the Stamp Act.

Again Pitt[2] moved to leave out the claim of right in all cases whatsoever. The analogy between Ireland and America was much insisted upon, and he renewed his opinion, that the parliament had no right to tax America, while unrepresented. "This opinion," said he, "has been treated, in my absence, as the child of ignorance, as the language of a foreigner, who knew nothing of the constitution. Yet the common law is my guide; it is civil law that is the foreigner. I am sorry to have been treated as an overheated enthusiastic leveller, yet I never will change my opinions. Wales was never taxed till represented; nor do I contend for more than was given up to Ireland in the reign of King William. I never gave my dissent with more dislike to a question, than I now give it."

The amendment was rejected, and henceforward America would have to resist in the parliament of England, as France in its king, a claim of absolute, irresponsible, legislative power.

[1] "Mon peuple n'est qu'un avec moi." [2] De Guerchy to Praslin, 7 March.

The final debate on the repeal ensued. Grenville and his party still combated eagerly and obstinately. "I doubt," said Pitt, who that night spoke most pleasingly, "I doubt if there could have been found a minister who would have dared to dip the royal ermine in the blood of the Americans." "No, sir," replied Grenville, with personal bitterness, "not dip the royal ermine in blood, but I am one who declare, if the tax was to be laid again, I would do it; and I would do it now if I had to choose; it becomes doubly necessary, since *he* has exerted all his eloquence so dangerously against it." It marks the times and the character of that House of Commons, that with the momentous discussion on questions interesting to the freedom of England, America, and mankind, was mingled a gay and pleasing conversation on ministerial intrigues, in which it was assumed of the actual ministry, and openly spoken of in their presence, that they, by general consent, were too feeble to have more than a fleeting existence. A letter was also read foretelling that Pitt was to come into power. "How," said Pitt, "could that prophet imagine any thing so improbable, as that I, who have but five friends in one house, and in this am almost single and alone, should be sought for in my retreat?" But Pitt had never commanded more respect than now. He had spoken throughout the winter with the dignity of conscious pre-eminence, and had fascinated his audience; and being himself of no party, he had no party banded against him.

At midnight the question was disposed of by a vote of two hundred and fifty against one hundred and twenty-two. So the House of Commons, in the Rockingham ministry, sanctioned the prin-

CHAP. XXIV. ciples of Grenville, and adopted half-way, the policy of Pitt.

1766. Mar. On the next day, Conway, and more than one hundred and fifty members of the House of Commons, carried the bill up to the House of Lords, where Temple and Lyttelton did not suffer it to receive its first reading without debate.

On Friday, the seventh of March, the declaratory bill was to have its second reading. It was moved, though no division took place, to postpone it to the bill for the repeal, for if the latter should miscarry, the former would be unnecessary; and if the latter passed, the former would be but "a ridiculous farce after deep tragedy."[1]

"My lords, when I spoke last on this subject," said Camden, opposing the bill altogether, "I thought I had delivered my sentiments so fully, and supported them with such reasons and such authorities, that I should be under no necessity of troubling your lordships again. But I find I have been considered as the broacher of new-fangled doctrines, contrary to the laws of this kingdom, and subversive of the rights of parliament. My lords, this is a heavy charge, but more so, when made against one, stationed as I am, in both capacities as peer and judge, the defender of the law and the constitution. When I spoke last, I was, indeed, replied to, but not answered.

"As the affair is of the utmost importance, and its consequences may involve the fate of kingdoms, I took the strictest review of my arguments; I re-examined all my authorities, fully determined, if I found myself mistaken, publicly to own my mistake, and give up my opinion; but my searches have more and more

[1] Hammersley to Sharpe, 22 March, 1766.

convinced me that the British parliament have no right to tax the Americans.

"The declaratory bill, now lying on your table, is absolutely illegal; contrary to the fundamental laws of nature; contrary to the fundamental laws of this constitution: a constitution grounded on the eternal and immutable laws of nature; a constitution, whose foundation and centre is liberty, which sends liberty to every subject, that is, or may happen to be, within any part of its ample circumference. Nor, my lords, is the doctrine new; it is as old as the constitution; it grew up with it; indeed it is its support; taxation and representation are inseparably united; God hath joined them; no British parliament can separate them; to endeavor to do it, is to stab our very vitals. My position is this; I repeat it; I will maintain it to my last hour; taxation and representation are inseparable. Whatever is a man's own, is absolutely his own; no man hath a right to take it from him without his consent, either expressed by himself or his representative; whoever attempts to do it, attempts an injury; whoever does it, commits a robbery.

"Taxation and representation are coeval with, and essential to this constitution. I wish the maxim of Machiavel was followed, that of examining a constitution, at certain periods, according to its first principles; this would correct abuses, and supply defects. I wish the times would bear it, and that men's minds were cool enough to enter upon such a task, and that the representative authority of this kingdom was more equally settled."

"I can never give my assent to any bill for taxing the American colonies, while they remain unrepresented; for, as to the absurd distinction of a virtual

CHAP. XXIV. 1766. Mar.

representation, I pass it over with contempt. The forefathers of the Americans did not leave their native country and subject themselves to every danger and distress, to be reduced to a state of slavery; they did not give up their rights; they looked for protection, and not for chains, from their mother country; by her, they expected to be defended in the possession of their property, and not to be deprived of it. For should the present power continue, there is nothing which they can call their own; 'for,' to use the words of Locke, 'what property have they in that which another may by right take, when he pleases, to himself?"'[1]

Thus did the defence of the liberties of a continent lead one of the highest judicial officers of England, in the presence of the House of Lords, to utter a prayer for the reform of the House of Commons, by a more equal settlement of the representative authority.[2] The reform was needed; for in Great Britain, with perhaps, at that time, eight millions of inhabitants, less than ten thousand, or as some thought, less than six thousand persons, many of whom were humbled by dependence, or debauched by corruption, elected a majority of the House of Commons, and the powers of government were actually sequestered into the hands of about two hundred men. Camden spoke deliberately, and his words were of the greater moment, as they were the fruit of a month's reflection and research; yet he mistook the true nature of representation, which he considered to be not of persons, but of property.

The speech printed in the following year, found

[1] Locke on Civil Government. Book ii. ch. xi. § 138, 139, 140.

[2] Compare Lord Charlemont to Henry Flood, 13 March, 1766.

an audience in America, but in the House of Lords, Mansfield compared it to words spoken in Nova Zembla, and which are said to be frozen for a month before any body can get at their meaning; and then with the loud applause of the peers, he proceeded to insist that the Stamp Act was a just assertion of the proposition, that the parliament of Great Britain has a right to tax the subjects of Great Britain in all the dominions of Great Britain in America. But as to the merits of the bill which the House of Commons had passed to ascertain the right of England over America, he treated it with scorn, as an absurdity from beginning to end, containing many falsehoods, and rendering the legislature ridiculous and contemptible. "It is," said he, "a humiliation of the British Legislature to pass an act merely to annul the resolutions of a lower house of Assembly in Virginia." "It is only assertion against assertion; and whether it rests in mere declaration, or is thrown into the form of a law, it is still a claim by one only, from which the other dissents; and having first denied the claim, it will very consistently pay as little regard to an act of the same authority."

In this debate Egmont spoke with ingenuity and candor; reasoning that the powers of legislation, which were exercised by the colonists, had become sanctioned by prescription, and were a gift which could not be recalled, except in the utmost emergency.

Yet the motion for a postponement of the subject was not pressed to a division, and the bill itself was passed, with its two clauses, the one affirming the authority of parliament over America, in all cases whatsoever; and the other declaring the opposite re-

CHAP. XXIV. 1766. Mar.

solutions of the American Assemblies to be null and void.

The bill for the repeal of the Stamp Act, was read a second time upon Tuesday, the eleventh of March.[1] The House of Lords was so full on the occasion, that strangers were not admitted. Ten peers spoke against the repeal, and the lords sat between eleven and twelve hours, which was later than ever was remembered.

Once more Mansfield and Camden exerted all their powers on opposite sides; while Temple indulged in personalities, aimed at Camden.

"The submission of the Americans," argued the Duke of Bedford, who closed the debate, "is the palladium, which if suffered to be removed, will put a final period to the British empire in America. To a modification of the duties I would not have been unfavorable; but a total repeal of them is an act of versatility, fatal to the dignity and jurisdiction of parliament, the evil consequences of which no declaratory act can avert or qualify."[2]

The House of Lords divided. For subduing the colonies, if need be, by sword or fire, there appeared sixty-one, including the Duke of York, and several of the bishops; in favor of the repeal there were seventy-three; but adding the voices of those absent peers, who voted by proxy, the numbers were one hundred and five against seventy-one. Northington, than whom no one had been more vociferous that

[1] Chatham Corr. ii., 384, note. The date of every one of the letters of W. G. Hamilton is wrongly given. For 15 Feb., read 8 March; for 17 Feb., read 10 March; for 19 Feb., read 12 March, &c., &c. How could these dates have been so changed?

[2] Wiffen's House of Russell, ii., 571.

the Americans must submit, voted for the repeal, pleading his unwillingness to act on such a question against the House of Commons.

CHAP XXIV. 1766. Mar.

Immediately, the protest which Lyttelton had prepared against committing the bill, was produced, and signed by thirty-three peers, with Bedford at their head. Against the total repeal of the Stamp Act, they maintained that such a strange and unheard of submission of King, Lords, and Commons to a successful insurrection of the colonies would make the authority of Great Britain contemptible; that the reason assigned for their disobeying the Stamp Act, extended to all other laws, and, if admitted, must set them absolutely free from obedience to the power of the British legislature; that any endeavor to enforce it hereafter, against the will of the colonies, would bring on the contest for their total independence, rendered, perhaps, more dangerous and formidable from the circumstances of the other powers of Europe; that the power of taxation to be impartially exercised must extend to all the members of the state; that the North American colonies, "our colonies," as they were called by the discontented lords, were able to share the expenses of the army, now maintained in them at the vast expense of almost a shilling in the pound land tax, annually remitted from England for their special protection; that parliament was the only supreme legislature and common council empowered to act for all; that its laying a general tax on the American colonies was not only right but expedient and necessary; that it was "a most indispensable duty to ease the gentry and people of this kingdom, as much as possible, by the due

CHAP. XXIV. exertion of that great right of taxation without an exemption of the colonies."

1766. Mar. Having thus placed themselves in direct and irreconcilable hostility to America, the protesting peers glanced also with jealousy at the immense majority of the people of England; and further opposed the repeal of the Stamp Act, "because," say they, "this concession tends to throw the whole British empire into a state of confusion, as the plea of our North American colonies, of not being represented in the parliament of Great Britain, may, by the same reasoning, be extended to all persons in this island who do not actually vote for members of parliament."

Such was the famous Bedford protest, to which a larger number of peers than had ever signed a protest before, hastened in that midnight hour to set their names. Among them were four in lawn sleeves. It is the deliberate manifesto of the party which was soon to prevail in the cabinet and in parliament, and to rule England for two generations. It is the declaration of the new tory party, in favor of the English constitution as it was, against any countenance to the extension of suffrage, the reform of parliament, and the effective exercise of private judgment. It is the modern form of an ancient doctrine. Oxford had said unconditional obedience to the king was the badge of loyalty; this protest substituted unconditional obedience to the legislature of the realm, as constituted in 1688. The first had, in the spirit of the mediæval monarchy, derived the right to the throne from God; the second, resting on principles that had grown up in opposition to the old legitimacy, deified established law, and sought to bind its own and coming ages by statutes which were but the wisdom of a less enlightened generation that had long slumbered in their graves. CHAP. XXIV.

1766. Mar.

The third reading of the repeal bill took place on the seventeenth of March. Bute, in whose administration the taxing of America had been resolved upon, spoke once more to maintain his opinion. He insisted that, as minister, he had done good to his country; in retiring, he had consulted his own character and tastes; and since his retreat he had not meddled with public business, and was firmly resolved for the future to maintain the same reserve. Yet he wished that an administration might be formed by a junction of the ablest men from every political section.[1]

The bill passed without a further division; but a second protest, containing a vigorous defence of the policy of Grenville, and breathing in every line the sanguinary desire to enforce the Stamp Act, was introduced by Temple, and signed by eight and twenty peers. Five of the bench of bishops were found ready in the hour of conciliation, to record solemnly on the journals of the house, their unrelenting enmity to measures of peace. Nor was the apprehension of a great change in the fundamental principles of the constitution concealed. "If we pass this bill against our opinion," they said, meaning to assert, and with truth, that it was so passed, "if we give our consent to it here, without a full conviction that it is right, merely because it has passed the other house, by declining to do our duty on the most important occasion which can ever present itself, and when our interposition, for many obvious reasons," alluding to the

[1] De Guerchy to Praslin, 18 March, 1766.

CHAP. XXIV. 1766. Mar.

known opinion of the king, "would be peculiarly proper, we in effect annihilate this branch of the legislature, and vote ourselves useless." The people of England had once adopted that opinion. It was certain that the people of America were already convinced that the House of Lords had outlived its functions, and was for them become worse than "useless."

On the morning of the eighteenth day of March, the king went in state to Westminster, and gave his assent, among other bills, to what ever after he regarded as the well-spring of all his sorrows, "the fatal repeal of the Stamp Act."

He returned from signing the repeal, amid the shouts and huzzas of the applauding multitude. There was a public dinner of the friends of America in honor of the event; Bow bells were set a ringing; and on the Thames the ships displayed all their colors. At night a bonfire was kindled, and houses were illuminated all over the city.

An express was dispatched to Falmouth with letters to different provinces, to transmit the news of the repeal as rapidly as possible to the colonies, nor was it at that time noticed, that the ministry had carried through the mutiny bill,[1] with the obnoxious American clauses of the last year; and that the king, in giving his assent to the repeal[2] of the Stamp Act, had also given his assent to the act declaratory[3] of the supreme power of parliament over America, in all cases whatsoever.

While swift vessels hurried with the news across the Atlantic, the cider act was modified by the minis-

[1] 6 Geo. iii. c. xviii. [2] 6 Geo. iii. c. xi. [3] 6 Geo. iii. c. xii.

try, with the aid of Pitt; general warrants were declared illegal; and Edmund Burke, already famed for "most shining talents," and "sanguine friendship for America,"[1] was consulting merchants and manufacturers on the means of improving and extending the commerce of the whole empire. When Grenville, madly in earnest, deprecated any change in "the sacred Act of Navigation," Burke bitterly ridiculed him on the idea that any act was sacred, if it wanted correction. Free ports were, therefore, established in Jamaica and in Dominica,[2] which meant only that British ports were licensed to infringe the acts of navigation of other powers. Old duties, among them the plantation duties, which had stood on the statute book from the time of Charles the Second, were modified; and changes were made in points of detail, though not in principle. The duty on molasses imported into the plantations was fixed at a penny a gallon; that on British coffee was seven shillings the hundred weight; on British pimento, one half-penny a pound; on foreign cambric, or French lawn, three shillings the piece, to be paid into the exchequer, and disposed of by parliament.[3] Thus taxes for regulating trade were renewed in conformity to former laws; and the Act of Navigation was purposely so far sharpened as to prohibit landing non-enumerated goods in Ireland.[4] The colonial officers did not relax from their haughtiness. Under instructions given by the former administration, the Governor of Grenada claimed to rule the island by prerogative; and Sir Hugh Palliser,[5] at Newfoundland, arrogated the monopoly of the fisheries to Great Britain and Ireland.

[1] Holt's N. Y. Gaz. 1228, for 17 July, 1766.

[2] 6 Geo. iii. c. xlix.

[3] 6 Geo. iii. c. lii.

[4] 6 Geo. iii. c. lii.

[5] Ordinances of 3 April, 1766.

CHAP. XXIV. 1766. April.

The strength of the ministry was tested on their introducing a new tax on windows. "The English," said Grenville, "must now pay what the colonists should have paid;"[1] and the subject was referred to a committee by a diminished majority.

Great Britain not only gave up the Stamp Tax, but itself defrayed the expenses[2] of the experiment out of the sinking fund. The treasury asked what was to be done with the stamps in those colonies where the Stamp Act had not taken place?[3] and they were ordered to be returned to England,[4] where the curious traveller may still see bags of them, cumbering the office from which they were issued.

At the same time the merchants of London wrote to entreat the merchants of America to take no offence at the declaratory act, and in letters, which Rockingham and Sir George Saville[5] corrected, the ministers signified to the dissenters in America, how agreeable the spirit of gratitude would be to the dissenters in England, and to the Presbyterians to the north of the Tweed.[6]

A change of ministry was more and more spoken of. The nation demanded to see Pitt in the government; and two of the ablest members of the cabinet, Grafton and Conway, continued to insist upon it. But Rockingham, who, during the repeal of the Stamp Act, had been dumb, leaving the brunt of the battle to be borne by Camden and Shelburne, was determined it should not be so;[7] and Newcastle and Win-

[1] De Guerchy to Choiseul, 21 April.

[2] Treasury Minute of 4 April.

[3] Treasury Minute Book, xxxvii. 414. C. Lowndes to Beresford, Treasury Letter Book, xxiii., 296.

[4] Treasury Minute Book, xxxvii. 214.

[5] Ms. draft of a letter with the corrections in my possession.

[6] Moffat to Stiles, 18 March, 1766.

[7] Grafton to Conway, 22 April, 1766.

CHAP. XXIV. 1766. April.

chelsea and Egmont concurred with him.[1] To be prepared for the change, and in the hope of becoming, under the new administration, secretary for the colonies, Charles Townshend assiduously courted the Duke of Grafton. Pitt, on retiring to recruit the health which his unparalleled exertions in the winter had utterly subverted, made a farewell speech, his last in the House of Commons, wishing that faction might cease, and avowing his own purpose of remaining independent of any personal connections whatsoever; while the ships bore across the Atlantic the glad news of the repeal, which he had been the first to counsel, and the ablest to defend.

May.

The joy was, for a time, unmixed with apprehension. South Carolina voted Pitt a statue; and Virginia a statue to the king, and an obelisk, on which were to be engraved the names of those who, in England, had signalized themselves for freedom. "My thanks they shall have cordially," said Washington, "for their opposition to any act of oppression." The consequences of enforcing the Stamp Act, he was convinced "would have been more direful than usually apprehended."

Otis, at a meeting at the Town Hall in Boston, to fix a time for the rejoicings, told the people that the distinction between inland taxes and port duties was without foundation; for whoever had a right to impose the one, had a right to impose the other; and, therefore, as the parliament had given up the one, they had given up the other; and the merchants were fools if they submitted any longer to the laws restraining their trade, which ought to be free.

[1] De Guerchy to Choiseul, 1 April, 1766.

CHAP. XXIV. 1766. May. A bright day in May was set apart for the display of the public gladness, and the spot where resistance to the Stamp Act began, was the centre of attraction. At one in the morning the bell nearest Liberty Tree was the first to be rung; at dawn, colors and pendants rose over the housetops all around it; and the steeple of the nearest meeting-house was hung with banners. During the day all prisoners for debt were released by subscription. In the evening the town shone as though night had not come; an obelisk on the Common was brilliant with a loyal inscription; the houses round Liberty Tree exhibited illuminated figures, not of the king only, but of Pitt, and Camden, and Barre; and Liberty Tree itself was decorated with lanterns, till its boughs could hold no more.

All the wisest agreed that disastrous consequences would have ensued from the attempt to enforce the Act, so that never was there a more rapid transition of a people from gloom to joy. They compared themselves to a bird escaped from the net of the fowler, and once more striking its wings freely in the upper air; or to Joseph, the Israelite, whom Providence had likewise wonderfully redeemed from the perpetual bondage into which he was sold by his elder brethren.

The clergy from the pulpit joined in the fervor of patriotism and the joy of success. "The Americans would not have submitted," said Chauncey. "History affords few examples of a more general, generous, and just sense of liberty in any country than has appeared in America within the year past." Such were Mayhew's words; and while all the continent was calling out and cherishing the name of Pitt, the greatest statesman of England, the conqueror of Canada and the Ohio, the founder of empire, the apostle of freedom;—"To you," said Mayhew, speaking from the heart of the people, and as if its voice could be heard across the ocean, "to you grateful America attributes that she is reinstated in her former liberties. The universal joy of America, blessing you as our father, and sending up ardent vows to heaven for you, must give you a sublime and truly godlike pleasure; it might, perhaps, give you spirits and vigor to take up your bed and walk, like those cured by the word of Him who came from heaven to make us free indeed. America calls you over and over again her father; live long in health, happiness, and honor. Be it late when you must cease to plead the cause of liberty on earth."

END OF VOL. V.

www.ingramcontent.com/pod-product-compliance
Lightning Source LLC
LaVergne TN
LVHW020933110826
845150LV00004B/854

* 9 7 8 1 4 2 5 5 5 3 4 6 3 *